Government of the Shadows

Books are to be returned on or before
the last date below.

GOVERNMENT OF THE SHADOWS

Parapolitics and Criminal Sovereignty

Edited by
Eric Wilson

PLUTO PRESS
www.plutobooks.com

First published 2009 by Pluto Press
345 Archway Road, London N6 5AA and
175 Fifth Avenue, New York, NY 10010

www.plutobooks.com

Distributed in the United States of America exclusively by
Palgrave Macmillan, a division of St. Martin's Press LLC,
175 Fifth Avenue, New York, NY 10010

British Library Cataloguing in Publication Data
A catalogue record for this book is available from the British Library

ISBN   978 0 7453 2624 5   Hardback
ISBN   978 0 7453 2623 8   Paperback

Library of Congress Cataloging in Publication Data applied for

This book is printed on paper suitable for recycling and made from fully managed and sustained
forest sources. Logging, pulping and manufacturing processes are expected to conform to the
environmental standards of the country of origin. The paper may contain up to 70 per cent post
consumer waste.

10   9   8   7   6   5   4   3   2   1

Designed and produced for Pluto Press by
Chase Publishing Services Ltd, Sidmouth, England
Typeset from disk by Stanford DTP Services, Northampton, England
Printed and bound in the European Union by
CPI Antony Rowe, Chippenham and Eastbourne

For Selina,
who came to learn to love to listen to
Charley Patton, screamin' and hollerin' the blues

Contents

Acknowledgements

The production of this volume involved a three-day international conference held in the Law School at University of Melbourne in August 2006, jointly convened with Monash University's Law School. The aim of the conference was to allow for round-table discussions to fine-tune draft chapters already prepared by the contributors who now appear in this volume. Speakers attended from Australia, USA and Europe and debate was, as the euphemism has it, 'full and frank' – and productive.

The conference was funded by a grant from the Deputy Vice Chancellor (International) of Monash University, Professor Stephanie Fahey; a grant from the University of Melbourne Law School's Research Committee; and an Australian Research Council Federation Fellowship grant to Tim Lindsey. I am grateful to all three sponsors, without whose support the conference – and thus this volume – would have been impossible.

The conference was managed with exceptional aplomb and exemplary patience by Kathryn Taylor, the Manager of Melbourne's Asian Law Centre, assisted by Helen Jung Hee Ryu and Naomita Royan, both Research Assistants in that Centre. From Monash, both Shing Khoo and Sanah Banahali also helped. I also wish to thank the speakers, many of whom had to endure long journeys from exotic semester-break destinations to attend.

The editing process benefited greatly from the efforts of Kathryn Taylor and, in particular, Shing Khoo. Shing's enthusiasm for the project, keen attention to detail and impressive capacity for hard work were admirable, and I thank her for efforts well beyond the call of duty.

Finally, I hope this volume will spark interest in more sustained scholarly consideration of events and ideas that I feel have for too long been considered only marginal when they are, as I hope this collection of essays shows, deeply embedded in the heart of modern state systems. There is much to be done in the study of parapolitics and shadow governance and I hope this volume will suggest the next steps for research.

Eric Wilson
Melbourne, January 2007

'Though in many of its aspects this visible world seems formed in love, the invisible spheres were formed in fright.' – Herman Melville, *Moby Dick*

Introduction: Parapolitics, Shadow Governance and Criminal Sovereignty

Robert Cribb

I am not what I am. – Iago, *Othello*

'Parapolitics' is a new term.[1] It emerged in scholarly discourse only in the early 1990s to capture a set of observations which suggest a strange, powerful, clandestine and apparently structural relationship between state security-intelligence apparatuses, terrorist organisations and transnational organised criminal syndicates. This relationship often involves spaces on the globe that are, for practical purposes, outside the formal international state system, including weak states, failed states, de facto states and unrecognised states (commonly separatist movements that control territory but which have not secured formal international recognition).

The term 'parapolitics' both creates a conceptual link between phenomena that have not normally been linked analytically and suggests a research agenda to identify more precisely how these links operate. Parapolitics is a new field and it is premature to say just how significant it will prove to be. At very least, however, it is likely to make a significant contribution to understanding contemporary global politics and to ask serious questions of the dominant liberal view of modern democratic systems.

INTELLECTUAL ROOTS

The intellectual roots of parapolitics as a field of investigation lie, on the one hand, in the deep conservative-liberal suspicion of government that is especially prevalent in the United States and, on the other hand, in the European anarchist tradition of hostility to the state as an instinctively oppressive institution. A distinctive feature of parapolitics, however, is its identification of clandestinity as a state attribute. Clandestinity is, of course, as old as politics, but until the 1960s it was generally assumed to be the preserve of forces opposed to the state order – rebels, revolutionaries and criminals. The distinctive view of parapolitics was that clandestine activity by state institutions and by institutions linked to the ruling elite played a major role in sustaining illiberal and anti-democratic features of the system.

1

Evidence of systematic clandestinity on the part of Western liberal states emerged first during the Cold War. At first this evidence was fragmentary, but it pointed to the likelihood that the US government was involved in activities at odds with human rights and political accountability. This evidence related, amongst other things, to projects such as MK-ULTRA, a CIA-sponsored programme to investigate the potential of drugs, hypnotism and electromagnetic radiation. The aim of these experiments was initially to produce selective amnesia (so that captured Soviet agents, for instance, could be released, not realising that they had been interrogated). In its later stages, the programme aimed at transmitting and implanting commands that would override the recipient's free will. This programme was developed in direct response to perceptions that the Soviet Union had mastered forms of mind control and it thus constituted an aspect of the Cold War era arms race.[2] More broadly, it related to a vast programme of clandestine dirty tricks, including (attempted) assassinations of foreign leaders, the promotion of coups and the financing of political groups considered to be sympathetic to US official interests. The programme was largely exempt from any kind of legal review or congressional oversight.

A special characteristic of this clandestine action has been the manufacture of apparent hostile acts in order to manipulate public opinion within the democratic system. Thus, it is now known that the Piazza Fontana bombing of 1969 in Italy, and the Bologna Railway Station bombing of 1980, were the work of a select group controlled by Italian military intelligence (and with links both to the American CIA and to Propaganda Due).[3] The CIA also took part in a campaign to blacken the name of the Indonesian Communist Party after a failed left-wing military coup in 1965, in order to fuel a massacre in which half a million people died. This intra-state conflict over the use of violence led observers to talk of a dual state, 'one open and democratic, the other clandestine and reactionary'.[4] Ola Tunander contrasts these two aspects of the advanced Western state as the 'democratic state' versus the 'deep state' or 'security state'.[5]

The parapolitical approach took definitive shape, however, in the path-breaking work of Alfred McCoy in the 1970s and 1980s that showed the complicity of the CIA in opium cultivation and heroin production and trade in Indochina.[6] McCoy's impeccable research showed the sustained involvement of Western security-intelligence organisations (both American and French) in operations which intertwined organised crime (in this case, gangs involved in heroin manufacture and smuggling) and the subversion of democratic processes. McCoy's work remains the archetype for parapolitical research. *The Politics of Heroin in Southeast Asia* is a stunning book, but its impact was relatively limited. It is useful at this stage, therefore, to explore the reasons why parapolitical insights have had relatively little effect on conventional political analysis. There appear to be two reasons.

First, parapolitics has been seriously compromised by its inability to distinguish itself sharply from grand conspiracy theory. The term 'grand conspiracy theory' refers to a category of beliefs that posit a vast, durable and enormously powerful conspiracy involving unexpected combinations of economic, political and religious groups which effectively constitute a hidden government of the world. Grand conspiracies are typically thought to be several centuries old and to rest on a remarkable degree of secrecy and collusion between disparate groups. They commonly reject a great deal of public evidence as fraudulent and rely on the anonymous testimony of dismayed insiders. They often attach great significance to symbols such as pyramids and number sequences and they sometimes attribute to the conspirators connections with Satan and/or beings from outer space. Small wonder that the earliest parapolitical insights were often not taken seriously.

Second, parapolitics failed to mesh well with conventional political science. McCoy's book aroused indignation that the democratic authorities in the US should have connived in such activities, but it did not articulate a way in which the dominant paradigms governing American political science ought to change as a result of its findings. The principal dynamic of parapolitics appeared to be a personal lust for extraordinary power – and a drive to maintain that power – on the part of parapoliticians. This meant that the individuals engaged in parapolitics were most easily portrayed as 'rogue elements' or 'evil geniuses'. Analysts of parapolitics did not offer any explanation for why the normal process of political competition, especially related to succession, failed to operate within the parapolitical world. Broadly speaking, parapolitics failed as a field to identify the structures that might explain the phenomena it identified.

This book is the first in a series which attempts to remedy this deficiency by marking out parapolitics as a sober, analytical field of investigation. It would be too early to claim in this first essay that the field has reached maturity, but we know enough to sketch out some defining characteristics.

THE STATE AND PARASTATES

Parapolitics as a field of study arises from shortcomings in the dominant approach to politics and international relations, which treats the state as a special institution in human affairs, having structure, intention, agency and even personality, as well as attributes such as sovereignty, in a way that other human institutions do not. This special reification of the state has tended to create an almost unbridgeable systemic and intellectual distinction between domestic politics and international relations. It also obscures the connections between them and focuses attention away from institutions which in some respects resemble states but which are not part of the international club of fully-recognised, functioning sovereign states. The pernicious effect of this distinction can be seen in the contradiction between the attempts of the US, along with Britain, France and the Soviet Union, to use drug networks as assets or proxies in the Cold War, while simultaneously attempting to suppress the drugs trade within their own borders.

At the same time, international relations struggles to cope with states which do not quite match up to the expectations of membership in the international community. US Secretary of State Madeleine Albright identified as 'failed states' those countries with a weak or non-existent central authority.[7] Others have talked of 'weak' or 'weakened states', which fail to exercise the authority expected of them;[8] of complex states, defined as countries with two or more linked wars or crises;[9] and even of 'collapsed states', 'a mere geographic expression, a black hole into which a failed polity has landed'.[10] Others have written of 'rogue states', defying international order, and of 'microstates', some of which are called 'states of convenience' (like

Vanuatu and the Cayman Islands), whose prime purpose is to provide territoriality for relief from the legal obligations required by public states.

There are also important state-like entities that control territory and exercise many, or most, of the functions of a state, without being recognised as a state for international relations purposes. These 'unrecognised states' include Abkhazia, Anjouan, Puntland, the Shan States, Somaliland, South Ossetia and Waziristan, as well as the semi-internationalised territories of Kurdistan and Kosovo. There are also countries such as Lebanon, Colombia, Afghanistan, Burma/Myanmar and the Philippines, where significant regions are completely beyond the control of the central government, even if they are not generally recognised to be separate.

For a long time it has been recognised that mafias provide rudimentary services in urban ghettos or inaccessible rural areas, but the recent rise in the number of failing states has been accompanied by the rise of a number of alternative groups, or 'quasi-states', often revolutionary in character.[11] To maintain their popularity, these quasi-states try, like the state, to satisfy the citizens whom they tax. For example the Christian Phalange, a pro-government militia in Lebanon, 'provided all public services, including street cleaning, transportation, planting of trees, retail price control, street patrols, etc.'[12] The anti-government Muslim Hezbollah in South Lebanon, like Hamas in Palestine, has provided similar services.

The most important innovation of parapolitics, however, is to treat as state-like entities a range of institutions which do not, at first glance, resemble states but which nonetheless possess some of the important characteristics of states. These entities include:

- covert entities, semi-autonomous intelligence agencies, cabals, secret societies, and elite power groups (such as the Greek KYP, Pakistan's ISI, P2, Opus Dei or the Safari Club) which seek to control or manipulate state violence independently from within;
- criminal structures (mafias, drug networks, militant organised religious networks, Russian criminal entrepreneurs),[13] which exist in parallel symbiosis with the state; and
- revolutionary and terrorist movements, which seek to overthrow one or more existing states, but whose territorial control is limited to sanctuaries, often in the territory of others, and to the equivalent of safe houses.

Recognising the growing power in the world of these entities, and above all of drug networks and of terrorist groups, conventional political science has come to speak of non-state actors. But Loretta Napoleoni has shown that the distinction between states and non-state actors is artificial and misleading. In today's world, some terrorist organisations (notably the PLO and Hamas) have had larger budgets, bureaucracies and armies than some of the states among which they live.[14] What, then, to call them? Napoleoni coins the term 'State-shell', but this term might be taken to imply external form without internal content, the reverse of what is meant. Other possibilities include 'incipient state' or 'partial state', but both terms imply a tendency to end up as full states, which is not necessarily the case. In this introduction, we use the term 'parastates', partly because it creates a link with parapolitics, partly because it avoids teleology.

As Napoleoni's analysis makes clear, economics is crucial in sustaining parastates. In 1998, the International Monetary Fund estimated that illicit funds, worldwide, amounted to between $800 billion and $2 trillion – 2 to 5 per cent of the world's GDP.[15] In some states the black economy, or Gross Criminal Product, exceeds the formal economy. In Pakistan, for example, the black economy was, by the late 1990s, three times the size of the formal economy, and twice as much money from foreign remittances passed through the informal *hawala* system as through the formal banking system.[16] In developed states the black economy can be partially integrated, through money-laundering, into the formal economy. For a half-century, laundered profits from drug trafficking have been recycled into American and Canadian real estate, notably in Florida and Nevada.[17] And it is significant that before the US offered an emergency bailout to Mexico in 1982, thus preventing a default on payments to over-extended US banks, the CIA first verified that drug trafficking represented a significant source of the Mexican foreign exchange earnings needed for repayment.[18]

Conventional political theory, with its focus on the state as an arena and on its institutions as agents in domestic politics, fails to direct our attention towards parapolitics. So does conventional international relations theory, with its emphasis on sovereign states as coherent agents in international affairs. As Clifford Geertz's comments on 'the State' suggest, there may be a growing willingness to accept that there are limits to the usefulness of the 'state' as an analytical concept: 'the enormous variety of [the state's] forms and expressions and the multiplicity of the regimes it houses and of the politics it supports render the very idea elusive, awkward, protean, and problematical'.[19] Parapolitics, with its attention to divided sovereignty, to illegal trade as a substitute for taxation, and to a world of 'safe zones', analogous to the 'safe houses' of domestic organised crime, is well placed to develop a new agenda. What will distinguish the parapolitical approach is a perspective which does not take the point of view of the state itself. Instead, it sees the state as competing for power and legitimacy with alternative power groupings, especially parastates, which themselves exhibit some of the same power features as the state. There is room in this neutral approach for both criticism and defence of traditional notions of state power and legal sovereignty.

HISTORICITY

Parapolitics is not just a new term but also a recent historical phenomenon. Although future investigation may show otherwise, current research suggests that parapolitics is primarily a phenomenon of the period since the First World War. It is intimately connected with the character of ostensibly democratic politics, with the rise of regulatory frameworks and with the character of the international system. These shallow roots suggest in turn that parapolitics will be a dynamic field in which scholars need to be alert to changing patterns, as well as underlying structures.

Parapolitics appears to have emerged from a confluence of three historical trends. The first of these trends is the spread of democracy during the twentieth century, including the enfranchisement of women, the poor and, through decolonisation, former colonial subjects. At one level, this enfranchisement has increased the likelihood of at least occasional democratic outcomes, which threaten important, entrenched political, social and economic interests. At another level, it has focused attention on the potential effectiveness of manipulating public opinion so as to achieve desired outcomes from the democratic system. Awareness of the power of propaganda in the broadest sense to manage (that is to say, manipulate) public opinion has been deeply subversive of confidence in democracy and has given rise to a sustained effort by states to counter what they term 'subversion', by means of the clandestine management of public opinion. In particular, state security-intelligence organisations have been recruited on numerous occasions to stage phoney events designed to create public alarm for political purposes.

The second historical trend has been the massive growth of government regulation of society and the economy, especially of morality and the environment. This regulation has created niches for organised criminality where few or none existed in earlier times. That is to say, the law, by creating a barrier which excludes many or most people from participating in a certain activity, effectively reserves that activity for those who are strong enough, clever enough or daring enough to cross that barrier. Environmental protection measures and moral protection measures represent especially fertile areas for organised crime, because they restrict profitable or enjoyable human activity for highly-generalised social benefits. The classic example is Prohibition in the US, during which laws banning the sale and consumption of alcohol created a barrier which organised crime was best equipped to surmount. The consequences of Prohibition in creating a base for organised crime in the US have lasted well beyond the end of the ban on alcohol. We can now point to a large number of comparable cases, falling into four major categories: drugs (heroin, cocaine, marijuana and methamphetamines); sex (including prostitution and pornography); technology (including software and arms); and environmental contrabands (illegal logging, the trade in endangered species, the re-labelling and disposal of toxic waste and the illegal trade in chlorofluorocarbons [CFCs]). In short, greater regulation in recent historical times has created more niches for criminality.

The third historical trend is caused by the tension between contradictory principles in international law and practice. The so-called 'Westphalia system' of sovereign states spanning every square centimetre of land (and an increasing proportion of the sea) does not cope easily either with aspirations for national self-determination that do not coincide with existing state boundaries or with the reality that significant regions may be beyond the power of state authorities. The convention of territorial integrity, intended to outlaw conquest as a tool of national aggrandisement, makes secession difficult, unless it can be grounded in historical borders.

The consequence is a significant number of unrecognised states across the globe. These states, cut off from normal international commerce, often under constant military threat and commonly located in relatively underdeveloped regions, provide a ready territorial base for criminal activity. One of the clearest cases of early parapolitics is the involvement of the Japanese puppet state of Manchukuo in clandestine opium trade. Manchukuo was carved by the Japanese Kwantung Army in 1932 from Manchuria and parts of Inner Mongolia which had been under

Chinese sovereignty. It was internationally recognised only by Japan's allies, and became a key player in the international illegal narcotics trade.[20]

STRUCTURE OR CONTRADICTION?

These observations on the historicity of parapolitics highlight a key unresolved tension within the parapolitical approach. Scholars of parapolitics are united in asserting that parapolitics is not simply a collection of strange tales from the margins of politics which serve only to mark out the extreme limits of human behaviour. That is to say, parapolitics does not blame rogue elements or evil geniuses (even though the subject matter of the approach is abundantly peopled with colourful characters). Rather it examines global political, social and economic structures to identify those features which permit or encourage the growth and maintenance of parapolitics. (This assumption implies, incidentally, that parapolitics will be remedied – if at all – by structural and policy changes, rather than by the pursuit of miscreants, although prosecution way well play some role in this process. Remediation, however, does not yet have a significant place in the parapolitical research agenda.)

Nonetheless, the historical discussion of parapolitics above suggests that it exists at the ragged intersection of political theories. Thus, the intervention of state security-intelligence apparatuses to manipulate public opinion lies at the uncomfortable discontinuity between democratic theory and theories of opinion management. Similarly, the role of state regulation in creating niches for crime may refer simply to the limits of state authority and to the tension between recognising the important public goods that a legal system normally brings to society and the fact that laws tend to reflect and defend the interests of the powerful. Likewise, the existence of unrecognised states clearly reflects the tension between the rival principles of state sovereignty and national self-determination.

The central question in parapolitics is, however, the extent to which moments of historical opportunity – Prohibition, the Cold War, environmental regulations – have permitted the emergence of structures that have become embedded in national and global systems. In other words, to what extent have criminal organisations (that is, organisations based in illegal trade and/or organisations which seek to subvert the democratic process by illegal means) acquired some, or even most, of the important functions of governmentality.

Specifically, we ask whether the resort of state security-intelligence organisations to the assassination of political enemies and the calculated manufacture of public alarm warrants a greater acceptance of Tilly's proposition that the modern state has its roots in a form of protection racket: states emerged as powerful institutions which extracted wealth from those they controlled, returning little but the promise to limit the extent of plunder and to keep other plunderers at bay.[21] We ask whether state authorities manage the barrier between crime and non-crime precisely in order to create opportunities for organised crime. And we ask whether the existence of unrecognised states in various parts of the world, far from being a product of systemic failure, a product of unrequited tensions between sovereignty and self-determination, might not instead be a key part of a world-system characterised by a pronounced division of labour between different territories, and the increasing challenge to some traditional states from the transnational forces.

We characterise this state of affairs as 'criminal sovereignty' because there has emerged a form of authority which is criminal both in its subversion of the formal political process and in its dependence on illegal trade, but which has important attributes of sovereignty by virtue of veto power within established polities and its control of territory which is then used for criminal purposes. Although 'criminal sovereignty' is sometimes used to refer to the sovereign authority of the state to define and prosecute crime, we believe that the term better expresses this new form of authority.

Parapolitics, then, is the study of criminal sovereignty, of criminals behaving as sovereigns and sovereigns behaving as criminals in a systematic way. It is not just a topic but an analytical conclusion. On the one hand, it goes significantly beyond the proposition that relations between security and intelligence organisations, international criminal networks and quasi-states are occasional and incidental, the work of 'rogue elements' and the like. On the other hand, it falls significantly short of grand conspiracy theory: it does not suggest that the world of visible, 'normal' politics is an illusion or that it is entirely subordinated to 'deep' politics. Rather, it proposes that the tripartite relationship between security and intelligence organisations, international criminal networks and quasi-states is systematic, extensive and influential. The task of parapolitics as a discipline is to identify the dynamics of that relationship and to delimit precisely the influence that it has, or does not have, on public politics.

Parapolitics is not a theory of everything. It is not comparable to the classic Marxist theory that the state in all its doings and manifestations is a consequence of underlying class relations, nor to that feminist theory which traces the fundamental character of society to patriarchy. We use the term 'shadow governance' as a synonym for parapolitics to indicate that the substance of the field is actual political practice, rather than a generalised understanding of the functioning of human society. Nonetheless, parapolitics as a field sharply challenges the often-uncomplicated understandings of 'the state' prevalent in liberal political theory and conventional international relations. It does this by asking how it is possible to use terms such as 'legitimacy', 'democracy' and 'sovereignty' when there exists a multitude of powerful institutions which have many of the attributes of states (including territoriality, a monopoly on the means of violence, taxation, a public bureaucracy and some form of the rule of law) but are not internationally recognised as a 'legitimate' state.

Parapolitics, then, offers the world a rich research agenda. The essays in this volume represent a step in delivering the fruits of that research.

NOTES

1. The word 'parapolitics' does not appear in the current edition of the *Oxford English Dictionary* and appears to be a back-formation from the term 'parapolitical'. Even that term, however, dates only to 1965, when the American political scientist David Easton coined it as an adjective referring to open and legal political sub-systems functioning within, and structurally dependent on, larger political systems. As a noun, 'parapolitics' gained currency in the 1970s, to denote a system or practice of

politics in which accountability is consciously diminished. Peter Dale Scott, a contributor to this volume, so used the term in 1972; he has also contributed to this Introduction. Journals in Britain, France and America helped to popularise this use of the term, now widely used on the Internet.

2. John Marks, *The Search for the Manchurian Candidate: The CIA and Mind Control* (New York: Times Books, 1979).

3. See Ganser, this volume.

4. Italian EU parliamentarian Enrico Falqui, quoted in Ganser, this volume.

5. Tunander, this volume.

6. Alfred W. McCoy, *The Politics of Heroin in Southeast Asia* (New York: Harper Colophon Books, 1973).

7. Robert I. Rotberg defines 'failed states' as those which are 'tense, deeply conflicted, dangerous and contested bitterly by warring factions'. *State Failure and State Weakness in a Time of Terror* (Washington: World Peace Foundation, 2003), p. 5.

8. Rotberg defines 'weak states' as countries with a shorter list of dimensions of failure. Rotberg, *State Failure*, p. 5.

9. Ted Gurr, Barbara Harft and Monty G. Marshall, *State Failure Task Force Report: Phase III (Polity IV)* (McLean, VA: Science Applications International Corporation, 2003); as reported in Peter Reuter and Edwin M. Truman, *Chasing Dirty Money: The Fight Against Money Laundering* (Washington: Institute for International Economics, 2004), p. 157. Reuter and Truman group 'failed' and 'complex' states together as failing states. Ibid.

10. Robert I. Rotberg, 'The New Nature of Nation-State Failure', *Washington Quarterly* (Summer 2002), p. 90; quoted in Loretta Napoleoni, *Terror Incorporated: Tracing the Dollars behind the Terror Networks* (New York: Seven Stories Press, 2005), p. 145.

11. Wole Soyinka defines the 'quasi-state' as 'that elusive entity that may cover the full gamut of ideologies and religions, contends for power but is not defined by physical boundaries that mark the sovereign State'. Wole Soyinka, Reith Lectures, BBC, 2004, at www.bbc.co.uk/radio4/reith2004/lecture2.shtml (accessed 1 September 2006). He cites the example of Hezbollah in Lebanon.

12. Napoleoni, *Terror Incorporated*, p. 72.

13. See for example Vadim Volkov, *Violent Entrepreneurs: The Use of Force in the Making of Russian Capitalism* (Ithaca, NY: Cornell University Press, 2002).

14. Napoleoni, *Terror Incorporated*, p. 67; citing Christopher Pierson, *The Modern State* (London: Routledge, 1996): 'According to Professor Christopher Pierson, professor of politics at the University of Nottingham, a modern state displays nine main characteristics. Of these the "State-shell" [her term for a terrorist movement] shares four: a monopoly on the means of violence; territoriality; taxation; and public bureaucracy. The remaining five – sovereignty; constitutionality; the rule of law; impersonal power; and the legitimacy of authority and citizenship – are absent.' Napoleoni's notion of a 'State-shell' is modelled chiefly on the PLO and Hamas. We see greater variety among terrorist organisations, and prefer the less restrictive term 'incipient state' to describe any such organisation that aspires to acquire more state characteristics. But we accept her demonstration that 'State-shells' are not 'non-state actors'.

15. William Wechsler, 'Follow the Money', *Foreign Affairs* (July/August 2001), p. 45; Fabre, this volume.

16. Napoleoni, *Terror Incorporated*, pp. 106, 218.

17. Peter Dale Scott, *Drugs, Oil, and War: The United States in Afghanistan, Colombia, and Indochina* (Lanham, MD: Rowman & Littlefield, 2003), pp. 198, 207.

18. Before the first loan was issued in 1982, the US government had already ascertained from the Drug Enforcement Administration and the CIA that the profits from drug exports for Colombia and Mexico 'probably represent 75 percent of source-country export earnings': James Mills, *The Underground Empire: Where Crime and Government Embrace* (New York: Dell, 1978), pp. 1135, 1181.

19. Clifford Geertz, 'What Was the Third World Revolution?' *Dissent* (Winter 2005), at www.dissentmagazine.org/article/?article=268 (accessed 1 September 2006).

20. See John M. Jennings, 'The Forgotten Plague: Opium and Narcotics in Korea under Japanese Rule, 1910–1945', *Modern Asian Studies*, 29/4 (1995), p. 795.

21. Charles Tilly, 'War Making and State Making as Organized Crime', in Peter Evans, Dietrich Rueschemeyer and Theda Skocpol (eds), *Bringing the State Back In* (Cambridge: Cambridge University Press, 1985), p. 169.

Part I

Theoretical Perspectives

1
Deconstructing the Shadows

Eric Wilson

> The human mind in its day-by-day operations cannot bear to look the truth
> of politics straight in the face. It must disguise, distort, belittle and embellish
> the truth – the more so, the more the individual is actively involved in the
> process of politics, and particularly in those of international politics. For
> only by deceiving himself about the nature of politics and the role he plays
> on the political scene is man able to live contentedly as a political animal
> with himself and his fellow men.
>
> Hans W. Morgenthau, *Politics Among Nations*

Law is the respectable face of crime. At first glance, this statement is absurd; a
facetious 'joke' of questionable taste and wit. That it definitely *is* a joke, however,
a subversive conjunction of appositional terms, reveals far more than is apparent
at first glance. Once we dispense with the strictly binary logic underpinning our
collective understanding of legality, the paradoxical effect of the assertion evaporates
and new insights emerge. Not the least important of these are new understandings
of the complex dynamic between macro- and micro-levels of political analysis;
'macro', denoting the allegedly unified entity the 'state' and its equally unified – and
unifying – juridical corollary the 'law', and 'micro', denoting the particular and
the private, the zone of pragmatic but ultimately uncertain application of formally
enunciated rules and procedures.

> A fundamental weakness of current sociological theory [which includes legal
> sociology] is that it does not relate micro-level interactions ['the small group'] to
> macro-level patterns ['political structures'] in any convincing way... the analysis
> of processes in interpersonal networks provides the most fruitful micro–macro
> bridge. In one way or another, it is through these networks that small-scale
> interactions become translated into large-scale patterns, and that these, in turn,
> feed back into small groups.[1]

The anthropological term for the interstitial figure that strategically regulates
the multiform flow of exchanges between the micro- and macro-levels is the

'power broker', or 'middleman', whose role is 'to bridge a gap in communications between the larger and the smaller structures'.[2] Consequently, the middleman is a consummately *political* creature, whose function 'lies in his capacity to acquire and maintain control over the paths linking the local infrastructure...to the superstructure of the larger society'.[3] From a purely anthropological perspective, the judge may convincingly be seen as analogous to the middleman, as he (or she) performs the mediatory role of applying the general law (the macro-political structure) to the particular person (the micro-small group). So, however, does the mafia chieftain – under certain circumstances.

> In every society there should always be one class of person who sets things right when they get out of hand. Generally these people are called civil servants, but when the state is non-existent or too weak, the job is done by private individuals. Don Calo is one of these, the only one entitled to be called 'Don'; all the rest are called 'zu' (uncle).[4]

The ordinary assumption of a unified state presence expressed through the legal principle of *concession*, that 'no other authority or form of association properly exists in society except insofar as it is conceded the right to existence by the particular sovereign',[5] is the main source of intellectual resistance to such a casual conflation of the legal with the criminal mediatory role. The criminal assumes a (pseudo-) legal role only if the 'state', which is equal to 'law', is weak or absent; indeed, the absence of the state is conventionally assumed to be identical with the presence of crime.[6] However, contrary to expectations, the mafia *capo* is meticulous in his compliance with legal form; it is no exaggeration that the essence of his identity as *mafioso*[7] lies precisely with his efficacy as legal agent.

> What differentiates from, and in a certain sense contrasts the spirit and organization of the Mafia with banditry[8] is the fact that the Mafia...never or almost never sets itself against the law, [or] directly proposes to break the law or protest against its ordinances, as is the case with the bandit in popular myth; but on the contrary presents itself as concerned with order and of course formal respect for the law.[9]

If we were to represent the dyadic relationship between the judge and the mafia chieftain as a formula, we would get:

(1)   Judge = Law = Politics = Power = Coercion[10]
(2)   Mafia Chieftain = Violence[11] = Honour[12] = Power = Coercion

The crucial link between the two coercing agents lies within the concise formulation offered by Henner Hess: 'All power is ultimately based on the ability to use force.'[13] A parallel, or 'mirror', logic is established between the illicit *capo* and the legal civil servant as was the case with Don Calo; 'The monopoly of honour implies power; and among the distinctions that derive from holding power is included that of supplanting the official powers in the administration of justice.'[14] Not surprisingly, the lexicon of legality permeates the language of the *mafiosi*.

> The conviction that the law is an instrument of physical force has deep roots in mafia culture. When an enemy threatens him with recourse to the State's laws, the *mafioso*...replies that 'law is force, and can never be separated from force.' Force and supremacy, here, create the law much more than they represent the efficacy of any law valid in itself. Of all historical and social worlds, none demonstrates more clearly than the world of the *mafioso* the extent to which physical force can be independent of any pre-established distributive justice. Individual *mafiosi* were perfectly aware of the ultimate foundation of their power, and on some occasions took care to emphasize how *the concrete 'justice of force' prevailed over the ideal force of justice*.[15]

Consistent with our dyadic formula, 'honour' corresponds to 'violence' as 'law' does to 'politics/power'.

> The socio-economic system [of Calabria] faced a constant and real threat of disintegration, and there was thus an urgent need for some supra-individual and public power, capable of creating even a semblance of public order... This need for some self-regulation of the system met with the sense felt by the *uomini di rispetto* to maintain their honour, and as a result the latter came to be entrusted with a series of important functions, protecting traditional laws, arbitrators and executioners, exercising in their own persons many sensitive powers that were normally the prerogative of the State. Honour was thus transformed into legitimate power, into authority. The latter then appeared in its turn as a means by which honour was itself confirmed and extended.[16]

The terrible logic at work in mafia discourse is that, in the final analysis, law can indeed be effectively reduced to power – or 'force' – obviating altogether the otherwise crucial factor of the legal agent's social identity.

Jacques Derrida, in his seminal essay, 'The Mystical Foundations of Authority', has re-drawn our attention to the brutal interrelationship between law and power and its implication for deconstruction.[17] Through its primary focus of inverting, or 'de-constructing', socially accepted hierarchies of meaning, revealing thereby the absence of a unifying 'metaphysics of presence',[18] deconstruction forces attention onto the extreme iterability[19] of all systems of meaning, now governed by a 'rhetoric of reversibility'. All textual meanings, or sign-systems, are dependent for their efficaciousness upon a prior tactical deployment against an opposite/oppositional meaning, this 'reversibility of placement' serving as the ground of meaning for each individual word/meaning. 'Law' or 'judge' depends upon the intelligibility of 'crime' and 'criminal' in order to be able to operate within any system of discourse; the meaning of any individual word is exhaustively determined by its strategic place within the text.[20] As every sign necessarily requires the existence/presence of its 'other', any conventionally accepted hierarchy of meaning ('the judge is the mediator of the state applying the law'), is always subject to a radical form of inversion/

subversion ('The mafia *capo* is just like a judge'). Every manifest term necessarily invokes its opposite; 'the essential property of the sign is its iterability'.[21]

In this way, a transversal of meaning is accomplished; from constituting 'associations of armed strongmen and their followers who exercise jurisdiction on the local level in conjunction with formal authority',[22] the mafia *familia*[23] may also be intelligibly defined as 'a pragmatic extension of the state'.[24]

The relevance of deconstruction to our problem becomes self-evident when greater attention is paid to the complexities of the middleman, the transversal figure that bridges two political orders, micro and macro. For Charles Tilly, middlemen

[c]onsist of those who simultaneously carry on active roles in the community and in the national structures that intersect it. [This] elite are the mediators, the brokers, between those national structures and the relevant activities within the community. *They gain power through their extraordinary access to information and to powerful individuals on the outside, and frequently have a good deal of influence over the contacts of other community members with 'outsiders'.*[25]

Similarly, for Eric R. Wolf, middlemen, or 'brokers'

[s]tand guard over the crucial junctures or synapses of relationships which connect the local system to the larger whole... [Brokers] must serve some of the interests of groups operating on both the community and the national level, and they must cope with the conflicts raised by the collision of these interests. *They cannot settle them, since by doing so they would abolish their own usefulness to others. They thus often act as buffers between groups, maintaining the tensions which provide the dynamic of their actions.*[26]

As middlemen, both judges and mafia *capo* derive their respective identities – 'their mutual conceptual interdependence' – from an underlying constitutive force linking law with crime; namely, power.[27] Without pressing the analogy between deconstruction and psychoanalysis too far, the *sub-text* – that which 'governs' the expression(s) of the surface text – may be interpreted as the 'unconsciousness' of the text. As with the human unconscious, the sub-text contains the polar inversion of the manifest meaning; every invocation of the law necessarily invokes the defining 'presence' of crime.

The repressed 'presence' of 'the other' is never consciously acknowledged; this facilitates the interpretative re-construction of texts, with the critical reader performing the role of terminally suspicious 'psychoanalyst'.[28] The very real possibility of deep and hitherto unacknowledged correspondences between the lawful state and its alleged binary opposite, the criminal cartel, elucidates the mechanisms of repression and denial that psychoanalysis posits as the foundation of neurosis. In precisely this way was Freud able to postulate murder as the originary act of cultural formation.

Certain transformations [go to] work on [historic memory], falsifying the text in accord with secret tendencies, maiming and extending it until it was turned into its opposite... The distortion of a text is not unlike a murder. The difficulty lies not in the execution of the deed but in the doing away with the trace. One could wish to give the word 'distortion' the double meaning to which it has a right, although it is no longer used in this sense. It should mean not only 'to change the appearance of', but also 'to wrench apart', 'to put in another place'. That is why in so many textual distortions we may count on finding the suppressed and abnegated material hidden away somewhere, though in an altered shape and torn out of its original connection. Only it is not always easy to recognize it.[29]

The self – culture – owes its existence to the presence of the other: violence.

POLITICAL PLURALISM: THE POST-MODERN IS THE PRE-MODERN

The nature of man cannot be confined by any single value, expressed by any single kind of relationship. The potential diversity of the human mind must be matched by a diversity of types of community within the social order, each as autonomous as possible within its own sphere of function, each with a measure of authority of its own based upon its unique function and no more disposed to transgress upon the function and authority of any other community than to have its own function and authority invaded.

Robert Nisbet, *The Social Philosophers*

It is the presumed unitary nature of the state signified by the legal doctrine of concession that guarantees the legitimacy of the commonly accepted binary opposition of 'crime' with 'law'. Mainly because of its Platonic heritage, Western political theory has fetishised the unified state; 'the idea of sovereignty, which clearly implies but one absolute power laying in the social order, with all relationships, all individuals indeed, ultimately subject to it, has been the characteristic approach to the political community'.[30] The belief in political monism has caused Western jurisprudence to conflate law with reason, establishing a chain of signifiers that demarcate the parameters of orthodox – or 'acceptable' – juro-political discourse. Monism logically presupposes that that which is not constitutive of reason – the 'irrational' – cannot exist as a necessary attribute of the 'true' state. Consequently, the history of Western political philosophy is marked by the ruthless denial of all pluralistic forms of political discourse.

It has been the fate of pluralism in Western thought to take a rather poor second place to philosophies which make their point of departure the premise of, not the diversity and plurality of things, but, rather, some underlying unity and symmetry, needing only to be uncovered by pure reason to be then deemed the 'real', the 'true', and the 'lasting'.[31]

This has been all the more surprising when one remembers how recent an innovation the 'state' and its necessary attributes, such as the 'public domain', actually are. Prior to the fairly late figure of Thomas Hobbes (1588–1679), the 'state', or *stato* or *status*, denoted the personal position or private estate of the sovereign, signifying the absence of any clear demarcation between the 'private' and the 'public'. Throughout the fifteenth and sixteenth centuries, *stato* was deemed equivalent to the typology of the prevailing regime, expressed through territory and institutions; 'when *status* and *stato* are employed by [pre-modern] writers to denote an apparatus of government, the power structure in question is not in fact viewed as independent of those who have charge of it'.[32]

Significantly, pluralism constituted a robust form of political discourse in the centuries immediately preceding that grand historical construct known as 'the Enlightenment'; that is, the era of the formation of the modern nation-state.

> The properly medieval system of thought started from the idea of the whole and the unity, but to every lesser unit down to and including the individual, it ascribed an inherent life, a purpose of its own, and an intrinsic value within the harmoniously articulated organism of the world-whole filled with the Divine Spirit. Thus in accordance with the medieval scheme of things it attained a construction of the social whole which in effect was federalistic through and through... Between the highest Universality or 'All-Community' and the essential unity of the individual there is a series of intermediate unities, in each of which lesser and lower units are comprised and combined. The political theories endeavour to set up a definite scheme descriptive of this articulation of mankind; for the church they follow the existing hierarchical system, and for secular societies they set up a parallel system by enlarging the Aristotelian gradation of communities.[33]

Due to its feudalistic pedigree, political pluralism operates as a freestanding refutation of the Myth of Enlightenment, foundationally premised upon a meta-historical supra-session of the archaic/pre-modern by the progressive/modern.[34] For Immanuel Wallerstein, the central component of the ideological system, or 'geo-culture', of the modern world-system is continuous, self-directing political transformation. In world-system theory, 'liberalism' is virtually identical with 'modernity' which is, in turn, premised upon an incessant and unconditional rupturing of the capitalistic present with all lingering 'traces' of the pre-capitalistic past. One of the principal consequences of the French Revolution for the modern world-system was that it

> [m]ade acceptable for the first time the idea that change, novelty, transformation, even revolution, were 'normal', that is, not exceptional, phenomena of the political arena, at least of the modern arena... What at first appeared as statistically normal quickly became perceived as morally normal.[35]

Deconstruction, however, by illuminating the governing absence of all hierarchical differences present within the orthodox (self-) understanding of Western philosophy, subverts all allegedly objective demarcations between the pre-modern and modern worlds. The 'modern' is revealed as dangerously supplemented by the lurking – and, more importantly, the *lingering* – presence of the 'archaic'.

The empirical detection of the presence of fragmented, and fragmenting, political identities and associations within the heart of the post-feudal nation-state is, therefore, the cause of considerable cognitive dissonance. Take, for example, the coolly objective assessment of the contemporary political landscape of the United States offered by Eric R. Wolf, one that expressly links the 'criminal' with the 'legal'.

> [There are] resources and organizations which it would be either too costly or too difficult to bring under direct control, and in these cases the system yields its sovereignty to competitive groups that are allowed to function in its entrails... *We must not confuse the theory of state sovereignty with the facts of political life.* Many organizations within the state generate and distribute and control power, in competition with each other and with the sovereign power of the state. As examples one might cite the Teamster's Union of the United States, the Mafia, or the American Medical Association. Thus we could also draw a map of political power for any complex society in which the key centres of control appeared in red – showing strong concentrations of sovereign power – while the other political regions appeared in grey or white. We thus note that the formal framework of economic and political power exists alongside or intermingled with various other kinds of informal structure which are interstitial, supplementary, parallel to it.[36]

The discernible traces of political pluralism within the works of the foundational figures of modern political theory are an even greater source of anxiety. The first modern theorist of federalism, Johannes Althusius (1557–1638),[37] formulated a radically pluralistic theory of both corporatism[38] and multilevel governance.[39] The first edition of Althusius' seminal text the *Politica Methodice Digesta* (1603) expressly postulates the public domain as constitutionally derivative from – which is to say, metaphysically inferior to – the private civil society.

> The public association exists when many private associations are linked together, for the purpose of establishing an inclusive political order. It can be called a community, an associated body, or the pre-eminent political association.[40]

Even more subversive is the theory of *divisible sovereignty* expounded by the alleged 'father' of international law, Hugo Grotius, in his early major work, *De Indis* (1603–08), identified by Richard Tuck as the locus of 'the first modern political theory'.[41]

A signature characteristic of *De Indis* is the recurrent juxtaposition of contending forms of sovereignty; the binary opposition between monistic and 'divisible' sovereignty forms a cardinal antinomy of both *De Indis* in particular and of the Grotian corpus as a whole. As Edward Keene rightly points out, much of the 'statist myopia' of both international law and international relations is the end product of a superficial, if not actually naïve, understanding of the complex cross-currents of early modern history, which leads directly, in turn, to a facile belief in an essentialising statist 'presence'.

> Since [Jean] Bodin, indivisibility has been integral to the concept of sovereignty itself.[42] In international political theory, this means that whenever sovereignty is

used in a theoretical context to confer unity upon the state as an acting subject, all that it conveys is that this entity is an individual by virtue of its indivisibility, which is tautological indeed. What follows from this search for the locus of sovereignty in international political theory, however necessary to its empirical testability, is thus nothing more than a logical sideshow; the essential step towards unity is already taken whenever sovereignty figures in the definition of political order. Whether thought to be upheld by an individual or a collective, or embodied in the state as a whole, sovereignty entails self-presence and self-sufficiency; that which is sovereign is immediately given to itself, conscious of itself, and thus acting for itself. That is, as it figures in international political theory, sovereignty is not an attribute of something whose existence is prior to or independent of sovereignty; rather, it is the concept of sovereignty itself which supplies this indivisibility and unity.[43]

The main discursive differences between Bodin's *On Sovereignty*[44] and Grotius' *De Indis* may be attributable to the different roles played by their respective countries (France; Holland) within the core zone of the modern world-system. France, as a non-hegemon but a 'strong' state within the core, led Bodin to concentrate on the requirements of robust intra-state formation, yielding a textually constructed reification of political unity. Holland, as the nascent hegemon within the still crystallising modern world-system lay at the vital nexus between intra- and inter-state crosscurrents. As a result, Grotius was committed to a discursive strategy of formulating the hegemonic requirements of maritime supremacy and world-market penetration within an international schema that permitted a plurality of political actors and stratagems.

It is no exaggeration to say that in the seventeenth century, it was the more speculatively metaphysical system-builders [Bodin] who believed in the indivisibility of sovereignty, while the more pragmatic and constitutionally-minded experts on the law of nations [Grotius] were the ones who upheld the empirically verifiable doctrine that sovereignty was divisible... [Grotian Divisibility Theory] recalls the complex hierarchies of overlapping jurisdictions that...were symptomatic of medieval Christendom, and precisely the opposite of the modern world where political authority is believed to come in neat territorial packages labelled 'sovereignty'... The imperial constitution, the territorial sovereignty of the states and the reserved right of the emperor made it hard for lawyers to ignore the fact that, whatever the attractions of the Bodinian theory in principle, sovereignty was divided in practice.[45]

As Advocaat-Fiscal of Holland and as political confidant of the Grand Pensionary Johannes van Oldenbarnevelt (1547–1619), Grotius' ruminations of primitive international legal scholarship were inevitably governed by domestic political and constitutional considerations; ordinarily, this meant legitimising the self-proclaimed national independence of the United Provinces.[46] *De Indis* provides a radically republican conception of divisible sovereignty, serving as a crucial textual/discursive linkage between the Just War waged by the Dutch East India Company (the VOC) and the republican precepts of the lawful war of national liberation. 'The power that has been bestowed upon a prince can be revoked, particularly when the prince exceeds the bounds defining his office, since in such circumstances he ceases *ipso facto* to be regarded as a prince.'[47] Herein, divisible sovereignty and republicanism are neatly fused with the self-grounding legitimation of Dutch national independence.

> Since the State has no superior, it is necessarily the judge even of its own cause. Thus the assertion made by Tacitus...was true, namely that by a provision emanating from the Divine Will, the people were to brook no other judge than themselves.[48]

Throughout his corpus, Grotius devotes considerable space to highly detailed empirical considerations of *actus summae potestatis*, those necessary 'marks' or signs of sovereignty; intriguingly, 'right' is clearly associated with 'power'.

> Those that no one may rescind by virtue of any higher right, for example, the supreme right to introduce legislation and to withdraw it, the right to pass judgement and to grant pardon, the right to appoint magistrates and to relieve them of their office, the right to impose taxes on the people, etc.[49]

Accordingly,

> [i]f some marks [*acti*] rest with the prince, and others with the senate, or rather with the prince and the senate, one cannot claim that full sovereignty is either with the prince or with the senate, but [only] with the prince and the senate [together]. The prince and the senate, however, are not one but several.[50]

It is tempting to discern a (sub-) textual Derridean joke operating here. The iterability, or radical reversibility, of the 'mark' of sovereignty as itself constitutive of sovereignty, unintentionally belies the wholly constructivist – and, therefore, contingent – nature of the alleged 'sovereign'. *De Indis* treats the 'mark' in a manner that is remarkably deconstructionist. The *actus* is inherently ambiguous, not identical with either *potestatis* or *ius*, but an operationally 'free-floating signifier' of the lurking 'presence' of sovereignty;[51] 'the term actus suggests not a diagnostic criterion which serves to indicate who possesses sovereign power, but the active exercise of some part of that power; the rendering function might be equally important'.[52] The radically contextualist nature of the *acti* highlights the extreme iterability that governs the Grotian alterity between 'public' and 'private' actors. Within this discursive frame, both states and persons – which include corporations[53] – are both fully able to respectively exercise the 'sovereignty function' and, thereby, acquire the signature 'mark'.

For Tuck, *De Indis* constitutes a seminal ('essentialising'?) moment in the Grotian Heritage.

> Grotius...made the claim that an individual in nature (that is, before transferring any rights to a civil society[54]) was morally identical to a state, and that there were

no powers possessed by a state which an individual could not possess in nature. The kind of state he had in mind, moreover, was one which was sovereign in a strong sense... *supra republicam nihil est.*[55]

The problem here as concerning the mark(s) of sovereignty, is that *any* agency capable of exerting effective control over organised violence is, by that fact alone, potentially eligible for legal personality. The subversive potential of this co-joining of divisible sovereignty and organised violence has received classic treatment by Frederic Lane in his theory of 'the protection industry'.

The use of force may be productive of a utility. That utility is protection. Every economic enterprise needs and pays for protection, protection against the destruction or armed seizure of its capital and the forceful disruption of its labour. In highly organized societies the production of this utility, protection, is one of the functions of a special association or enterprise called government. Indeed, one of the most distinctive characteristics of governments is their attempt to create law and order by using force themselves and by controlling through various means the use of force by others. The more successful a government is in monopolizing all use of force between men within a particular area, the more efficient is its maintenance of law and order. Accordingly, the production of protection is a natural monopoly. The territorial extent of this monopoly is prescribed more or less loosely by military geography and historical circumstances. Breaks in the monopoly occur, as when there is an insurrection or a boom in the rackets of gangsters, but such rival enterprises in the use of force substitute monopolies of their own if successful. These illegal monopolies may be quite transitory and highly localized... [When] no protection is given against immediate additional seizure by some bandit or some other user of violence, it is a clear case of plunder.[56] Both the history of nations and the stories of gangsters contain plenty of borderline cases, but clearly force is not only used in plundering but also in preventing plundering, and a government which maintains law and order is rendering a service in return for the payment it collects.[57]

Lane's approach is radically nominalist, the demarcation between licit and illicit organised violence wholly an exercise of taxonomic classification. The effective monopolisation of violence is not merely a derivate attribute of an 'objective' sovereignty, but the primary signification of sovereignty itself, subverting any hierarchical distinction between 'government' and 'governance'. The 'appropriation' of public functions by organised criminal cartels in Colombia,[58] Sicily,[59] and Russia[60] are outstanding empirical examples of the state as a self-legitimating 'pariah entrepreneur'[61] based upon effective provision of the commodity of protection; 'a private agent who manages to achieve monopoly over violence in a specific territory eventually becomes a public actor'.[62] Successful 'state building' is thus invariably equated with the successful monopolisation of violence[63] coupled with a self-sustaining collection of 'protection rent', either in the form of 'tribute' or, in a more bureaucratised form, of 'taxation'.[64]

The irreducible plurality of civil society serves as the necessary precondition of the emergence of 'private' parapolitical structures and relationships. Criminal cartels in particular signify the 'presence' of a pluralist multi-centric order; it is therefore possible to interpret the corruption of governmental structure as the heteronomous 'privatisation' of public authority.[65] This point is supremely well expressed by Tilly in his introduction to Anton Blok's seminal cultural anthropological work, *The Mafia of a Sicilian Village, 1860–1960.*

The processes Anton Blok has witnessed in Sicily are, in fact, standard state-building processes: consolidation of control over the use of force, elimination of rivals, formation of coalitions, extension of protection, routinised extraction of resources. If one *mafia* network managed to extend its control over all of Sicily, all concerned would begin to describe its actions as 'public' rather than 'private', the national government would have to come to terms with it, outsiders and insiders alike would begin to treat its chiefs with legitimate authority. It would be a government; it would resemble a State. With outside recognition of its authority [i.e. a treaty-making capacity], plus the development of differentiated and centralized instruments of control, it would *be* a State... The difficulty [identified by Blok] is simply that Sicily now has many such proto-states... Sicily's problem is not a shortage, but a surfeit of such government[s].[66]

Now compare Tilly's insight with this rather lengthy passage from Althusius.

For it cannot be denied that provinces are constituted from villages and cities, and commonwealths and realms from provinces. Therefore, just as the cause by its nature precedes the effect and is more perceptible, and just as the simple or primary precedes in order what has been composed or derived from it, so also villages, cities, and provinces precede realms and are prior to them. For this is the order and progression of nature, that the conjugal relationship, or the domestic association of man and wife, is called the beginning and foundation of human society. From it are then produced the associations of various blood relations and in-laws. From them in turn come the sodalities and collegia, out of the union of which arises the composite body that we call a village, town, or city. And these symbiotic associations as the first to develop can subsist by themselves even without a province or realm. However, as long as they are not united in the associated and symbiotic and universal body of a province, commonwealth, or realm, they are deprived of many of the advantages and necessary supports of life. It is necessary, therefore, that the doctrine of the symbiotic life of families, kinship associations, collegia, cities, and provinces precede the doctrine of the realm or universal symbiotic association that arises from the former associations and is composed of them.[67]

In the simplest terms, Althusius is arguing that 'civil society' in its non-statist form is itself is the bearer of all of the signs of political authority. Intriguingly, Diego Gambetta locates the historical origin of the Sicilian mafia – the parapolitical 'other' to the Italian state[68] – in the provision of protection to professional guilds and trade unions.[69]

An obvious objection to be made at this point is that one cannot extrapolate universal conditions from the local climate of western Sicily. The reader should keep in mind that the Sicilian mafia is deployed here as a Weberian 'ideal type' for purposes of discussion; obviously, some of what is discussed has to be understood as particular to Italian political culture. Nevertheless, once the iterability between state/crime is established – in Sicily or elsewhere – then the scope for deconstructive 'joking' – the subversive co-joining of appositional signs – becomes virtually limitless. To take an obvious, but irresistible, example rich in deconstructive potential: 'family'. In the most general sense, family is a kinship-based unit of sexual reproduction, devoid of broader political significance. As we have just seen, however, for the pluralist Althusius

> [t]he family is…a social unit in every sense of the word… Althusius regards study of the family as being just as much a part of the discipline of politics as is that of any other form of association, including political government itself: 'Certain writers eliminate, wrongly in my judgement, the doctrine of the conjugal and kinship private association from the field of politics and assign it to economics.'[70]

'Family', in Italian, is *'familia'*, the basic unit of familism – both moral and amoral – an alternative order of civil society parallel to the Italian state.[71] Two points are of especial concern here. Firstly, amoral familism, with its accompanying phenomenon of purely instrumental friendship and kinship,[72] signifies the pervasiveness of a 'culture of distrust', an endemic feature of the political culture of the Mezzogiorno.[73] Hess has convincingly identified this Sicilian 'sub-cultural system' as an anti-colonialist phenomenon, a 'dual morality' stressing resistance, silence (*omertà*) and distrust;[74] consequently, the mafia is able to exploit anti-colonialist resistance to its own advantage, while presenting itself as a 'protector', or 'trust provider',[75] of the Sicilian *populo*, generating authority and legitimacy for itself. Secondly, *familia*, as is well known, is, at its most instrumentalised, the basic unit of mafia organisation.

> Although the single mafia family or *cosca* is strongly centralized, this takes the form of a series of dyadic relationships between the *capo-mafia* and each of the individual members. The mafia as a whole is thus seen as a complex of social networks, held together by traditional bonds of honour, kinship and 'instrumental friendship'. Typically the activities of the *cosca* are limited to a well-defined territory, over which it enjoys a monopoly of protection and control. To the extent that a structure going beyond the *cosca* exists, it is a loose 'federal' structure[76] in which each *cosca*, autonomous in its own territorial or sectoral sphere of influence, enters into alliances or coalitions with its neighbours in the pursuit of larger-scale economic interests.[77]

No less an authority of the Sicilian mafia than Giovanni Falcone has drawn out the full implications of the multiform convergences of family/*familia* and familism.

> I believe that it is the lack of a sense of State, of State as an interior value, which is the root cause of the distortions in the Sicilian soul: the dichotomy between society and State, the consequent over-reliance on family ['amoral Familism'], on group, on clan; the search for a rationalisation that will allow everyone to live and work in perfect anomie, without reference to the rules of collective life.[78]

Note, however, Judge Falcone's wholly *negative* evaluation of familism; it is a virus, the sign of a normative pathology, preventing the (southern) Italian people from embracing unconditionally the morally and socially progressive concept of the monist state. Contrast Falcone's judgement with the anthropologically sophisticated assessment by Hess.

> Because of the weakness of the coercive machinery of the state there is an absence of a legal order and of the sanctions which lend dependability and durability to relationships in heteronomous groups. But this lack has no bearing on the possibility or stability of relationships in autonomous groups whose norms are not sanctioned by public law... The bonds within these primary groups or informal groupings are felt clearly and as an obligation.[79]

For Hess, amoral familism is not a deficiency – an *absence* of something desirable – but an alternative mode of social order – the *presence* of a pluralistic politics.

ANTI-ESSENTIALISM: POWER, AUTHORITY, LEGITIMACY

The deconstruction of the unifying presence of the state radically 'de-essentialises' the three primary signs of the statist object: *power*, *authority*, and *legitimacy*.

Power

For Steven Lukes, power is defined neither essentially nor substantively but operationally, the pre-emption of resistance and dissent through the successful manipulation of cultural norms to preclude the conceptualisation of an alternative political order.

> The supreme and most insidious exercise of power [is] to prevent people, to whatever degree, from having grievances by shaping their perceptions, cognitions and preferences in such a way that they accept their role in the existing order of things, either because they can see or imagine no alternative to it, or because they see it as natural and unchangeable, or because they value it as divinely ordained and beneficial.[80]

Luke's account explains well the successful integration of *mafiosi* into Sicily's sub-cultural normative system of distrust and amoral familism. Consistent with norm manipulation, the mafia is best understood not as a corporate entity but as a totalising mode of cultural behaviour; '*Mafia* is neither an organisation nor a secret society, but a method.'[81] Only in this way can that complex chain of mafia signs collectively defined as 'honour' be fully understood. It is a sign-system that signifies a dyadic relationship between 'self-help' and physical violence embedded within a political landscape governed by distrust; 'A *mafioso* is not the man who regards himself as one, but he who is regarded as one. It is the public that makes him a *mafioso*.'[82] In a famous passage replete with Machiavellian overtones, Pino Arlacchi has written

> To achieve such fundamental social control, the archaic virtues of courage, ruthlessness and force, which favoured his rise to power, were no longer enough. The mafioso had to be able to exercise the activities of a government if he wanted to die in bed honoured and revered as a gentleman. To the lion he had to add the fox. Now he had to prove his prudence, balance and astuteness if his power were to be accepted and recognised by the population. The people had to see in his person not only the strong, victorious man capable of annihilating any adversary whatever but also a form of superior authority. He had to act as father of all, friend of all, the protector, mediator, counsellor and judge.[83]

Through this passage, Arlacchi draws our attention to extra-statist power as a form of governance, inseparable from wider considerations of authority and legitimacy.

Authority

Authority has been defined by Joseph Raz as 'a right to make laws and regulations, to judge and punish for failing to conform to certain standards, or to order some redress for the victims of such violations, as well as the right to command'.[84] Thanks to the post-modern applicability of Grotius' pre-modern 'iterability of signs', it should be clear by now that authority can be legitimately exercised by a pirate, a *mafioso*, a civil servant, a terrorist, or a revolutionary, depending upon the total socio-historical context of the coercive act. As that supremely logo-centric admirer of the state Judge Falcone[85] famously remarked: 'When you think closely about it, in character, the mafia is nothing other than the expression of a longing for order and thereby for government.'[86]

It must be emphasised at this point that the coherence of this notion of mafia as a 'parallel state' is directly dependent upon the degree that the state has been convincingly 'deconstructed'. If belief in presence is maintained, then the joke that began this chapter does not work.[87] It is important to remember, however, that deconstruction, through its endless subversion of hierarchies, never works to privilege an 'anti-hierarchy' of its own; it strategically contests all total and essentialist systems of meaning and value. Deconstruction does not need to positively demonstrate the para-statist essence of the mafia; merely, it must subversively play with the analogous similitudes governing the relationship(s) between 'crime' and 'law' in order to ironically contest any exhaustively juridical conception of the state that pretends to be self-validating, or 'self-grounding'. In any event, the historical survival and protean mutability of the mafia should, in itself, provide prima facie evidence for a doubling of identities and functions, both 'legal' and 'criminal'. Whatever theoretical arguments that can be made against deconstruction, the force of such an objection is greatly weakened when one considers the Sicilian experience in purely empirical terms; because of entrenched structural weaknesses, the Italian state has actively appropriated – or 'captured' – the mafia as a proxy agent.[88] In this way, the authority of the mafia is symbiotically dependent upon the authority of the state.

> Far from putting themselves in the State's place or constituting a State within a State…the traditional *mafiosi* actually depend upon the State insofar as their power derives in part from the privileged access they enjoy to the levers of State power.[89]

Consequently, the functions 'discharged by the mafioso frequently enable him to present himself to the state organs as a collaborator in their tasks'.[90] Of these functions that the formal state was not able to execute effectively, one of the most important was to serve as 'middleman' between the state and the 'dangerous classes'.[91]

> We must now emphasize the exceedingly important function which the *mafioso* discharges for the landowner. The protection which the *mafioso* provides for the property of his padrone is principally directed against *ladri* [thieves] and *banditi*; that is against elements wishing, within the existing system, to improve their personal prospects. The punitive actions of *mafioso* protective power are terror actions and as such simultaneously have a deterrent effect… Acts which enter the official statistics as criminal actions, measured by the criterion of formal law, are better understood as sanctions of an informal legal system if one realises the general problem of sub-cultural peculiarities and the need for self-help within the sub-cultural system.[92]

The exercise of authority, in turn, fits in perfectly with the *mafioso*'s self-perception as a juridical agent.

> The *uomo di rispetto* liked to take upon himself the preservation of order, and he found a second extensive field for the exercise of his power within the local community in the repression of non-conformist behaviour.[93] By taking on this function, the *mafioso* was enabled to present himself to the local society and to the State authorities as a guardian of public order.[94]

Most importantly, mafia power is deployed in a self-consciously statist fashion: full compliance with the critical variables of neutrality and objectivity guaranteed through the theatricality of the application of coercive force.

> The *mafioso* defended established positions, and was a member of the local power elite. However, the ways in which he intervened to safeguard the economic status quo hardly ever brought him to identify altogether with the perspective of those who held official power and wealth. A contractual element always persisted. In all the workings of 'protection', the *mafioso's* role was kept clearly distinct from

that of any patron or client. Mafia power was an independent power, with its own autonomous bases of legitimation, and the agents through whom it operated were never too restricted in their scope. *Even when it was most obvious that some private interest was being pursued, the intervention of the mafia always had the aspect of something undertaken in the name of order and of the overall stability of things.*[95]

Judith Chubb has described this symbiotic relationship between state and mafia as 'organic interpenetration'.[96] Within this arrangement, *mafiosi*

[u]ltimately secure their long-term position only through...an alliance with the ruling class or ruling cliques and by rendering appropriate services, from the defence of the landowners against bandits and land-hungry peasants to the protection of businesses or the supply of votes for politicians who, in turn, protect the *mafiosi* against law enforcement. *Mafia* is not just the criminal enemy of the state or in some respects a sort of competing para-state, it also reaches into the state with a subtle web of friends-of-friends.[97]

As a result, 'public safety was entrusted to the mafia, thus handing society over to it'.[98]

Legitimacy

The problem of legitimacy is essentially that of *consent*; it is here that we encounter the most intractable objection to our deconstructive 'joking'. The (parallel) state can never be an objectively 'true' one because it will always lack the necessary prerequisite of the (singular) legal state: popular consent.

What this apparently irrefutable objection elides, however, is the two-fold nature of the problem of statist legitimacy. In the *negative* sense, it is obvious that clearly 'lawful' states frequently lack consent; 'a state by its nature is not free'.[99] In the *positive* sense, it is equally obvious that parallel statist structures are, as a matter of social fact, frequently invested with large amounts of popular consent. The crucial issue, as has been perceptively elucidated by Hess is that 'essentially legitimation stems...from popular morality and from functional necessity'.[100] Through his monopolisation of physical violence, the *mafioso* 'assures himself not only of a personal material or prestige gain but also discharges certain functions within the sub-cultural system by entering the service of others'.[101] Through repetitive performance, this leads, over time to the 'institutionalised legitimacy' of mafia power: 'honour is institutionalised and transformed into a *power* acknowledged as legitimate'. Although his 'behaviour is regarded as illegitimate by the codified law of the superimposed state [it] conforms with the sub-cultural norms and enjoys legitimation by public normality'.[102]

PARAPOLITICS, SHADOW GOVERNANCE AND CRIMINAL SOVEREIGNTY

To deconstruct the monistic state, it is not necessary to demonstrate that criminal cartels always bear the 'sovereign marks' of authority and legitimacy; it is enough merely to show that, under local and specific conditions, they *may* do so. It is this vital contingency that fractures the logo-centric monism of the post-Platonic state, creating a fissure through which the always latent potential for political pluralism may be realised. This insight, in turn, leads to a far more interesting and subversive consideration, which is the formal topic of this book: that the 'legitimate' but fissured state actively seeks to appropriate and to deploy for purposes of its own forms of criminal activity that are otherwise lacking authority. The crucial point is not that the state and crime are identical, but that they are reversible – which is to say, iterable. Employing the logic of deconstruction, it is truly possible to see crime as a continuation of the state by other means. We call this state of affairs *parapolitics*.

'Western European states have seemingly been characterised by the existence of a regular "democratic state", on the one hand, and a "security state" on the other.'[103] The central analytical concept of 'parapolitics' is the notion of political pluralism: the fragmentation, by *différance*, of the nation-state into competing sub-statist entities that, under the appropriate local conditions, have been capable of serving as the bearer of a divisible sovereignty. Some of these entities originate from within the state apparatus; others began as their opponents. In the end, however, they may become states, quasi-states or 'shadow states' in themselves, exerting functions of governance even if devoid of the formal signs of the state. This is termed 'shadow governance', the acquisition of the functions of governmentality by sub-statist groups or structures by means both judicial and extra-judicial. The successful operation of shadow governance, in turn, provides scope for the establishment of 'criminal sovereignty', the investiture of extra-legal groups with a de facto autonomy through the acquisition of the requisite marks of sovereignty.

For Ola Tunander,[104] all of this reveals the bad faith of mainstream liberal political science. 'Liberal political science has been turned into an ideology of the "deep state" because undisputable evidence for the [national security] "deep state" is brushed away as pure fantasy or "conspiracy".' Tunander shows the liberal state to be coeval with the 'deep state' which has deployed a 'liberal' form of political culture that legitimates itself through a systematic denial of the operational presence of its dangerous supplement – clandestine, or 'shadow', government. His chapter seeks to prospectively map out new forms of international juro-political landscape, composed of multiple and cross-sectional political complexes that defy conventional analysis in terms of government, the 'rule of law' or political transparency.

Central to this book is a thorough re-examination of the intellectual legitimacy of the orthodox division of constitutional government into the clearly demarcated spheres of 'public' and 'private'. The inherently pluralistic nature of heterogeneous civil society, suffused by divisible sovereignty, leads to the proliferation of what Guilhem Fabre[105] appropriately labels 'legal illegality'. This book consists of a series of case studies, both theoretical and empirical. Unifying the chapters are three overlapping areas of concern: parapolitics, shadow governance, and criminal sovereignty. Consistent with the principles announced at the beginning of this chapter, criminal sovereignty is seen as corresponding to the intra-state/micro-level of analysis; global governance with the inter-state/macro-level of analysis; and parapolitics as the transversal 'bridge' that discursively links the two levels of interpretation, providing the other terms with 'mutual conceptual interdependence'.

Combined, all three units, or 'levels', of analysis serve to form the interstitial poetic metaphor that is the title of this book: 'Government of the Shadows'.

PARAPOLITICS: THE BRIDGE

Parapolitics is the lurking presence to all of the chapters of this volume. Peter Dale Scott has provided the formal definition of this 'shadow' presence.

> 1. a system or practice of politics in which accountability is consciously diminished. 2. generally, covert politics, the conduct of public affairs not by rational debate and responsible decision-making but by indirection, collusion and deceit. Cf. *conspiracy*. 3. the political exploitation of irresponsible agencies or para-structures, such as intelligence agencies.[106]

Just as politics as a field ('political science') studies the overt politics of the public state, so parapolitics as a field studies the relationships between the public state and the political processes and arrangements outside and beyond conventional politics. However, conventional, or liberal, political science assumes the normalcy of the state, both in its constitutional and its normative dimensions, as a given and studies political phenomena from the perspective of the state. Parapolitics, in contrast, constitutes a radically nominalist critique of conventional political studies. Parapolitics uses the varying levels of interaction between conventional states and quasi-statist entities as the basis for formulating an analytical perspective that privileges neither the state nor its alternatives as legitimate international actors. Although of no determinative political bias, parapolitics does foster a basic scepticism regarding the coherence of orthodox liberal understandings of the state. This analytical perspective also serves to critique the purportedly self-grounding principles of recognition offered by the doctrine of effectiveness. In this context, the term 'parapolitical structure' does not connote an essence but nominally denotes an entity possessing cognisably political characteristics that can validly serve as an object within the study field, or paradigm, of parapolitics. In turn, it is the observable and traceable patterns of constructive interaction between the political and parapolitical structures that validates parapolitics' foundational hypothesis of the inherently covert nature of the state. Parapolitics' recognition of criminal sovereignty is signified by its location of statist and para-statist interaction at the centre of 'national security'; the successful conduct of extra-legal activity within this domain is not of incidental but of primary importance to the state. It would not be an exaggeration to claim that such interactions serve as one of the driving motors of the formation of national security policy, the hallmark of the parapolitical 'dual state' that is simultaneously legal and extra-legal. To express it in wholly pedestrian terms: *why* is it exactly that states always seem to require 'back doors'? Simply put: parapolitics constitutes a continuation of both political science and international law by other means.

One of the basic premises of *Government of the Shadows* is that parapolitical structures are neither 'parasitic' nor 'deviant', but functionally central to the routine operation of global governance and private authority; this is argued by Peter Dale

Scott in his contribution. The presence of the fragmentary – and fragmenting – parapolitical within the modern nation-state compels critical self-reflection on the traditional categories of liberalism, government, governance, accountability, responsibility, transparency and the rule of law. To what degree is the successful functioning of allegedly 'rational' models of liberal government in praxis dependent upon successful negotiations with parallel economies governed by parapolitical complexes? What are the precise benefits that nation-states derive from effective extra-statist regulation of the parallel world-economy (for example, transnational narco-trafficking as a parapolitical means of servicing Third World debt)? In what ways are state policies, either foreign or domestic, shaped by a nation-state's own covert intervention into global underground economies?

The most obvious and, perhaps, the most important, nexus between parapolitics and the ostensibly liberal state is the market place: arguably, national parapolitical systems exist and are implicitly tolerated – if not actually encouraged – in order to provide both extra-statist and extra-juridical regulation of underground, or 'shadow', economies.[107] As Hennner Hess[108] and Vincenzo Ruggiero[109] make clear in their respective contributions,

> [t]rans-national crime may well transcend conventional activities and mingle with entrepreneurial and, at times, governmental deviance… in this respect, it is appropriate to identify trans-national organized crime as the result of a partnership between illegitimate and legitimate actors.[110]

If law invokes government, then corruption invokes governance;[111] within the transnational economy, criminal organisations transverse from a predatory to a symbiotic mode of being.

> Most of the time, corruption entails a confusion of the private with the public sphere or an illicit exchange between the two spheres. At both the policy-making and law-enforcement levels, corrupt practices involve *public officials acting in the best interests of private concerns*, regardless of, or against the public interest. Therefore, corruption can be defined as the *covert privatisation of government functions*.[112]

Over time, 'illicit privatisation' may result in the complete fusion of criminal and statist forms.

> The ability to corrupt is…dependent on how integrated the individual or group is into the 'legitimate' society. If they have secure positions of influence and power and therefore have entwined themselves into the power structure through either the economic sphere, political alignments, or the enforcement/criminal justice field, their activities are more easily defined as legitimate. With this integration comes invisibility in that decisions taken, policies passed and agreements signed are not defined as corruption but rather as 'normal' operations of business or enterprise.[113]

This is highly reminiscent of the 'Smith Thesis'; organised crime represents 'in virtually every instance an extension of a legitimate market spectrum into areas normally proscribed... [It derives] from the same fundamental considerations that govern entrepreneurship in the legitimate marketplace: a necessity to maintain and extend one's share of the market'.[114]

> Paralleling the de-legitimation of the extant political order, the old instruments and institutions of economic organization are also obsolete. In one country after another not only is the 'underground' – the informal, unrecorded and unregulated – part of the economy growing faster than the official part, but in many countries of the developing world it is now larger in absolute terms. It is not a matter merely of unlicensed street vendors but of entire large-scale production units that are operating in an environment over which the formal state apparatus has no control. It was not accidental that, in the past, insurgencies thrived in precisely those societies where the de-legitimation of the state was paralleled by the spread of underground economic authority. And it will not be accidental that, in the future, the spread of the underground economy will be a political and financial breeding ground for the forces most anxious to challenge the status quo distribution of power and wealth.[115]

The highest stage of juro-political evolution of the criminal cartel is the 'symbiotic phase'. In this phase

> [c]riminals become an integral, functional part of the society off which they formally preyed, and the distinction between illegal and legal activities starts to blur. Rather than their income and wealth being a direct deduction from that of legitimate formal society, the income and wealth of both increase together as the criminal sector supplies goods and services which, for a variety of reasons, the formal society's legitimate enterprises cannot be seen as providing. This symbiosis goes beyond the merely economic. It is a commonplace observation that much of the covert funding for political parties in those democratic systems that impose limitations on campaign financing comes from or through underworld sources... [These] links are more than financial. More overtly corrupt regimes... can actually endorse the stranglehold of powerful criminal syndicates...on a wide range of businesses in return for those criminal groups deploying their muscle to keep political rivals of the government at bay.[116]

As Arlacchi points out, the 'seriousness of the mafia phenomenon today lies... precisely in the fact that it is no longer an unproductive, subordinate element in the economy, but has become a productive force embedded in the socio-economic structures' of the world-economy.[117]

> Mafia entrepreneurs know full well that they hold a good share of regional economic power, and constitute a largely autonomous economic force. *For all their conflicts with part of the State apparatus* and with the non-mafia elements in the entrepreneurial elite, they feel themselves to be members of

the ruling class, and have come to realise that their needs require appropriate political expression.[118]

A global economic system premised upon 'ceaseless capital accumulation'[119] exacerbates irrational economic drives in both the official and the underground economies. Historically, mafia-type entrepreneurial activity was constrained by the inherent imbalance 'between the rapid pace of capital accumulation and the restrictive narrowness of territorial markets'.[120] However, now that 'the mafia's activities obey forces tending towards a ceaseless expansion of power, this balance of generational succession has been disturbed, and continual conflict between *mafiosi* has become inevitable'.[121]

Arlacchi's significant comment – *'For all their conflicts with part of the State apparatus'* – attains an even deeper resonance when read in conjunction with Scott's notion of the parapolitical, both parapolitics and predatory entrepreneurial-ism signifying expanding orbits of the economically and the politically irrational. In his more recent writing, Scott has come to see the parapolitical as a free-floating sign of a political irrationality not expressly circumscribed by statist forms.

> The investigation of *Parapolitics*, which I defined (with the CIA in mind) as a 'system or practice of politics in which accountability is consciously diminished'… I still see value in…[it as a]…definition and mode of analysis. But Parapolitics as thus defined is itself too narrowly conscious and intentional… it describes at best only *an intervening layer of the irrationality under our political culture's rational surface.* Thus I now refer to Parapolitics as only one manifestation of *deep politics*, all those political practices and arrangements, deliberate or not, which are usually repressed rather than acknowledged.[122]

Note how Scott's concept of 'deep politics' parallels the honour culture of Hess' para-statist *mafiosi*; honour is both irrational *and* deeply determinative. Read in the strongest sense, 'deep politics' directly echoes Schopenhauer's parodic inversion of Hegel's metaphysics: the real is the irrational, the irrational is the real. Through its convergence with a more generic illiberal political irrationality, 'deep politics' is dyadic to a globalised predatory entrepreneurialism utilising a para-logic of its own.

> If the *mafioso's* entrepreneurial activity is marked at once by an economic-rational dimension and by an aspect that is irrational and extra-economic, he is not alone in this… Far from progressively enlarging the sway of values and conduct of a rational-capitalist type, the entrepreneurial practices of the *mafiosi* extend the domain governed by archaic and predatory practices.[123]

Arlacchi deliberately evokes Susan Strange's observations on the interpenetration of 'market' with 'state' forms.[124] If the monist identity of the state has been fractured by para-structures and the market strives to operate in an extra-juridical manner, then it is precisely those same para-structures that will strive to assimilate the potent but unpredictable extra-statist dimensions of the economy. An 'irresponsible' economy serves as the natural habitat of irresponsible agencies. Conversely, if the world-economy, an inherently irrational process of ceaseless capital accumulation,[125] has truly penetrated *everywhere*, then the most successful predatory structures of capital accumulation will be able to evolve into 'legitimate' forms of political agency.

WORLD-SYSTEM THEORY

The symbiotic convergences between criminal cartels and transnational economies underscore the necessity of understanding intra-state developments of the parapolitical as encapsulated within inter-state developments; the transversal between the micro-level to the macro-level transferred to the global level of analysis. This is the main argument of the chapter by Howard Dick.[126] By positing a structural equivalence between the North and the South – or, the 'core' and the 'periphery' – world-system theory provides us with a vital interpretative model with which to conceptualise parapolitics.[127]

> The architecture of the global economy features an asymmetrically interdependent world, organised around three major economic regions[128] and increasingly polarized along an axis of opposition between productive information-rich, affluent areas, and impoverished areas, economically devalued and socially excluded.[129]

In world-system terms, the parapolitical convergence of core zone states via transnational shadow economies strictly parallels the exploitative assimilation of peripheral and semi-peripheral states within the world-system; 'The governance networks linking North and South…largely reflect the internationalisation of [northern domestic] public policy and reflect the South's subordination.'[130] For Mark Duffield,

> [i]n terms of the international North–South flows and networks, there is a noticeable duality. While patterns are uneven and great differences exist, the shrinkage of formal economic ties has given rise to two opposing movements. Coming from the South, there has been an expansion of trans-border and shadow economic activity [i.e., parapolitics] that has forged new local–global linkages with the liberal world system and, in so doing, new patterns of actual development and political authority – that is, alternative and non-liberal forms of protection, legitimacy and social regulation. Emerging from the North, the networks of international public policy have thickened and multiplied their points of engagement and control. Many erstwhile functions of the nation state have been abandoned to these international networks as power and authority have been reconfigured. *The encounter of the two systems has formed a new and complex development-security terrain.*[131]

In a similar vein, Manuel Castells has famously argued,

[a] new world, a Fourth World, has emerged, made up of multiple black holes of social exclusion throughout the planet. The Fourth World comprises large areas of the globe, such as much of Sub-Saharan Africa, and impoverished rural areas of Latin America and Asia. *But it is also present in literally every country, and every city, in this new geography of social exclusion.*[132]

The necessary linkage between parapolitics and a globally fragmenting political pluralism is provided by the two signature characteristics of the modern world-system itself. These are: (1) a radically heterogeneous inter-state system that yields an endless proliferation of transnational actors and identities;[133] and (2) a strict verticality of North–South flows.[134] The recent permutations within both the modern world-system and its economic corollary, the capitalist world-economy, have spawned entire classes of anomalous political entities that resist orthodox analysis. Ambivalent terminology signifies doctrinal dissent: 'rogue states'; 'weak states'; 'failed states'; 'states of concern'; 'quasi-states'; 'deep states'; and 'dual states'.[135]

The geo-spatial (sub-)divisions of an unevenly integrated world-system serve as the necessary precondition for the emergence of global parapolitical structures. Duffield's tantalising phrase 'new and complex development-security terrain' provides the venue for the direct insertion of parapolitical bodies and criminal cartels into the primary patterns of global governance.

While antagonisms exist with regards to the state's official regulatory authority over these regional economies, complicity is also evident insofar as the state is dependent upon these regional economies for rents and the means of redistribution. Likewise, while these networks can be described as trans- or sub-national, they make important, or even essential contributions to the national political economy. Moreover, while these regimes of power and wealth may be described as novel realms of thought and action, they are none the less inscribed in the same logical – or epistemological – order as that of the nation-state.[136]

These 'shadow networks'[137] constitute an outstanding example of 'blowback', the re-direction of hostile covert activities back towards the sending state.

The threat of an excluded South fomenting international instability through conflict, criminal activity and terrorism is now part of a new security framework. Within this framework, underdevelopment has become dangerous… On the one hand, evidence suggests that the South has been increasingly isolated and excluded by the dominant networks of the conventional global informational economy… At the same time, however, formal economic exclusion is not synonymous with a void, far from it. *The South has effectively reintegrated itself into the liberal world system through the spread and deepening of all types of parallel and shadow trans-border activity. This represents the site of new and expansive forms of local-global networking and innovative patterns of extra-legal and non-formal North–South integration.*[138]

We do well to conclude this section by recalling the words of Peter Dale Scott on the correlation between blowback and vertical North–South flows.

> Covert power is like nuclear power: it produces noisome and life-threatening by-products [that] cumulatively are more and more threatening to the environment supposedly served. The by-products of covert power include trained terrorists who in the end are more likely to target their former employers, the incriminating relations to government [that] hinder the terrorist's prosecution, and the ensuing corruption of society at large. The result is deep politics: the immersion of public political life in an immobilizing substratum of unspeakable scandal and bad faith. The result in practice is 9/11.[139]

SHADOW GOVERNANCE: THE MACRO-LEVEL

The scope for and significance of parapolitical structures is directly proportionate to the degree that the modern world-system is identical with the world-economy. Herein may lie the explanation for the global recurrence of parapolitics: *it precisely is the extra-statist and extra-juridical governance of a world-economy that is constituted equally by sub-system legal and 'shadow' economies*. Again, a new series of questions are posed. Under what conditions can parapolitical complexes be invested with juro-political legitimacy and authority? To what degree is invisibility a necessary precondition for effective parapolitical governance?

Here, highly subversive alternatives to the conventional models of modernity and development begin to suggest themselves. It is submitted that a (potentially) new index for the qualitative measuring of levels of national development is the degree to which the parapolitical complexes have been either effectively co-opted by or integrated into the de jure nation-state. Far from eliminating 'organised crime', developed states have merely been (comparatively) successful in rendering cartels institutionally invisible, through a strictly teleological trajectory of historical development: from predatory models of cartel function to the parasitical and, finally, the symbiotic.[140] Conversely, a 'developing' state may be defined as one in which adequate mechanisms of parapolitical assimilation are lacking, rendering criminal governance transparent; for example, the tributary/exaction model of African warlord-ism as a visible – and, therefore, 'primitive' – system of protection/taxation; these are discussed by William Reno in this volume.

The definition of 'governance' – 'shadow' or otherwise – employed here broadly follows that formulated by James N. Rosenau; 'the command mechanism of a social system and its actions that endeavour to provide security, prosperity, coherence, order and continuity to the [socio-political] system'.[141] Governance is both extra-governmental and anti-hierarchical: while it encompasses formal institutions, it also expressly includes all private actors who utilise command mechanisms in regulating the production and distribution of outcomes. The issue of *private agency* is of central importance to us.

Governance is also inextricable from the wider phenomenon of legitimacy, voluntary obedience to consensus-generated inter-subjective systems of rules. As we have already shown in our cursory discussion of the Sicilian mafia, although not necessarily supported by formal legal authority, legitimacy exists wherever some sort of system of governance guarantees the completion of 'those tasks that have to be performed to sustain the routinized arrangements of prevailing order and that may or may not be performed by government'.[142]

This thoroughly pragmatic nexus between legitimacy and outcome-performance creates 'authority', both private and public, consistent with our discussion above. It is at precisely this juncture that 'legal illegality' emerges; the rise of legitimate private authority invests extra-judicial, or non-legal, actors with the symbolic construction of political order as is argued by Mark Findlay.[143]

This book deliberately employs the phrase 'shadow governance' in relation to parapolitical structures as a way to highlight the centrality of covert action for international politics, what might be deemed as the continuation of 'informal Empire' by other means.[144] It is in this sense, and this sense only, that 'conspiracy theory' is a topic of concern for the contributors to this volume. Stripped of its speculative and sensationalist armature, 'conspiracy theory' stands revealed as the merely self-consciously parapolitical realisation that covert agencies and actions are an integral part of the practical exercise of governance within both national and transnational spaces. Global governance is never politically neutral or morally innocent as it is always highly prone towards the fostering of deep politics, even within its most innocuous forms; throughout the late twentieth century, 'there has been a noticeable move from the hierarchical, territorial and bureaucratic relations of government to more polyarchical, non-territorial and networked relations of governance'.[145] A primary example of this is what Duffield has labelled 'the liberal peace', which is

> [p]art of the complex, mutating and stratified networks that make up global liberal governance. More specifically, liberal peace is embodied in a number of flows and modes of authority within liberal governance that bring together different *strategic complexes* of state–non-state, military–civilian and public–private actors in pursuit of its aims. Such complexes now variously enmesh international NGOs, governments, military establishments, IFIs, private security companies, IGOs, the business sector and so on. They are strategic in the sense of pursuing a radical agenda of social transformation [i.e. 'Developmentalism'] in the interests of global stability. In the past, one might have referred to these complexes as representing the development or aid industry; now, however, *they have expanded to constitute a network of strategic governance relations that are increasingly privatised and militarised.*[146]

Within this general convergence of 'strategic complexes' and parapolitical structures, it is the element of 'private' that most concerns us, causing a transversal shift from licit to illicit or 'shadow' forms of governance.

SHADOW GOVERNANCE AND PRIVATE AUTHORITY: THE MERCANTILE COMPANIES

As we have already discussed, successful 'state building' within the euro-centric core zone of the modern world-system was invariably equated with the successful monopolisation of violence within a specific territory coupled with a self-sustaining collection of 'protection rent', either in the form of 'primitive' tribute or rationalised 'taxation'. What is generally under-appreciated is the degree to which the currently asymmetrical world-system operates within the 'trace' of a more primitive but highly efficacious world-system of private authority and governance established by the great mercantile companies of the seventeenth century. The political and economic realities of the early modern period served as sufficient grounds for legitimising the status of the trading companies, such as Grotius' Dutch East Indies Company (the VOC), as an autonomous military – and, therefore, *political* – force.[147]

Pivotal to the global success of the VOC was the systematic internalisation of 'protective costs'; the institutional integration of military and paramilitary activity within the lawful scope of company activities so as to ensure the secure transit of capital assets, 'guaranteed' or 'forced' access to new markets, and the efficient subsidisation of costs through the enforced guarantee of advantageous rates of return on capital outlays. An exact counterpart of those contemporary international private security companies that constitute an outstanding example of Duffield's strategic complexes,[148] the armed mercantile company efficiently subsidised 'low-intensity warfare',[149] leading directly to the institutionalised 'over-lapping' of public and private functions.

> The managers of the Company, confronted with conflicting political and economic considerations, created a new kind of balance between non-economic means and economic ends. Against the demands of the participants, the directors carried through an aggressive policy, a policy of consolidation and a policy of dividends. But they did not identify the Company with the State and they did not make the aim of the State their own. In the long run they did not forget that the Company was a privately owned business and that its owners were meant to make a profit. The result of this situation was a hybrid, neither a simple partnership for trade nor a state strategy; profit remained the ultimate aim, but under conditions which tended to make the presentation and growth of the capital as important as, or more important than, the payment of demands. At least as early as 1609, but probably already in 1606, the Heeren XVII realized that the non-economic means might be used for economic ends, and that the acts of war in the East might be turned into a profitable investment. Even if it might be a waste of time to combine the functions of soldier and merchant in one person, the Company found that it was no waste to combine economic and non-economic activities in one enterprise. The instruments of violence under the control of the Company were to some extent used for the purposes of organized plunder; they were in general used to safeguard and further economic activities, but they did not become an end in themselves.[150]

Many historians have regarded the endemic corruption of the VOC as a primary cause of the company's long-term decline.[151] 'The VOC's success was to no small extent achieved because of the secrecy of its affairs and its decentralization at home – either of which could with hindsight appear as weaknesses.'[152] The economic transgressions of the VOC are thus strongly reminiscent of contemporary trends.

Illicit wealth is dangerous because it is cumulative. With higher rates of return, it grows faster than legal. Because it is associated with the de-legitimation of the state and the discrediting of the prevailing distribution of legal income and wealth in the eyes of citizens, underground accumulation can go hand in hand with the general breakdown of social cohesion and the spread of more predatory forms of economic behaviour. Legitimate wealth will then tend to imitate its behaviour – seeking out higher rates of return in the underground economy and stashing surpluses in short term, anonymous and speculative assets rather than in long term productive investment.[153]

Strikingly, the dawning recognition of the iterability between official and underground economies marks a comparative 'deconstructive turn' in criminology.

The notion that legitimate markets shape the way in which illicit goods are simultaneously marketed found it very hard, and perhaps still does not gain currency. Admitting to such a close connection between legitimate and illegitimate commercial undertakings amounts, in some quarters, to acknowledging that economic development brings, along with wealth and social opportunities, parallel opportunities for the acquisition of illegally produced wealth.[154]

The point of this historical excursus has been to highlight the way in which the foundational conduits through which the modern world-system evolved were, in the most generic sense, both 'private' and 'corrupt'; which is to say, parapolitical. As we have seen elsewhere, the seventeenth century provided an extensive staging ground for twenty-first-century developments. Thanks to the global penetration of the capitalist world-economy, the macro-level North–South vertical axis is now paralleled by micro-level divisions North-to-North and South-to-South. The 'shadow economies' of the South constitute 'black holes of informational capitalism' replicated globally throughout the world-system.[155] The emergence of an international informational capitalist class, generating ever-higher levels of transnational convergence, increasingly leads to the criminalisation of domestic structures and to an ever-widening collapse of the political into the parapolitical.[156] The growing parallel linkages between North and South create new parapolitical structures to guarantee acceptable political outcomes in the absence of responsive or controllable state institutions. The more a state's vital interests are determined by extra-territorial factors, the greater the need for extra-juridical forms of covert action and deep politics.[157]

Instead of complex political emergencies [e.g. Humanitarian assistance], global governance is encountering *emerging political complexes* on its borders. *Such complexes are essentially non-liberal*. That is, they follow forms of economic logic that are usually antagonistic towards free-market prescriptions and formal regional integration. At the same time, politically, the new forms of protection and legitimacy involved tend to be socially exclusive rather than inclusive. *However, for those that are included, such political complexes nevertheless represent new frameworks of social representation and regulation. In other words, political complexes themselves are part of a process of social transformation and system innovation, a characteristic that embodies the ambiguity of such formations. While their economic and political logic can find violent and disruptive expression, in many cases such complexes are the only forms of existing or actual authority that have the powers to police stability.*[158]

THE SUB-STATE

Rosenau expressly identifies post-international politics with the unregulated proliferation of 'sub-groupism'.[159] This leads directly to a new set of questions: can parapolitical complexes evolve into either de jure or de facto polities and, if so, how? This involves consideration of the proliferation of the sub-state, the quasi-sovereign territorial fragment of the radically parapolitically sub-divided nation-state; in this volume William Reno discusses examples of this phenomenon from Africa, while Rensselaer Lee and Francisco Thoumi focus on Afghanistan and South America respectively. The sub-state, in turn, exerts transnational effects through its multiple nexuses with the parallel world-economy, which, symbiotically, creates and sustains the parapolitical territorial unit.[160]

One of the main areas of concern here will be tracing the effects of 'reversible colonisation'. To the extent that First World countries form transnational relationships with localised Third World political complexes (for example, the 'penetration' of the Italian Christian Democratic Party by the Sicilian Mafia), the 'developed' state undergoes a degree of politically archaic regressive 'de-evolution', collapsing the conventional dichotomies between politics/economics and public/private that are the universally accepted signs of modernity and development. While this phenomenon may be the effect of 'reverse colonisation' by the South, it is of the greatest importance to note that the North frequently has both the will and the opportunity to adopt practices allegedly restricted to the South as their own; the ultimate anti-hierarchical conflation of northern 'Self' with southern 'Other'. Given the deeply symbiotic relationship between North/South within the world-system, the proliferation of horizontal flows within the centres of global governance will initiate a parallel movement within the peripheries.

In the case of the new wars [or, 'humanitarian crises'], *market deregulation has deepened all forms of parallel and trans-border trade and allowed warring parties to forge local–global networks and shadow economies as a means of asset realisation and self-provisioning.* The use of illicit alluvial diamonds to fund conflict in West and South Africa is a well-known example of a system that has a far wider application. *Rather than expressions of breakdown or chaos, the new wars can be understood as a form of non-territorial network war that works through and around States.* Instead of conventional armies, the new wars typically oppose and ally the trans-border resource networks of state incumbents, social groups, diasporas, strongmen, and so on. These are refracted through legitimate and illegitimate forms of state–non-state, national–international and local–global flows and commodity chains. Far from being a perpetual aberration, network war reflects the contested integration of stratified markets and populations into the global economy. Not only can the forms of innovation and state–non-state networking involved be compared to those of liberal peace; more generally, *they stand comparison with the manner in which Northern political and economic actors have similarly adapted to the pressures and opportunities of globalisation. In this respect, as far as it is successful, network war is synonymous with the emergence of new forms of protection, legitimacy and rights to wealth. Rather than repression, the new wars are organically associated with a process of social transformation: the emergence of new forms of authority and zones of alternative regulation.*[161]

The key question that now emerges is: how, and to what degree, is it possible to give formal juro-political expression to parapolitical governance? The demonstrable linkage between parapolitics, criminal cartels and anti-systemic movements of national liberation throughout the South forces us to reconceptualise the entire problem of international political identity and legal personality.[162]

Robert H. Jackson's theory of the 'quasi-state' is most useful here.

Most African countries, even the smallest ones, are fairly loose patchworks of plural allegiances and identities somewhat reminiscent of medieval Europe, with the crucial difference that they are defined and supported externally by the institutional framework of sovereignty regardless of their own domestic conditions. Ironically, they are 'medieval' and 'modern' at the same time.[163]

For Jackson, quasi-states are a striking confirmation of Raz's radically anti-essentialist concept of authority.

They do not disclose the empirical constituents by which real states are ordinarily recognised. [Juridical States] frequently lack the characteristics of a common or public realm; state offices possess uncertain authority, governing organizations are ineffective, and plagued by corruption, and the political community is highly segmented ethnically into several 'publics' rather than one.[164]

Quasi-states are, in turn, subject to infinite juridical sub-division; 'violence in illegal markets is a mechanism of dispute resolution'.[165] Accordingly, the legitimation of non-statist criminal gangs is achieved increasingly through the establishment of effective 'regulatory authority' over proliferating insurgent 'trans-border' economies.[166]

While antagonisms exist with regards to the state's official regulatory authority over these regional economies, complicity is also evident insofar as the state is dependent upon these regional economies for rents and the means of redistribution. Likewise, while these networks can be described as trans- or sub-national, they make important, or even essential contributions to the national political economy. Moreover, while these regimes of power and wealth may be described as novel realms of thought and action, they are none the less inscribed in the same logical – or epistemological – order as that of the nation-state.[167]

Duffield identifies struggles of this kind as *'post-modern conflict'*, which

> [a]ddresses the emergence within the past couple decades of political projects in the South, including qualified state systems, *which no longer seek or even need to establish territorial, bureaucratic or consent based political authority in the traditional sense*. It reflects the re-emergence of globalised political economies no longer reliant on an inclusive nation-state competence.[168]

Two things follow from this. Firstly, as Reno reminds us, this 'connection between domination of societal networks, accumulation and power makes nonsense of efforts to mark firm distinctions between state and society'.[169] Secondly, the patrimonial state is revealed as standing in a relationship of extreme iterability with that of the criminal cartel, a pointed confirmation of Tilly's assertion that 'banditry, piracy, gangland rivalry, policing, and war making all belong on the same continuum'.[170] Far from constituting a symptom of 'pathology' or 'regression', criminal organisations may be plausibly read as signs of alternative forms of juro-political organisation precisely to the degree with which they have been invested with the requisite degree of authority.[171]

CRIMINAL SOVEREIGNTY: THE MICRO-LEVEL

These questions lead to the final substantive area of concern – criminal sovereignty understood as a mode of extra-legal authority. In many ways, this is the most difficult topic to discuss, as it is the one most buried in the 'shadow' of deep politics. It is also the topic addressed least directly by the contributors, being deeply embedded within the bridging mechanism of parapolitics. Herein, the methodological challenges – and criticisms – are most weighty; it is difficult, if not impossible, to exhaustively treat that which, by its very nature, is inherently invisible. The most obvious response in defence of parapolitical studies is provided by way of an analogy with theoretical physics in its attendant discussions of 'black holes' or 'dark matter', both quintes-sentially 'shadow' phenomena; the existence of the invisible may be deductively inferred by otherwise inexplicable anomalies in the behaviour of visible events.

It is our contention that parapolitical structures, acting either unilaterally or in conjunction with clandestine national security and intelligence agencies, may be understood as *positive* phenomena, insofar as they constitute alternative modes of authority by providing security/protection or effective dispute resolution, especially where the state is unwilling or unable to do so. The fatal flaw of orthodox liberal political theory is that it relies upon a foundational misconception of the true nature of the nation-state. The highest expression of political modernity in territorial form, the state is ultimately unable to perform the single most important task assigned to it: to serve as a self-validating basis of a legitimacy and authority that is free from internal contradiction. This 'freedom from internal contradiction' is commonly referred to as 'transparency'; yet, the objective nature of the state signifies the precise absence of any such transparency.

The source of this lack of transparency lies within History. The critical moment was the conflation of sovereignty with statism that occurred in the mid seventeenth century, not coincidentally the era of both Althusius and Grotius. Sovereignty, understood within its historical dimensions, clearly antedates its modern territorial construction. Although always identified with executive power and zones of control, sovereignty was never exhaustively defined by such terms. In its pre-modern form, sovereignty is a quintessentially Natural Law concept, signifying the presence of authority as the basis for legitimate law making. Indeed, both law making and legitimacy may be interpreted as virtual synonyms of sovereignty. Understood this way, territory, as a container or demarcation of sovereignty, is wholly dispensable. Historically, sovereignty has resided within the People, the Church, the Papacy, the Empire, the Guilds, the City, and the Family; it may be expressed through a wide variety of constitutional formulas, including republicanism, monarchy, and oligarchy.

The critical moment for criminal sovereignty, however, was reached with the rise of the Westphalian System and the early-modern formation of the society of nation-states. Eschewing the subjective criteria of political, cultural, or religious identity as the basis of sovereignty, the Peace Settlement of 1648 marks a collective shift towards the objective criterion of territoriality as the true basis of internationally recognised legal personality juridically expressed through the positive recognition of legal personality.

The re-conceptualisation of sovereignty on the basis of a thoroughly secular or 'post-theological' notion of territoriality served as the juridical lynchpin of the Westphalian System. Given that the Peace of 1648 marked the end of the ultra-sectarian Thirty Years' War, we should not find the aggressively secular, or 'positivist', nature of modern international legal discourse surprising. Secular – here, meaning 'objective' – territoriality received its highest legal expression through the concept of 'effectiveness'. The vital criterion for sovereignty is now control: the state 'is the spatial framework within which a general legal authority is exercised'.[172] From this, it follows that the Westphalian sovereignty is to be factually, or 'positively', constituted by a 'state of affairs where an international actor displays actual control *and* general legal authority over a certain territory'.[173] It is important to note here the express identification of authority with *control*. As we have seen, there is absolutely no reason why this must self-evidently be so. Yet, within contemporary international law, or 'the law of nations', the effective exercise of

[t]erritorial jurisdiction, in other words of general legal authority over a certain territory, is normally accompanied by the presumption that the subject exercising such jurisdiction has a right to do so. This is due to the role that the concept of effectiveness has played in the way international law has developed its basic concepts.[174]

It is precisely this postulated linkage between sovereignty and territory, legally mediated by effectiveness, which explains the endlessly self-subverting nature of liberal political discourse. It is of great significance that international law is marked by two outstanding 'gaps' or *lacunae* in its treatment of the state. The first is that international law has no actual conception of the state, relying upon the factual, and essentially circular, finding of a series of empirical signs demonstrating the presence of effective control. The second is that espionage – or, more generally, *the covert* – is not expressly recognised as a form of state practice, even though it constitutes one of the most basic forms of inter-state relations. When both *lacunae* are combined, we are left with the rather bewildering reality that international law provides no means to adequately treat entire categories of alternative modes of political behaviour directly expressive of both legal personality and extra-legal interaction.

History explains why this is so. In his seminal essay, 'War Making as State Making', Tilly persuasively argues that taxation, the supremely statist function, also effectively doubles as a 'protection racket'.

> If protection rackets represent organized crime at its smoothest, then war making and state making – quintessential protection rackets with the advantage of legitimacy – qualify as our largest examples of organized crime. Without branding all generals and statesmen as murderers and thieves, I want to urge the value of that analogy. At least for the European experience of the last few centuries, a portrait of war makers and state makers as coercive and self-seeking entrepreneurs bears a far greater resemblance to the facts than do its chief alternatives: the idea of a social contract, the idea of an open market in which operators of armies and states offer services to willing consumers, the idea of a society whose shared aims and expectations call forth a certain kind of government.[175]

The *lacunae* exhibited by international law now become readily explainable: sovereignty as the meta-normative principle of constitutional order cannot be allowed to become the exclusive possession of an entity that is inherently violent in origin and, therefore, essentially covert in nature. To admit to the capture of the constitutional by the covert is to subvert the internal coherence of the foundational principle of the rule of law itself through a two-fold conflation: (1) the collapse of the public into the private; and (2) the collapse of the objective into the subjective. Most dangerous of all, such subversion allows for – and, perhaps, even *legitimates* – the wholesale substitution of the community and the national interest with the preferences of those classes and elites most adept at covert action. Insights such as these reveal the radically un-contingent nature of the centrality of intelligence services in the conduct of the national policy of incorrigibly class-based polities such as the United Kingdom. Nevertheless, it is Liberalism's insistence upon a wholly secular conception of the state as defined by territorial effectiveness, pressing an inherently covert entity into serving as the meta-normative basis of legitimacy, that itself yields that supreme parapolitical 'paradox' of criminal sovereignty: the dual state. Precisely to the degree that the state is able successfully to manufacture a shadow duplicate of itself is it able to comply with all of the legal demands of formal legitimacy while pursuing its true *raison d'état*, which, given its genealogical descent, remains inherently covert.

This paradox is only worsened when one examines in more detail the deficiencies of the doctrine of effectiveness: if legal personality is reducible to the practical exercise of control, then potentially any entity is capable of achieving the status of sovereign. Historically, Grotius implicitly grasped this with his theory of *actus summae potestatis*, the iterable marks of sovereignty. In contemporary international legal theory, the establishment of effectiveness will produce formal legal recognition as a sovereign by other actors who are equally adept at demonstrating a similar degree of effective control. This yields an international legal system that is thoroughly circular in both nature and effect.[176] On the basis of the doctrine of effectiveness, it is impossible to determine in advance what entity may or may not constitute a state. Recognition by itself fails to be self-grounding as the agent affording recognition to others itself exists nowhere outside of its own capacity for effective control which is itself 'recognised'. As Enrico Milano has demonstrated, the concept of effectiveness 'can be equated to the exercise of territorial jurisdiction by a certain international person, normally a State but possibly also an international organization, a national liberation movement, and potentially even a terrorist group'.[177] Effectiveness as the sole criterion of international legal personality creates the scope for a potentially unlimited proliferation of international actors and agents, both statist and non-statist, licit and illicit.

Criminal cartels regulate forms of social and economic activities that the state may have an active interest in maintaining but which, because of their very nature, are excluded from conventional forms of political discourse; for example, gambling in the Philippines as both an extra-juridical source of political finance as well as an informal, but highly efficacious, mode of 'moral policing' as discussed by Alfred McCoy.[178] Accordingly, the state may be viewed as colluding in actively maintaining parapolitical structures as necessary regulatory agencies of domains that obviate official institutions and practices. This topic is addressed directly by Daniele Ganser[179] from both a developing and developed world perspective; the primary element unifying these diverse forms of political complexes is globalisation and the concomitant inversion of traditional distinctions between First and Third World forms of institutional governance.

The complex acceleration of the world-economy results in a global interpenetration of local and regional parallel ('underground') economies. These convergences effect a parallel and simultaneous re-configuration, largely unrecognised, of formal governmental and political structures. The creation of a parallel quasi-legal world-economy, the source of tremendous political and economic potential, entices states to undertake new forms of extra-statist regulatory actions, either through their own clandestine organisations (for example, intelligence agencies) and/or through the more informal medium of non-statist proxies (i.e. transnational organised criminal cartels). The result is a global model of 'shadow governance', practically realised and coordinated through a dispersed, multilayered, transnational network of parapolitics.

Although the topic of the inter-relationship between criminal sovereignty and intelligence agencies is far too vast a topic to be exhaustively dealt with here, several tentative observations may be offered. Continuing with the dyadic joking that opened this chapter, it is striking to note the highly analogous middleman functions performed by both criminal cartels and secret services within the modern world-system. Both entities conduct a mediatory role between the 'local community' – in this instance, the state itself – and the larger exogamous political structure, which is the world-system as a whole.[180] Following F.G. Bailey,[181] we find an equivalent example of 'encapsulation' operating within the world-economy itself; states serve as the 'small group' structures that 'exist within larger encapsulating structures', necessitating the intervention of middlemen.[182] Writing in non-anthropological terms, Duffield has shown that the 'politics of liberal governance was associated with the transformation of nation states in both the North and the South "from being buffers between external economic forces and the domestic economy into agencies for adapting domestic economies for the exigencies of the global economy"'.[183] From this arises the proliferation of non-statist strategic complexes; 'This transformation has been achieved through the emergence of new cross-cutting governance networks involving state and non-state actors from the supranational to the local level.'[184] As a result,

> [t]he growth of such networks is associated with the attenuation of the ability of state incumbents to govern independently within their own borders. Governments now have to take account of new supranational, international and even local constituencies. However, this does not mean that states have necessarily become weaker (although many have, especially in the South); it primarily suggests that the nature of power and authority has changed.[185]

Intelligence agencies and criminal cartels converge at precisely that point at which extra-statist forms of both mediation and regulation are required by the inherently 'shadow' nature of the capitalist world-economy. If we recall Gambetta's observations concerning the corollary between distrust and competition, this makes perfect sense; the higher the degree of competition within an arena devoid of either trust or security the greater the impetus for the creation of a 'protection industry'.[186] It does no intellectual violence to Gambetta's insight about Sicily by extending it to the entirety of the world-system.[187] In terms of economics, this involves the successful monopolisation and regulation of transnational underground economies; in terms of national security – increasingly inseparable from the world-economy – this necessitates the penetration, appropriation, and manipulation of criminal and parapolitical structures. The steady expansion of the middleman role of intelligence agencies enlarges the scope of operation of the inherent functional 'dualism' of deep politics; it services both political and economic covert imperatives both within the statist and extra-statist systems, leading to an inevitable growth of extra-institutional autonomy and a decline of institutional oversight and accountability.

This takes us to our final, albeit brief, observation. Just as the mafia protector must always generate distrust in order to guarantee the artificial demand of protection, so must parapolitical structures regulate global governance in such a way as to maintain the demand for their services. The recent events of Gulf War II have wholly validated Tilly's chilling pronouncement: 'Since governments themselves commonly simulate, stimulate, or even fabricate threats of external war...governments themselves often operate in essentially the same way as racketeers.'[188] This leads us to our final critical innovation; an appreciation of the manner in which the operational requirements of the covert security apparatus itself becomes a primary driver of the formation of national policy. This, then, is the true domain of the 'Government of the Shadows'.

NOTES

1. Mark S. Granovetter, 'The Strength of Weak Ties', *American Journal of Sociology*, 78/6 (1973), pp. 1360–80.
2. F.G. Bailey, *Stratagems and Spoils: A Social Anthropology of Politics* (Oxford: Basil Blackwell, 1980), p. 167; cf. Chapter 8, passim.
3. Anton Blok, *The Mafia of a Sicilian Village 1860–1960: A Study of Violent Peasant Entrepreneurs*, with Foreword by Charles Tilly (Cambridge: Polity Press, 1974), p. 7.
4. Michele Pantaleone, *The Mafia and Politics* (London: Chatto & Windus, 1966), p. 228; interview by Sicilian journalist Indro Montanelli with the ostensible 'chieftain' of the Sicilian *Cosa Nostra* in the 1940s and 1950s, Don Calo Vizzini. 'The mafia has been said to despise the police and the judiciary. This is inaccurate. The mafia has always respected the judiciary – the law – and bowed to its verdicts; nor has it obstructed the judges' work. In hunting bandits and outlaws…it even sided with law enforcers.' Pino Arlacchi, *Mafia Business: The Mafia Ethic and the Spirit of Capitalism* (London: Verso, 1987), pp. 59–60.
5. Robert Nisbet, *The Social Philosophers: Community and Conflict in Western Thought* (London: Heinemann, 1974), p. 122.
6. Cf. Vincenzo Ruggiero, 'Criminal Sovereignty in Italy: Testing Alternative Definitions', *Social & Legal Studies*, 2 (1993), pp. 131–48.
7. Succinctly defined by Blok as a 'violent entrepreneur, middleman'. Blok, *The Mafia of a Sicilian Village 1860–1960*, p. 265. See below.
8. For the tortuous and highly ambiguous relationship between mafia and banditry, see Raimondo Catanzaro, *Men of Respect: A Social History of the Sicilian Mafia* (New York: The Free Press, 1988), pp. 23–4.
9. S.F. Romano, quoted in Catanzaro, *Men of Respect*, p. 24.
10. 'State-power is in the last analysis coercive power.' Raymond Geuss, *History and Illusion in Politics* (Cambridge: Cambridge University Press, 2001), p. 14.
11. The mainstay of the *mafioso*. Cf. Henner Hess, *Mafia and Mafiosi: Origin, Power and Myth* (Bathurst: Crawford House Publishing, 1998), p. 52, for the testimony of 'a Castellammare peasant': 'I recognise the *mafioso* by his *mafioso* behaviour, no matter what it is, and I believe that *mafia* in all its forms means the commission of an act of violence against another person.'
12. Honour as the sign of 'the man of respect'; intriguingly, one who 'with a single gesture, wasting few words, is able to settle dispute'. Catanzaro, *Men of Respect*, p. 27.
13. Hess, *Mafia and Mafiosi*, p. 50. Cf. Giovanni Falcone, *Men of Honour: The Truth about the Mafia* (Warner Books: London, 1992), p. 57: The 'logic of the Mafia is never obsolete or incomprehensible. It is nothing more than the logic of power, to be understood purely in terms of the attainment of their goals.'
14. Catanzaro, *Men of Respect*, p. 29. As the *pentiti* Antonino Calderone remarked, 'Mafia bosses have a weakness for the law. They send their sons to university and make sure they study law.' Pino Arlacchi, *Men of Dishonour. Inside the Sicilian Mafia: An Account of Antonino Calderone* (New York: William Morrow, 1992), p. 39. The integration of the lawyer into the mafia unit is an established feature of the 'modern' mafia group, or *cosca*. Arlacchi, *Mafia Business*, pp. 141–7.
15. Arlacchi, *Mafia Business*, p. 14. Emphasis added.
16. Pino Arlacchi, *Mafia, Peasants and Great Estates: Society in Traditional Calabria* (Cambridge: Cambridge University Press, 1983), pp. 114–15.
17. Jacques Derrida, 'Force of Law: The "Mystical Foundations of Authority"', in Drucilla Cornell, Michel Rosenfeld and David Gray Carlson (eds), *Deconstruction and the Possibility of Justice* (New York: Routledge, 1992), pp. 3–67.
18. Jonathan Culler, *On Deconstruction: Theory and Criticism after Structuralism* (London: Routledge & Kegan Paul, 1983), pp. 100–9, 159–87, 200–5.
19. Rudolphe Gasche, *The Tain of the Mirror: Derrida and the Philosophy of Reflection* (Cambridge: Harvard University Press, 1986), pp. 212–17.
20. Jonathan Culler, *Saussure* (London: Fontana Press, 1976), pp. 29–34.

21. J.M. Balkin, 'Deconstructive Practice and Legal Theory', *Yale Law Journal*, 96 (1987), pp. 743–86 at 744.

22. Blok, *The Mafia of a Sicilian Village 1860–1960*, p. 94.

23. See below.

24. Blok, *The Mafia of a Sicilian Village 1860–1960*, p. 96.

25. Quoted in ibid., p. 25. Emphasis added.

26. Quoted in ibid., pp. 7–8. Emphasis added.

27. Commenting on the parallel middleman functions performed by both *mafiosi* and state officials, criminologist Paolo Pezzino has remarked, 'between local society and politics it was the *mafioso* who did the mediating; between *mafioso* and institutions this was the job of the politician'. Quoted in Paul Ginsborg, *Italy and its Discontents: Family, Civil Society, State, 1980–2001* (London: Penguin Books, 2001), p. 203.

28. 'A trace represents a *present* mark of an *absent* (presence).' Rudolphe Gasche, *Inventions of Difference: On Jacques Derrida* (Cambridge: Harvard University Press, 1994), p. 45.

29. Sigmund Freud, *Moses and Monotheism*, trans. Katherine Jones (New York: Vintage Books, 1939), p. 52.

30. Nisbet, *The Social Philosophers*, p. 386. Cf. ibid., Chapter 2, passim. For the inherently inchoate nature of the modern state, see Geuss, *History and Illusion in Politics*, passim; 'the state is not best and fully understood as a teleological entity directed exclusively at attending some single end or as having a single function'. Ibid., p. 61.

31. Ibid., p. 385.

32. Quentin Skinner, 'The State', in Terence Ball, James Farr and Russell L. Hanson (eds), *Political Innovation and Conceptual Change* (Cambridge University Press: Cambridge, 1989), pp. 90–131, 102–3.

33. Otto von Gierke, *The Development of Political Theory* (New York: H. Fertig, 1966), pp. 257–8.

34. Marshall Berman, *All That is Solid Melts into Air: The Experience of Modernity* (New York: Penguin Books, 1982), passim.

35. Immanuel Wallerstein, *After Liberalism* (New York: New Press, 1995), p. 74.

36. Eric R. Wolf, 'Kinship, Friendship, and Patron–Client Relations in Complex Societies', in Micheal Banton (ed.), *The Social Anthropology of Complex Societies* (London: Tavistock Publications, 1966), pp. 1–2. Emphasis added.

37. Carl Joachim Friedrich, 'Introduction', in Johannes Althusius, *Politica Methodice Digesta of Johannes Althusius* (Cambridge: Cambridge University Press, 1932), pp. ix–cxviii.

38. T.O. Hueglin, *Early Modern Concepts for a Late Modern World: Althusius on Community and Federalism* (Waterloo, Ont.: Wilfrid Laurier University Press, 1999), pp. 66–7.

39. Ibid., pp. 3, 197–229.

40. Frederick S. Carney, *The Politics of Johannes Althusius* (London: Eyre & Spottiswoode, 1965), p. 34.

41. Richard Tuck, *The Rights of War and Peace: Political Thought and International Order From Grotius to Kant* (Oxford: Oxford University Press, 1999), p. 232.

42. It is important, however, not to over-emphasise Bodin's monistic tendencies, as he sought to guarantee a politically circumscribed autonomy for the family. Cf. Nisbet, *The Social Philosophers*, pp. 131–5.

43. Jens Bartelson, *A Genealogy of Sovereignty* (Cambridge: Cambridge University Press, 1995), p. 28.

44. Julian H. Franklin, 'Sovereignty and the Mixed Constitution', in J.H. Burns and Mark Goldie (eds), *The Cambridge History of Political Thought 1450–1700* (Cambridge: Cambridge University Press, 2001), pp. 298–328.

45. Edward Keene, *Beyond the Anarchical Society: Grotius, Colonialism and Order in World Politics* (Cambridge: Cambridge University Press, 2002), p. 105.

46. For greater discussion, see Eric Wilson, *The Savage Republic: De Indis of Hugo Grotius, Republicanism, and Dutch Hegemony within the Early Modern World-System (ca. 1600–1610)* (Leiden: Brill/Martinus Nijhoff, forthcoming).

47. Hugo Grotius, *[De Indis] De Iure Pradae Commentarius. Comentary on the Law of Prize and Booty*, trans. Gwladys L. Williams and Walter H. Zeydel (London: Wildy & Sons, repr. 1964), p. 289.
48. Ibid., pp. 24–5.
49. Hugo Grotius, *Commentarius in Theses XI: An Early Treatise on Sovereignty, the Just War, and the Legitimacy of the Dutch Revolt*, ed. with a Critical Introduction, Peter Borschberg; 'Foreword to the English Edition', Philip H. Burton (New York: Peter Lang, 1994), p. 225.
50. Ibid., p. 229.
51. Borschberg, 'Critical Introduction', in Grotius, *Commentarius in Theses XI*, p. 55.
52. Burton, 'Foreword to the English Edition', in Grotius, *Commentarius in Theses XI*, p. 205.
53. Otto von Gierke, *Natural Law and the Theory of Society 1500 to 1800, With a Lecture on the Ideas of Natural Law and Humanity by Ernest Troeltsch*, trans. with Introduction, Ernest Baker (Cambridge: Cambridge University Press, 1958), pp. 70–8.
54. The Batavians.
55. Tuck, *The Rights of War and Peace*, p. 82. For Grotius, a remarkably 'positivist' sentiment.
56. The critical linkage between *banditi* and *mafiosi* is their involvement in the 'protection industry'. 'Criminal Sovereignty is not an anti-state, [but]…can only exist when a state exists but is ineffectual. In fact, it is only when there exists a mechanism of public protection unable to function properly that the conditions for private protection can arise. The rise of the Mafia in Sicily during the building of the Italian nation-state is clear confirmation of this… Conversely, if public protection does not even exist on paper, the mechanisms are triggered that in the long term induce citizens to choose among the various private subjects competing to provide them with protection, until one of these emerges as the agent able to offer protection as a public good. Historically, this has been the process whereby public authority in nation-states has formed.' Raymondo Catanzaro, 'Violent Social Regulation: Organized Crime in the Italian South', *Social and Legal Studies*, 3 (1994), pp. 267–79 at 270.
57. Frederic C. Lane, *Venice and History: The Collected Papers of Frederic C. Lane* (Baltimore: Johns Hopkins Press, 1966), pp. 383–4. Cf. Frederic C. Lane, *Profits from Power: Readings in Protection Rent and Violence-Controlling Enterprises* (Albany: State University of New York Press, 1979), pp. 1–36.
58. Simon Strong, *Whitewash: Pablo Escobar and the Cocaine Wars* (London: Pan Books, 1995), pp. 6, 43–8, 82–4, 114–15, 136, 157, 219–20, 323–5; Manuel Castells, *End of Millennium: The Information Age: Economy, Society and Culture*, iii (Oxford: Blackwell Publishers, 1998), pp. 190–201.
59. 'In essence, Mafiosi operate in the economic transactions and agreements where trust, while of paramount importance, is nevertheless fragile, and where it is either inefficiently supplied or cannot be supplied at all by the state: typically, in illegal transactions in otherwise legal goods, or in all transactions in illegal goods.' Diego Gambetta, *The Sicilian Mafia: The Business of Private Protection* (Cambridge, MA: Harvard University Press, 1993), p. 172. It is important to note that Gambetta virtually reduces the mafia to a service provision industry specialising in commodified protection. Gambetta, *The Sicilian Mafia*, passim.
60. Federico Varese, 'Is Sicily the Future of Russia? Private Protection and the Rise of the Russian Mafia', *European Journal of Sociology*, 9 (1991), pp. 224–58, passim; Castells, *End of Millennium*, pp. 180–90.
61. Castells, *End of Millennium*, pp. 166–205.
62. Catanzaro, 'Violent Social Regulation', p. 270.
63. 'All state organization was originally military organization, organization for war.' Otto Hintze, 'Military Organization and the Organization of the State', in *The Historical Essays of Otto Hintze*, ed. Felix Gilbert (Cambridge: Cambridge University Press, 1975), pp. 180–215 at 181.
64. 'Even in our day, the government is primarily an institutional arrangement that sells protection and justice to its constituents. It does so by monopolizing the definition and enforcement of property rights over goods and resources and the granting of rights to the transfer of these assets. In return for this service, the state receives payment in the form of taxes.' Douglass C. North and Robert Paul Thomas, *The Rise of the Western World: A New Economic History* (Cambridge: Cambridge University Press, 1973), p. 97. Cf. Chapter 8, passim.

65. 'Most of the time, corruption entails a confusion of the private with the public sphere or an illicit exchange between the two spheres. At both the policy-making and law-enforcement levels, corrupt practices involve *public officials acting in the best interests of private concerns*, regardless of, or against the public interest. Therefore, corruption can be defined as the *covert privatisation of government functions*.' Nikos Passas, 'A Structural Analysis of Corruption: The Role of Criminogenic Asymmetries', *Transnational Organized Crime*, 4 (1998), pp. 42–55 at 44–5.

66. Charles Tilly, 'Introduction' in Blok, *The Mafia of a Sicilian Village 1860–1960*, p. xxiii.

67. Althusius, *Politica Methodice Digesta of Johannes Althusius*, pp. 201–2.

68. See below.

69. 'They were conglomerates – a mixture of cartels, unions, and syndicates – which for a variety reasons benefited from protection, either by supplying it or by making use of it.' Gambetta, *The Sicilian Mafia*, p. 89. Gambetta, however, is somewhat dismissive of the notion of political pluralism as the basis for a viable mode of government. Cf. ibid., pp. 4–6.

70. Nisbet, *The Social Philosophers*, p. 403.

71. Cf. Paul Ginsborg, *History of Contemporary Italy: Society and Politics 1943–1988* (London: Penguin Books, 1990), pp. 2–3, 17–18, 24–5, 108, 139, 146, 171, 180–1, 216, 235, 240, 342, 359; Ginsborg, *Italy and its Discontents*, Chapters 4 and 7, passim. The connection between familism and *clientelism* is especially important here; the Italian anthropologist Amalia Signorelli has defined the latter as 'a system of interpersonal relations in which private ties of a kinship, ritual kinship, or friendship type are used inside public structures, with the intent of making public resources serve private ends... [facilitating a] mass socialization in the practices of illegality.' Quoted in ibid., pp. 100–1.

72. Cf. Catanzaro, *Men of Respect*, passim. 'The Cosa Nostra...demands each affiliate's absolute loyalty and submission to the family and its representative body. A man of honour acquires status through a commitment "for life", symbolically expressed in a blood oath.' Arlacchi, *Men of Dishonour*, p. 8.

73. Ginsborg, *History of Contemporary Italy*, p. 34; Gambetta, *The Sicilian Mafia*, passim. 'Nepotism, the practice of favouring relatives in the conferring of public offices and contracts, stood in relation to familism much as corruption did to clientelism. Within the framework of a set of uneasy relationships between family, civil society and the state, characterized by strong and cohesive family units, a historically weak civil society, and scant respect for a negligent state, it was to be expected that individual families, both powerful and powerless, would view the public sphere as a plundering ground.' Ginsborg, *Italy and its Discontents*, p. 184.

74. Hess, *Mafia and Mafiosi*, pp. 14–38; Gambetta, *The Sicilian Mafia*, passim. Cf. Blok, *The Mafia of a Sicilian Village*, pp. 95–6; Catanzaro, *Men of Respect*, pp. 8, 52, 82–4.

75. Gambetta, *The Sicilian Mafia*, passim.

76. The parallels with Althusius are obvious.

77. Judith Chubb, *The Mafia and Politics: The Italian State Under Siege*, Western Societies Program Occasional Paper No. 23 (Center for International Studies Cornell University, 1989), p. 3. 'Instead of a uniform organisation the existence of [*Cosa Nostra*] has to be assumed of a great number of separate *associazioni* or *cosche*, each with a *capo* of its own. Relations between *cosche* are not uniform or regulated; there may be hostility or cooperation. A customary distinction is that of *alta* and *bassa mafia*, higher and lower *mafia*. Included in the *alta mafia*, in addition to the *capo*, are usually a number of persons who cooperate with the *cosca* without themselves displaying any *mafioso* attitudes – that is, the protectors. The *bassa mafia* comprises the executors, the *sicari*, who often do not even know the meaning and purpose of an action committed by them at the behest of another person.' Hess, *Mafia and Mafiosi*, pp. 79–80. Gambetta attempts to bridge the differences between instrumental and kinship *familia* by emphasising the importance of protection provided by both units to its respective members: Gambetta, *The Sicilian Mafia*, pp. 57–8.

78. Falcone, *Men of Honour*, p. 56.

79. Hess, *Mafia and Mafiosi*, p. 37.

80. Steven Lukes, *Power: A Radical View* (London: Macmillan, 1974), p. 24.

81. Hess, *Mafia and Mafiosi*, p. 132.

82. Ibid., p. 56.

83. Arlacchi, *Mafia, Peasants and Great Estates*, p. 114. Note the striking confirmation of Luke's radical theory of power offered by General Della Chiesa's damning indictment of mafia authority: 'I have understood something, very simple but perhaps decisive. A large part of the protection and the privileges for which citizens pay the mafia dearly are nothing but their elementary rights. Let us assure the citizens of these rights, let us take this power away from the mafia, and we will turn its dependents into our [the state's] allies.' Quoted in Chubb, *The Mafia and Politics*, p. 53.

84. Joseph Raz, 'Introduction', in idem (ed.), *Authority* (New York: New York University Press, 1990), pp. 1–19 at 2.

85. See below.

86. Falcone, *Men of Honour*, p. 56.

87. For example, cf. Ginsborg, *Italy and its Discontents*, p. 195. 'The Mafia did not even resemble a pre-modern state, for it had no absolute monarch and no dependence on a landowning class.'

88. See below.

89. Arlacchi, *Mafia Business*, p. 40. Cf. ibid., pp. 38–44, 69–75, 161–86.

90. Hess, *Mafia and Mafiosi*, p. 67. 'It is impossible to understand the origins and evolution of the Mafia without acknowledging that the Mafia's power system protects a certain number of important interests and performs functions essential to the perpetuation of specific social arrangements. The Mafia could never have lasted, much less prospered, as long as it has without such a purpose.' Catanzaro, *Men of Honour*, p. 12; ibid, pp. 67–77.

91. Fernand Braudel, *The Wheels of Commerce* (vol. ii of *Civilization and Capitalism 15th–18th Century*), trans. Sian Reynolds (New York: Harper & Row Publishers, 1982), pp. 506–12. There is a 'fundamental opposition between the power of the mafia, which is repressive and conservative by nature, and the typically anomic, rebellious and utopian character of the various primitive forms of social revolt and deviant behaviour.' Catanzaro, *Men of Respect*, p. 29.

92. Hess, *Mafia and Mafiosi*, p. 147.

93. This may include theft, banditry, vagabondage, homosexuality, and prostitution. Arlacchi, *Mafia Business*, p. 28.

94. Ibid., p. 28.

95. Ibid., pp. 27–8. Emphasis added.

96. Chubb, *The Mafia and Politics*, passim.

97. Hess, *Mafia and Mafiosi*, p. xi.

98. Villari, quoted in Catanzaro, *Men of Respect*, p. 72.

99. Geuss, *History and Illusion in Politics*, p. 127. Cf. ibid., pp. 57–69, especially on the fatal weaknesses of social contract theory. 'To assume that the absence of grievance equals genuine consensus is simply to rule out the possibility of false or manipulated consensus by definitional fiat.' Lukes, *Power*, p. 24.

100. Hess, *Mafia and Mafiosi*, p. 70.

101. Ibid., p. 175.

102. Arlacchi, *Mafia Business*, pp. 21, 22. Cf. Blok, *The Mafia of a Sicilian Village 1860–1960*, p. 172: 'most Sicilians realized that State sovereignty existed mainly on paper. For security and protection they had to rely on private power.'

103. Tunander this volume.

104. This volume.

105. This volume.

106. Peter Dale Scott, *The War Conspiracy: The Secret Road to the Second Indochina War* (Indianapolis: Bobbs-Merrill, 1972), p. 171.

107. 'In general terms, it can be suggested that organized crime exists in contexts where relationships or overlaps are observed between legal and illegal entrepreneurial procedures. As for other subjects, organized crime should be acknowledged to have an identity which depends, *inter alia*, on the interactions it establishes with other actors. The focus of analysis, in other words, could fruitfully be removed from its internal apparatus and centred upon that "relationship". This entails a *mutual provision of services and a mutual entrepreneurial promotion* with the legal economy... Organized Crime acts as a supplementary infrastructure for the legal economy, a sort of parallel or clandestine tertiary sector, assigned the role of stepping up the circulation of commodities.' Vincenzo Ruggiero, *Organized and Corporate Crime in Europe: Offers that Can't*

Be Refused (Dartmouth: Aldershot, 1996), p. 143. Conversely, the 'official' economy provides the 'shadow' economy with vital services including finance trafficking, investment opportunities, entrepreneurial partnerships and financial loans. Ibid. 'With respect to traditional analysis, there no longer exists a juxtaposition between legal, submerged, a-legal, illicit and mafia economy. We are faced with a "bad" economy, made up of continuities, contacts and overlaps among them all.' Mario Centorrino, quoted in ibid., p. 141.

108. This volume.

109. This volume.

110. Vincenzo Ruggerio, 'Global Markets and Crime', in Margaret E. Beare (ed.), *Critical Reflections on Transnational Organized Crime, Money Laundering and Corruption* (Toronto: University of Toronto Press, 2003), pp. 171–82 at 177.

111. 'The growing importance of networks and cross-cutting linkages is central to the transition from government to *governance*. It denotes a situation in which the political decision making has become more polyarchical governance'. That is, 'Hierarchical patterns of negotiation and decision-making are replaced by co-operative network like types of negotiation and bargaining.' Mark Duffield, 'Post-modern Conflict: Warlords, Post-adjustment States and Private Protection', *Civil Wars*, 1 (1998), pp. 65–102 at 69. Governance is defined in greater detail below.

112. Passas, 'A Structural Analysis of Corruption', pp. 44–5.

113. Margaret E. Beare, 'Corruption and Organized Crime: Lessons from History', *Crime, Law and Social Change*, 28 (1997), pp. 155–72 at 158.

114. Dwight C. Smith, 'Organized Crime and Entrepreneurship', *International Journal of Criminology and Penology*, 6 (1978), pp. 161–77 at 164. 'Analytically, the corrupt activities of ordinary businesses and criminal businesses are indistinguishable.' Passas, 'A Structural Analysis of Corruption', p. 42.

115. R.T. Naylor, 'The Insurgent Economy: Black Market Operations of Guerilla Organizations', *Crime, Law and Social Change*, 20 (1993), pp. 13–51 at 47.

116. Ibid., p. 21.

117. Arlacchi, *Mafia Business*, p. 115. Cf. Chapter 4, passim, for predatory entrepreneurialism and 'mafia capital accumulation'.

118. Arlacchi, *Mafia Business*, p. 166. Emphasis added.

119. Immanuel Wallerstein, *The Modern World-System I: Capitalist Agriculture and the Origins of the European World-Economy in the Sixteenth Century* (New York: Academic Press, 1974).

120. Arlacchi, *Mafia Business*, p. 157.

121. Ibid., p. 156.

122. Peter Dale Scott, *Deep Politics and the Death of JFK* (Berkeley: University of California Press, 1993), pp. 6–7.

123. Arlacchi, *Mafia Business*, p. xvii.

124. Susan Strange, *States and Markets*, 2nd edn (New York: Pinter Publishers, 1994); Susan Strange, *The Retreat of the State: The Diffusion of Power in the World Economy* (Cambridge: Cambridge University Press, 1996).

125. Wallerstein, *The Modern World-System I*.

126. This volume.

127. Wallerstein, *The Modern World-System I*.

128. In world-system theory, these are the core, the semi-periphery, and the periphery.

129. Castells, *End of Millennium*, p. 145.

130. Mark Duffield, *Global Governance and the New Wars: The Merging of Development and Security* (London: Zed Books, 2001), p. 8.

131. Ibid., p. 9. Emphasis added.

132. Castells, *End of Millennium*, p. 164. Emphasis added.

133. Immanuel Wallerstein, 'Inter-State Structure', in S. Smith et al., *International Theory: Positivism and Beyond* (Cambridge, 1996), pp. 87–107 at 89.

134. 'If globalisation has a meaning in this context it is the consolidation of several distinct but interrelated economic systems as the core of the formal international economy. Moreover, rather than continuing to expand in a spatial or geographical sense, the competitive financial, investment, trade and productive networks that link these regionalised systems have been *thickening and*

deepening since the 1970s. Although there are, of course, many differences that separate them, these core regionalised systems of the global informational economy are here figuratively described as the "North". Correspondingly, the areas formally outside or only partially or conditionally integrated into these regional networks are loosely referred to as the "South". The inclusion of the South within the conventional economic flows and networks of the global economy – even when raw materials and cheap labour are available, even as unequal and exploited subjects – can no longer, as in the past, be taken for granted.' Duffield, *Global Governance and the New Wars*, pp. 3–4.

135.   Cf. Scott, this volume.

136.   Janet Roitman, 'New Sovereigns? Regulatory Authority in the Chad Basin', in Callaghy et al. (eds), *Intervention and Transnationalism in Africa: Global–Local Networks of Power* (Cambridge: Cambridge University Press, 2001), pp. 240–63 at 241.

137.   Carolyn Nordstrom, 'Shadows and Sovereigns', *Theory, Culture & Society*, 17/4 (2000), pp. 35–54, passim.

138.   Duffield, *Global Governance and the New Wars*, pp. 2, 5. Emphasis added.

139.   Peter Dale Scott, 'The CIA's Secret Powers: Afghanistan, 9/11, and America's Most Dangerous Enemy', *Critical Asian Studies*, 35/2 (2003), pp. 233–58 at 233.

140.   'We can expect "quiet", effective, and well-organized illegal markets and corrupt practices in exactly those countries that are conventionally regarded as corruption free. Whenever outlaws commodities or illegal services are in high demand and whenever criminogenic asymmetries are at play, relatively stable and strong governments are fertile ground for corrupt practices facilitating the most sophisticated and best criminal cartels.' Passas, 'A Structural Analysis of Corruption', p. 51.

141.   James N. Rosenau, *Along the Domestic–Foreign Frontier: Exploring Governance in a Turbulent World* (Cambridge: Cambridge University Press, 1997), p. 145.

142.   James N. Rosenau, 'Governance, Order, and Change in World Politics', in James N. Rosenau and Ernst-Otto Czempiel (eds), *Governance without Government: Order and Change in World Politics* (Cambridge: Cambridge University Press, 1992), pp. 1–29 at 4.

143.   This volume.

144.   Chalmers Johnson, *Sorrows of Empire: Militarism, Secrecy, and the End of the Republic* (London: Verso, 2004).

145.   Duffield, *Global Governance and the New Wars*, p. 11. Although beyond empirical demonstration, it would be fascinating to ascertain whether there has been a quantitative increase in the size and scope of covert action following 1945 concomitant to the global implementation of decolonisation.

146.   Ibid., p. 12. Emphasis added.

147.   'Armed merchantmen were not considered at all unusual in the European Middle Ages and Renaissance, and in both their charters, the Dutch and English companies had the right to their own armed forces, which today is the exclusive prerogative of material power.' George D. Winius and Marcus P.M. Vink, *The Merchant-Warrior Pacified: The VOC (the Dutch East India Company) and its Changing Political Economy in India* (Delhi: Oxford University Press, 1991), p. 9. Cf. Marjolein 't Hart, *The Making of the Bourgeois State: War, Politics and Finance During the Dutch Revolt* (Manchester: Manchester University Press, 1993), pp. 187–215; William H. McNeil, *The Pursuit of Power: Technology, Armed Force, and Society Since A.D. 1000* (Chicago: University of Chicago Press, 1982), pp. 102–16; Janice E. Thomson, *Mercenaries, Pirates, and Sovereigns: State-Building and Extraterritorial Violence in Early Modern Europe* (Princeton: Princeton University Press, 1994), pp. 35–41, 59–67, 97–105.

148.   Cf. Juan Carlos Zarate, 'The Emergence of a New Dog of War: Private International Security Companies, International Law, and the New World Disorder', *Stanford Journal of International Law*, 34 (1998), pp. 75–162, passim. Although widely regarded as a 'shocking anachronism', the revitalisation of corporate mercenaries operates in tandem with core zone exploitation of peripheral zones; 'in most states where mercenaries were involved, there seemed to be vital economic interests at stake, usually mining and oil interests'. Zarate, 'The Emergence of a New Dog of War', pp. 87, 89. 'Analytically, this is the road back to feudalism.' Immanuel Wallerstein, *The End of the World as We Know It: Social Science for the Twenty-First Century* (Minneapolis:

University of Minnesota Press, 1999), p. 132. In this way, the localised 'new world disorder' fostered by the modern world-system 'has given birth to [security companies], which act as surrogates for state power'. Zarate, 'The Emergence of a New Dog of War', p. 81.

149. Defined as actions that 'occupy a grey area on the spectrum of conflict, representing a state that is neither war nor peace'. Uyeda, cited in Zarate, 'The Emergence of a New Dog of War', p. 81, n. 30.

150. Neil Steensgaard, 'The Companies as a Specific Institution in the History of European Expansion', in Leonard Blusse and Femme S. Gaastra (eds), *Companies and Trade* (Leiden: Leiden University Press, 1981), pp. 245–64, 251–2.

151. R.J. Barendse, *The Arabian Seas: The Indian Ocean World of the Seventeenth Century* (London: M.E. Sharpe, 2002), pp. 415–16.

152. Ibid., p. 416.

153. R.T. Naylor, 'From Underworld to Underground: Enterprise Crime, Informal Sector Business and the Public Policy Response', *Crime, Law and Social Change*, 24 (1996), pp. 79–150 at 140.

154. Ruggerio, 'Global Markets and Crime', p. 171.

155. Castells, *End of Millennium*, pp. 161–205. 'Consistent with the logic of this view – that exclusion leads to the breakdown of normative order – Castells has argued that the only export from the global black holes that rivals the informational economy in terms of its innovations and networked character is the new "perverse" connection of a global criminal economy.' Duffield, *Global Governance and the New Wars*, p. 7.

156. The parapolitical implications of a global digital economy are discussed by Saskia Sassen, 'Digital Networks and the State: Some Governance Questions', *Theory, Culture & Society*, 17/4 (2000), pp. 19–33.

157. 'For weak state rulers, these [transnational] relationships constitute a new form of extra-territorial power. They manipulate commercial connections and recruit foreign firms as allies in battles with local challengers.' William Reno, 'How Sovereignty Matters: International Markets and the Political Economy of Local Politics in Weak States', in Thomas M. Callaghy, Ronald Kassimir and Robert Latham (eds), *Intervention and Transnationalism in Africa: Global–Local Networks of Power* (Cambridge: Cambridge University Press, 2001), pp. 197–215 at 198.

158. Duffield, *Global Governance and the New Wars*, pp. 14–15.

159. James N. Rosenau, *Turbulence in World Politics: A Theory of Change and Continuity* (Princeton: Princeton University Press, 1990), pp. 403–12.

160. 'Weak states exist within the state system because they and their private firm partners continue to benefit from and manipulate their juridical equality with other states, even though these states lack centralized systems of government and do not provide much in the way of collective goods to citizens... the marginality of very weak states constitutes the primary tool that rulers can use to extend non-bureaucratic control within commercially viable parts of their realms through a lucrative private diplomacy.' Reno, 'How Sovereignty Matters', pp. 214–15.

161. Duffield, *Global Governance and the New Wars*, p. 14. Emphasis added.

162. Nordstrom, 'Shadows and Sovereigns', passim.

163. Robert H. Jackson, 'Quasi-States, Dual Regimes, and Neoclassical Theory: International Jurisprudence and the Third World', *International Organization*, 41/4 (1987), pp. 519–49 at 528.

164. Ibid., pp. 526–7. Quasi-States 'are states mainly by international courtesy', correlating with the concept of Juridical Statehood, which is 'derived from a right of self-determination – negative sovereignty – without yet possessing much in the way of empirical statehood, disclosed by a capacity for effective and civil government – positive sovereignty.' Ibid., pp. 528, 529.

165. Passas, 'A Structural Analysis of Corruption', p. 52.

166. Duffield, *Global Governance and the New Wars*, pp. 140–60, 171–8.

167. Roitman, 'New Sovereigns?', p. 241; passim.

168. Duffield, 'Post-modern Conflict', p. 76. Also, see William Reno, 'Reinvention of an African Patrimonial State: Charles Taylor's Liberia', *Third World Quarterly*, 16/1 (1995), pp. 109–20.

169. Reno, 'Reinvention of an African Patrimonial State', p. 109.

170. Charles Tilly, 'War Making and State Making as Organized Crime', in Peter B. Evans (ed.), *Bringing the State Back In* (Cambridge: Cambridge University Press, 1985), pp. 169–91 at 170.

171. Duffield, *Global Governance and the New Wars*, pp. 128–201; Reno, 'How Sovereignty Matters', passim.

172. Enrico Milano, *Unlawful Territorial Situations in International Law: Reconciling Effectiveness, Legality and Legitimacy* (Leiden: Martinus Nijhoff Publishers, 2006), p. 6.

173. Ibid.

174. Ibid., p. 8.

175. Tilly, 'War Making and State Making as Organized Crime', p. 169.

176. Here, as elsewhere, international public order collectively holds itself hostage to fortune through its naïve faith in the indefinite continuation of the world-system as a specifically *liberal* system. That is, the actors within the system will never, on the basis of state practice, recognise as a sovereign any entity that neither ideologically nor institutionally resembles the recognizing agent that, in turn, is always presumed to be liberal-statist. Even if this were the case, it also remains true that international law is suspiciously under-developed in this regard. The objective requirements of institutional development provided by the Montevideo Convention are scant, there are no express requirements of liberal political identity, and the paramount indicator of legal personality remains the voluntary recognition of the other actors within the system.

177. Milano, *Unlawful Territorial Situation*, p. 6.

178. This volume.

179. This volume.

180. 'The encounter of a global actor – firm or market – with one or another instantiation of the national state can be thought of as new frontier zone. It is not merely a dividing line between the national economy and the global economy. It is a zone of politico-economic interactions that produce new institutional forms and alter some old ones.' Saskia Sassen, 'Excavating Power: In Search of Frontier Zones and New Actors', *Theory, Culture & Society*, 17/1 (2000), pp. 163–70 at 164.

181. Bailey, *Stratagems and Spoils*, pp. 144–55.

182. Ibid., p. 146.

183. Robert W. Cox, quoted in Mark Duffield, *Global Governance and the New Wars*, p. 8.

184. Duffield, *Global Governance and the New Wars*, p. 8.

185. Ibid.

186. Gambetta, *The Sicilian Mafia*, passim.

187. Nordstrom, 'Shadows and Sovereigns', pp. 47–9.

188. Tilly, 'War Making and State Making as Organized Crime', p. 171.

2
Democratic State vs. Deep State: Approaching the Dual State of the West

Ola Tunander

In a 1955 study of the United States State Department, Hans Morgenthau discussed the existence of a US 'dual state'.[1] According to Morgenthau, the US state includes both a 'regular state hierarchy' that acts according to the rule of law and a more or less hidden 'security hierarchy' – which I will refer to here as the 'security state' (also known in some countries as the 'deep state')[2] – that not only acts in parallel to the former but also monitors and exerts control over it. In Morgenthau's view, this security aspect of the state – the 'security state' – is able to 'exert an effective veto over the decisions' of the regular state governed by the rule of law.[3] Indeed, the 'democratic state' and the more autocratic 'security state' always 'march side by side'![4] While the 'democratic state' offers legitimacy to security politics, the 'security state' intervenes where necessary, by limiting the range of democratic politics. While the 'democratic state' deals with political alternatives, the 'security state' enters the scene when 'no alternative exists', when particular activities are 'securitised'[5] – in the event of an 'emergency'. In fact, the security state is the very apparatus that defines when and whether a 'state of emergency' will emerge. This aspect of the state is what Carl Schmitt, in his 1922 work *Political Theology*, referred to as the 'sovereign'.[6]

Logically speaking, one might argue that Morgenthau's 'dual state' is derived from the same duality as that described in Ernst Fraenkel's conception of the 'dual state', which Fraenkel described as typifying the Nazi regime of Hitler's Germany. In the Nazi case, though, this duality was overt, combining the 'regular' legal state with a parallel 'prerogative state', an autocratic paramilitary emergency state or *Machtstaat* that operated outside or 'above' the legal system, with its philosophical foundation in the Schmittian 'sovereign'. Fraenkel refers to Emil Lederer, who argues that this *Machtstaat* ('power state', as distinct from the *Rechtstaat*) has its historical origins in the European aristocratic elite, which still played an important role within European society after the triumph of democracy. This elite acted behind the scene in the 1920s, but considered it necessary to intervene in support of the Nazi Party in the 1930s to prevent a possible socialist takeover. However, this autocratic *Machtstaat* – the Nazi SS-state – was arbitrary, because of its individualised command.[7]

In his analysis, Morgenthau draws a parallel between Nazi Germany and the US dual state. Indeed, in his view, the autocratic 'security state' may be less visible and less arbitrary in democratic societies such as the US, but it is no less important. Morgenthau argues that

> the power of making decisions remains with the authorities charged by law with making them, while, as a matter of fact, by virtue of their power over life and death, the agents of the secret police... [and what I would call the security state: author] at the very least exert an effective veto over [these] decisions.[8]

Below, I will demonstrate that the activity of the 'security state' – or the 'deep state' – concerns not just the vetoing of democratic decisions, but also the 'fine tuning of democracy',[9] for example through the 'fostering' of war or terrorism to create fear and increase public demands for protection. The 'security state' is able to calibrate or manipulate the policies of the 'democratic state' through the use of a totally different logic of politics – a kind of politics that in this book is referred to as 'parapolitics' and which operates outside the law to define the limits of the legal discourse. The argument presented here is not meant as a normative statement, but rather as an attempt to describe and analyse the Western state as it actually operates, both inside and outside the law.

This argumentation has already appeared in Italy both among parliamentary investigations and scholars. Franco de Felice re-introduced the concept of dual state in Italy in his 'Doppia lealtà e doppio stato' (1989). He argues that the dual state is born from an incapacity of the regular state to reconcile domestic policies with foreign policies.[10] Paolo Cucchiarelli and Aldo Giannulli have written in their *Lo Stato Parallelo* (1997) about the dual state or 'parallel state' as a state that operates both inside and outside the law;[11] and Rosella Dossi has written about the dual state in *Italy's Invisible Government* (2001).[12] These Italian scholars, however, refer back to Ernst Fraenkel, not to Hans Morgenthau. Morgenthau's analysis is very useful, however, because it is able to combine the concept of democracy with an autocratic *Machtstaat* or 'shadow government', thus putting a finger on an aspect of the state that is often neglected in political science.

Morgenthau was a traditional 'realist' who inherited important ideas from Carl Schmitt,[13] and was able to flesh out Schmitt's rather abstract analysis of the sovereign. My ambition in this chapter is to continue along that path, to give yet more substance to this line of thinking and, at the same time, make it accessible to a wider audience.

THE SOVEREIGN AS THE 'DEEP STATE'

Let us approach the idea of the 'sovereign' as the security side of the state – what some would call the 'deep state' – by looking at a few examples.

Recent trials and parliamentary investigations in Italy have established that bombing campaigns in the late 1960s and 1970s in that country – and probably elsewhere in Europe – were run not by various anarchist or other left-wing groups, as had been generally believed at the time, but were instead carried out by action squads known as *Nuclei di Difesa della Stato* (Nuclei for Defence of the State, or NDS) in accordance with a policy known as the 'Strategy of Tension'. Already in 1964, William Harvey, then CIA station chief in Rome, had recommended Colonel Renzo Rocca, Chief of Italian Military Intelligence Division R (Gladio: the Italian Stay-Behinds),[14] to use his 'action squads' to 'carry out bombings against Christian Democratic Party offices' in order to implicate the Italian Communist Party (PCI). These 'gladiators' had been 'recruited from the Italian former naval Special Forces Decima MAS and other militant fascist organizations'.[15] From 1966, US and Italian intelligence started to recruit action squads for a 'parallel Gladio', or NDS, from the fascist organisation Ordine Nuovo.[16] Subsequently, while masquerading as left-wingers, anarchists and Maoists, Italian NDS squads, in collaboration with Avanguardia Nazionale activists, carried out a bombing campaign that resulted in the deaths of hundreds of people, in direct collaboration with the CIA and 'US factions' of the Italian intelligence and security services.

Later, Carlo Digilio, who had worked with the CIA in Italy, would recount in court hearings how he had collaborated with activists from Ordine Nuovo and how the bombing campaign had been linked to a US plan to introduce a state of emergency in Italy in order to exclude the political left from government. The same view was presented by Italian Chief of Counter-Intelligence, General Gianadelio Maletti, who confirmed in court that US intelligence had provided Ordine Nuovo with explosives for the first major Italian bomb attack (Milan in 1969). Digilio also described how he passed on details of planned bomb attacks to his CIA contact, Captain David Carrett, who had also told him that the bombing campaign was part of a US plan to establish a state of emergency in order to control Italian domestic politics.[17]

In 1974, however, after several years of bombings in Italy, a number of activists from Ordine Nuovo and Avanguardia Nazionale were forced to flee the country. This led to a pause in their bombing campaign, with no major operations being carried out until 1980, when a bomb at Bologna's railway station left 85 dead and more than 200 wounded. However, also in the early 1970s, as General Maletti and others have confirmed, Italian and US intelligence and secret service agents were able to assume vital positions at the highest levels of Italy's Red Brigades.[18] In 1974, the left-wing leadership of the Red Brigades had been arrested, facilitating the 'takeover' of the organisation by the US and Italian services. This resulted in the launch of a range of professional military operations, a period of 'blind terror' and a radical increase in the number of attacks being carried out within Italy.[19]

It thus seems that the Italian 'deep state' switched to using the Red Brigades as its major extra-legal instrument following the flight of right-wing activists in 1974.

After the murder of Aldo Moro in 1978, his wife recounted how a senior US official had threatened to use 'groups on the fringes' of the official services to kill her husband 'if he did not abandon his policy' of a 'historical compromise' with the left. Notably, the 'Red Brigade' kidnapping of Moro in March 1978 took place on the very day on which his 'compromise' was to go to the vote in the Italian parliament.[20] Later, it was discovered that an apartment and printing press used by the 'Red Brigades' at this time belonged to SISMI, Italy's military intelligence.[21]

It is now indisputable that the use of terrorism was an element of US policy with respect to Italy. US policy was not just to infiltrate and monitor extremist groups, but also 'to instigate acts of violence', to quote General Gianadelio Maletti. A similar strategy, Maletti believed, was also carried out in other European countries.[22] Thus, although a bomb attack in 1972 was first blamed on the Red Brigades, it later transpired that the attack had been carried out by Ordine Nuovo's Vinunzo Vinciguerra. While Vinciguerra described himself in court as genuinely fascist, he argued that Ordine Nuovo no longer was: it had been turned into a covert military arm of the 'state'.[23] Here, in using the term 'state', Vinciguerra is speaking of the 'security state' – the 'deep state' that is prepared to use extra-legal violence to force the general population to trade democratic freedoms for security and protection, establishing a political order that limits the range of democratic discourse and the rule of law.

Similarly, in Turkey, terrorists detonating bombs were exposed as agents of gendarmerie intelligence. Former Turkish Prime Minister Suleyman Demiral argued, 'In our country there are two [states]: one deep state and one other state [the legal state].' This 'deep state' allegedly detonates bombs under cover of being terrorists to justify emergency measures.[24] As stated by Cucchiarelli and Giannulli, in Italy this 'deep state' or clandestine 'parallel state' makes an illegitimate use of power not to subvert, but rather to preserve, the current system of power.[25] The terrorist acts are explicitly carried out in defence of the state (*Nuclei di Difesa della Stato*).

In the final analysis, it is the deep state that is the state structure that decides when and when not to use illegal measures to keep order. In Schmitt's words, it is this 'state' that is the actual 'sovereign', the entity that is able to establish order and the rule of law through operations outside the law: 'The sovereign is he who decides on the exception... For a legal order to make sense, a normal situation must exist, and he is sovereign who definitely decides whether this normal situation actually exists.'[26]

THE HISTORICAL ORIGIN OF EUROPEAN TERRORISM

In his *Theory of the Partisan* (1963), Schmitt describes the irregular fighter or anti-state insurgent as a 'partisan', and in the battle between the state and insurgents, he argues, the state will 'fight like a partisan wherever there are partisans'.[27] Schmitt continues, 'In the vicious circle of terror and counter-terror, the combat of the partisan is often simply a mirror-image of the partisan battle itself.'[28] Schmitt refers to the example of French General Raoul Salan, head of the Organisation d'Armée Secrète (OAS) that from 1961 carried out a campaign of mass terror against the insurgency in Algeria. Salan introduced the ideas of 'revolutionary war' to fight the insurgency using its own methods.[29] Already from late 1950s, French settlers and the French Secret Service set up an organisation, the Red Hand, for the assassination of nationalist Algerians trying to buy small arms abroad. The Red Hand poisoned their targets or let Algerians carry out the killings to suggest an internal Algerian feud,[30] but from early 1960s the OAS also attacked French citizens, in order to lay the blame for such attacks on the Arab insurgency. In Italy from the mid 1960s, the 'sovereign' employed similar terror tactics against the Italian population, laying the blame on the left and the increasingly democratic PCI.

The general ideas for the bombing campaign in Italy, the Strategy of Tension and the concept of 'revolutionary war' were presented at a seminar in May 1965 – financed by Colonel Rocca's Gladio division of Italian military intelligence – at the Alberto Polio Institute for Military Studies in Rome.[31] Among the participants at that seminar were top-ranking Italian military officers and politicians linked to NATO and the US. A central figure was General Adriano Magi Braschi, Chief of Division for Unconventional Warfare of the Italian Military Intelligence. He had been close to the OAS and had, according to the court case in Milan in 2001, played an important role in the initiation of the *Nuclei di Difesa della Stato*. Among the speakers presenting the concepts of the Strategy of Tension and 'revolutionary war' were two 'journalists': Pino Rauti, leader of Ordine Nuovo, and Guidi Giannettini, a fascist intelligence operative and liaison to the OAS. Both were writing a strategy booklet sponsored by the Chief of Staff General Giuseppe Aloja and were subsequently involved in the bombing campaign of the late 1960s and early 1970s.[32]

In 1966, the international fascist intelligence network Aginter Press was established to implement the Strategy of Tension, with support from the Portuguese security service PIDE and the CIA. This network included a unit specialising in the infiltration of anarchist and pro-Chinese groups and its 'correspondents' would use such organisations as a cover for carrying out bombings and other violent attacks. Aginter Press also included a strategic centre for subversion and intoxication operations, along with an executive action organisation that carried out assassinations[33] (most likely the same 'pool of assassins' that William Harvey, CIA Station Chief in Italy, had recruited in Europe for the CIA's 'Executive Action Capability').[34] All of these divisions of Aginter Press were under the leadership of French OAS officer and former US liaison officer Captain Yves Guillou (alias Yves Guerin Serac), in collaboration with Robert Leroy, a former French SS officer, and Otto Skorzeny, a senior German SS officer.

Their network brought together Nazi and fascist activists from intelligence services and security services all over Europe (West Germany, France, Italy, Spain, Portugal and Greece) and Latin America, South Africa and the US. Italian 'correspondents' for Aginter Press included the co-founder Stefano delle Chiaie (leader of Avanguardia Nazionale), Pino Rauti and Guidi Giannettini, who collaborated with French OAS leader Pierre Lagaillarde[35] (also involved in the assassination attempt on the French President, Charles de Gaulle).[36] Some of these, such as delle Chiaie and Rauti, were also linked to the US-dominated World Anti-Communist League (WACL). Braschi was later Italian representative of WACL.[37] An Aginter Press document from 1969 (found in Lisbon in 1974) paints a picture identical to that presented by Giannettini earlier in 1965, with proposals for 'selective terrorism… eliminating certain carefully selected persons' (including assassination of political leaders) and 'indiscriminate terrorism', including 'randomly shooting down people with firearms' and the use of bombs in public squares or buildings, in accordance with the Strategy of Tension bombing campaign.[38] The intention was to dramatise political life in order to 'securitise' issues previously open to public debate, thus limiting the range of the democratic discourse.[39]

From the late 1960s, fascist activists in Italy conducted terrorist operations in collaboration with US intelligence in order to manipulate public opinion and limit the range of the democratic discourse. In the early and mid 1980s, attacks similar to those that had taken place in Italy were also conducted in Belgium, including the random shooting of 28 people in supermarkets outside Brussels in 1983–85. A 'left-wing' terrorist group known as the Cellules Communistes Combattantes (CCC) was accused of having carried out these operations. Later, however, it transpired that the attacks had been conducted by fascist and Nazi groups, with US support. Like Aginter Press before it, the neo-Nazi organisation Westland New Post operating in Belgium contained both an intelligence division and a special operations division. It was run by Belgian agent Paul Latinus in collaboration with US intelligence and the WACL.[40] Around the same time, US Army special forces began a programme of targeting Western/NATO installations in Belgium, while disguising themselves as terrorists. Indeed, the CCC may have simply been a cover for this form of 'deep state' extra-legal activity.[41] Notably, the CCC was supported by prominent Belgian neo-fascist Jean-Francois Thiriart, who had founded a 'Belgium OAS', had close ties to the OAS and had initiated the European-wide fascist organisation Jeune Europe, a forerunner of Aginter Press.[42]

THE SOVEREIGN DEFINING THE LIMITS OF THE DEMOCRATIC DISCOURSE

Drawing on these two examples of Italy and Belgium, we see that Western European states have seemingly been characterised by the existence of a regular 'democratic state', on the one hand, and a 'security state' – what Vinciguerra simply calls the 'state', a US-linked security structure – on the other. This is what the Italian Parliamentary Commission on the Massacres from 1991 meant by 'il Doppio Stato' or 'the dual state'.

As mentioned, de Felice argues that this dual state is born from the incapacity of the regular democratic state to reconcile domestic politics with foreign policies, primarily its responsibility to the US and NATO.[43] Within such a context, NATO is not just something in between an alliance of sovereign nation-states and a super-state in its own right, but also something of both – with the US 'supranational political-military authority' unifying the policies of the individual states. For example, in Italy in the 1960s and the 1970s, two chiefs of military intelligence (SIFAR and later SID) – General Giovanni de Lorenzo and General Vito Miceli – led military 'coup attempts' while they were liaison officers to the US. Both of these men had been appointed on the recommendation of the US ambassador and both later became members of parliament for the Italian fascist party, MSI.[44] When Licio Gelli – a former fascist intelligence officer, US liaison officer and head of the Italian quasi-masonic lodge 'Propaganda Due' (P2)[45] – was interviewed about the Strategy of Tension, he suggested that 'dictatorship and democracy always march side by side, because democracy is being undermined by dictatorship and dictatorship is being undermined by democracy', adding that we have not yet 'reached an equilibrium'.[46] For Gelli, the activity of the Italian 'security state' during the Cold War was close to what the Turkish military elite would describe as the 'deep state' correcting the course of democracy – or the political 'fine tuning' of democracy.[47]

In Italy, a number of 'coup attempts' took place (in 1964, 1970, 1973 and 1974), though all were called off at critical moments once the government had been reminded of the existence of the 'state' – or rather the 'security state': the real 'sovereign'. In these cases, various liaison officers, generals and fascist leaders exerted an effective veto on government policy by informing the prime minister that a coup had been set in progress, warning that he would have to suffer the consequences if he did not back down on his policy.[48] In 1964, for example, a governmental shift to the left was interrupted by General de Lorenzo's 'coup' in collaboration with Prince Junio Valerio Borghese, the 'Black Prince' who had headed the Italian naval special forces Decima MAS during the Second World War. To achieve his aims, De Lorenzo set in motion 'Plan Solo', which had originally been devised for counter-insurgency purposes (just as Colonel George Papadopulous, the Greek liaison officer to the US, would similarly activate Greece's 'Prometheus' plan three years later, launching a military coup in Greece to prevent NATO critic Georgios Papandreou from returning as Prime Minister).[49] In December 1970, another 'coup' was launched in Italy. This time, Borghese's people – led by Stefano delle Chiaie – had already taken over the Ministry of Interior when the coup was aborted. Borghese's collaborator, Gaetano Lunetta, later insisted that 'the truth is that it was a coup and that it succeeded'. He said that the

political result that those who organized the attack sought to attain was achieved: the deep-freezing of the [centre-left] policies of Aldo Moro, the removal of the PCI from the government arena, [and] the assurance of [Italy's] total pro-Atlantic and pro-American loyalty.[50]

After this followed the Rosa dei Venti 'coup' led by General Magi Braschi in 1973 and the so-called 'White coup' led by Count Edgardo Sogno in 1974. General Maletti described in court his conversation with Sogno. After Sogno had presented his case to the CIA Station Chief in Rome in July 1974, Maletti had asked Sogno if the Americans would support the coup. Sogno responded, 'the United States would have supported any initiative tending to keep the communists out of government'.[51] In the court case following the Rosa dei Venti 'coup', the coup plotters were accused of 'having promoted, set up and organized a secret association made up of civilians and military personnel, with the purpose of provoking an armed insurrection and, as a consequence, an illegal alteration of the Constitution and of the form of government through the intervention of the armed forces'.[52] In October 1974, Chief of Italian Military Intelligence, General Vito Miceli was arrested accused of political conspiracy. However, in court, he argued that the secret organisation accused of overthrowing the government had been formed under a secret agreement with the US and within the framework of NATO.[53] In the later court case in 2001, General Maletti said that Count Sogno had close ties with the CIA.[54]

All the 'coups' were carried out in close collaboration with the Americans, and notably, two of the major actors in this game – Federico Umberto D'Amato, chief of the secret service UAR (the Interior Ministry Office of Special Affairs), and

Prince Junio Valerio Borghese, leader of the National Front and former president of the fascist party MSI – had been close collaborators with the US postwar liaison to Italy, CIA counter-intelligence chief James Jesus Angleton, since the end of the Second World War. Indeed, Angleton maintained his contacts with Borghese and D'Amato up to the 1970s; and, as CIA Station Chief in Rome in the mid 1960s, William Harvey was Angleton's close collaborator.[55]

THE SOVEREIGN AND THE *GROSSRAUM*

The organisation that General Miceli had spoken about in 1974 was Gladio – the Italian 'Stay-Behind' army – that would not only 'stay behind' in case of a Soviet occupation, but that would also conduct clandestine domestic operations to counter domestic communist forces.[56] The Stay-Behinds were coordinated in Brussels by the very secret Allied Clandestine Committee (also known as the Allied Coordination Committee, ACC) and by the equally secret Clandestine Planning Committee (CPC).[57] In addition, there was a parallel structure. Former chief of the Italian Stay-Behinds, General Gerardo Serravalle (from 1971 to 1974), said that when he heard how Vinciguerra, in court, had presented the Stay-Behinds 'with such a precision and in such detailed terms' he concluded that Vinciguerra was an insider and that it must have been a parallel structure (later confirmed as the NDS) that he himself was not informed about. Serravalle stated that there was a part of the Stay-Behinds that he did not control and that he was forced by the Americans to carry out this domestic campaign to blame the left in order to receive material support from the CIA.

> Mr Stone [the CIA] stated, quite clearly, that the financial support of the CIA was wholly dependent on our willingness to put into action, to program and plan, these other – shall we call them internal measures [terrorist operations blaming the Communists: author]. I said this was not in the orders for the Stay-Behinds. Nor had it been foreseen by *Gladio* when the original discussion took place.

But this was CIA policy, Serravalle said.[58]

In addition to these US-led formal structures, there existed an informal 'US network'. The US created and maintained special intelligence ties and clandestine ties with individuals not only in Italy and Belgium but all over Europe. These local 'US elites' were more tuned to US interests and were often able to influence local state policies, and even to veto or manipulate policies and individuals in conflict with US interests.[59] Such elites formed part of what we have called the 'security state' – the 'sovereign' – which included informal groups and their network of extra-legal executives.

One such 'entirely informal group' was the Cercle Pinay,[60] which brought together Atlanticist ultra-right-wing political leaders, industrialists and intelligence chiefs. It was named after former French Prime Minister Antonio Pinay but was, in practical terms, run by its secretary, the French fascist intelligence operative Jean Violet. Italian Prime Minister Giulio Andreotti has named other participants: US State Secretary Henry Kissinger, US Vice-President Nelson Rockefeller (host), German

CSU leader Franz Josef Strauss, Andreotti himself and Pinay's 'good friend', Carlo Pesenti,[61] who was the main financial backer of the Aginter Press 'correspondent' Stefano delle Chiaie.[62] Jean Violet also had direct links to Aginter Press.[63] This suggests that the Cercle Pinay acted as some kind of parapolitical 'board' to the extra-legal executives of Aginter Press.

Thus, the Schmittian 'sovereign' cannot be identified with NATO as a formal organisation, but is rather the parallel hierarchy of informal Western structures with their military/intelligence centre in the US. And it was this informal security structure, or 'security state', that intervened if necessary to guarantee US or 'Western' interests. Indeed, the central actors of this Western security network appear as the real 'sovereign', in the Schmittian sense, that decides on the exception in the Euro-Atlantic area, or what Schmitt would call *Grossraum*.

This idea of a *Grossraum* led by a central power, or *Reich*, was first introduced by Schmitt in the late 1930s,[64] and further developed in his 1950 work *Nomos of the Earth*.[65] Distinct from Karl Haushofer's *Lebensraum*,[66] Schmitt's vision of a German *Grossraum* covered a bloc of independent states under German leadership and protection. Its realisation would have created an economic sphere of interest for Germany, just as the British colonies had come to represent a similar sphere for England. Schmitt based his idea on the US Monroe Doctrine, which denied European and other powers the right to interfere in North and South American affairs. Schmitt sought to apply this approach to Central Europe, a bloc of independent states under German leadership and protection, orchestrated around German political ideas.[67] However, after Germany's defeat in the Second World War and the Red Army's advances in the East, it was the US that emerged as Europe's protecting power.

Western leaders established a Euro-Atlantic 'bloc of states', a *Grossraum* that we call 'NATO', orchestrated around Western political ideas and protected by its *Reich*, the US. Cold War NATO was a 'bloc of states' intended to exclude Soviet intervention. It was led by its central power and unified by its hegemonic political ideas: democracy, market liberalism, national pluralism, the rule of law and collective defence. However, the glue that held Cold War NATO together was not just ideas. Equally important were the informal super-national structures – or rather a hierarchy of such structures under the sovereign's hegemony. Under this view, NATO – or the Western security community – may have been a more unified entity than even Schmitt's concept of *Grossraum*.

THE DUAL STATE AND THE DUAL SECURITY STRUCTURE

To guarantee the stability and defence of the NATO area, or *Grossraum*, the US developed a 'dual security structure' that included both defensive forces and offensive units that would regularly challenge the defensive force structures. In 2000, former US Secretary of Defense Caspar Weinberger (1981–87) confirmed that during the Cold War the US had specifically tasked units to play the role of enemy forces. These would secretly attack Western defences worldwide in order 'regularly' and 'frequently' to test their capabilities and increase their state of readiness, so that counter-forces to potential Soviet capabilities could be developed prior to their emergence.[68] Referring to covert US/UK submarine operations in Swedish waters in the 1980s, Weinberger stated that

> it was necessary to test frequently the capabilities of all countries, not only in the Baltic [Sea] – which is very strategic of course – but in the Mediterranean and Asiatic waters and all the rest... And it was not just done in the sea. It was done on air defences and land defences as well [see Belgium above: author]... and all this was done on a regular basis and on an agreed upon basis.[69]

In collaboration with local security elites, the US 'security state' used special forces that tested and reinforced the defensive capabilities of US allies and friends worldwide. In the case of the submarine intrusions into Swedish waters in the 1980s, a couple of admirals trusted by the US were informed about the operations in advance, but the mass media, local military forces and even the host country government were led to believe that the operations were carried out by the 'enemy', the Soviet Union. In the 1970s (up to 1980), only 5 to 10 per cent of the Swedish population believed in a direct Soviet threat. In 1983, however, after a series of submarines turned up within densely populated Swedish archipelagos, more than 40 per cent of the population viewed the Soviet Union as a direct threat; and the percentage of people viewing the Soviet Union as unfriendly went from 27 per cent to more than 80 per cent over the same period.[70] Thus, in collaboration with trusted individuals within Sweden, US forces seem to have been able to change the mindset of the population and the government almost overnight.[71] Members of the Swedish 'security state', or 'deep state', acted in collaboration with their US counterparts to deceive the Swedish government and public. These PSYOPs – psychological or 'perception management' operations – were run outside the law.

In that sense, there is a correspondence between the dual state and the 'dual security structure' (offensive/defensive forces) of the Western powers. In Italy, for example, the same US officers who ran US operations to 'test the readiness' of Italian coastal defences (Delfino Attivo and Delfino Sveglio) simultaneously organised the terrorist campaign aimed at raising the awareness of and 'changing the mindset' of the Italian population as a whole.[72]

In a similar development, US Rear-Admiral James Lyons, Deputy Chief of Naval Operations for Plans, Policy and Operations, in 1984 set up a 'terrorist unit' – known as the Red Cell – recruited from his own naval special forces (SEAL Team Six), to attack naval bases worldwide. This unit set off bombs, wounded US personnel and took hundreds of hostages as part of its operations. According to Lyons, it was necessary for US forces to get 'physical' experience of the terrorist threat in order to 'change the mindset' and 'raise the awareness' of the troops to prevent a possibly even more devastating attack.[73]

Once again, the US was developing a security system that included both sides of the coin. With the end of the Cold War and the decline of the Soviet threat, however, many Europeans believe this 'dual structure' – with its specifically tasked terrorist units – may have evolved into an instrument for establishing not only internal Western stability but also US hegemony. In such a world, war is no longer waged between the large armies of major powers, but by 'special units' to create 'a special mental atmosphere…to keep the structure of the society intact', to quote George Orwell's *1984*.[74]

CONCLUSIONS

The above examples show that the 'sovereign' – the 'security state' or what some would call the 'deep state' – is able not to just limit the range of the democratic discourse but also to manipulate or 'fine tune' such discourse.

- *First*, the secret armies of the 'sovereign' (the Stay-Behinds and the 'parallel Stay-Behinds' or NDS) were recruited from the defeated fascist forces of Southern Europe in France, Italy, Spain, Portugal and Greece. In Northern Europe, hundreds of Nazi SS officers were recruited for a similar purpose.[75] Fascist leader Prince Junio Valerio Borghese was rescued and recruited by the later CIA liaison to Italy, James Jesus Angleton, at the very end of the war, and Angleton's man, Federico Umberto D'Amato, was given the task of recruiting forces from the fascist Republic of Saló to the Ministry of Interior, the army and the secret armies in order to combat the Italian communists. The brutal 'black' terrorist, Stefano delle Chiaie, collaborated with both Borghese and D'Amato.[76] These secret fascist and Nazi armies were recruited and developed as part of a 'historical compromise' between the winning Anglo-Saxon democrats and the losing autocrats of the Axis powers. But, more importantly, the 'sovereign', as it developed after the Second World War, turned these secret armies into a sophisticated military arm for PSYOPs to limit the range of democratic discourse and to 'fine tune', calibrate and manipulate that discourse.
- *Second*, by letting fascist forces carry out the preliminary stages of military coups, the 'sovereign' was able to force governments to resign or accept a change of policy on a number of occasions. Once a change of policy had been accepted, as during all the Italian 'coup attempts' in the 1960s and 1970s, the 'sovereign' then aborted the military coup and the use of extra-legal measures was no longer considered necessary. The Borghese–delle Chiaie 'coup' of December 1970, for example, was allegedly aborted after interventions by General Vito Miceli – or, according to Remo Orlandini, a close collaborator with Borghese, by US President Richard Nixon himself.[77] In each case, the Italian government was presented with a *fait accompli*, giving the 'sovereign' a de facto veto over policy. The elected government, the 'democratic state', was forced either to yield to the 'sovereign', the 'security state', or to confront it by mobilising popular support and legitimacy – something the 'security state' is only able to do through the introduction of its 'game' of fear and protection. In the final analysis, with the exception of Aldo Moro, Italian prime ministers always chose to back down.
- *Third*, the 'sovereign' may decide to carry through a military coup in order to take over government responsibility, as in Greece in 1967. To a certain extent, the same CIA network (including the CIA station chief and the leader of the Italian Ordine Nuovo) was involved both in Italy and in the 1967 coup

in Greece. In the Greek case, the 'sovereign' was able to veto the anti-NATO policy of Greek Prime Minister Georgios Papandreou.[78] However, it later proved to be more difficult to return to democratic politics, and over time US officials grew less happy with the Greek generals. For the 'sovereign', fascist or military rule was never a goal in itself. The 'coup' was rather an instrument to re-establish order in accordance with the Machiavellian formula of fear and protection: first, let a 'cruel and efficient governor' eliminate all opposition; then, publicly eliminate the same governor to regain legitimacy.[79] In comparison with Greece, the return to regular politics was smoother in Turkey, where the army had widespread legitimacy and military coups have been more or less institutionalised. However, in most of Europe, the overt *coup d'état* appears to have been too clumsy an instrument for controlling domestic politics.

- *Fourth*, the 'sovereign' may raise the 'security temperature' through the use of 'indiscriminate terrorism' – dramatising politics, as happened during the bombing campaign in Italy. Fear of bomb attacks has enormous psychological impact, compelling people to turn to the state for protection and to blame the perceived enemy. In the event of such attacks, mass media will often respond hysterically, blaming whomever the authorities say is responsible. Such an instrument is thus ideal for calibrating government policy, in other words as a means to 'fine tune' democratic politics and to 'securitise' what used to be open to public debate, bringing the democratic political sphere more into line with the political vision of the 'security state'. Through the use of a brutal bombing campaign, it is possible to create events that the mass media will interpret as an 'enemy attack', that will enable the 'sovereign' to externalise conflicts to provide internal stability. The Strategy of Tension, as it was developed in Italy, was used to discredit critics and to 'correct' the political line of the democratic state. Most important was the exercise of control over domestic Italian politics in a way that could not be achieved through the use of legal means.

- *Fifth*, if necessary, the 'sovereign' may turn to 'selective terrorism' to take out a political leader, either as a way of vetoing the policies of that leader or to blame anti-US forces for such 'terrorist' actions. In the case of Aldo Moro's murder in 1978, both of these goals were achieved. Moro's wife accused the Americans of responsibility for her husband's death, claiming that they had previously threatened to kill him, and Moro himself was given a private funeral. Moro's murder enabled the 'sovereign' to veto his 'historical compromise', and at the same time to blame left-wingers – the so-called Red Brigades – for the operation. Both General Maletti and secret service chief D'Amato have confirmed that the Red Brigades had been penetrated at the top. Indeed, Maletti has even confirmed that the top echelon of the Red Brigades was run by Western intelligence.[80] Until 1974, the 'sovereign' could rely on the assassination squads of Aginter Press, but when it began using the Red Brigades it needed special forces support. The killing of Aldo Moro was a special forces operation, involving the use of ammunition from special forces supplies.[81]

- *Sixth*, the 'sovereign' may use specifically tasked units (army or navy special forces) to attack its own forces or allied or friendly forces throughout the Western world in order to increase readiness and raise public awareness of a common threat. Such dramatic operations are conducted as realistic exercises ('train as you fight'), but in the mass media they are presented as enemy attacks or intrusions, which thus shape and influence the mindset of the general public and local military forces and even the policies of the host country government. Such attacks create fear and demands for protection; they externalise conflicts to provide internal stability; and they may force governments to back away from particular policies. The 'enemy attacks', as they are reported in the mass media, are turned into PSYOPs that alter world opinion and influence decisions in international forums such as the UN. Such a strategy gives the 'sovereign' an ideal instrument for calibrating the ruling mass media discourse as well as government policy in various countries.

- *Seventh*, the 'sovereign' spans the entire Western world. By this is meant that the dual state divide between the 'democratic state' and the 'security state' seemingly corresponds to a divide between democratic nation-states and a protective central power – or, to use Carl Schmitt's terminology, between the states of the Western *Grossraum* and the US *Reich*. In every state, US intelligence has recruited loyal officers and civil servants who have acted as direct liaisons to US authorities – such as General de Lorenzo and General Miceli in Italy. Licio Gelli set up P2 as a parallel 'security state' or shadow government, and in practice it was a high-level US–Italian network.[82] A similar picture is emerging in other European states. These local 'US elites' played the game of fear and protection to set the agenda, to influence local governments and even to veto policies or individuals in conflict with US interests. This presence of the *Reich* in various host countries gives the hegemonic power, in this case the US, an even more dominating role than Schmitt had anticipated. The central actors of the Western informal security network appear as the real 'sovereign', in a Schmittian sense, that decides on the exception in the NATO area or *Grossraum*.

- *Eighth*, in the world of democracies, the 'sovereign' – the 'deep state' – must always implement its game of fear and protection covertly and its very existence is always denied in public. Thus, the problem with liberalism in political science and legal theory is not its ambition to defend the public sphere, political freedoms and human rights, but rather its claim that these freedoms and rights define the Western political system. Liberal political science has been turned into an ideology of the 'sovereign', because undisputable evidence for the 'sovereign' – what Vinciguerra simply calls the 'state' – is brushed away as pure fantasy or 'conspiracy'. Schmitt has been described as an apologist for the autocratic emergency state in Germany, but when we look closer he rather emerges as a scholar unveiling the dual state – the hidden autocratic security force parallel to the democratic state. Some might argue that this dual state is defensible, others not, but we should be aware that the liberal denial of its very existence is based on an illusion.

NOTES

1. Hans J. Morgenthau, *The Decline of Democratic Politics* (vol. i of *Politics in the Twentieth Century*) (Chicago: University of Chicago Press, 1962), p. 400. This section of Morgenthau's work – Chapter 29, entitled 'The Corruption of Patriotism' – had previously been published in 1955 in the *New Republic* and the *Bulletin of the Atomic Scientists*.

2. In Turkey, but also elsewhere, the concept of the 'deep state' is used frequently to refer to a kind of security structure able to operate outside the law. See, for example, Shahram Chubin, Jerrold D. Green and Ian O. Lesser, 'Turkish Society and Foreign Policy in Troubled Times', RAND Conference Proceedings, Geneva, Switzerland, 25–27 April 2001, Center for Middle East Public Policy and Geneva Centre for Security Policy, available at www.rand.org/pubs/conf_proceedings/2005/CF171/pdf (accessed 2 January 2007).

3. Morgenthau, *The Decline of Democratic Politics*, p. 400.

4. See quote from Licio Gelli below, n. 38.

5. Ole Wæver, 'Securitization and Desecuritization', in Ronnie D. Lipschutz (ed.), *On Security* (New York: Columbia University Press, 1995); Ole Wæver, 'European Security Identities 2000' in J. Peter Burgess and Ola Tunander (eds), *European Security Identities: Contested Understandings of EU and NATO* (International Peace Research Institute Oslo, PRIO Report no. 2, 2000).

6. Carl Schmitt, *Political Theology* (Cambridge, MA: MIT Press, [1922] 1985).

7. Ernst Fraenkel, *The Dual State: A Contribution to the Theory of Dictatorship* (New York: Octagon Books, [1941] 1969).

8. Morgenthau, *The Decline of Democratic Politics*, p. 400.

9. One Turkish general famously referred to the 'fine tuning of democracy'; see Ralph Boulton, 'Turkey's New Govt Faces Challenge', *Dawn*, 30 January 2003.

10. Franco de Felice, 'Doppia lealtà e doppio stato', *Studi storici*, 3 (1989), pp. 493–563.

11. Paolo Cucchiarelli and Aldo Giannulli, *Lo Stato Parallelo: L'Italia 'Oscura' Nei Documenti e nelle Relazioni delle Commissione Stragi* (Rome: Gamberetti, 1997).

12. Rosella Dossi, *Italy's Invisible Government*, CERC Working Papers, 1 (2001), The University of Melbourne.

13. Alfons Söllner, 'German Conservatism in America: Morgenthau's Political Realism', *Telos*, 72 (Summer 1987), pp. 161–77; Tarak Barkawi, 'Strategy as a Vocation: Weber, Morgenthau and Modern Strategic Studies', *Review of International Studies*, 24/2 (April 1998), pp. 159–84; Hans-Karl Pichler, 'The Godfathers of "Truth": Max Weber and Carl Schmitt in Morgenthau's Theory of Power Politics', *Review of International Studies*, 24/2 (April 1998), pp. 185–200.

14. See Ganser, this volume.

15. Jeffrey McKenzie Bale, 'The "Black" International: Neo-Fascist Paramilitary Networks and the "Strategy of Tension"' (doctoral dissertation) (Ann Arbor: UMI Dissertation Service, 1994), pp. 272–3. See also Philip Willan, *Puppet Masters: The Political Use of Terrorism in Italy* (London: Constable, 1991).

16. Tribunali Civile e Penale di Milano (Sentenza – ordinanza del Guidice Istruttore presso il Tribunale Civile e Penale di Milano, dr Guido Salvini, nel procedimento penale nei confronti di ROGNONI Giancarlo ed altri, 1995–2001), available at www.strano.net/stragi/tstragi/salvini/index.html (accessed 2 January 2007).

17. Agents linked to the CIA – including Italians Giovanni Bandoli, Carlo Digilio and Sergio Minetto, as well as US Navy Captain David Carrett and his replacement in 1974, Captain Theodore Richard – were involved in this NDS terrorist activity. See Tribunali Civile e Penale di Milano (1995–2001). See also Daniele Ganser, *NATO's Secret Armies: Operation Gladio and Terrorism in Western Europe* (London and New York: Frank Cass, 2005); Bale, 'The "Black" International'; The Italian Parliamentary Investigation on Terrorism (1998), available at www.parlamento.it/parlam/bicam/terror/stenografici/indicese.htm (accessed 2 January 2007). On General Gianadelio Maletti's statements, see Philip Willan, 'Terrorists "Helped by the CIA" To Stop Rise of Left in Italy', *Guardian*, 26 March 2001; Franco Ferraresi, *Threats to Democracy: The Radical Right in Italy after the War* (Princeton, NJ: Princeton University Press, 1996); and a number of interviews in the BBC documentary 'Gladio: Parts I–III', first shown on British television in June 1992.

18. Maletti, quoted in Willan, *Puppet Masters*, p. 199. See also Ganser, *NATO's Secret Armies*; and an interview with Fedricio Umberto D'Amato, former chief of the Interior Ministry Division of Special Affairs (secret service) and close confidant of CIA master spy James Jesus Angleton, in the BBC documentary 'Gladio: Part III: The Foot Soldiers', 10 June 1992.

19. See Ferraresi, *Threats to Democracy*; Willan, *Puppet Masters*; and the BBC documentary 'Gladio: Part III: The Foot Soldiers', 10 June 1992.

20. Quoted in Willan, *Puppet Masters*, p. 220. See also the statement by Aldo Moro's wife to the Italian Parliament in the BBC documentary 'Gladio: Part III: The Foot Soldiers', 10 June 1992.

21. Willan, *Puppet Masters*.

22. Willan, 'Terrorists "Helped by the CIA" To Stop Rise of Left in Italy'.

23. Quoted from the BBC documentary 'Gladio: Part II: The Puppeteers', June 1992; see also Ganser, *NATO's Secret Armies*.

24. Jon Gorvett, 'Turkey's "Deep State" Surfaces in Former President's Words, Deeds in Kurdish Town', *Washington Report on Middle East Affairs*, January/February 2006.

25. Quoted from Dossi, *Italy's Invisible Government*, p. 6.

26. Schmitt, *Political Theology*, pp. 5, 13.

27. Carl Schmitt, *The Theory of the Partisan: A Commentary/Remark on the Concept of the Political* (East Lansing, MI: Michigan State University Press, [1963] 2004), pp. 8–9.

28. Schmitt, *The Theory of the Partisan*, p. 9; see also Andreas Behnke, 'Terrorising the Political: 9/11 Within the Context of the Globalisation of Violence', *Millennium*, 33/2 (2004), p. 289.

29. Schmitt, *The Theory of the Partisan*, pp. 43–5.

30. Joachim Joesten, *The Red Hand* (London: Robert Hale, 1962).

31. Bale, 'The "Black" International', pp. 155, 180–2.

32. Ferraresi, *Threats to Democracy*, p. 74.

33. Ibid., pp. 125–88; Tribunali Civile e Penale di Milano (1995–2001).

34. 'Sometime in early 1961 [Allan Dulles's Deputy Director for Plans, Richard] Bissell instructed [William] Harvey, who was then Chief of the CIA foreign intelligence staff (and soon afterwards CIA station chief in Rome), to establish an "Executive Action Capability", which would include research into a capability to assassinate foreign leaders.' The Senate Intelligence Committee stated that an agent, QJ/WIN [probably an OAS activist], was recruited in Europe and put under Harvey's supervision to hire killers and to identify individuals with criminal and underworld connections in order to create 'an available pool of assassins'. See Senate Intelligence Committee Report on Foreign Assassinations, *Alleged Assassination Plots Involving Foreign Leaders: An Interim Report of the Select Committee to Study Governmental Operations with respect to Intelligence Activities* (New York: Norton, 1976), pp. 181–2.

35. Bale, 'The "Black" International'. See also Tribunale Civile e Penale di Milano (1995–2001); and Ganser, *NATO's Secret Armies*.

36. E.H. Cookridge, *Gehlen: Spy of the Century* (London: Corgi, 1972).

37. Scott Anderson and Jon Lee Anderson, *Inside the League* (New York: Dodd, Mead, 1986).

38. Quoted in Bale, 'The "Black" International', pp. 139, 179, 186.

39. On 'securitisation', see Wæver, 'Securitization and Desecuritization'.

40. Ganser, *NATO's Secret Armies*, pp. 125–47.

41. Interview with Lucien Dislaire, in the BBC documentary 'Gladio: Part III: The Foot Soldiers', 10 June 1992. See also Ganser, *NATO's Secret Armies*, p. 137.

42. Bale, 'The "Black" International', pp. 106–25.

43. See Dossi, *Italy's Invisible Government*, pp. 1, 7; de Felice, 'Doppia lealtà e doppio stato'.

44. Ferraresi, *Threats to Democracy*.

45. See Ganser, this volume.

46. Quoted in Willan, *Puppet Masters*, p. 211.

47. Boulton, 'Turkey's New Govt Faces Challenge'.

48. Ferraresi, *Threats to Democracy*; Bale, 'The "Black" International'; Ganser, *NATO's Secret Armies*.

49. Bale, 'The "Black" International', pp. 272–3; Ferraresi, *Threats to Democracy*, pp. 74–83; Ganser, *NATO's Secret Armies*, pp. 212–23.

50. Quoted in Bale, 'The "Black" International', p. 459.

51. Willan, 'Terrorists "Helped by the CIA" To Stop Rise of Left in Italy'.
52. Quoted in Dossi, *Italy's Invisible Government*.
53. Ganser, *NATO's Secret Armies*, p. 8.
54. Willan, 'Terrorists "Helped by the CIA" To Stop Rise of Left in Italy'.
55. See Ferraresi, *Threats to Democracy*; Bale, 'The "Black" International'; and interviews in the BBC documentary 'Gladio: Parts I–III', shown on British television in June 1992. In 1961, when MI5 officer Peter Wright was invited to Washington, both Harvey and Angleton were primarily interested in recruiting assassins and learning techniques for assassinations. Wright told them about the OAS experience and pointed out that the Americans had made use of the Italian mafia during the war. Peter Wright, *Spycatcher: The Candid Autobiography of a Senior Intelligence Officer* (New York: Viking, 1987), pp. 159–61.
56. See also Ganser, this volume.
57. Ganser, *NATO's Secret Armies*; Willan, *Puppet Masters*, pp. 26–7, 116–18; the Belgium Senate Investigation on the stay-behinds from October 1991 quotes a French document from 1958: 'The ACC is a six-power regional committee for providing mutual consultation and developing policy guidance on matters of common interest regarding stay behind matters in the Western European countries concerned.' However, Paris continued to be represented in the ACC, even after France had ended its military cooperation with NATO. The ACC also included the neutral countries.
58. BBC documentary, 'Gladio: Part II: The Puppeteers', June 1992.
59. Ola Tunander, *The Secret War Against Sweden: US and British Submarine Deception in the 1980s* (London and New York: Frank Cass, 2004).
60. Giulio Andreotti, *The USA Up Close: From the Atlantic Pact to Bush* (New York: New York University Press, 1992), pp. 61–2.
61. Ibid.
62. Stuart Christie, *Stefano delle Chiaie: Portrait of a Black Terrorist* (London: Anarchy/Refract, 1984).
63. Bale, 'The "Black" International', pp. 441–2, 506–7.
64. Carl Schmitt, *Völkerrechtliche Grossraumordnung mit Interventionsverbot für Raumfremde Mächte: Ein Beitrag zum Reichsbegriff in Völkerrecht* (Berlin: Deutcher Rechtsverlag, [1939] 1941).
65. Carl Schmitt, *The Nomos of the Earth: In the International Law of the Jus Publicum Europaeum*, trans. with introduction Gary Ulmen (New York: Telos, [1950] 2003).
66. Karl Haushofer, *Grenzen in ihrer geographischen und politischen Bedeutung* (Berlin Grünewald: Kurt Vowinckel Verlag, 1927).
67. Schmitt, *Völkerrechtliche Grossraumordnung mit Interventionsverbot für Raumfremde Mächte*, p. 23. For a discussion of Schmitt's *Grossraum* concept, see, for example, Gary L. Ulmen, 'American Imperialism and International Law: Carl Schmitt on the US in World Affairs', *Telos*, 72 (Summer 1987) (Special issue on Carl Schmitt), pp. 43–71. Since the late 1980s, there has been a wave of articles and books on Carl Schmitt. The journal *Telos* has since 1987 hosted an extensive debate on Schmitt, including several special issues. An article by Paul Piccone and Gary Ulmen contains a long and detailed discussion of some of these contributions: 'Uses and Abuses of Carl Schmitt', *Telos*, 122 (Winter 2002), pp. 3–32. See also John McCormick's book *Carl Schmitt's Critique of Liberalism: Against Politics as Technology* (Cambridge: Cambridge University Press, 1999). At the Schmitt panel for the 5th Pan-European International Relations Conference at the Hague, 9–11 September 2004, Christoph Burchard presented a paper entitled 'Puzzles and Solutions: Appreciating Carl Schmitt's Work on International Law as Answers to the Dilemmas of his Weimar Political Theory', in which he discussed the *Grossraum* concept at some length.
68. Interview with former US Defense Secretary Caspar Weinberger, *Striptease*, Swedish TV2, 7 March 2000; transcribed in Tunander, *The Secret War Against Sweden*, pp. 325–9.
69. Interview with former US Defense Secretary Caspar Weinberger (see above).
70. Opinion Poll by the Swedish Board for Psychological Defence: Göran Stütz, Opinion 87 – *En opinionsundersökning om svenska folkets inställning till några samhälls- och försvarsfrågor hösten 1987* (Stockholm: Styrelsen för psykologiskt försvar, December 1987). See also, Tunander, *The Secret War Against Sweden*.
71. Tunander, *The Secret War Against Sweden*, p. 287.
72. Tribunali Civile e Penale di Milano (1995–2001).

73. See interviews with Captain Richard Marcinko and Admiral James Lyons in the video documentary 'Red Cell: Secret SEAL "Terrorist" Operations' (Boulder, CO: Paladin Press, 1996); see also Tunander, *The Secret War Against Sweden*, and www.specialoperations.com/Navy/Red_Cell/Default.htm (accessed 2 January 2007).

74. George Orwell, *1984* (London: Everyman's Library, [1948] 1992), p. 207.

75. Interview with Erhard Dabringhaus, a special agent for US Counter-Intelligence Corps in West Germany (1948–49), in the BBC Documentary 'Gladio: Part I: The Ring Masters', June 1992; see also Ganser, *NATO's Secret Armies*, pp. 189–211. The National Security Archive has also published a number of documents on CIA recruitment of Nazis: see www.gwu.edu/~nsarchiv/NSAEBB/NSAEBB146/index.htm (accessed 2 January 2007).

76. Interview with D'Amato in the BBC documentary 'Gladio: Part I: The Ring Masters', June 1992; see also Bale, 'The "Black" International'.

77. Bale, 'The "Black" International', pp. 403–7, 454; see also Ganser, *NATO's Secret Armies*, p. 77.

78. Ferraresi, *Threats to Democracy*, pp. 74–83; see also Ganser, *NATO's Secret Armies*.

79. Niccolo Machiavelli, *The Prince* (Harmondsworth: Penguin, [1514] 1995), pp. 23–4.

80. Quoted in Willan, *Puppet Masters*, p. 220; see also the statement by Moro's wife to the Italian Parliament, in the BBC documentary 'Gladio: Part III: The Foot Soldiers', 10 June 1992.

81. Willan, *Puppet Masters*; see also the BBC documentary 'Gladio: Part III: The Foot Soldiers', 10 June 1992.

82. Bale, 'The "Black" International', p. 438; Ganser, *NATO's Secret Armies*, pp. 73–4.

3
Governing Through Globalised Crime

Mark Findlay

This chapter moves beyond the suggestion that crime is a problem for global governance. Instead it advances crime – and terrorism in particular – as instrumental in the promotion of the 'new' globalisation and 'para-justice' control regimes. Along with the argued utility of crime in global governance, the fear of crime and the valorisation of crime victims are identified as vital forces over the crime/ governance nexus. With international terrorism justifying a risk/security focus for global governance, criminal justice is both relied upon, and contorted, in the achievement of violent control agendas.

While it is accepted that crime may frame the broader role of regulatory power,[1] it is now apparent in the global context that crime and control have become central planks of international governance, in a divided world. Essential for this is:

- the magnification of crime (through terror) as a threat to legitimate world order;
- the construction of the crime victim as 'humanity';
- the representation of the victim as the idealised citizen subject of the global community;
- the responsibility of the representatives of the 'global community' to fight crime, as part of a process to restore post-conflict societies; and
- taking the political subjects of the global community beyond idealised fictions, into a realm of security, away from terrorist threat as defined by the dominant political hegemony.[2]

Central to this domain of threat and security is the vast and imagined possibility of victimisation. If the fear of crime and terror as a prevailing threat predetermines global political control agendas, then any dominant hegemony claiming the right to identify the terrorist, and the capacity to protect the citizen will retrieve their political currency, even if this does not progress beyond narrative representation.[3] Further, as the recent relationship between global governance and international criminal justice suggests, the fragile legitimacy of dominant political alliances has inspired concurrent resort to 'para-justice'[4] strategies, wherein violence and oppression run contrary to the protective limitations that demark conventional justice responses.

Jonathan Simon[5] has developed the paradigm that crime metaphors are crucial to state-centred governance. In this chapter, I move outside a state-centred jurisdictional focus to engage with globalisation, international criminal justice and global crime as contexts for global governance. I also argue that, while metaphor is relevant for conceptualising governance through crime, morphology is a more incisive paradigm from which to address crime and governance in globalisation.

Simon identified two metaphorical directions crucial to a particular legislative reliance on crime as governance:

- the rise of the 'street' as the nexus for a 'war on crime'-style governance; and as a consequence,
- the extraordinary emphasis this placed on policing in managing virtually all organisations, public and private.[6]

From an international/global as opposed to a local/jurisdictional/state-based perspective this chapter augments these directions towards:

- the rise of the 'global community' as the *habitas* for crime (and eventually control);
- the indication of 'humanity' as the global crime victim; and
- the particularisation of a dominant global political hegemony as 'policing' international security against crime, especially terrorism.

International crime control has become the discourse of the 'liberal democratic' interlocutor. The idealised political subject (the 'global community' or 'humanity') is realised through the definition of 'actual' threats, and legitimate responses.[7] Presidents and Prime Ministers speak on behalf of victim communities and determine what qualifies as crimes of aggression and crimes against humanity. These political discriminations accord legitimacy to idealised victims and alienate and delegitimise the motivations and actions of those who challenge the dominant political hegemony.

The dependencies of global governance on international criminal justice, and in turn on a risk/security environment for globalisation, have developed reactively. They are repressive, recursive and regressive. International terrorism has necessitated for the dominant political hegemony a shift away from late-modern economic culturation, towards a containment model which relies on criminalisation and justice/control supports (often following military or violent intervention) to counter the challenge of alternative cultural and political alignments.

This evolution has not been without its radical coincidences, or its long-standing antipathies. The destruction on September 11, grounded in part in the struggle between fundamentalism and the 'liberal' ideologies and perceived economic imperialism of the West, has become the backdrop for a 'new age of globalisation'. Crime and control within this transition appear as:

- a process, to consolidate political victory for a coalition of dependent states, through an emergent and formal international criminal justice;[8]
- a consequence of an opposed political alignment or challenge to the dominant hegemony, wherein religion, economy and morality are determined as the enemy for war discourse at many levels;
- a recognition of the need by the dominant hegemony for legitimacy through 'justice' as well as force, in the face of violent challenge;
- a critical growth in specialised technologies and exclusive knowledge that, in turn, fuel governing through crime/control; and
- the defining of a new set of privileged subjects for government, together with an old set of enemies for exclusion.

Valorisation counterbalances demonisation. The 'streets' to be 'policed' are now populated by the global community and are beyond state jurisdiction, legislation and dominion.[9] The security of the idealised citizen/victim is the justification for meeting the terrorist risk. The locally/culturally relative motivations for terrorist violence are thereby subsumed in a more simplistic anti-crime discourse. The indicia of good global governance are successes in the 'war on terror' fought in the tribunals and not the trenches.

Yet legitimacy is fragile. This hegemony is a loose and negotiated order. It lacks true legislative, juridical or executive authority beyond metaphor or concession. The citizenship it serves is ceded to it rather than democratically included. Its normative foundation has few deep or common cultural roots. It is searching for a framework of governance. The risk/security nexus particularly mirrored in international terrorism has, to some extent, recently provided this.

However, the legitimating potential of international criminal justice has, in certain control contexts, been supplemented by the dominant global political alliance, with a 'para-justice' paradigm. The violent and oppressive nature of this second level of 'justice' has challenged the legitimacy of control interventions as a consequence of denying some central justice 'balances' which international criminal justice propounds. The assumed necessity and expediency of 'para-justice' has made the legitimating capacity of international criminal justice more potent and less negotiable.

In the context of parapolitics (where both organised crime and terrorism are said to have their place) the characteristics of 'para-justice' are predominant in control strategies. The adoption of 'para-justice' by the dominant political alliance in this new phase of globalisation reveals an intriguing intersection between the aims and activations of both political forms.

The conflict language of this dominant political hegemony, and the emergence of its strong military imagery in its control discourse ('para' and conventional), are paradoxical at a global level. Wars against crime are designed to replace military intervention with criminal justice. While war imagery invokes a simplistic and dominant process of demonisation as a consequence of 'victor's justice', systematic measures against the criminalised enemy see international criminal justice, as well as military intervention, engaging both the moral and political threats that they represent.

Accepting the potential for crime to facilitate governance at the state level, this chapter explores the recent and apparent synergy between globalisation, a risk/security nexus and the structure and form of international criminal justice and governance, particularly in the context of international terrorism. It also speculates on the tension between the legitimating capacity of international criminal justice as a crucial agency of governance, as against the reversion to violent and intimidatory control practices of *para-justice*.

THE 'NEW' GLOBALISATION[10]

In *The Globalisation of Crime*[11] I envisaged globalisation as the 'collapsing of time and space' in a political age where modernisation and materialism promoted common culturation through economic development. The 'new' globalisation considered here takes mass communication as a given and modernisation as the medium for the advancement of international political hegemony. A risk/security nexus which has emerged from the domination by (and violent challenges to) this hegemony, provides a contemporary international context for both crime control and governance issues. With the present (somewhat limited) legitimating potential of international criminal justice above military intervention in post-conflict states,[12] the connection between criminalisation and governance, in a world where legitimacy is violently contested, is inextricable.

It is an age of risk and security. From the perspective of 'liberal' Western democracies vying for global hegemony, 9/11 was the crunch point – the 'apocalypse now'. In these scenarios of terrorism lie the seeds of the 'new' globalisation. The radical conflation which was '9/11' complemented long-standing antipathies and ushered in a regime of 'war' against ideology, dominion and a redefinition of global citizenship. The restructuring of jurisdiction, standing, citizenship, humanity, community and exclusion, essential for the new age of globalisation, have their justifications and projections in 9/11. Global governance through reaction became the reluctant priority. Battle lines were redrawn. Global crime agendas were re-ordered. Security priorities realigned. States of war were more universalised. Crime victimisation and the legitimate claims to global citizenship were conflated. The fissures of exclusion and inclusion were revealed against criminality and victimisation across global communities. Governance became defined by criminalisation and the restoration of global security.

Along with this, the 'risk society' has surpassed modernisation as the organising framework for globalisation. 'Victim communities' identified at risk and valorised as without blame require the intercession and security proffered by the dominant political 'culture', as, with modernisation, 'underdeveloped' and transitional cultures required material advancement through the dominant economy.[13]

The common push toward a mono-culture in globalisation, similar to earlier mercantile epochs, has had to defer economic priority in order to address the violent challenges of contesting cultures.[14] Rather than engage with the complexity of this resistance, a methodology of criminalisation is employed by the dominant political hegemony and the immediate motivations for globalisation become redefined in response to crime risk, as security/control.

CAN GLOBALISED CRIME CONSTRUCT GOVERNANCE?

About governance Foucault suggests that the task of acting on the actions of others (government) is bound up with ways of *reasoning about governing*.[15] In the sense of globalised governance within the 'new' globalisation, the dominant political hegemony has tended to define what is 'knowable' *and 'more importantly to produce truth selectively'*.[16] This 'truth' has emerged as a by-product of its own strategies of intervention and their legitimacy through the earlier-argued crime/security nexus. A particular notion of governance has been rationalised both through challenges to international security and 'exclusive' approaches to its restoration.

Therefore, the 'ways of reasoning about governing' in the recent global context have in significant measure focused around:

- new emergent crime risks;
- consequent challenges to international security;
- actual harm of the global citizen and global communities;
- requiring a force-based response from the 'democratic' international hegemony;
- legitimating a particular form of international justice intervention; and
- repositioning ongoing concepts of sovereignty, citizenship, legal standing and alien attack.[17]

The translation of this reasoning through epithets and campaigns such as the 'war on terror' has moved the nexus between crime and governance from the politics of the ideal, into processes whereby criminal justice and the control potentials it offers significantly reconstruct and determine the legitimate interlocutors of global conflict.[18] In fact, global conflict and the re-institution of post-conflict states are in part now dependent on the arena of international criminal justice for legitimate resolution. Resistance through violence, no matter how destructive, is marginalised and relegated by the determination of the criminal liability of its principal perpetrators. The tribunal has become essential to the restoration of governability post military intervention.

Global governance around a political discourse of the 'war on terror' seems now reliant on risk/security balances. An investigation of the structures which are said to achieve and maintain these balances (morphology) align with and support the central structures and institutions of global governance where globalisation addresses risk (crime) and concerns for security (control).

The structures of the relationship between risk and security, mirrored in contemporary global governance, include:

- jurisdiction – international alliances beyond 'super' states and regions;
- location – the global 'community';
- citizenship – idealised members of that community;
- standing – power to determine the legitimate victim, to empower the interlocutor, to authorise the judiciary and to disenfranchise the perpetrator;
- dominion – the dominant political hegemony;

- authority – control over the institutions of international justice first through 'victor's' status and then through control of international organisations;
- enforceability – initially through violent military intervention followed by monopoly over investigation, policing, trial and punishment;
- amnesty – monopolisation over rewarding complicity and awarding mercy; and
- reconciliation – metering the availability of retributive and restorative outcomes.

Employing the example of terrorism and its containment, from the perspective of the dominant hegemony:

- jurisdiction is the attack against democracy and 'liberal' values;
- location is within those communities which enjoy democratic government;
- citizenship is accorded to the idealised victim and denied to the perpetrator;
- standing is only as a consequence of victimisation within the context of citizenship;
- dominion comes as a consequence of 'liberal' democracy;
- authority is initially force-based but eventually legitimated through monopoly over justice paradigms;
- enforceability comes from superior force, widest communication and control over 'knowledge' and through the support of alliances and coalitions with mutual risk/security agendas;
- amnesty is denied as a consequence of terror, except where it is perpetrated within the hegemony; and
- reconciliation is marginalised in favour of retribution and deterrence.

This summarises a passage of crime control and governance within the contemporary international risk/security agenda. To move on and detail the institutions and processes responsible for international criminal justice resolutions of risk would identify further the synergy between justice in this context and identifiers of global governance.[19] These would include (but not exhaustively):

- prevailing constitutional legality;
- 'supra-national' legislative power;
- a set of rules and regulations for administering criminal liability and punishment;
- a fabric of public and private policing;
- state monopoly over prosecution;
- power to appoint and authorise judges; and
- executive responsibility for the nature and duration of penalty.

It is not difficult to identify, determine and confirm the separation of powers implicit in this structure which is said to confirm democratic government. However, in the practice of governance this neat division of authority and responsibility is not so simple to maintain.

This holds also for the consideration of 'para-justice' responses to crimes such as terrorism, which is characterised by:

- prevailing authority to create and maintain alternative 'legalities';
- 'supra-national' exclusion of both the perpetrators and the mechanisms for their containment beyond the conventional jurisdiction of the state;
- extraordinary rules and regulations for administering criminal liability and punishment, which, in turn, rely on complex discretionary delegations and largely anonymous activation;
- a process of investigation and policing which is covert, co-optive, compulsory and confrontational;[20]
- state monopoly over prosecution, and more importantly, when to detain and punish without prosecution;
- power to sanction and penalise without the confirmation of judicial authority;
- enforceability through superior force and through the construction of control 'technologies', plus the clandestine application of terror against terror, torture against aggression;
- collapsing of military and quasi-judicial powers and the translation of perpetrators into combatants; and
- executive responsibility for the nature and duration of penalty.

The application of conventional and para-justice paradigms is not essentially a question of choice. But insofar as they may be known to operate against the same 'risk' for the restoration of global security, they may tend to challenge legitimacy, each to each.

CAN CRIME CONTROL DETERMINE CONSIDERATIONS OF RISK AND SECURITY?

Garland,[21] as did Cohen[22] before him, argues that community protection is now the dominant theme of penal policy. The risk here is unidirectional. Crime poses a threat to the security of the individual and the community, and the state is therefore obliged to minimise that risk through control. The public supports this. On the other hand:

[i]n these matters (harsh state control interventions) the public appears to be (or is represented as) decidedly risk-averse, and intensely focused on the risk of depredation by unrestrained criminals. The risk of unrestrained state authorities, of arbitrary power and the violation of civil liberties seems no longer to figure prominently in public concern.[23]

Garland says more than that new crime control developments have 'adapted' and 'responded' to the late modern world and to its political and cultural values. He advances these developments as 'creating that world, helping to constitute the meaning of late modernity'.[24] Along with managing problems of crime and insecurity, he argues, crime control 'institutionalises a set of responses to these problems that are themselves consequential in their social impact'.[25]

Transposed to a global context, and with the risk being terrorism, and the control response being both violence and 'justice',[26] strong messages for the managing of risk and the 'taming of chance' travel through the new institutions of international criminal justice. These, in turn, lead on to an environment of international governance in which the citizen accepts restrictions of liberty that would have been intolerable in an era of globalisation outside this risk/security nexus, particularly when democracy was marketed as the ideology of modernisation. Now:

> spatial controls, situational controls, managerial controls, system controls, social controls, self-controls – in one realm after another, we now find the imposition of intensive regimes of regulation, inspection and control and, in the process, our civic culture becomes increasingly less tolerant and inclusive, increasingly less capable of trust. After a long term process of expanding individual freedom and relaxing cultural and social restraints, control is now being reemphasised in every area of social life – with the singular and startling exception of the economy, from whose deregulated domain most of today's major risks routinely emerge.[27]

Prophetically, in the global context Garland identifies along with the rise of this partial concern for risk/security, control agendas as the characteristic of political reaction. A new sense of international disorder pervaded the close of the twentieth century and was accompanied by a renewed interest in global order and world governance. Crucial to governance and order internationally, as seen from the perspective of the dominant political hegemony, was the addressing of:

- dangerously inadequate controls; and
- rapidly and violently emergent challenges to the control of that hegemony.

Initial responses were militaristic, but as is always the case, these were unsustainable. Criminal justice has been conscripted to take management of the control of global risk.[28] Of course, this is not an exclusive control responsibility and more violent repression will always be on call in a climate of risk and security where the threat is erratic and incisive. International criminal justice is, however, the attractive medium-term response, because of its perceived potential to enhance the legitimacy of the dominant political hegemony.

Another important feature of the control profile internationally is the redefinition of 'community' and, along with it, notions of jurisdiction, citizenship and standing. Immersed in community is the potential both for legitimacy and resistance.

In a recent Australian context, the previous Federal government's policy on asylum seekers and the use of criminal justice to 'protect national borders' and quarantine citizenship is a case in point. This initially was built on a denial of the discourse of political correctness that allowed for the re-emergence of racially based migration constructions. 'Boat people' became a threat to national integrity and, when they were demonised as willing to sacrifice their children in illegal efforts at entry, the Australian electorate got behind a party with tough policies that criminalised people who later proved to be valid refugees.

'Multiculturalism' was an associated victim of government policy that 'played the race card' in the context of national security and international risk. Cultural integrity was degraded and dismissed as ethnic individualism. Particularly when focused on Islamic communities and their failure to embrace 'Australian values', it was not difficult to equate the threat beyond with the threat within. Whole communities became the target of crime and control identification because of their 'otherness'; a difference which was synonymous with the cultural stereotyping of international terror. The crime was as much seen as inherent in a culture or religion claimed by the terrorist, rather than evidenced by particular risks to security and real threats to sovereignty and citizenship. The application of crime and control to internal, rather than international, security concerns helped also to endorse exclusive and exclusionist notions of nationhood, citizenship and national identity readily compatible with Australia's place in the dominant political hegemony.

So too, the 'para-justice' processes employed in Guantanamo Bay have received a remarkably tolerant response from the conventional institutions of justice governance in the United States, even if not so amongst its alliance partners.[29] Arguably this is due to what Garland identifies as a modification of citizenship and the liberties of the democratic state in the face of heightened risk and more problematic global security. Paradoxically, we see para-justice compromising freedom, for its protection.[30]

WHERE DOES LEGITIMACY FIT WITHIN THIS RELATIONSHIP – CONTESTED REASONING FOR GOVERNANCE?

Predominant and prevailing notions of 'truth' are essential in the struggle over the legitimacy of international governance. Dominant *reasoning* presupposes predominance over 'truth' as a delineator of the government and the governed.

When it comes to considerations of 'truth' in (for instance) the context of terrorist struggle, the contested nature of truth is obvious, even if also regularly glossed over. Truth is what the suicide bomber is said to die for and what the military and criminal justice responses are set to protect. Can it be the same truth? If not then its relativity becomes a contested objective of the relationship between terror and 'justice' responses. How is the subjectivity of truth here to be managed beyond the force-based authority and supremacy of victor's justice?[31]

In the terrorism/response context it is not so much the nature of truth but its contest which is the connection. The protection of truth is the common justification for the exercise of violence on both sides. Even violent retaliation against, say, 'genocide', through terrorism, claims its legitimacy against 'guilty' or 'blameworthy' violence where truth is at risk. Yet again, the relativity of guilt and blame challenge the advance and democratic dominance of a single 'truth' on which the justice response relies.

In contest, where responses to terrorism claim the legitimate use of violence, is 'moral standing'. Those, on the other hand, who promote re-integrative techniques as against retribution to more effectively manage original violence, recognise that restorative justice relies on the context of a supportive community, if shaming is to be positively applied to offenders.[32] Without a supportive context, dependent on a common acceptance of the moral standing of the preferred response, attempts at shaming break down as stigmatising rather than re-integrative. Resort to violence is soon reiterated.

However, in the situation of terrorism/response relationships, moral standing is at the centre of the contest for legitimacy. Reflective communities in which both the terrorist and the justice responses are marketed may oppose the moral legitimacy of each other. These communities are, in part, galvanised through resistance to the external and oppositional claims for moral standing.[33]

Particularly damaging to the justice response is the resistance of terrorist 'communities' over the basis of moral standing. Dworkin's[34] components of the moral standing of law (determinacy, integrity, coherence and wholeness)[35] are difficult for the violent justice response to export when new institutions and processes of incarceration, interrogation, trial and punishment are directed at the terrorist opponent. These novel entities generally contradict, or at least strain, some of the central protections which make criminal justice in general fair and 'just'.[36]

HOW DO GLOBALISED CRIME PRIORITIES INFORM THE POLITICAL DISCOURSE OF GLOBALISATION?

As mentioned previously, concepts of crime have traditionally relied on some cultural or jurisdictional situation for their relevance and impact. Implicit in this is the expectation that crime stops at national borders, or at least that it has localised interests.

The jurisdictional boundaries of crime, however, can only be explained in terms of legal convenience and legislative limits. As piracy, smuggling, abduction, gun-running and counterfeiting have been crime problems for centuries, so too the laws of individual nations have been powerless to control them.

Transnational crimes such as terrorism are new only in their technologies and reach, along with the manner in which law enforcement and international agencies have recently identified it as a priority. Again, the selective political representation of crime is the explanation for such a trend. For instance, as governments realise the potential for criminal enterprise to endanger world market structures, capital transfer, national security and international transport and communication, so particular crime targets are selected for cooperative action while others – such as environmental degradation on a scale well beyond the reach of harm ever caused through terror attacks – are largely ignored. Strategies have been developed for example, to prevent and prosecute commodity futures fraud and abuses, but an international approach to crimes against the environment is yet to be convincingly settled.

The other difference with transnational crime, represented as a recent problem for globalisation, is the manner in which crime control is reshaped in order to address the difficulties with jurisdiction. Crime control is, in this context at least, a bi-lateral endeavour. However, in many control strategies for transnational crime, the bi-lateral efforts are stimulated by globalised representations of crime and control priorities.

It is the threat posed both by terrorism and organised crime that is motivating local jurisdictions to adopt international control agendas. Normally this would be resisted on the basis of the autonomy of criminal justice as a state domain, even in the face of international crime threats.[37] By concentrating on representations of organised crime and terrorism, as well as the state response through criminalisation, the local authorities have translated the international significance of crime threat to justify local interventions which may have little real impact within the jurisdiction concerned. It is an example of the impact of internationalism on localised/criminal justice policy.

The threat of global terrorism as a challenge to 'legitimate' political ordering has stimulated the development of extra-ordinary control responses in a similar fashion to the way that organised crime justified extra-legal state reactions under threat.[38] Organised crime and their economies, enterprises and market manipulations were determined throughout the last century as challenging legitimate political and economic governance. Further, the application of violence and intimidation by organised crime in its control aspirations were said to require a response in kind by the state. With global terrorism today, the dominant political alliance emphasises the risk of terrorism to legitimate governance and its capacity to compromise the protections of conventional justice to its own ends. Para-justice paradigms are promoted in return and legitimated against the nature of the threat and its own methods of 'governance'.

HOW DOES INTERNATIONAL CRIMINAL JUSTICE RELATE TO GLOBAL GOVERNANCE?

New levels of law enforcement cooperation across borders have been fostered in a climate of acute threat and exaggerated retaliation.[39] By concentrating on the violent and intimidatory behaviours of terrorism, rather than on their organisational structures or expressed motivations, the community is more ready to accept strong medicine to prevent terror in its midst. Interestingly, the state has employed the 'terror' of fear concept to facilitate what might otherwise be law enforcement responses that would meet vocal resistance.[40] Para-justice paradigms gain similar purchase in the strategies for national, regional and global security against the representation of risk, which emphasises the challenge to legitimate governance.

Fear or reality, both justice and governance issues depend on constituencies as well as jurisdiction. For international criminal justice and global governance, the focus recently is with 'victim communities'. This notion engages:

- individual victims;
- the communities of these victims which share their harm;
- where wider communities or groups of victims suffer harm;
- where the crime is directed at community cohesion or cultural integrity; and
- when violence is motivated by the destruction of what makes communities or cultures (language, art, religion, family structure etc.).

A justification for international criminal justice is 'crimes against humanity'. In this sense 'humanity' has a community or cultural location. Justice should reflect 'humanitarian' concerns in its mandate to protect humanity. Such concerns are only partial, sectarian or selective in the way contemporary global governance views 'humanity'. Anything outside the legitimate citizenship of the dominant hegemony tends to be removed from the protective ambit of its humanity. The excluded are worthy of destruction rather than protection. The followers receive the patronage, so long as they ascribe to the dominant order.

The dominant hegemony in this climate of international terrorism (be it manifested in the genocide of Rwanda, the ethnic cleansing of the Balkans, or the anticipated and illusory weapons of mass destruction in Iraq) has significantly transferred militaristic intervention (at least in part) to the jurisdiction of international criminal justice. This is a transition that carries with it expectations for global governance and the legitimation on which it depends. But in keeping with the agenda and exclusive instrumentation of this political alliance, the morphology of international criminal justice for this purpose is made reliant on common notions of the crimes against humanity, the legitimate victim communities and appropriate retributive responses. This has, in fact, meant that the formal institutions of international criminal justice have presented limited pathways of access, exacerbated by professionally removed modes of representation, which, in turn, have not well integrated and connected with these communities. The consequence for global governance has been to limit the influence of international criminal justice in restoring post-conflict societies.

But it is not only about victims and harm as it is not merely about governance outside context. Much of what we have explored is at least stimulated by the contest of legitimacy. As international criminal justice transforms to better address the needs of victim communities, then its legitimacy, and its power to legitimate as a crucial component of global governance, will be enhanced.

The connection between international criminal justice and global governance is both symbolic and applied. We will leave symbolism aside for another day. In terms of its designated and located context in an age of global insecurity, the power of international criminal justice in global governance is in recuperating the tattered authority of the dominant hegemony as a consequence of military intervention. And at this level, the justice/governance link is reliant on, and determined by, the failings of the hegemony, as much as by the transformational strength and consistency of international criminal justice.

CRIME, CONTROL AND GOVERNANCE – MORE THAN METAPHOR

Roberts'[41] 'cultural assemblage' well covers the dominant political hegemony that is currently master of international governance, at least at a formal/economic level. It has come together largely within projects of regional government. Its claims to the indicia of 'government' are, as yet, fragile and primitive beyond military victory. The international organisations said to house global governance while representative, are without authority, absent the support of this hegemony. The legislature, judicial institutions and executive bureaucracies that emerge from these international organisations are dependent (particularly in resource terms) on this hegemony.

The endorsement and protection of global citizenship currently resides with the hegemony, not in terms of democratic inclusion and representation, but rather through patronage. Roberts rightly cautions against rewarding these 'negotiated orders' with the established juridical, legal or jurisdictional order required of the nation-state. 'Today, under an onslaught of jural discourse and institutional design, the distinctive rationalities and values of negotiated order, while arguably deserving to be celebrated, are effectively effaced.'[42]

Globalisation invites the discussion of governance in terms such as law, justice, and bureaucracy, without or above the state. For law at least, this requires severance from a narrow notion of legislative jurisdiction. In the 'war on terror' discourse there is an invocation to protect 'civilisation' and 'democracy' against violent assault. It is compatible with this celebration of preferred international political paradigms, to view law as 'cosmology'. In this sense, law and its institutions are engaged in the enterprise of 'imagining and articulating what we want the social world to be'.[43] Law in governance in this sense links the discursive formulation of rules and process to an articulation of preferred world order.

Law as cosmology is also supportive of governance through 'leaders and followers', ideas which go well beyond the inclusive occupation and responsibilities of democracy. While democracy is celebrated as worthy of protection by the dominant international hegemony, its aspirations to global governance are not democratic but oligarchic. Justice within this oligarchy tends to be institutionalised, formal, non-accountable and professionalised. It is thereby consistent with, and supportive of, oligarchic governance.

If globalisation – even in an age of risk and security – retains a commitment towards a single culture,[44] the preferred justice is exclusive and not pluralist in its authority, coverage, or outreach. Justice also tends to legitimate oligarchic governance, rather than to seek legitimacy from it. This is because the trajectory of international criminal justice (even if not its procedures) is towards a concern for humanity and its communities of victims. This then becomes another ground on which the dominant political hegemony claims the legitimacy of its constituency and their patronage.

This trajectory sees an intersection between the conventional and the 'para' justice paradigms for the advancement of hegemonic interests. Interestingly, common claims for the predominance of security as the framework of governance justify conventional and 'para' justice responses. Where the paradigms depart is around the procedural conditions for justice outcomes, particularly those which are said to give international criminal justice its force in state reconstruction and peace-making.[45]

Presumptuous as it may seem in fact, the dominant political hegemony has represented its version of global order as legal order and this is supported by a crude but emergent general jurisprudence.[46] The jurisprudence of international criminal law has a particular place in international governance when compared with other fields of international law. For instance, international commercial law sees courts with national legal orders applying commercial conventions originating at a supra-national level. International criminal law has, in contrast, developed for itself a tribunal/court structure which requires the determination of state authority. The negotiated order that will be the province of the International Criminal Court will act as law at least for subscribing states and will operate across a ceded international jurisdiction. A globalised legal order managing criminal justice is not simply taken for granted. As with states and their jurisdiction, international criminal justice and its institutions become indicia of governance (local, regional or international).

I would argue that Foucault's observation on law's decreasing capacity to code power to serve as its system of representation does not hold for international criminal justice and its jurisprudence. The reasons for this I have suggested are uniquely contextual and inextricable with the new globalisation and a very particular enterprise of global governance. This is much more than what Roberts explains as the 'extended space claimed by jural discourse and institutional forms'.[47] International criminal justice is now incorporated into the 'reasoning' of global governance, I would assert, much more so than Simon gives it credit for at a state level as metaphor.

In the context of a security/risk nexus, the 'reasoning' of contemporary governance is created recursively. A formative and fragile institutional hegemony legitimises globalised forms of 'truth' through control mechanisms specifically designed to minimise threats to its authority. Hence, although 'libertarian' arguments trumpet justice as an integral element of the democratic credo (and thereby through their application internationally, as indicia of global governance), the reverse seems to represent reality. Bi-lateral intimidation, regional coercion and military incursion are the preferred international relations.

The reduction of risk (in whosever name) is accompanied by a reduction in civil liberties, a denial of plurality and a marginalisation of civil society. Individual autonomy, so central to the normative politics of the dominant hegemony and their idealised 'community', is subjugated through the sacrifices required to maintain 'civilisation' and 'humanity'.

At this point, the analysis of global governance need not leave concerns for metaphor, but in a very practical sense, globalised crime problems and control responses (as we have seen with international terrorism), are neither simply metaphoric of, nor represented by, the struggle for global order.

The secularisation of international criminal justice has led to the emphasis on formal retributive paradigms to resolve conflict, and the abandonment of reason to fear on a globalised scale. This may be as much due to fragile and transitional frameworks of global governance, as it is a consequence of the vacuum resulting from relativity and moral pluralism and a failure to find expression in a shared belief system that would underpin globalised forms of justice. Dominant political hegemony and ideological oppression fill the gap, so that the institutional control of behaviours which threaten it are justified in amoral terms – terms which do not rely on any notion of a shared reason, experience or shared value system. In this sense, international criminal justice as the theatre in which the crime/risk-control/security nexus is tested has been profoundly compromised. It is a justice largely unconfirmed by universal moralities. As such, it retains limited legitimacy and its potential to legitimate wider global governance and conflict resolution, while present, will continue to have limited sweep.

Risk and security as threats and needs are procured to essentially justify harsh control, and the only morally coherent basis for global governance they can provide is through a reactive denunciation of those who challenge the hegemony. For instance, in order to justify an extreme punishment response, the violence and violent potential of terrorism is highlighted. However, a moral assessment of terrorism in terms of 'mindless' violence is compromised by any corresponding excessive violence of punishment, particularly where this has consequences for innocent communities in a 'law of war' scenario. In addition, its 'mindlessness' challenges the deterrent impact of violent punishment, which is offered as the reason for requiring violent punishment.

If they are to stand alongside recognised indicia of governance and claim a more long-lasting legitimation, the 'new drivers' for globalised justice should be developed from a renewal of humanistic principles as they find expression in what Henham and I have referred to elsewhere as 'communities of justice'.[48] To sustain and complement these communities, the foundations for international criminal justice need to rediscover the deeper and more grounded rationality for penality, as expressed in the sharing of values and experiences over time and place.

In this way, the 'contexts of control' within the globalisation project may be more convincingly identifiable as coherent and resilient value systems essential to (and more tolerant of) relative forms of human existence. As such, partial and hegemonic justice will be diminished in its role and will no longer provide either a metaphor for, or structural implementations of, justice in global governance. A natural consequence of this transition will be the diminution of the risk/security imperative, leaving international criminal justice to offer a more accessible, heuristic and normatively convincing role in global governance and conflict resolution.

NOTES

1. David Garland, *The Culture of Control: Crime and Social Order in Contemporary Society* (Oxford: Oxford University Press, 2001).
2. Due to limits of space, it is not possible here to fully argue the nature of this hegemony or to appropriately problematise its entity and significance. Against the 'war on terror' metaphor (post 9/11) and accepting the place of Western 'liberalism' behind the modernising era of globalisation, this hegemony is equated with the loose (and often unwilling) coalition supporting the US Iraqi intervention.
3. Mark Findlay, 'Terrorism and Relative Justice', *Crime, Law and Social Change,* 47/1 (2007), pp. 57–68.
4. As with parapolitics, the concept of 'para-justice' has no definitional certainty. Here I am employing the notion to encapsulate those control responses that follow on from proscribed behaviours, which, in other circumstances, might be processed through conventional criminal justice. Violence, intimidation and a denial of due process are characteristic of para-justice. Rather than being dismissed as institutional injustice, para-justice makes claims for institutional and process credibility through the determinations of military tribunals in particular and justifies excessive responses through the necessities of war.
5. Jonathan Simon, 'Governing through Crime Metaphors', *Brook Law Review*, 35 (2001–02), p. 1053.
6. For an example in the domestic legislation of the time, see President Johnson's Safe Streets Act.
7. Findlay, 'Terrorism and Relative Justice'.
8. Mark Findlay and Ralph Henham, *Transforming International Criminal Justice: Restorative and Retributive Justice in the Trial Process* (Collumpton: Willan Publishing, 2005).
9. Simon Roberts, 'After Government? On Representing Law Without the State', *Modern Law Review* 68/1 (2005), p. 1.

10. For the purposes of this argument I am not critiquing the reality or utility of 'globalisation' as an analytical concept.

11. Mark Findlay, *The Globalisation of Crime: Understanding Transitional Relationships in Context* (Cambridge: Cambridge University Press, 1999).

12. Findlay and Henham, *Transforming International Criminal Justice*, especially Chapter 7.

13. Findlay, *The Globalisation of Crime*, Chapter 2.

14. The similarities might be extended in contrast with the militaristic mercantile companies in Asia and the New World, chartered by their sponsoring states to make war, colonise, and deliver criminal justice along with the predominant commitment of wealth creation. None of this, however, operated in the same atmosphere of internationalisation as we see it today.

15. Michel Foucault, 'Govenmentality', in James Faubion (ed.), Vol. 3 of *Essential Works of Foucault 1954–1984* (New York: New Press, 2000).

16. Simon, 'Governing through Crime Metaphors', p. 1063.

17. Findlay, 'Terrorism and Relative Justice'.

18. Findlay and Henham, *Transforming International Criminal Justice*.

19. Ibid.

20. For a discussion of these styles of policing, see Mark Findlay and Uglješa Zvekic, *Alternative Policing Styles: Cross-cultural Perspectives* (Deventer: Kluwer, 1993), Chapter 2.

21. Garland, *The Culture of Control*.

22. Stanley Cohen, *Visions of Social Control* (Oxford: Polity Press, 1985).

23. Garland, *The Culture of Control*, p. 12.

24. Ibid., p. 194.

25. Ibid.

26. Findlay, 'Terrorism and Relative Justice'.

27. Garland, *The Culture of Control*, pp. 194–5.

28. Findlay and Henham, *Transforming International Criminal Justice*.

29. Ronald Meister, 'The Supreme Court, Guantanamo Bay and Justice Fix-it', *Cornell Law School Berger International Speaker Series*, Paper 4; Helen Duffy, 'Case Study: Guantanamo Bay Detentions under Human Rights and Humanitarian Law', in *The War on Terror and the Framework of International Law* (Cambridge: Cambridge University Press, 2005), pp. 379–442.

30. Gerard Clark, 'Military Tribunals and the Separation of Powers', *Suffolk University Law School Faculty Publications*, Paper 111 (2002); Erwin Chemerinski, 'Detainees (Wartime Security and Constitutional Liberty)', *Albany Law Review*, 68/4 (2005), p. 119.

31. There is a need here for a more detailed consideration of Weber's conditions for the authority of the state.

32. John Braithwaite, *Crime, Shame and Re-integration* (Oxford: Oxford University Press, 1989).

33. Moral standing as a legal/constitutional claim to legitimate voice is discussed in Steven Winter, 'The Metaphor of Standing and the Problem of Self Governance', *Stanford Law Review*, 40 (1988), p. 1371.

34. As in West; see n. 35.

35. For a discussion of these see Robin West, 'Taking Moral Argument Seriously', *Chicago Kent Law Review*, 74 (1999), p. 499 at 500.

36. For a discussion of the detail of these changes in US criminal justice and their impact on due process see, Emanuel Gross, 'Trying Terrorists – Justification for Differing Trial Rules: The Balance between Security Considerations and Human Rights', *Indiana International and Comparative Law Review*, 13/1 (2002), pp. 1–98.

37. Mark Findlay, 'International Rights and Australian Adaptations: Recent Developments in Criminal Investigation', *Sydney Law Review*, 17/2 (1995), pp. 278–97.

38. Findlay, *The Globalisation of Crime*, Chapter 5.

39. Emilio Viano (ed.), *Global Organised Crime and International Security* (Aldershot: Ashgate, 1999).

40. Jude McCulloch, '"Counter-terrorism", Human Security and Globalisation – from Welfare to Warfare State', *Current Issues in Criminal Justice*, 14/3 (2003), pp. 283–98.

41. Roberts, 'After Government?'

42. Ibid., p. 1.

43. Ibid., p. 6.
44. Findlay, *The Globalisation of Crime*.
45. Findlay and Henham, *Transforming International Criminal Justice*, Chapter 8.
46. Claims for the existence and operation of international criminal law are consistent with this.
47. Roberts, 'After Government?', p. 24.
48. Findlay and Henham, *Transforming International Criminal Justice*, Chapter 7.

4
Prospering from Crime:
Money Laundering and Financial Crises

Guilhem Fabre

In 1998 the International Monetary Fund estimated that illicit funds, worldwide, amount to between $800 billion and $2 trillion – 2 to 5 per cent of the world's GDP.[1] These facts are not a great surprise any longer. Leading journals have published articles on the magnitude and processes of money laundering.[2] The incredulity of those who act as if they have just discovered corruption in emerging nations brings to mind the police officer in the film *Casablanca*, who is shocked to find gambling in a casino. Instead of merely condemning such open secrets, public officials ought to investigate just how it is that illicit profits are, in fact, recycled into the legal economy – how criminals prosper from crime.

What, for example, is the relationship between offshore companies recycling 'dirty money', the Central Bank of Russia, the Bank of New York, governments of developing countries and the vicissitudes of international financial assistance? The answer is hardly self-evident, but an increasing body of evidence suggests that there is a link between money laundering and financial crises.

The post-Cold War financial system rests upon two assumptions that contradict one another. The first is that free capital flows – like international trade – optimise the allocation of global resources. This assumption is dubious, both theoretically and empirically.[3] Although a massive increase in direct foreign investments has contributed to economic development in the South, larger bank loans and other short-term financial measures have produced the opposite effect, diverting investment from productive sectors to areas of potentially rapid capital appreciation, such as highly speculative stock markets and real estate.[4] This damages the export competitiveness of developing countries, the supposed basis for repaying foreign loans. So, for example, increasingly frequent recourse to foreign loans for the purpose of financing public debt (supposedly to reduce the risk of inflation) aggravated the risk of currency crises and default on loans in Mexico, Russia and Turkey.

The second assumption is that the legal and institutional infrastructure that enabled free financial flows between North America, Europe and Japan was of secondary importance. In the post-Cold War euphoria, decision-makers accepted uncritically the idea of a self-regulating market. They underestimated the importance of legal standards that were instrumental to the development of the capitalist economy over the last two centuries, as well as the significant burden imposed by the lack of such institutions in transitional economies.

In the result, the coexistence of free international capital flows and weak national institutional and regulatory systems created a void in which transnational economic and financial delinquency flourished.[5] Transitional economies privatised state-owned firms without allowing market competition or creating the necessary institutional and legal infrastructure for effective markets. Tax evasion accounts for the most important share of crime; but other problems include capital flight in countries where exchange controls are inadequate; counterfeiting (which represented, according to the Davos Global Economic Forum, 9 per cent of world commerce in 2000);[6] insurance fraud; and contraband. Thus, corruption grows with new opportunities in North–South exchange and in the legal void of countries in transition, which, while instituting privatisation policies, accept the market economy's idea of profit but not the complementary ideal of market competition.

THE GROWTH OF 'GREY' AND 'BLACK' MARKETS

The sizeable development of the 'grey economy' in the context of finance-driven globalisation favoured the spectacular expansion of offshore markets and tax havens, through which nearly half of the world's money supply is currently funnelled.

In 1979 there existed only 75 offshore funds. In 1996, they numbered more than 3,300.[7] These havens institutionalise tax evasion, especially by the world's great fortunes – a third of whose holdings, estimated at $5.5 trillion (or 18 per cent of the world's GDP), are placed in offshore funds.[8]

Sheltered from central bank supervision, these new extra-territorial spaces are the home of choice for the 9,000 hedge funds in 2006 that manage some two-thirds of their assets from tax havens.[9] Although all hedge funds combined amount only to some $1,000 to $1,500 billion – some 3 to 5 per cent of the global capital held by the major financial institutions (insurance firms, pension funds, banks) – they have privileged access to credit and this multiplies risks to the financial system.[10] In the autumn of 1998 the last-minute rescue of Long Term Credit Management (LTCM), a Wall Street darling located in Connecticut but officially headquartered in the Cayman Islands,[11] proved to the world that a single institution with assets of less than $5 billion could threaten the entire financial system by taking positions in excess of $200 billion, thanks to the credit received from major banks and brokerages.[12]

Globalisation has been accompanied not only by the growth of the grey economy, but that of a black economy as well. According to the United Nations, organised and unorganised crime together now generate annual sales in the order of 3 per cent of the world's GDP – about $1 trillion – half of which is in drug sales, which have boomed over the last decade, stimulated by an abundant supply and diversification into synthetic narcotics.[13] Other profits from crime are drawn from multi-service activities such as the control of legal and illicit gambling establishments, the arms trade, human smuggling, trafficking in body organs, car theft, prostitution and racketeering. These profits boost demand for money laundering, which favours offshore markets because of their secrecy and immunity from legal oversight.

In response to the demand for money laundering services, tax havens and offshore markets have developed into international hubs for three kinds of 'illegal legality': (1) the 'white' economy of banks, investors and fund managers; (2) the 'grey' economy of tax evasion and corruption; and (3) the profits that organised crime seeks to recycle. The boundaries between these three domains are nebulous, since the illegal activity occurs prior to transfer of funds to offshore markets. In addition, it is usually impossible to distinguish between tax evasion and profits from crime, because the recycling techniques are identical.[14]

THE FUNCTIONS OF MONEY LAUNDERING

Beyond the evasion of legal regulation, offshore markets in the post-Cold War period are of concern because money laundering played a significant role in the financial crises of nation-states after the Cold War. The experience in Russia, recorded in abundant detail through a sequence of scandals closely tied to political back-stabbing, suggests that there are intricate links between capital flight, embezzlement, racketeering, pillaging of public assets, corruption and organised crime. As I have demonstrated in my book *Criminal Prosperity*, significant profits derived from organised crime and corruption were deposited in Swiss banks and re-invested in Russia to finance growing national debt.[15] Corruption and criminal activities played a major part in creating public debt and diverting funds to speculative overseas financial markets: the Russian Central Bank estimated, for example, that $74 billion was transferred from Russian banks to offshore accounts in 1998, the year of the devaluation.[16] A predatory, kleptocratic and, in the end, mafia-style pattern of abuse created substantial demand for money laundering on international capital markets, including the demand for Russian Treasury bonds and thus was an important factor in the Russian financial crisis of 1998.

There are other examples, as well, which are typically overlooked in neoclassical economic analyses that remain limited to empirical testing of limited models. Yet such examples reveal the sometimes incestuous relations between the laundering of 'funny money' and financial crisis. So, for example, the Mexican crisis of 1994–95 and the 'tequila effect', or the repercussions which it triggered in Latin American countries through the regionalisation of exchanges, can only be understood if the 'cocaine effect' is also taken into account. Starting in the 1990s, Mexican drug dealers took charge of one-half of the Colombian drug trade with the United States, thereby repatriating some $3 billion to $8 billion per year, amounts which exceeded the value of Mexico's oil exports.[17] Part of these funds went to the ostentatious consumption of luxury goods from the US, thereby increasing the country's dependence on imports. The rest was recycled in small businesses, luxury real estate and the securities and 'grey' currency markets that levy some 10 to 15 per cent for their money laundering services. The hasty privatisation initiated by Mexican President Carlos Salinas also provided opportunities for recycling narco-profits, especially in the banking sector where the state sold a series of firms for $12 billion. After the crisis, these banks were saddled with debts in excess of $60 billion, which were subsequently assumed by the state.

In Mexico, money laundering was combined with international short-term capital flows to create excess liquidity and a stock market and real estate bubble. Although at the outset they corresponded to only 1 to 3 per cent of GDP, the mass of narco-dollars distorted competition to the advantage of organised crime in small business and banking. The 'laundering premium' which they earned made it possible for them to be more competitive and, on occasion, to absorb their competitors while emphasising short-term speculative investments. Moreover, their access to credit made it possible to recycle and expand capital of dubious origin. Far from improving the general competitiveness of the export economy, or helping to reduce external debt, laundering accentuated imports of consumer goods and emptied the productive sphere in favour of short-term investments. The injection of narco-dollars thus contributed to the deterioration of foreign trade and precipitated payment defaults, devaluation and the financial crisis of 1994–95.

As in Russia and Mexico, the Thai economic crisis, which triggered the Asian crisis of 1997, was no stranger to money laundering. According to a study published in 1997 by three researchers at Chulalongkorn University,[18] the equivalent of 8 to 11 per cent of Thai GDP was controlled, at the onset of the crisis, by organised crime, which derived its profits mostly from gambling and prostitution, as well as drug trafficking out of Burma.

Accelerated democratisation of the Thai political system during the 1990s gave a clear advantage to the provinces over the Bangkok region. Bangkok was the stronghold of the modernist democratic party and generated half the GDP. The peripheral regions were under the control of local 'godfathers', frequently of Sino-Thai origins, who combined certain legal monopolies with illegal activities such as gambling, prostitution, drug trafficking and contraband in wood and precious stones. When the provinces acquired the decisive role in fragile government coalitions, political patronage encouraged money laundering. Once again, it focused on speculative real estate and stock market investments, in a context of insider trading scandals tied to privatisation.

As in Mexico, the inflow of foreign short-term capital, most often transited through the Bangkok Offshore Banking Facility, accelerated local speculation by limiting investments at the expense of the productive and export sectors. The deterioration of the external accounts that ensued was aggravated by the rise of the dollar and the slowdown of the electronics export markets in 1996.[19] This precipitated the exchange crisis and the devaluation of the baht.

The pressure created by short-term investments, or by the results and figures drawn from the formal economy, does not, however, explain the magnitude of the crisis. The local political and financial system also played a part, in that it strongly favoured the laundering of profits from crime. By the end of 1999, two years after the crisis, Thai GDP had contracted by 10 per cent in 1998 alone, and the surplus on the real estate market was estimated at 300,000 units in the Bangkok region, but real estate prices did not fall.[20] This stability remains incomprehensible if one analyses real estate prices according to traditional market criteria, but the puzzle disappears when one factors in the need for money launderers to funnel massive amounts of funds into real estate, as well as the delays which they caused in the reconstruction of the financial sector.

JAPAN: THE *YAKUZA* RECESSION

The role of money laundering is also evident in developed economies, for example, in Japan, the world's second largest economy. To understand the social legitimacy of the *yakuza*, Curtis Milhaupt and Mark West have shown that 'in Japan, the activities of organised criminal firms closely track inefficiencies in formal legal structures, including both inefficient substantive laws and a state-induced shortage of legal professionals and other rights-enforcement agents'.[21]

The role that the *yakuza* played in the speculative bubble of the 1980s is now known.[22] Through their control of drug trafficking, prostitution and employment in the building sector and public works, as well as their interests in the very lucrative business of *pachinko* – electric billiard games which generate one and a half times the turnover of the Japanese automobile sector, some 6 per cent of the GDP – organised crime has invaded the real estate co-operatives (*jusen*), the leading brokerages and the shareholders' meetings of certain large companies.[23] Their access to credit enables them to launder their illicit profits in speculative businesses, where they tend to prefer high-risk operations.

When the speculative bubble burst at the beginning of the 1990s, stock and real estate prices dropped, and bad debts swamped the banks and other financial institutions. The former director of Japan's National Police Agency, Raisuke Miyawaki, estimates that 10 per cent of these debts are *yakuza*-related and an additional 30 per cent have probable links with other organised crime, which would put non-recoverable debt attributable to gangsters at somewhere between $75 billion and $300 billion, that is, 6.5 per cent of GDP.[24]

After having speculated on the upside, the *yakuza* then speculated on the downside, trying to buy up real estate assets at fire sale prices and by blocking, through targeted operations, the liquidation of the liabilities of certain firms that resort to their illegal services in order to escape their obligations. This explains why the fall in real prices of real estate – between 30 to 70 per cent since the beginning of the 1990s – did not coincide with a corresponding rise in transactions and thus retarded the reconstruction of the financial sector and the supply of credit, and, in the end, new growth.

There are, of course, other factors that explain Japan's economic difficulties; however, the '*yakuza* recession', in the words of Raisuke Miyawaki,[25] should not be taken lightly. Despite the government's numerous expansionist policies, which increased the GDP by several percentage points, the exceptional length of the Japanese crisis is fully understood only when one takes account of money laundering and the activities of organised crime. These socialised the costs and privatised the profits of organised crime, thereby distorting the competitive environment. From 1985 to 1995, the Japanese GDP grew by 52 per cent, while total financial assets grew by 85 per cent. The difference between these two figures demonstrates the persistence of the speculative bubble[26] centred in the real estate market, the *yakuza* sector of choice for their invisible manoeuvres, which delay market adjustment.

SEPTEMBER 11 AND BEYOND

The cases of Russia, Mexico, Thailand and Japan do not prove that there exists an automatic link between money laundering and financial crises. That argument would be strengthened by further research on other examples of financial crises, such as those of Argentina, Turkey and Nigeria in 2000–01. The accumulation of such crises and their probable links to money laundering demonstrate, however, how the forces that prosper from crime – however marginal in comparison to the formal economy – can provoke decisive political repercussions.

Although it is clear that the masses in the Arab world have been subdued – under humiliating conditions – by Western nations and by their own governments, the September 11 massacre of 2001 does not reflect an act of revenge for this state of affairs. On the contrary, it illustrates, with unprecedented drama, the political strength of criminal networks whose power, in this case, stems from the systematic destruction of 'enlightenment Islam' and the symbolic manipulation of a sect of wahhabi origin, supported by rent-seeking families of Saudi Arabia.[27] Yet political will and political means should take into account these realities and overtake this opaque system, where the methods of supervision and the rules of the game are at least a decade behind the rapidity of financial flows and the existing capacities for circumvention.

Without significant changes in the regulatory superstructures of financial institutions worldwide, the links between those who prosper from crime, money laundering and financial crises are likely to proliferate, protected by the fear they inspire and the silence they maintain.

NOTES

1. William F. Wechsler, 'Follow the Money', *Foreign Affairs*, July/August 2001, p. 45.
2. Wechsler, 'Follow the Money'; Nigel Morris-Cotterill, 'Money Laundering', *Foreign Policy*, May/June 2001. Nigel Morris-Cotterill is editor of *World Money Laundering Report*.
3. Jagdish Bhagwati, 'The Capital Myth', *Foreign Affairs*, May 1998.
4. China, in this respect, is an exception because it focuses on foreign direct investment and relies marginally on short-term capital flows. See Alejandro Lopez-Mejia, 'Large Capital Flows: A Survey of the Causes, Consequences, and Policy Responses', IMF Working Paper 99/17 (1999).
5. Jean de Maillard, *Un monde sans loi, La criminalité financière en images* (Paris: Editions Stock, 1998).
6. *Global Counterfeiting Background Document*, 27 January 2002. See also *Newsweek*, 24 October 2005.
7. *Resident Abroad*, 'The International Investor in 1997', *Financial Times Magazine*, p. 18.
8. Guilhem Fabre, *Criminal Prosperity: Drug Trafficking, Money Laundering and Financial Crises After the Cold War* (London and New York: Routledge Curzon, 2003), pp. 77–8.
9. Barry Eichengreen and Donald Mathieson, *Hedge Funds and Financial Market Dynamics*, IMF Occasional Paper 166 (May 1998); *Le Monde Economie*, 3 October 2006, p. 3.
10. *Le Monde Economie*, 3 October 2006, p. 2; *Financial Stability Review*, June 2006, European Central Bank, p. 198, www.ecb.int (accessed 8 January 2006).
11. Robert M. Morgenthau, 'On the Trail of Global Capital', *New York Times*, 11 September 1998.
12. Franklin R. Edwards, 'Hedge Funds and the Collapse of Long-Term Capital Management', *Journal of Economic Perspectives*, 13/2 (Spring 1999).
13. *World Drug Report*, United Nations International Drug Control Programme (Oxford: Oxford University Press, 1997), pp. 123–43.

14. Morris-Cotterill, 'Money Laundering'.
15. Fabre, *Criminal Prosperity*, pp. 163–4.
16. Wechsler, 'Follow the Money', p. 47.
17. For more details on Mexico, see Fabre, *Criminal Prosperity*, Chapter 5.
18. Cf. Pasuk Phongpaichit, Sungsidh Piriyarangsan and Nualnoi Treerat, *Guns, Girls, Gambling, Ganja: Thailand's Illegal Economy and Public Policy* (Chiang Mai: Silkworm Books, 1998).
19. For more details on the Thai crisis, see Fabre, *Criminal Prosperity*, Chapter 6.
20. Odile Cornet, *Le MOCI (Moniteur du Commerce International)*, 3 November 1999.
21. Curtis J. Milhaupt and Mark D. West, 'The Dark Side of Private Ordering: An Institutional and Empirical Analysis of Organized Crime', *University of Chicago Law Review*, 67 (2000), p. 41.
22. Philippe Pons, *Misère et crime au Japon du 17ème siècle à nos jours*, ed. Gallimard (Paris: Bibliothèque des Sciences Humaines, 1999).
23. For more details on Japan, see Fabre, *Criminal Prosperity*, Chapter 4, 'The *Yakuza* Recession'.
24. Miyawaki even estimates that 'up to 50% of the bad debt held by Japanese banks could be impossible to recover because they involve organized crime and corrupt politicians'. See Velisarios Kattoulas, 'The Yakuza Recession', *Far Eastern Economic Review*, 17 January 2002.
25. *Far Eastern Economic Review*, 17 January 2002.
26. Teruhiko Mano, 'New Moves in the Money and Capital Markets', *Japan Review of International Affairs*, 4 (1998).
27. Fethi Benslama, 'Islam: quelle humiliation?', *Le Monde*, 28 November 2001.

5
The Shadow Economy: Markets, Crime and the State[1]

Howard Dick

> Capitalism did not take up all the possibilities for investment and progress that economic life offered. It was constantly watching developments in order to intervene in certain preferred areas – in other words, it was both sufficiently informed and materially able to choose its sphere of actions… the very fact that it had the means to create its own strategy or to alter that strategy if necessary, defines capitalism as a superior force.
>
> Braudel, *The Wheels of Commerce*

An alarmist view has it that modern democratic states are being overwhelmed by a surging tide of transnational organised crime. Titles such as Allum and Siebert's *Organized Crime and the Challenge to Democracy* (2003), Freemantle's *The Octopus: Europe in the Grip of Organised Crime* (1995) and Sterling's *Thieves' World: The Threat of the New Global Network of Organized Crime* (1994) convey the flavour. Criminal interests have certainly seized the opportunities of globalisation. Nevertheless, as with the complementary 'war on terror', it must be asked whether fear and the political manipulation of that fear has not got in the way of clear observation and thinking.[2]

The problem may be portrayed in terms of an upside-down triangle between markets, the state and (underground) crime. Public attention is directed to the vertical and allegedly subversive relationships between crime and markets and between crime and the state. Yet it is state legislation that distinguishes economic crime from other market transactions. The fundamental relationship is between the state and markets. Unlike markets, the state is not free-standing. It does not earn its own subsistence.[3] Rather, the rise of the nation-state was financed by markets and grew with them.

During the second half of the twentieth century, the state impinged more and more upon the economy by means of compulsory reporting, taxation and regulation. The most effective form of resistance to the insistent claims of the state was to under-report or not to report at all, thereby giving rise to what has become known as the 'shadow economy'. There is much debate on how broadly this phenomenon should be defined and how to measure what is 'missing'. One recent estimate, which notably excludes the 'black economy' of criminal activity (theft, drugs) and tax evasion, reckons the shadow economy to average about 17 per cent in OECD countries and around 40 per cent in developing and transitional countries.[4] In the case of Thailand, a fairly careful estimate by Phongpaichit et al.[5] estimates *illegal* economic activity excluding tax evasion as around 20 per cent of GDP. Although definitions are contested and measurement is crude, such estimates suggest that the black and grey components together could add up to a fifth of measured GDP in OECD countries and twice that in developing or transitional economies. Under- or non-reporting is facilitated if the profits can be transferred to offshore tax havens. In the case of criminal activity and tax evasion, such transfers take the form of money laundering, but legitimate business may also quite legally channel funds though offshore tax havens as a way of minimising tax. Fabre[6] estimates the equivalent of 18 per cent of world GDP to be held in offshore funds.

Intellectually, it is hard to justify ignoring the shadow economy. Evidence suggests both that the shadow economy may be growing faster than world GDP and that it has its own logic, which should not be equated with criminality. Rather it is the logic of globalisation, of the increasingly sophisticated spatial differentiation of economic activity. The main actors are not only criminals but also corporations, whose leaders are in constant engagement with states and state actors. What is being contested and negotiated in this process is the extent to which big business will be subject to and regulated by formal state laws and processes and in which jurisdictions. The shadow economy has its counterpart in shadow politics, as surely as the duality of male and female.

This chapter sets the 'threat' of transnational organised crime in a Braudelian perspective on markets, capitalism and the world economy. French economic historian Fernand Braudel in his three-volume magnum opus *Civilization and Capitalism* (1981–85) offered a magisterial perspective on the emerging world economy of the fifteenth to eighteenth centuries. While this much less sophisticated world might seem remote, it is a challenging intellectual exercise to juxtapose the current era of waning nation-states with the era when nation-states were first asserting themselves. This wide-angle lens allows us to focus more clearly on markets and the global economy without the bulky but often ineffectual apparatus of the nation-state being always in the foreground. Nation-states do still matter, but it is an open question whether they control or respond to global markets.

The chapter argues that crime flourishes within the global market economy like fish in the sea. The black economy of crime disguises itself within a much larger grey economy. Crime occurs most obviously in the form of illegal activities, including so-called black markets, and may be aided by corruption of the organisations of law enforcement. It may also occur by circumventing or leap-frogging their jurisdiction. Transnational crime has much in common with the transnational corporation in its lack of transparency and accountability. Both are hydra-headed in their jurisdictional scope and skilful in their legal and political defences, whether to minimise payment of tax or to withhold information. Business and crime both take advantage of porous global money markets to hide and launder flows of funds and of diffuse global logistics to hide and launder flows of goods and people. This is not, however, the whole story. Crime is also symbiotic with the state, which determines the institutions that govern markets through the specification of legislation and the manner of its enforcement. Failures of control are embedded in the power relations of the global economic and political system. At the commanding heights of the global economy and at the intersections with national sovereignty, ambiguity is the very essence of the relationship between money and power.

CAPITALISM, MARKETS AND CRIME

Braudel envisaged society as a house of three levels: a base of simple material life as subsistence or household economy; a middle level of market economy; and an upper level of capitalist economy that transcends competitive markets.[7] In the market economy, small and medium-size firms predominate and profits are quickly competed down to a normal level; in the capitalist economy, supra-normal profits tend to persist along with the market power. Capitalism proves so flexible and trans-formative because, like bees to nectar, it searches out super-profits and reinvests them, relentlessly 'accumulating', as Karl Marx so keenly noted.

The distinction between business and capitalism gives some insight into the phenomenon of crime. In the above quote from Braudel, at the beginning of this chapter, the word 'capitalism' could be substituted by 'crime' without doing any violence to the meaning. That might suggest that crime is very like capitalism, but it may be more insightful to suggest that some crime is capitalism, albeit of a perverted form. An equivalent Braudelian distinction can be made between petty or local crime, which is akin to small business, and organised and transnational crime, which we may identify with capitalism. The emergence of capitalism itself was accompanied by a good deal of criminal activity and not necessarily by thug-like pirate gangs and mafia-like syndicates. On the contrary, the 'criminals' were often respectable members of their own societies. Petty criminals are likely to be locked up, but successful corporate heads who pay very little tax may be feted as public heroes and dine with the leaders of government.

Transnational criminals are the capitalist adventurers of the modern age. They drive a double wedge into the state, not only engaging in activities which are quasi-legal or illegal but also using different corporate identities to evade and avoid tax. The criminal stereotype is of hard-faced, brutal men like the Russian mafia and Chinese triads who use ruthless standover tactics to run their various rackets. At the other extreme, however, is the respectable professional who has money to invest at a higher return, perhaps with the spice of some extra risk, by dabbling on the fringes of the law. Up-and-coming young business people who want to get rich fast can find it expedient to take risks and short-cuts. The market has room for all of them. Its concern is not to distinguish between who is and who is not criminal but only between who does and who does not fulfil their contracts, for without that the market cannot function.

One perspective on the relationship between crime and capitalism is that it is symbiotic. The capitalist economy and weaknesses in the enforcement of law, especially across jurisdictions, create both market incentives and opportunities for criminals to gain a share of the super-profits. This is a plausible model which has its biological equivalents. The policy implication is straightforward: the bad animals that prey on the good animals should be stopped. Problems arise, however, if the bad animals and the good animals are not easily distinguished, or indeed may sometimes be one and the same. I will argue below that this is indeed the case, especially if the definition of transnational crime embraces, as it should, tax avoidance and evasion. In other words, crime is contingent. Those who make super-profits from transnational criminal activity may launder it through legitimate businesses, while otherwise perfectly respectable business people may, on occasion, by dint of temptation or pressure of circumstance, step outside the law. Sometimes, as with tax evasion, the practice may be such a normal business practice that only in extreme cases is it regarded as 'criminal'.

The symbiotic model may therefore be more misleading than helpful. We need to think more carefully through the relationship between transnational crime and capitalism in an era of rapid globalisation. The key word is *ambiguity*. When we look behind the morality play of the world as it is meant to be seen in the public domain and into the shadows off stage, we lose the sharp clarity of figures and roles. We observe much cross-dressing and illicit intercourse and it is by no means apparent that those who break the rules are those who would, in the light of day, be regarded as criminals.

THE STATE, CORPORATIONS AND CRIME

The essence of the state is encapsulated in the bargain between security in return for tax – or is it tax in return for security? Does the state provide security for its citizens, in return for which it levies tax, or does it assert the right to levy tax, in return for which it provides a measure of security? Those who view the state as a benevolent commonwealth tend to the former view; cynics including Charles Tilly[8] and Mancur Olson[9] give more credence to the latter. The question becomes even more interesting if one takes the new institutionalist view that a third essential role of the state is to set the 'rules of the game'.[10] This adds to 'law and order' a distributional aspect. If one takes the issue of tax, it becomes a matter of whom to tax and by how much. Conversely, who is exempt, and to what extent? The simple rule of thumb is that those who control the state tax their friends and allies less heavily than the rest. Whatever the rhetoric of public interest, herein may be found a prime motive for winning government, whether in a democracy or an autocratic regime. Discretion applies not only in who is taxed but also how the laws are framed and how they are applied. As in George Orwell's succinct phrase, 'some are more equal than others'.[11]

While economists have steadfastly promoted the benefits of competition, capitalism has moved relentlessly in the opposite direction. The key institution has been the corporation, a collective economic actor and fictive legal person formally representing the bounded financial stakes of its shareholders. Historically the corporation, like the city, held a set of privileges and exemptions granted by state charter in order to mobilise resources, primarily capital. Such charters were granted only in exceptional circumstances, at first mainly for high-risk overseas ventures. Since the nineteenth century, however, the package of commercial and legal privileges has been standardised at law and been made available as of right by mere application. As ownership rights were increasingly vested in these corporations, they accumulated profits, swallowed rivals and gave birth to new subsidiaries. At first the rise of the corporation proceeded *pari passu* with the rise of the nation-state. As the state consolidated its political power, so did the corporation consolidate its market power within national markets. In recent decades, however, as the corporation has become more adept at assuming multi-national identities, the leverage of the state has diminished. These 'legal persons' have become super economic beings that have colonised the global economy and consolidated market power on a global scale. Most leading global industries are now dominated by fewer than 20 large firms and the trend towards consolidation has by no means run its course. And although ideology has it that these corporations are controlled by their shareholders, the reality is very often, as Berle and Means[12] long ago recognised, that their managers act with a great deal of autonomy.

The advantage that corporations have over individuals is that they have more means to avoid and evade tax. Having more money exposed to appropriation, they can afford to employ very good accountants and lawyers to exploit and defend every last loophole. Because business is conducted across borders, they also have all the advantages of transfer pricing, whether through conventional trade, contracting, borrowing and lending, or various forms of investment. In short, corporations have become masters in transforming the identity of funds, whether in currency, timeliness, ownership or transactional status.

It follows that the relationship between the state and the corporation is highly ambiguous. On the one hand, the corporation is the legal citizen of the state in which it is registered and legally bound correctly to report and to discharge its tax liability. On the other hand, the corporation is also a chameleon which can at one and the same time manifest itself in different colours and behaviours in different states and transfer funds by elaborate pathways from one to another. Here the corporation has adapted to the market economy far more efficiently than the state, which remains bound by territoriality. At best, the state can trace the money trail across borders by auditing the corporation's financial statements and cross-checking financial transactions and tax records. By means of double-tax agreements between states, well-managed states may extend the audit reach, but they cannot prevent the shifting of tax liabilities from higher to lower tax rate states, nor can they collude sufficiently to surround determined corporations within a tight transnational tax regime. Ultimately the corporation wins this game because, should one country's tax regime prove too high or too onerous, it can shift headquarters – and perhaps even its main operations. States are therefore forced to compromise, both in setting the rates and in their enforcement. Corporations do pay tax but, by a kind of tacit negotiation, at effective rates that are a great deal lower than actual rates.

In fact, there are two battlegrounds between the corporation and the state. Besides the inevitable conflict over tax, there is a more subtle conflict over information. Here we may remember Braudel's insightful comment that capitalism (read 'the corporation') was '*sufficiently informed* and materially able to choose its sphere of actions'. In other words, the corporation is an efficient means for mobilising and deploying vast amounts of information. It tends to be overlooked that information ('intelligence') is the *sine qua non* of the market, the very corpuscles that activate the flows of funds and goods. Moreover, the flows of information are deployed to the private purpose of securing competitive advantage and earning profit. It follows that most of this information is by nature what is referred to as 'commercial in confidence' and therefore closely held. The public and the state have to judge whether the information that is released by way of public relations reflects the true situation or, at the other extreme, is simply misinformation. Potentially, agents of the state can obtain access to commercially privileged information, but to do so they need to invoke legal powers and withstand determined objection to them. If there is evidence of crime or malfeasance, police or other agents may subpoena certain categories of documents.

What the state cannot do, however, is to demand documents on mere suspicion of crime or malfeasance. In short, the corporation becomes a very effective means of hiding information from the state. If historically the corporation was a means for the individual to avoid liability for funds, now surely, and even more so, it is a means to hide information. As the regulatory demands by the state increase in fields such as health and environment, so these protections become all the more valuable.

It is therefore no accident that most corporate crime and scandal is uncovered after the event, that is to say after some catastrophe such as financial collapse opens the corporation to public scrutiny. Then, almost invariably, the media ask the very sensible question of why the regulatory agencies did not uncover evidence of wrongdoing before the event, given that corporate collapses seldom occur without warning signs. There are various answers that range from outright corruption or the milder 'regulatory capture' to political pressure and sheer laziness or complacency. The common thread is the sheer cost of gaining access to and processing the vast amount of information that a corporation generates. That is not to deny that intelligent regulators cannot ask good questions and require answers. But even should that occur, there is a high cost of verification.

MARKETS AND WORMHOLES

Markets are invariably in a state of tension between two countervailing forces. The first is a tendency towards localisation: states seek to lock resources within their jurisdiction in order to tax and maintain prosperity, hence rules are laid down and exit barriers set up. The countervailing tendency is for markets to globalise by seeking the most favourable jurisdiction. Funds globalise almost without friction because there is no physical element to the transaction. Ships move under their own power and can easily change their country of registry. Goods move more or less readily according to their mass and quantity. Drugs are the classic case of goods that are hard to trace because the mass is so small relative to the value.

Complexity arises because of the issue of visibility. The great disadvantage of visibility is liability to tax. If all or part of a transaction or the ownership of an asset can be rendered invisible to the voracious nation-state, then tax may be saved, net of the costs of doing so. The ideal is to register assets and to declare the income from them in the states which impose the lowest tax rates. Thus corporations and criminals have a vested interest in fudging or hedging jurisdiction. The higher the effective tax rates and the greater the spread across jurisdictions, the greater the incentive to do so. The existence of numerous microstates allows a wide choice. Moreover, sovereignty itself defines and protects property rights, even in outright tax havens.

Of the 191 nations that are full members of the United Nations, 41 or one-fifth may be described as microstates with populations in 2003 of less than 1 million.[13] The city-state of Singapore, which is usually regarded as a small nation, has a population of over 4 million and may better be described as a mini-state. By population size, it actually ranks ahead of 75 other nations. Indeed, the *median* population size of UN member states is just 6.5 million. All this is a remarkable turnaround from the 1950s, when the world consisted of declining Western empires and there were few independent mini- or microstates. Andorra, Liechtenstein, Luxembourg, Monaco and San Marino then stood out as curious relics of a bygone age. As the pace of decolonisation accelerated, however, even tiny islands in the Caribbean and the Pacific found their way to an often reluctant independence, with all the trappings of a nation-state.

Size matters because for microstates the problem of viability is acute. The 'overheads' of supporting a nation-state are usually higher than a colonial administration in relation to the size of the economy and the tax base. Even microstates require not only the basic infrastructure of policing, ports and roads, utilities, health and education but also the paraphernalia of a modern nation-state, on top of which a growing population has come to expect a higher standard of living than the country's resources can sustain. The exceptions are a few microstates with abundant resources such as the oil kingdoms of Bahrain, Brunei and Qatar or the fishing nation of Iceland. For the rest, foreign aid seldom closes the gap. They face the challenge of attracting resources to enlarge the tax base and the licit options are quite limited. Crops such as sugar and copra now deliver low returns; high labour costs preclude manufacturing.

In more innocent days, microstates supplemented their meagre earnings by philately. With more imagination and the advantages of location, Liechtenstein, Luxembourg and Monaco showed long ago what could be created out of nothing with tax-exempt companies, banking privileges and tourism, especially if there was the attraction of a casino. Allowing also for flag-of-convenience shipping registrations, offshore fishing licences and, most recently, sale of Internet rights, the microstates of the Caribbean and the Pacific have few other options apart from labour migration and remittances. Where licit means prove inadequate, however, there may well be scope for the illicit, such as money laundering and drug smuggling. Often the line is a fine one, as in the case of tax evasion, and many microstates, following the example of Liechtenstein, Luxembourg and Monaco, find it expedient not to look too closely as long as the revenue flows in.

Insofar as transnationals seek to hide behind foreign jurisdiction, microstates therefore offer a range of choices, low cost of entry and low transaction costs. Choice exists because microstates differ in location and politics and entry costs are low because they are competing with each other to attract business. Transaction costs are low because, increasingly, business can be done on-line or through on-shore agents: the client has no need to travel. For business that involves investment in hotels, resorts or casinos, as also physical smuggling, political influence and the necessary access to resources can be bought cheaply and without much fear of public scrutiny. In short, the 'diseconomies' of scale for microstates translate into economies of nationality for transnational business.

In terms of market dynamics, microstates become what might be termed 'wormholes' in the fabric of the global economy. In theoretical physics, a wormhole is 'a short-cut through space and time'.[14] Here we use it as a metaphor. Funds controlled by corporations or criminals that are legal persons in high-taxing and highly regulated OECD juridisdictions are readily transferred to offshore tax havens.[15] Even in the case of China, Yu[16] reports that 19 per cent of China's inward foreign direct investment is sourced to the British Virgin Islands, making it the second largest source after the internal tax haven of Hong Kong. Such investment is referred to as 'round-tripping'. The funds can be retrieved when required because, whatever devices are used to disguise beneficial ownership, the principals remain the same.

IT and the Internet facilitate these wormholes. Access is now so straightforward that interested parties to longer require a foreign consul or an intermediary but can go directly to websites such as the Cyprus-based www.flagsofconvenience.com and there register a company, ship or aircraft in any of a wide choice of jurisdictions across the world. One can even apply to become a franchise holder offering such services. Thus the legal nationality of companies, funds, ships and aircraft, along with the ownership of goods, may be transferred instantaneously through cyberspace at the click of a mouse.

A brief overview of several different kinds of markets helps to show how the system works. Each vignette seeks to demonstrate first the nature of the market, then the relationship between the offshore jurisdiction and the principals.

Banking

As financial intermediaries, banks not only move and store funds but can also make them disappear. Invisibility can be achieved very simply by registering funds to an offshore entity whose principals cannot readily be determined. If this is done through onc or more offshore financial centres – especially if that financial centre is also a tax haven – the costs of determining beneficial ownership become all but prohibitive in normal circumstances. In recent years, concern with international criminal and terrorist activity has focused attention on 'money laundering'. To ensure that suspect flows can be identified and traced, the United States especially is imposing more stringent reporting requirements on all international banks, with the threat of sanctions against banks and countries which do not comply. Nevertheless, Kapstein's view that '…gaps in supervision will always exist… and they will be exploited before one or more states takes action' seems still to apply.[17]

Historically Switzerland, Luxembourg and Monaco and, closer to the US, Cuba were the offshore refuges for shy money. High postwar tax rates and death duties led British capital to look longingly offshore: Bermuda emerged as an offshore tax haven in the mid 1950s and the Channel Islands from the late 1950s, followed by Gibraltar and the Isle of Man.[18] Meanwhile in 1959 the US lost access to its offshore haven of Cuba.[19] Attention turned briefly to the Dominican Republic and the tax-free Cayman Islands, then in 1964 to the self-governing Bahamas, later also Saint Vincent and the Grenadines, which became independent in 1979, followed by Antigua in 1981. The Dutch and French established similar offshore status in their Caribbean dependencies. As Swiss authorities under international pressure began to make concessions to transparency, banks began to proliferate in other countries more willing to maintain secrecy.[20] In the 1990s the model has been copied by islands in the South Pacific such as the Cook Islands, Vanuatu, Tonga and Nauru.

In an IT world, physical isolation is no longer such a disadvantage. Though it helps to maintain credibility, banks of convenience need not maintain physical offices in their offshore locations: a company registration and a nameplate at some 'official' address is all that is required. The principals need never set foot on the island and the funds never physically enter the jurisdiction, being no more than a computer transfer to a correspondent bank of a reputable financial institution in a large Western city. Here indeed is a wormhole, annihilating time and space.

Shipping

Globalisation has involved the large part of the world's shipping fleet being registered under 'flags of convenience'. This practice began in the period between the two world wars when US Prohibition, trade embargoes and conflicts such as the Spanish Civil War and the Sino-Japanese War made it expedient for smart shipowners to disguise their nationality and ownership.[21] The US client state of Panama emerged as the flag of choice, with consular officials empowered to register ships to dummy companies (*sociedad anonima*) in return for a modest fee. There were no requirements of seaworthiness or manning, in fact no physical inspections at all. At the end of the Second World War political instability in Panama and frustration at perceived extortion by its consular officials led former secretary of state, Edward R. Stettinius Jr, with a group of other former officials and oil industry leaders, to set up a new flag of convenience in the client West African state of Liberia.[22] This operation was very tightly controlled. Registration was handled by a private company, the International Trust Company with headquarters in New York and a trusted American CEO. This archetypal wormhole allowed US oil interests not only to reduce costs by circumventing the strict US requirements on seaworthiness, crewing with cheaper foreign nationals and paying minimal registration fees but, more importantly, to pay no tax on the earnings until and unless they were remitted back to the US. Soon the oil companies realised that they no longer needed to own their own fleets of tankers but could charter instead. American shipowner Karl Ludwig led the way and was followed by Greek shipowners such as Stavros Niarchos, Aristotle Onassis and John Livanos and a Norwegian, Erling Naess. By the mid 1950s, Liberia had become the leading flag of convenience, but the action was all in New York, not in West Africa. This was already globalisation, several decades before the phenomenon came to be widely recognised.

Whereas in the 1950s Panama and Liberia were *the* flags of convenience, followed by British-flag registration in Hong Kong, the number of flags and arrangements has proliferated with the independence of more and more microstates. In 1968, newly-independent Singapore greatly increased the attractions of its register by granting shipowners tax exemption. Britain added to Hong Kong offshore flags of convenience in Bermuda, Gibraltar and later the Isle of Man. The Netherlands and France did likewise with their colonies in the Caribbean. Lacking colonies, Norway set up what was officially called a second register, establishing a precedent for other OECD countries. Meanwhile, as Panama and Liberia yielded to pressures to tighten the conditions for their registries, new flags-of-convenience arose in Belize, Cambodia, Cyprus, the Maldives, the Marshall Islands, Tonga and various Caribbean islands, all of which were as lax as Panama and Liberia had once been and attracted many secondhand vessels of doubtful seaworthiness and uncertain ownership. Despite various international conventions, the maritime industry is now more diffuse and less well organised than at any time since the nineteenth century.

Commodity markets and trade

The movement of goods across borders is the very life blood of the international economy and gives rise through various channels to an enormous black and grey economy of contested jurisdiction. In the first instance, there is the black economy of trade in goods whose very production is illegal: drugs, counterfeit brands, pirated copies and poached or plundered natural resources such as fish, ivory and timber. Secondly there is illegal trade, which extends from the above to physical smuggling, under-invoicing and defiance of embargoes. Thirdly, because some countries still impose foreign exchange controls, there is opportunity to manipulate the buying, selling and remittance of foreign currency earnings. In many developing countries this has resulted in the total corruption of the customs service and the foreign exchange regime: almost the entire business community is guilty of criminal behaviour, which effectively legitimises it.

A different perspective is to look at the commodity markets themselves. Oil and metals are particularly interesting because, although consumption is worldwide, production is concentrated in rather few locations and in the hands of only a limited number of global firms. Moreover, sudden perturbations in supply or demand can have a dramatic effect on price. Thus, regardless of whether supply is actually regulated by a formal cartel, as has been the case in the oil and tin industries, there is scope for human agency to affect the market and profit from it. Leading firms and governments have large stakes in the outcome. Shadowy brokers with access to funds and top-level political connections can seek to influence or even 'rig' markets, while governments with geo-political agendas find it convenient to deal with such people, whose stock-in-trade is their discretion.

A WORLD-SYSTEMS PERSPECTIVE

Almost invariably nation-states are treated as discrete cases. To use a medical analogy, a Third World state with weak institutions is regarded as a patient with an illness that requires intervention, not as a manifestation of a wider epidemiological problem. Yet most of the funds that slosh through Third World tax havens, along with the pseudo company and shipping registrations, as indeed the tourists and their gambling, derive from the First World. Even in the case of drugs, the main demand is in the First World. Such is the contemporary, globalised form of dependency. If in the past, colonies and later independent nations were locked into highly unequal patterns of commodity trade, now they have more options but still within a nexus of dependency.

The microstates which provide the tax havens, registries and websites are not themselves substantial beneficiaries. The income which flows across their borders and the vast wealth that is stored within it leaves a very light footprint. Property rights are only nominally transferred. Apart from brass-plate offices for lawyers and accountants, there is little generation of local income. Even the rate at which the income and wealth may be taxed, if not directly then by establishment and registration fees, is highly constrained by competition from neighbouring microstates. In effect, microstates are just short-stay parking lots for international capital. All they have for sale is jurisdiction.

Despite the appearance of independent nationality, most microstates therefore remain economic satellites of the large economies. This can be seen very clearly in the case of the US, whose tax havens cluster in the Caribbean with outliers in Bermuda and Panama. For historic reasons, Britain, France and the Netherlands also make use of colonies in the Caribbean. Britain also has its own tax havens closer to home in the form of the dependencies of the Isle of Man and the Jersey Islands. All European countries can take advantage of Switzerland, Luxembourg, Liechtenstein and Monaco. France has established its own far-flung haven in the desolate Kerguelen Islands just above the Antarctic, taking things to the logical extreme by being uninhabited except for transient groups of scientists.

Transnational wormholes thus collapse one into another. It is well known, for example, that drug trading is highly correlated with money laundering and in turn intersects with the arms trade. An awkward fact is that most arms are produced in G8 countries. Even in something as mundane as the fishing industry, the problem of over-exploitation arises from beneficial owners, typically from EU countries or Taiwan, using flags of convenience, multiple or even unknown flags, to evade management and conservation regimes.[23] For registrations costing no more than around US$2,500 per vessel per annum with nations – including land-locked Bolivia and Mongolia – which have no intention or means of enforcing international maritime conventions, owners are able to catch illegal fish estimated very conservatively at a minimum of US$1.2 billion. Besides the poaching of environmental resources, gambling, counterfeiting, intellectual piracy and people trafficking also intrude into criminality. And then, of course, there are the wellsprings of tax avoidance and evasion. At a more legitimate level, there are multiple intersections between money flows, shipping and trade. Significant price and profit differentials across any of these markets generate arbitraging flows of funds, legal and illegal, as surely as water flows downhill.

This brings us to a political reality: strong nations seek to exercise hegemony over the weak. This phenomenon was widely remarked upon during the Cold War, when the US in particular supported many governments that had an appalling record on development and human rights but were pliably anti-communist. Since the fall of the Berlin Wall in 1989, the political agendas of the US and European powers have become more diffuse but hegemony remains in a new guise, backed by threat of military force. Governments that do not comply risk intervention and destabilisation.

It is actually easier for rich nations to enforce compliance upon small nations than to adopt tough policies in their own countries that might alienate key constituencies. A clear illustration is the reluctance of the US and various other rich nations to legalise and regulate the drug trade, lest it be seen by conservative lobbies as legitimising evil. Far easier to globalise a 'war on drugs' and to conduct paramilitary operations in the poor world, despite a host of unintended consequences.[24]

The 'cover' for the US and other rich nations is that they have great influence over the flow of information and the way political actions are perceived. Here we come to the last form of interdependence. The deliberate deceptions perpetrated by the US, Britain and Australia over the Iraq War illustrate the power of modern propaganda. How much greater is that power when paramilitary operations or discreet interventions are conducted in remote parts of the world where there are few, if any, foreign journalists and local views have almost no conduit to influence world opinion against the barrage of the propaganda or 'spin' machines.

PAX AMERICANA

The US has in recent decades been the country to act most aggressively and internationally against drug trafficking, terrorism and money laundering. It has done so through international agreements, through cajolery and pressure, through extraterritorial enforcement of US law, and through paramilitary and military actions. There is some acknowledgement here of interdependency. The US has sought to impose a kind of extra-territoriality that gives its laws international reach, backed up by sanctions of exclusion from the US market. The emphasis upon controls and punitive measures, however, fails to address the underlying problem of lack of resources and the low tax base of many 'Third World' nations.

At the same time, in response to perceived imperatives of national security, US policy has itself contributed to, if not given rise to, the evils which it avowedly seeks to control.[25] Arms have been shipped to allies who turned into enemies; hard-line Islam was fomented as a tactic to defeat the Soviet Union in Afghanistan, which it did, but also bred a new form of terrorism; the drug trade was from time to time clandestinely encouraged as a means of funding friendly insurgencies; and so on. Are such things random errors of foreign policy or something more systemic?

Here we come to the crucial relationship between the shadow economy and the shadow state. The tax–protection bargain between markets and the state breaks down when corporations are able to evade tax demands by 'going global'. This would appear to be a weakening of the state, as many have argued. However, it would be wrong to assume that powerful states, especially hegemonic ones, do not have a response. Indeed, state actors may be implicated in the cause as well as the response. This section considers several different forms of interaction between the shadow economy and shadow state. First, for reasons of state policy, state actors have themselves established wormholes, even pioneering the phenomenon. Secondly, state powerholders have often resorted to trusted brokers to forge deals that could not be achieved by official diplomacy. Moreover, former powerholders with their networks are now themselves engaging in high-level global business dealings.

None of these arrangements are necessarily criminal, but they may intersect with criminal activities.

Front companies and wormholes

The systematic interest of the US government in front companies and wormholes arose from the need to equip and fund special operations without implicating or compromising the sovereign government. The prototype seems to have been China Defense Supplies, which was set up in 1940 at the instigation of President Franklin D. Roosevelt through his trusted 'fixer' Tommy Corcoran to provide a kind of 'Asian Lend-Lease Program' to assist Chiang Kai-shek and his beleaguered Nationalist forces against the Japanese.[26]

This front company provided the channel to supply General Claire Chennault's Flying Tigers, in effect a clandestine volunteer air force. Within months of the war's end, Corcoran through a Panamanian nominee company combined with Chennault to set up the airline Civil Air Transport (CAT) in a joint venture with Kuomintang interests. From 1947 CAT was running covert airlifts for the newly formed Central Intelligence Agency (CIA). In 1950, after the Nationalist government had been forced to evacuate to Taiwan, CAT (later Air America) was bought out by the CIA and reregistered in Delaware as a CIA 'proprietary' or private front company to conduct special operations against mainland China.[27] Around the same time, Overseas Southeast Asia Supply Corporation (Sea Supply) was registered in Miami with headquarters in Bangkok to provide logistics support to Kuomintang forces in Indochina and Yunnan.[28] Most of the key figures involved in these special operations had shared a background in China during the Second World War as agents of the Office of Strategic Services (OSS), forerunner of the CIA.

The pointsman in the establishment of the CIA's civilian front companies was Paul Helliwell. Having served with OSS intelligence in China and Europe, in 1945 he returned to Washington as chief of the Far East Division of the Strategic Services Unit of the War Department.[29] Absorbed into the newly formed CIA, he soon 'retired', ostensibly to become a corporate lawyer in Miami. There he served as the first head of the CIA proprietary, CAT Inc., and was instrumental in setting up Sea Supply, which was registered in Miami and to which he became legal counsel.[30] Scott hypothesises a link with the narcotics trade and organised crime, for both of which Miami was a hub.[31] If New York was America's front door to the global world of finance, commodities and shipping, Miami was its backdoor to the underworld of drugs, gambling and money laundering. Helliwell would have had intimate knowledge of the Chinese drug trade from his OSS days and had a continuing association with the Nationalists and Southeast Asia through CAT, Sea Supply and his role as Thai consul. In Miami, Helliwell also served as counsel to New York gangster Meyer Lansky, who owned the casino in nearby Havana and with Lucky Luciano ran US drug operations. From his wartime service in Europe, Helliwell undoubtedly had connections also with the Italian Mafia. The timing of his 'retirement' and the commencement of his new enterprise in 1950/51 coincided with the launch of Operation Paper to support Nationalist forces in the Golden Triangle and would explain Helliwell's otherwise curious choice of a location to start his new life.[32]

Covert operations cannot be sustained without reliable channels to hold and distribute funds, namely banks. Details of how this was done initially remain obscure but it seems that friends on Wall Street were willing to assist in the national interest.[33] One specific channel may have been the International Bank of Washington, control of which was acquired in 1955 by retired Major General George Olmsted, followed in 1959 by Financial General Corporation, the seventh largest US holding bank.[34] Establishment of special purpose vehicles seems to have begun in the early 1960s, again through Paul Helliwell, who in 1960 was assigned to support covert operations against Cuba.[35] Having set up Mercantile Bank and Trust in the offshore tax haven of Bermuda, in the early 1960s, he and associates moved on to set up Castle Bank and Trust based in Nassau, in the Bahamas.[36] When the illegal operations of Castle Bank attracted the attention of US regulators in 1972, a new vehicle was needed. In the following year the Nugan Hand Bank was set up in Sydney by local lawyer Frank Nugan and probable CIA operative Michael Hand with a board of retired senior military and intelligence personnel and former CIA head William Colby as legal counsel.[37] Nugan Hand quickly established a global network but seems to have specialised in clandestine CIA business in Southeast Asia, as well as a good deal of drug dealing and money laundering for other parties.[38] The bank collapsed in 1980 with the unsolved murder of Frank Nugan and the 'disappearance' of Michael Hand.

After the Castle and Nugan Hand debacles, the CIA found a better arms-length vehicle in the Bank of Credit and Commerce International (BCCI), established in Dubai in 1975 before rapidly becoming a global phenomenon, including branches and affiliates in the US under the control of the very influential Democrat, Clark Clifford.[39] BCCI served as a conduit for funds involved in the Iran–Contra scandal of the Reagan administration. In 1991 regulators seized most of the bank's assets and enforced liquidation. Another CIA conduit for special operations in Europe was Banco Ambrosiano, controlled by the Vatican Bank and associated with the high-level state-linked network of the mysterious P2 Masonic Lodge.[40] Banco Ambrosiano came under criminal investigation in 1981, a year before its chairman, Roberto Calvi, was found dead hanging from London's Blackfriars Bridge, with subsequent indications of a mafia assassination.[41]

For conducting sensitive transactions such as arms deals, drug deals and funds transfers, the CIA also relied upon friendly international business figures who were rich and well-connected and could operate discreetly at the very top level of government in both the US and overseas. One such broker over several decades was Swiss-Israeli magnate Bruce Rappaport. Rappaport was from 1959 owner of Inter-Maritime Bank of Geneva, a founding shareholder in Castle Bank (Nassau), linked into the BCCI network; from 1982 owner of his own Antigua Bank; and from 1989 a substantial stakeholder in Bank of New York (BONY), which in 1990 arranged a share swap with the Inter-Maritime Bank of Switzerland.[42] The New York–Geneva nexus came into being around the time of the fall of the Berlin Wall and proved to be an efficient conduit for transfer of funds out of Russia, although it was not until 1999 that this became a public scandal, whereupon Rappaport sought to disassociate himself. Between the 1960s and 1990s Rappaport seems to have been involved in a series of dubious transactions that the US government did not wish to become public knowledge.[43]

Another allegedly long-term CIA associate was American-educated, Swiss-Israeli commodity trader Marc Rich, former principal of Glencore and Xstrata.[44] Like Rappaport, Rich made a lot of money trading with countries such as South Africa, Iran and Iraq.[45] In the late 1980s he forged good relationships with senior figures in the Soviet Union that in the 1990s placed him in good stead to sign lucrative contracts amidst the political turmoil. In 1983, he was indicted in the US on charges of tax evasion and fled the country never to return, though pardoned by President Clinton in his last hours in office. Clinton cited clemency pleas from the Israeli Prime Minister.[46]

Mention should also be made of Saudi financier and arms dealer Adnan Khashoggi. He achieved fame in the 1970s as virtually the sole arms dealer for the government of Saudi Arabia, earning fabulous commissions from American manufacturers.[47] His ability to network discreetly with heads of state and agencies around the world led in turn to his instrumental role in the Iran–Contra scandal of the mid 1980s during the Reagan administration.[48] After being implicated in the collapse of BCCI and being brought to trial with acquittal in the US, he has led a quieter but not inactive life in Monaco.[49] Others such as Russian-national Viktor Bout have taken his place.[50]

A third channel of economic and political influence has been private equity funds. The model is the Carlyle Group, the world's largest private equity firm, established in 1987 and, as of late 2006, managing $44 billion of funds across 16 countries.[51] Being 'spectacularly well-connected politically', Carlyle specialises in what Craig Unger refers to as 'access capitalism'.[52] Among its partners, advisers and counsellers are former heads of state (including George H.W. Bush and John Major), cabinet members, high officials and ambassadors. These luminaries do not necessarily do business deals, but they help to set them up and minimise the risk. As Unger argues, retired politicians and officials can thereby through equity deals earn a great deal more than in the past as mere consultants or lobbyists to corporate law firms. Moreover, '[a]s a private partnership, Carlyle is not subject to the same disclosure rules as public companies'.[53] According to Unger, Carlyle has been an efficient channel for American–Saudi business deals. Another channel, identified by Seymour Hersh, was Trireme Partners, a private venture capital fund headed by Defense Policy Board adviser Richard Perle with an advisory board including Henry Kissinger.[54]

Power elites

One way of exploring the relationship between shadow economy and shadow state in an era of globalisation is to go back to C. Wright Mills' concept of a 'power elite'.[55] Writing in the middle of the Eisenhower period, Mills argued that the New Deal period had seen the economic elite, once utterly opposed to big government, join with the new political elite. In the 1950s, he saw a shift to a more militarised elite, foreshadowing Eisenhower's concern at the emergence of a 'military–industrial complex'.

Since the 1980s there has been a marked trend back towards smaller government, but some of Mills' insights continue to apply. For example, he refers to the 'inner core' of the power elite as consisting 'of those who interchange commanding roles at the top of one dominant institutional order with those in another'. He refers to generals and admirals, corporate executives and 'statesmen', which he extends to include corporate lawyers and investment bankers.[56] With some broadening of the categories to include the oil industry and contractors, this is still a valid description of the merry-go-round of patronage and office that rotates every four to eight years according to the winners and losers in each presidential election.

Where C. Wright Mills is deficient is his lack of attention to the mechanisms of political funding. As the phrase attributed to the Californian Assembly Speaker Jesse Unruh has it, 'money is the mother's milk of politics'. In the 1950s, mass television advertising did not yet generate such massive demands upon political funding. In the 2004 presidential election, however, George W. Bush officially received $367 million and his rival John Kerry $301 million.[57] Corporate donors, of which the largest was Enron at $2.4 million, gave to both parties but with a heavy bias towards the Republican Party. And this is only funding accounted for by the Federal Electoral Commission. Through various loopholes, there is other soft money that is not reported. The consequence is a nexus between political funding, public appointments and policy that corrupts government at both the national and state level. While funding and appointments are fairly transparent, the resultant policy process and the distribution of the fruits of office are not.

Money politics typically derives from market power and contrived regulatory gaps in commercial markets. Thus, as has been seen under the recent Bush administration, interests associated with a particular industry – in this case oil – can hold sway in the White House, cronies can enjoy privileged access to the gravy train of war contracts (Bechtel, Halliburton) and corporate crooks can enjoy political protection (Enron). Ethnic lobbies in 'swing states', such as the Cuban lobby in Florida, buy enormous influence over policy.[58] The trial of Republican fund raiser and lobbyist Jack Abramoff and the indictment of House Leader Tom DeLay have given further insight into the webs of power, money and influence.[59] Sleaze taints the Bush administration, as it did the Clinton administration, and their predecessors.

Two implications may be drawn. First, members of a self-selected power elite, whether in or out of power, are likely to share common interests. For example, Peter Dale Scott documents that all seven of the early deputy directors of the CIA, including Allen Dulles, came from New York legal and financial circles.[60] It follows that they also had professional expertise in corporate law and finance. Networks in banking, shipping, oil, minerals and insurance all intersected. These men did deals to promote the national interest and make money at the same time. As Mills noted in the 1950s, they were not beholden to the bureaucracy or bureaucratic procedure. As with the setting up of the Liberian flag-of-convenience register in the late 1940s, so later with offshore banking and finance, the power elite have sought through various wormholes to remove their own assets from the taxing and regulatory powers of the state, while using state leverage to generate business, sometimes subtly but now quite blatantly. Abuse of power it may well be, power in the raw, but it is also a well-established and by default an accepted system of government.

Secondly, 'old boy' and club networks, as also service to the state, conferred protection, not least against prying bureaucratic regulators. Part of the explanation as to why the CIA's irregular banks were allowed so much leeway by regulators is that they were known to enjoy top-level patronage and their patrons or their associates were prepared if necessary to intervene in due process. Castle Bank and Nugan Hand had high-level CIA connections; Banco Ambrosiano was owned by the Vatican with links to the P2 Masonic Lodge and the Mafia;[61] BCCI enjoyed a close business relationship with President Carter's Director of Budget, Bert Lance, and donated generously to President Carter's charities; and the chairman of its main US subsidiary and legal counsel was Democrat grandee Clark Clifford.[62] Years later, it was to be the same story with Enron.

In the case of money laundering, the imperative to counter terrorism and crime does not necessarily extend to the collection of tax. The determination of the Internal Revenue Service has frequently been thwarted by intersecting business and political interests who have little more than acquaintance with the public interest. The power elite protect themselves and hide the evidence.

CONCLUSION

Recent decades have seen a seismic shift between political and economic power. After a half-century of containment, capital and big business has escaped the costly 'protection' and regulation of the nation-state and forced it to bargain on less favourable terms. The nation-state still sets the rules, but is more constrained and less and less willing or able to enforce them. Moreover, the proliferation of independent nations since the Second World War has led to many creations that are simply not viable as modern nations. These weak states are chronically short of revenue and willing clients for whoever is willing to pay the most, be it the US, Japan, China, Taiwan or Israel. For corporations and the mega-rich, they are jurisdictions for sale, happy hunting grounds for money, goods and ships needing a fresh and non-transparent identity. This offshore economy with its proliferating wormholes back to the centres of the world economy may be a kind of macular degeneration in which the blank spots of disorder impinge upon an over-extended world hegemony. But it may also denote a return to a less constrained version of capitalism as it existed before the crisis of the 1930s and still recognisable to Fernand Braudel or even Adam Smith.

Because this global economy is only intermittently subject to state control and taxation, powerful states seek to devise techniques to extend their reach. This may be achieved through cooperation in supra-national law enforcement, but there are strict limits to the willingness and ability of national agencies to do so. As the global hegemon, the US seeks to pursue its international interests by whatever *realpolitik* is seen at the time to be most expedient under the guise of national security. Nevertheless, the new world order also involves interplays with the perceived national interests of other large countries. In Russia under Vladimir Putin, the former shadow state of the KGB has consolidated its hold on power and its control over natural resources.[63] The still-totalitarian Chinese government is no less ruthless than the US in pursuit of its interests and maintains an enormous structure of semi-autonomous state corporations as non-transparent instruments of state power. European middle powers have shown themselves to be utterly amoral in pursuit of their national arms trade and commercial interests. Mention might also be made of Israel and Mossad's international web. These governments all have a record of subverting markets for the sake of 'national security', consolidating their own power, enriching their power-holders and their associates and overriding accountability at law. From time to time they cooperate in doing so.

The threats of terrorism and crime are not without substance but the more pressing reality is that they have exposed massive institutional weaknesses in the rich, democratic nations that are the beating hearts of the capitalist world order. Much-criticised institutional weaknesses in poor countries are complemented and indeed fed by institutional weaknesses in rich countries, nowhere more so than in the United States itself. Corruption cuts both ways. These weaknesses will not be relieved by wars. Notwithstanding the disabling effects of fear and the political manipulation of those fears, they demand renewal of civil society and more effective representative democracy.

NOTES

1. I am grateful to Peter Verhezen for comments on a previous draft.
2. Margaret E. Beare (ed.), *Critical Reflections on Transnational Organized Crime, Money Laundering, and Corruption* (Toronto: University of Toronto Press, 2003).
3. Howard Dick and John Butcher (eds), *The Rise and Fall of Revenue Farming: Business Elites and the Emergence of the Modern State in Southeast Asia* (New York: St Martins Press, 1993).
4. Friedrich Schneider, 'Shadow Economies Around the World: What Do We Really Know?', *European Journal of Political Economy*, 21 (2005), pp. 598–642.
5. Pasuk Phongpaichit, Sangsit Phiriyarangsan and Nualnoi Treerat, *Guns, Girls, Gambling, Ganja: Thailand's Illegal Economy and Public Policy* (Chiang Mai: Silkworm Books, 1998).
6. Fabre, this volume; Guilhem Fabre, *Criminal Prosperity: Drug Trafficking, Money Laundering and Financial Crises After the Cold War* (London and New York: Routledge Curzon, 2003), pp. 77–8.
7. Fernand Braudel, *The Wheels of Commerce* (vol. ii of *Civilization and Capitalism, 15th–18th Century*), trans. Sian Reynolds (London: Fontana, 1985).
8. Charles Tilly, 'War Making and State Making as Organized Crime' in Peter Evans, Dietrich Rueschmeyer and Theda Skocpol (eds), *Bringing the State Back In* (Cambridge: Cambridge University Press, 1985).
9. Mancur Olson, *Power and Prosperity: Outgrowing Communist and Capitalist Dictatorships* (New York: Basic Books, 2000).
10. Douglass C. North, *Institutions, Institutional Change and Economic Performance: Political Economy of Institutions and Decisions* (Cambridge: Cambridge University Press, 1990).
11. George Orwell, *Animal Farm: A Fairy Story* (London: Longman, 1945).
12. Adolph A. Berle and Gardiner C. Means, *The Modern Corporation and Private Property* (New York: Macmillan, 1932).
13. United Nations, *Human Development Report 2005: Demographic Trends*, www.hdr.undp.org/reports/global/2005/pdf/HDROS/HD1.pdf (accessed 21 April 2006).
14. Wikipedia, 'Wormhole' (accessed October 2006).
15. See Fabre, this volume.
16. Yu Yongding, 'Global Imbalances and China', Finch Lecture, University of Melbourne, 17 October 2006.
17. Ethan B. Kapstein, *Governing the Global Economy: International Finance and the State* (Cambridge, MA: Harvard University Press, 1994).
18. Mark Hampton, *The Offshore Interface: Tax Havens in the Global Economy* (Basingstoke: Palgrave Macmillan, 1996).
19. Jeffrey Robinson, *The Sink: Terror, Crime and Dirty Money in the Offshore World* (London: Constable & Robinson, 2003).

20. Hampton, *The Offshore Interface*; Robinson, *The Sink*.
21. Howard Dick, 'The Competitive Advantage of British Shipping in China Seas', in Richard Harding, Adrian Jarvis and Alston Kennerley (eds), *British Ships in China Seas: 1700 to the Present Day*, Papers presented at the Conference held at the Merseyside Maritime Museum in September 2002 (Liverpool: Society for Nautical Research and National Museums Liverpool, 2004), pp. 43–58.
22. Rodney Carlisle, *Sovereignty for Sale: The Origins and Evolution of the Panamanian and Liberian Flags of Convenience* (Annapolis, MA: Naval Institute Press, 1981).
23. Matthew Gianni and Walt Simpson, *The Changing Nature of High Seas Fishing: How Flags of Convenience Provide Cover for Illegal, Unreported and Unregulated Fishing*, Australian Department of Agriculture, Fisheries and Forestry, International Transport Workers' Federation and WWF International, Canberra, 2005, www.wwf.org.uk/filelibrary/pdf/flagsofconvenience.pdf (accessed 18 May 2006).
24. Juan G. Ronderos, 'The War on Drugs and the Military: The Case of Colombia', in Beare (ed.), *Critical Reflections on Transnational Organized Crime, Money Laundering, and Corruption*, pp. 209–36; Alfred W. McCoy and Alan A. Block, *War on Drugs: Studies in the Failure of U.S. Narcotics Policy* (Boulder, CO: Westview, 1992). See also, Thoumi, this volume.
25. Peter D. Scott, *Drugs, Oil, and War: The United States in Afghanistan, Colombia, and Indochina* (Lanham: Rowman & Littlefield, 2003).
26. Spartacus, Entries for: Tommy Corcoran, Paul Helliwell, www.spartacus.schoolnet.co.uk (accessed 21 October 2006).
27. Alan A. Block and Constance A. Weaver, *All is Clouded by Desire: Global Banking, Money Laundering and International Organized Crime* (Westport, CT: Praeger, 2004); Scott, *Drugs, Oil, and War*.
28. John Prados, *President's Secret Wars: CIA and Pentagon Covert Operations since World War II* (New York: William Morrow, 1986), p. 74.
29. Block and Weaver, *All is Clouded by Desire*, p. 37.
30. Scott, *Drugs, Oil, and War*, p. 198.
31. Ibid.
32. Alfred W. McCoy, *The Politics of Heroin: CIA Complicity in the Global Drug Trade* (Chicago: Lawrence Hill, 2003), pp. 168–9.
33. Joseph Trento, *Prelude to Terror: The Rogue CIA and the Legacy of America's Private Intelligence Network* (New York: Carroll & Graf, 2005).
34. The George and Carol Olmsted Foundation, 'General Olmstead's Biography', www.olmstedfoundation.org/public/biography-3.cfm (accessed 22 October 2006); Block and Weaver, *All is Clouded by Desire*, p. 41.
35. Trento, *Prelude to Terror*, also Spartacus, 'Tommy Corcoran', 'Paul Helliwell', www.spartacus.schoolnet.co.uk (accessed 21 October 2006).
36. Block and Weaver, *All is Clouded by Desire*.
37. Wikipedia, 'Nugan Hand Bank' (accessed October 2006).
38. Jonathan Kwitny, *The Crimes of Patriots: A True Tale of Dope, Dirty Money, and the CIA* (New York: Norton, 1987); McCoy, *The Politics of Heroin*.
39. Peter Truell and Larry Gurwin, *False Profits: The Inside Story of BCCI, the World's Most Corrupt Financial Empire* (New York: Houghton Mifflin, 1992); Mark Potts, Nicholas Kochan and Robert Whittington, *Dirty Money: BCCI: The Inside Story of the World's Sleaziest Bank* (Washington, DC: National Press Books, 1992); Jonathan Beaty and S.C. Gwynne, *The Outlaw Bank: A Wild Ride into the Secret Heart of BCCI* (New York: Random House, 1993).
40. See Ganser, this volume.
41. Wikipedia, 'Roberto Calvi' (accessed October 2006).
42. Block and Weaver, *All is Clouded by Desire*.
43. Ibid.
44. A. Craig Copetas, *Metal Men: Marc Rich and the 10-Billion-Dollar Scam* (New York: Putnam's Sons, 1985).
45. Australian Broadcasting Corporation (ABC), 'Swiss link undermines Xstrata's bid for WMC', AM Program, 11 February 2005, at www.abc.net.au/am/content/2005/s1300651.htm (accessed 10 October 2005).

46. Bill Clinton, *My Life* (New York: Knopf, 2004).
47. Said K. Aburish, *The Rise, Corruption and Coming Fall of the House of Saud* (London: Bloomsbury, 1995).
48. Lawrence E. Walsh, *Iran-Contra: The Final Report* (New York: Times Books, 1994).
49. Wikipedia, 'Adnan Khashoggi' (accessed October 2006).
50. Douglas Farah and Stephen Braun, 'The Merchant of Death', *Australian Financial Review*, 3 November 2006.
51. Carlyle, www.carlyle.com/eng/company/index.html (accessed 21 October 2006).
52. Craig Unger, *House of Bush, House of Saud: The Secret Relationship between the World's Two Most Powerful Dynasties* (New York: Scribner, 2004), pp. 156–7.
53. Carlyle, www.carlyle.com/eng/company/index.html (accessed 21 October 2006).
54. Seymour M. Hersh, *Chain of Command* (London: Penguin Books, 2005).
55. C. Wright Mills, *The Power Elite* (New York: Oxford University Press, New York, 1956).
56. Ibid., pp. 288–9.
57. Federal Election Commission, Financial Summary Reports, 2003–2004: Presidential candidates, http://herndon1.sdrdc.com/cgi-bin/cancomsrs (accessed 22 October 2006).
58. Ann Louise Bardach, *Cuba Confidential: Love and Vengeance in Miami and Havana* (New York: Random House, 2002).
59. Wikipedia, 'Jack Abramoff' (accessed October 2006).
60. Scott, *Drugs, Oil, and War*, pp. 187, 200, n. 14.
61. See Ganser, this volume.
62. Beaty and Gwynne, *The Outlaw Bank*.
63. Paul Klebnikov, *Godfather of the Kremlin: Boris Berezovsky and the Looting of Russia* (New York: Harcourt, 2000).

6
Transnational Crime and Global Illicit Economies

Vincenzo Ruggiero

Current global economies shape new patterns of transnational criminal activity. This chapter examines how recent economic development, along with unprecedented opportunities, fosters increasing demand for illegal goods and services. After describing the nature of such goods and services, a number of cases are discussed in which criminal organisations and official, economic or political actors compete in illegality or establish illegitimate partnerships with one another.

In this chapter, the notion that criminal organisations are poised to 'subvert global governance' is critiqued, and the hypothesis is put forward that, rather, official economic actors are incorporating philosophies and practices they have acquired, in a mutual learning process, from criminal organisations.

A brief history of the corporation allows the pinpointing of attempts, throughout this history, to divert risk and insecurity from top managers and large shareholders onto small shareholders and society at large. In a number of case studies an attempt is made to validate this hypothesis. Far from being unique, these cases demonstrate how corporations and entrepreneurs are becoming 'parapolitical' groups influencing national and international choices.

In a brief conclusion, a re-definition of the crimes of the powerful is presented in which the variable 'innovation' is attributed paramount significance. This variable, adopted by Schumpeter[1] with respect to entrepreneurs and by Merton[2] with respect to criminal entrepreneurs, is said to constitute a core notion against which developments in transnational crime and 'the government of the shadows' can be analysed.

TRANSNATIONAL CRIMINAL ECONOMIES

I am forced here to discuss the 'G word', 'globalisation', although I prefer using the term 'transnationalism'. The G word, as we know, is contested. Some commentators focus on revolutionary developments in communication and transport, and on internationalisation of trading and labour, as well as on growing coordination of tasks performed by groups and individuals worldwide.[3] With organisations attempting to position themselves globally, whether in relation to markets, media, or politics, enthusiasts claim that the world is becoming a single space in which new opportunities arise for all.

Critics,[4] however, argue that this process mainly involves the most advanced countries, namely countries engaged in all sorts of international interactions and exchange. Therefore, the benefits of this interconnectedness are rarely shared with developing countries and when they are, the unequal terms in which benefits are shared make 'transnationalism' seem, in large part, synonymous with 'Westernisation'.

True, geographical expansion is one of the historical necessities of business, the result of a constant urge to establish new markets. However, the recent intensification of this process and its effects can hardly go unnoticed. These include the formation of networks of interdependencies forging a new world-system, the corrosion of borders and the increasing 'placelessness' of the economy.[5] World flows of information, which constitute crucial elements of economic growth, are coupled with the growing mobility of goods and finances.[6] Institutional authorities, enforcement and legislations, it should be noted, provide a normative corollary to this mobility, allowing the movement of certain goods and people, while impeding the movement of others. Criminal business, particularly transnational crime, responds to this new normative corollary by establishing networks that by-pass national regulations. This response gathers momentum as demand for prohibited goods increases, along with the demand of localised people for mobility.

It is a widespread assumption among institutional agencies and conventional observers that transnational crime originates in developing countries and that its impact is suffered in developed ones. The following typology of transnational criminal activities shows that illicit business conducted by 'aliens' needs a receptive environment, along with a range of indigenous partners and agents, in the countries in which it operates. It also shows that crimes may originate in developed countries but have an impact in developing ones. The following list constitutes a very succinct phenomenology derived from the numerous episodes that have occurred over recent years.

- Joint ventures between members of organised crime, politicians and financial operators are necessary for money laundering operations to be successful: in such cases the official economy offers a service to criminal syndicates.[7]
- It is by now recognised that entrepreneurs and politicians are prime actors in the illegitimate transfer of money abroad. 'Hot money', which is almost automatically associated with the laundering of criminal proceeds, in reality includes money earned, legitimately or otherwise, by official actors.[8]
- Both large and small companies employ unregistered migrants. These workers are normally smuggled into developed countries by a variety of groups and actors. The companies employing such workers enjoy the smuggling services offered to them by these groups and actors.[9]
- Corporations operating in developing countries have often been charged with using quasi-slave, or forced, labour. In some cases they have been accused of human rights abuses in countries where trade unionism is criminalised and opposition groups violently repressed.[10]

- Some corporations have been found guilty of selling goods to criminal organisations, which then on-sell them, untaxed (tobacco products, clothes). In such cases they become partners of criminal groups, sharing with them the sums involved in the fiscal fraud.[11]
- Large international drug trafficking is often carried out by, or with the complicity of, import–export firms operating in the official domain. Concealing drugs with legitimate goods is a well-developed practice, particularly in respect of cocaine trafficking.[12]
- Research into illegal arms transfers suggests that a variety of organisations are involved and that international criminal groups may form business partnerships with producers and the political lobbies supporting them.[13]

The areas of activity listed above would suggest that transnational organised crime is not to be exclusively identified with the illegal activities of notorious large crime syndicates. Rather, the cases presented show that transnational crime may well transcend conventional activities and mingle with entrepreneurial and, at times, governmental deviance. This occurs when legally produced goods are illegally marketed, or when the illegal marketing of goods produced in one country is supported by the complicity of corrupt politicians in a country in which those goods are officially banned. It is therefore appropriate to identify transnational organised crime as the result of partnerships between illegitimate and legitimate actors.

The notion of 'partnership' implies that organised criminal groups both teach and learn from their legitimate counterparts in the economic arena. By investing illicit proceeds in the official economy, for example, they learn the techniques and the rationalisations adopted by white-collar and corporate offenders, thus being, in a sense, corrupted by the economy rather than corrupting it. We shall see in the second part of this chapter how the opposite can also be the case, that is, that official economic operators can learn the techniques and rationalisations commonly adopted by organised crime.

In brief, the encounter between organised crime and the official economy is not the result of an unnatural relationship between a harmonious entity and a dysfunctional one. Rather, it amounts to a joint undertaking of two loosely regulated worlds, both deviating from the rules they officially establish for themselves. For example, the rules of 'honour' are often ignored by criminal entrepreneurs, who claim their unconditional faith in them;[14] similarly, the rules of fair competition are often disregarded by those very legitimate entrepreneurs who claim their universal validity.[15]

SUBVERTING GOVERNANCE?

It is hard to infer from the above that global governance is being subverted by transnational crime, particularly if by this term we mean conventional and international organised crime. It would appear that subversion, if at all, may be brought about by alliances, partnerships and consortia between illicit and licit entrepreneurs. As Cribb suggests in the introduction to this volume, one of the attributes of such consortia is clandestinity, linking diverse elites irrespective of their background, which may fall in the terrain of legality or illegality. A crucial question arising, however, is to what extent transnationalism per se causes an increase in the crimes of the powerful? This apparently new question, in fact, brings us back to similar, old concerns, for example, does corporate crime increase in periods of economic stagnation or in periods of economic growth? Are small firms operating in competitive markets more likely to commit crime than large companies enjoying a monopolistic condition? Students of corporate criminality have discussed these issues for decades, but answers have proven inconclusive. The reason, perhaps, lies in the extreme versatility of the crimes of the powerful, which are capable of reproducing themselves within a wide range of diverse conditions.

There are three variables which provide the background to such versatility. The first falls in the normative domain, or rather it is associated with the lack of it. Transnational business enjoys what old colonialism has always enjoyed, namely the lack of clear, written rights protecting the populations it addresses. Like colonialism building the industrial revolution on predation, new corporations and states build their profits on deregulation. Both, however, enjoy various degrees of complicity on the part of local elites, who grant access to territories and peoples in exchange for status and private gains. We seem to be faced, in this respect, with a new 'compradorial' class in developing countries which encourages or allows deregulation to develop.

Here, the analysis put forward by Samir Amin[16] comes to mind, particularly his distinction between autocentric and extroverted economies. The former type of economies augment their potential for accumulation in deregulated conditions, and the constituent aspects of the accumulation they pursue are integrated in single national realities or in the multinational, developed, context in which they operate. Extroverted economies, by contrast, while giving shape to a new compradorial class in developing countries, display a form of 'extroversion' in that the effects of the accumulation pursued are found not so much in the world periphery, as in the developed world at large.[17] In brief, access to territories and peoples in present circumstances does not necessarily translate into beneficial effects for developing countries.[18] Far from reducing poverty, transnational economic activity generates criminal opportunities which lead to the type of conduct we currently witness: the use of forced and child labour; the export of dangerous or defective goods; the dumping of poisonous substances and waste; and the purchase of women's and children's bodies or, on demand, of their organs. Deregulation is an essential aspect of transnationalism, and epitomises an unbalanced economic development, a skewed system of opportunities allowing the removal of resources from poor environments and their transfer towards wealthy areas.[19] Among the justifications accompanying this transfer is the well-known 'trickle down principle', according to which the profits made by powerful economic actors will eventually benefit vulnerable groups and individuals as well. Resources, in this sense, do not belong to local or global collectivities, but to those who, in exploiting them, create wealth destined to 'trickle down' for the benefit of all.

The second variable for the understanding of the crimes of the powerful is mobility. This variable includes a notion of speed: financial and commercial conduits have to be quickly identified, if quick profits are to be made. The task consists of reaching specifically suitable places, with fast, short-term investments, before the effects of those investments are perceived. Such investments will be all the more remunerative in countries where a well-disciplined, undemanding workforce is available, often a workforce victimised by elite misconduct, rulers' abuse or military dictatorship. Investments, in these contexts, have to be resolutely fast, and, indeed, extremely mobile, because the vagaries of the political climate might bring change and therefore make regimes more unfavourable. New regulations may be introduced in developing countries; a new political climate may emerge; or the international community may expose unethical or criminal conduct by corporations, thus forcing corporations to quickly find new arenas of investment. Mobility, swiftness and speed in identifying new receptive territories are crucial. It should be noted that speed was, and is, also important for conventional criminals: the most successful, legendary, bank robbers of the past had an advantage on law enforcement in terms of mobility and speed: they bought the fastest cars. Similarly, the most successful drug dealers keep moving, exploring, penetrating new markets, and approaching new pools of customers. They repeatedly change their addresses, both official and informal, in order to escape detection. Moreover, it has been suggested that the white collars who are most inclined to commit crime are extremely mobile, they change employer quickly and frequently, so that they do not develop any sort of loyalty to the company employing them or, for that matter, to customers, the market and society at large.[20] Mobility is, typically, a resource that distinguishes powerful, or at least, wealthy people from marginalised individuals.

Invisibility is the third variable connoting transnationalism. Traditionally, invisibility is regarded as one of the characteristics of white collar crime, and relates to the offender as well as the victim – in this respect, some corporate crimes appear to be offences without offenders. Victims may also be invisible, or they may even be unaware of being victimised. This is due to the fact that white collar criminals often do not share the crime scene with their victim: the place in which the crime is committed and the place where its impact is experienced and suffered may not coincide. The same applies to time: the time when the crime is planned and the time when victimisation is experienced do not coincide. Invisibility, in the current times, also applies to the profits, which, along with the perpetrators and the victims, need to be hidden and therefore have to disappear in financial networks often inaccessible to public scrutiny.

It could be argued that all of this is neither novel nor unique to the history of international markets. However, it should be appreciated that the potential impact of the crimes of the powerful, while becoming increasingly international in nature, also becomes more easily concealable, as crimes are perpetrated in areas where statutory control is problematic. Crimes are committed 'abroad', where national or international legislation has little clout, while proceeds are enjoyed domestically. Here, the dream of reformers seems to come true: the task is not to get rid of crime, but to use it productively; not to eliminate it, but incorporate it in legitimate business; finally, not to suppress it, but to divert its impact.[21]

Recent episodes appear to prove that transnationalism, coupled with neo-liberal philosophies, does not simply equate with an encouragement to commit crimes, but with an untold guarantee of impunity. In this sense, the dilemma of previous forms of business and trade returns, albeit in a different guise. In the eighteenth century, traders and entrepreneurs, along with moral and political philosophers, were engaged in identifying the limit beyond which commercial practices amounted to unethical or criminal practices. Similarly, today, economic enterprise is struggling to establish a new moral justification for its activity. For this reason, every economic act, even if illegitimate, may become normative, in that it can establish new regulations and values, and promote new ethical codes and legitimacies.

As in the eighteenth century, what is at stake now is a definition of what is legitimate and what is not. Forcing the boundaries between legitimate and illegitimate economic behaviour is becoming crucial for the development of new forms of enterprise. Entrepreneurs experiment with new practices, then 'wait and see': reactions to their newly adopted practice may vary, and if they are weak or non-existent, the new *modus operandi* becomes routine and can subsequently spread.

In this sense, the crimes of the powerful encapsulate a normative element, and, while challenging legality, may end up establishing new norms and legislation. I am referring here to 'experimentation', namely attempts to change practices, to distort or outflank rules, to manipulate perceptions thereof: in brief, conduct that cannot be ascribed to a grand conspiracy, but rather to the day-to-day improvisation of powerful actors seeking to maintain and augment social and institutional position.

To sum up, transnationalism may encourage partnerships between conventional criminal organisations and official powerful actors, including large entrepreneurs, while it may simultaneously create an environment conducive to increasingly adventurous and illegitimate entrepreneurship. In the new environment, firms do not limit their interest to profit-making, they also engage in international neo-liberal pedagogy. For example, they translate International Monetary Fund ideas into practice, therefore enacting 'wide-scale privatisation, the curtailment of state regulation, the end to state subsidies geared toward the creation of a social good, such as the social safety net or the medical care'.[22] At the same time, by forcing the boundaries between legitimate and illegitimate practices, they indeed reshape or subvert global governance. All of this requires a constant readjustment of the features and nature of the corporation and the firm in general.

THE ADVENTURES OF THE CORPORATION

The history of the corporation is also the history of its endless attempts to sell wellbeing. Along with what they produce, prosperous businesses sell their image as successful enterprises to consumers, investors, and society at large. The entre-preneurial jargon is affected by this attempt and equates prosperity with safety, certainty of development with happiness: think of phrases like 'safe investment' and, in the financial vocabulary, of words such as 'securities', which implicitly stave off the general perception that economic life is unpredictable, and instability is the norm. Business entails, therefore, an in-built contention to repel notions of risk and to spread, in the collective imagination, the idea of safe, guaranteed, harmonic growth.

In the history of the corporation, one of the first moves aimed at increasing certainty of profits consisted of separating ownership from management. Despite the decentralisation of risk this implied, the move did not prove effective, as gigantic scandals erupted showing the vulnerability of the new arrangement.[23] Fraud and breach of trust affected investors, while a number of sensational bankruptcies caused tension not only within specific national contexts, but also in international relations.[24]

Working harder on the variable certainty, the corporation then resorted to the notion of limited liability: investors, in case of financial crisis, were only personally liable, and therefore financially exposed, for the amount of money they had invested and not for the whole loss of the firm. This, however, resulted in a consequent loss of power in the control of corporations by shareholders. With managers becoming the main decision-making force, shareholders tended to disappear from the scene, thus distancing themselves from the corporation they owned. In this way, risk associated with investment could grow rather than shrink, as lack of control by investors turned into lack of certainty for the finances they committed.

A proper history of the unaccountability of the corporation is yet to be written. This history, however, would have to pay particular attention to the crucial shift occurring towards the end of the nineteenth century, when through a bizarre legal alchemy, courts managed to transform the corporation into a person. The corporation thus assumed its own identity, separate from the people who owned it and managed it. Again, this made some people safer, but society as a whole more unsafe, as it became extremely difficult to identify responsibilities and culprits for malpractice and deviance: corporate crime became a crime without criminals.

In the 1980s, the emphasis on market freedom brought deregulation and privatisation, leading to the unprecedented international expansion of business. Freedom of enterprise came to be identified, among other things, with freedom from the bonds of location, and was enhanced through a number of international agencies or agreements: all measures that might restrict international trade were banned.

Certainty and interest for some translated into risk for entire populations, though the very concept of 'interest' underwent a subtle modification. In corporate jargon, for example, though interest is regarded as the only *raison d'être* of economic enterprise, the notion of 'corporate social responsibility' is gaining increasing currency. 'Interest with an attitude' is the new creed, as corporations try to show their philanthropic nature and reject imputations of greed and self-centredness. In the new climate, corporations may easily become a major force in responding to the environmental and social problems they have caused. Are we witnessing the development of a free market economy with a conscience? Tobacco giants, for example, are creating centres for Corporate Social Responsibility, while corporations seem to be set to compete against one another for higher ethical standards by setting up 'moral' business schools. The message is clear: corporations care about the environment and communities, they are not sheer profit-pursuers.

More realistically, however, economists such as Milton Friedman, when asked about recent developments, reiterate a concept that can hardly be escaped.

There is only one social responsibility for corporate executives: they must make as much money as possible for their shareholders. This is a moral imperative. Executives who choose moral and environmental goals over profits – executives who try to act morally – are, in fact, immoral.[25]

There is only one instance in which corporate social responsibility is acceptable; this is when responsibility is not an end in itself, but is yet another way to maximise profits.

In a recent definition, an 'irresponsible firm' is a firm which assumes that it cannot be called to account to any public or private authority, or to the public opinion, for the social, economic and environmental consequences of its activity.[26] Irresponsible firms prosper thanks to the emphasis on the maximisation at any cost, and in the short term, of their market value in the stock exchange, irrespective of their budget or revenues and of their productive capacity. Although 'maximisation at any cost' appears to benefit all shareholders, including small ones, in practice throughout the 1990s it resulted in the disproportionate creation of wealth for large shareholders and managers and in loss on the part of the small investors.[27] Further, irresponsible firms experience changes in their functioning and governing apparatus. Recent changes include the return to the direct power of the proprietors, along with family-type property and capital. New investors, however, also include institutional actors: private and public pension funds, investment funds and insurance companies.[28] The managerial phase of the firm, according to Gallino,[29] was superseded when proprietors realised that the decline of revenues (between the 1960s and 1980s) required more aggressive practices. Hence, proprietors started to exert increasing pressure on managers, who devised strategies prioritising the creation of stock value above any other objective, even if this was to the detriment of small investors.[30]

The corporate scandals of the 1990s took place against this backdrop, with hundreds of bankruptcies. The collapse of Crédit Lyonnais cost small investors €15 billion, proving that the real owners of a company are institutional investors (pension funds, investment funds, insurance companies) and 'fat cats', who can decide on strategies and determine the destiny of other investors. The Crédit Lyonnais case also showed that mergers are not based on any productive assessment of firms, but on the nominal, artificial increase in their stock value.[31]

Shell's reserves scandal came back to haunt the company after a new claim for damages was filed in the US. Institutional investors, led by Dutch pension fund ABP, launched a lawsuit for several hundred million US dollars, claiming compensation for losses suffered when Shell's shares fell, after the company admitted overstating the size of its estimated oil and gas reserves by up to a third. Shell had already paid $90 million to settle one lawsuit instigated by a US shareholder.[32]

Other notorious cases include the collapse of Enron (US 2001), a global leader in the production and distribution of energy and, at the time, the seventh-largest world conglomerate on the stock exchange, three times on the front cover of *Time* as one of the most dynamic firms in the world.[33] In Europe, this was followed by the cases of Kirsch Media Group (Germany 2002); Royal Ahold (the Netherlands 2003); Vivendi (France 2002); and finally Parmalat in Italy (late 2003), whose dimensions, in terms of capital evaporated – with some €20 billion in debts – were well beyond the losses in the Enron case.

Enron, in this sense, acted as a successful experiment, and was replicated by a number of other corporations throughout the world, all giving the impression of prosperous business through fraud or false accounting and all showing a constant increase in the market value of shares, irrespective of production performance. 'Most corporate investments are not done with cash, the currency of choice is stock: the more inflated the stock, the more it can buy.'[34]

The social cost of irresponsible conduct by firms is difficult to measure, and at times it is even hard to identify who exactly can be held to account for such conduct. For example, due to the intricate web of concessions, sub-concessions, contracts, subcontracts – in other words, to what is termed the 'placelessness' of production – it is difficult to establish responsibilities for imposing certain labour conditions or violating human rights. In more general terms, and limiting costs to the mere fiscal dimension, estimates suggest that the amount of money not paid by corporations in tax would guarantee universal primary education in developing countries, and is three times higher than the potential cost of universal health basic service.

In brief, it should be noted that while production, distribution and exchange of goods are becoming globalised, regulations and institutions are not. The result is a global society formed by a number of protectorates, where the absence of a credible central power, or a set of universally-accepted international norms, leaves nation-states with the mere task of protecting international transactions. In this way, while in the past states controlled their own territories in order to monitor the wealth produced, today it is no longer the state which decides how to tax wealth, but it is wealth itself which decides how and where it will be taxed.[35]

LEARNING PROCESSES

While in a previous section of this chapter it has been argued that parapolitical organisations subverting global governance are the result of partnerships between illicit and institutional actors, the argument developed here identifies corporations as the major candidates for a transnational 'government of the shadows'. It is now worth examining whether, and if so, how, corporations are able to de-link themselves from conventional organised criminals, and whether and how they retain, in their own conduct, a philosophy or *modus operandi* they have learned from them. The cases summarised below may provide a tentative answer.

Lord Conrad Black, the former owner of the *Daily Telegraph*, was elevated to the House of Lords in 2001. The following year, he was accused of looting large sums of money from Hollinger, the international publishing empire he built up. According to the investigators, he fraudulently diverted £30 million from the sale by Hollinger of one of its holdings in Canada. He lived an extravagant life style and colleagues described him as an ideal example of corporate kleptocracy, of self-righteous and aggressive looting. His company had engaged in bizarre arrangements called 'non-compete deals'. Under the terms of the deals, when the publishing group sold a newspaper it would sign a 'non-compete' agreement to stop it starting up another title in the area. The fees for such agreements were paid not to Hollinger but to a private holding company called Ravelston which was controlled by Lord Black and his close associates.[36] This amounted to extortion in exchange for the promise not to compete. In July 2003 Lord Black was convicted on three charges of fraud and one of obstructing justice and in the appeal court in February 2008 he lost his attempt to delay the start of his six-and-a-half year jail sentence.[37]

The Bank of Italy scandal can be summarised as follows. General director Antonio Fazio accepted the bid made by banker Gianpiero Fiorani, despite the fact that a non-Italian competitor had made a more advantageous offer to buy the Antonveneta Bank. Behind the national sentiment mobilised by Fazio in explaining his choice, there emerged a long-term partnership between him and Fiorani in numerous mutually-enhancing financial operations. In a tapped telephone conversation the latter expressed his gratitude with the desire 'to kiss his friend on the forehead'.[38] After an official reprimand by European partners against the Italian elite, which was said to officially adhere to the principles of free competition, while perpetuating nepotistic and corrupt practices, Fazio resigned from his senior job in what was once regarded as the most independent Italian institution.[39]

The cases of Lord Black and Antonio Fazio show how the official paladins of the free market, in fact, have no faith in such freedom. The business practices of the former and the rigging of the financial market performed by the latter resemble the long-standing traditions of organised crime business, which over the years has developed sophisticated techniques for discouraging competitors and winning contracts. The two cases, however, are not unique, as hidden exchange between entrepreneurs and politicians is the rule in many advanced democracies. In the US, for example, payments offered by the former to the latter ensure that candidates can invest in their political campaigns and that entrepreneurs can be repaid in the form of contracts or purchasing commitments.[40]

We are thus faced with a 'mutual learning' process, whereby organised crime acquires the techniques of entrepreneurial venture and entrepreneurs appropriate the techniques successfully utilised by organised crime. Sarcastically, one should also note the symbolic importance of the 'kiss on the forehead' episode, an act of affection which has numerous precedents in the kisses that the *mafiosi* exchange with one another and, at times, also offer to businessmen and politicians.

As I have already argued, the crimes of the powerful seem to be inspired by an 'experimental' logic, according to which some illicit practices are adopted with the awareness that they are indeed illicit, but with an eye to the social and institutional reactions that might ensue. It is the intensity of such responses which will determine whether violations are to become part of a 'viable' routine or are to be carefully avoided. Although in a different fashion, Derrida[41] makes a similar point when he remarks that some violations possess a 'founding force'; that is, they are capable of transforming the previous jurisprudence and establishing new laws and new types of legitimacy. The crimes of the powerful restructure the legal and the political spheres. Examples of this 'founding force' are far from being confined to economic activity. Recent episodes of torture, military invasion, secret flights, kidnappings by secret services and the use of prohibited weapons appear to confirm that the crimes committed by powerful actors can re-write international law and re-found the principles of justice.

INNOVATION AND CRIME

In much Western literature bourgeois characters enjoy a kind of horrified intimacy with their diabolical counterparts: Faust with Mephistopheles, Ahab with Moby Dick, and Leopold Bloom with Stephen Dedalus.[42] Rivalry and affinity between these coupled characters suggest a form of secret complicity between the entrepreneur and the criminal.[43] Although 'the new bourgeois order must draw a veil of oblivion over its ignominious beginnings',[44] entrepreneurs are in perpetual agitation, they possess an inherent transgressive force. There is a crucial term that encapsulates this transgressive force, summing up the difficulties, ambiguities and shortcomings of the debate on economic crime, but also, ironically, of the debate on 'the economy and crime' as two distinct entities. This term is 'innovation' and it is used and cherished by economists, as well as sociologists of deviance.

When Schumpeter[45] identified the main characteristics of the entrepreneurial spirit, he relied on the variable innovation to distinguish between those economic actors passively following tradition and those more inclined to adopt new technologies. Only the latter were granted the definition of entrepreneurs, as the economic process, in his view, is an evolutionary one, and, when forced to remain stationary, it should not be described as a process in the first place. The fundamental impulse setting and keeping the economic engine in motion, according to Schumpeter, derives from new consumer goods, new methods of production or distribution, new markets and new forms of industrial organisation. The author resorted to a biological metaphor to illustrate the process of economic mutation. This, he argued, revolutionises the economic structure from within, incessantly destroying the old, incessantly creating the new. This process of 'creative destruction' is the essential fact of market economies.

It is not surprising that the term 'innovation' found its way into the vocabulary of the sociology of deviance. In effect, the term, while capturing the entrepreneurial spirit in a nutshell, also encapsulates the disquieting gist of entrepreneurial deviance. Economic actors, in order to be actors at all, must avoid the habitual flow, escape from stagnant conditions and deviate from mainstream behaviour: they must fight against the whirl of conformity. This is still Schumpeter, though his argument is as close as it could be to the elaboration of Merton,[46] who includes 'innovation' among the available deviant adaptations to strained social and economic conditions.

In his words, the history of the great American fortunes is threaded with various strains of institutionally-dubious innovation, and for those located in the lower reaches of the social structure, the culture makes incompatible demands: on the one hand, they are asked to pursue wealth and success, while on the other, they are largely denied effective opportunities to do so legally. Within this context, with society placing a high premium on affluence and social ascent, and with the channels of vertical mobility being closed or narrowed, Al Capone represents the triumph of amoral intelligence over morally-prescribed failure. But let me take this analysis of variable innovation a little further.

If this variable epitomises the ambiguity of 'economic development' and 'crime' as discrete spheres of human activity, how does it apply to the sphere of 'economic crime'? Economic crime innovates both in Schumpeter's sense and in Merton's sense. Deviant entrepreneurs, in other words, introduce new combinations of productive factors, while devising deviant adaptations to economic strain, therefore pursing legitimate goals through illegitimate means. There is, however, one final aspect of innovation that deserves to be highlighted, an aspect that belongs more strictly to the ideological dimension of entrepreneurship.

Economic criminals innovate by avoiding the 'criminal' label and directing it instead to competitors. Innovation in economic crime, in other words, entails changes in the perception of business, whereby those who, indeed, innovate successfully claim that their activities and practices are ethical, while those of competitors are unethical. Innovation thus entails the vindication of one's economic activity as value-bound (or safe) and the displacement of the criminal stigma onto the activity of others as value-free (or unsafe). It consists of decreasing marginal morality while criminalising others as responsible for such decrease. It amounts to promoting an ethical race to the bottom, while deflecting moral judgement from oneself. Innovation and economic crime, in brief, aim for the production of a new market spirit, whereby those more successful in criminalising others can also claim that their own interests correspond to those of the collectivity.

I would describe this type of innovation, and the 'criminal sovereignty' it generates, as parapolitics aimed at establishing a 'government of the shadows'.

NOTES

1. Joseph Schumpeter, *The Theory of Economic Development* (New York: Oxford University Press, 1961).
2. Robert K. Merton, *Social Theory and Social Structure* (New York: Free Press, 1968).
3. Anthony D. King (ed.), *Culture, Globalization and the World-System: Contemporary Conditions for the Representation of Identity* (Basingstoke: Palgrave Macmillan, 1991).
4. Ulf Hannerz, *Transnational Connections: Culture, People, Places* (London: Routledge, 1996); David Harvey, *Justice, Nature and the Geography of Difference* (Oxford: Blackwell, 1996).
5. Paul L. Knox and Peter J. Taylor (eds), *World Cities in a World System* (Cambridge: Cambridge University Press, 1995).
6. Manuel Castells, *The Informational City: Economic Restructuring and Urban Development* (Oxford: Blackwell, 1989).
7. Petrus C. van Duyne and Michael Levi, *Drugs and Money: Managing the Drug Trade and Crime Money in Europe* (London: Routledge, 2005).
8. Margaret E. Beare (ed.), *Critical Reflections on Transnational Organized Crime, Money Laundering and Corruption* (Toronto: Toronto University Press, 2003).
9. Stefano Becucci and Monica Massari, *Globalizzazione e criminalità* (Rome/Bari: Laterza, 2003).
10. Andrew Higginbottom, 'Globalisation and Human Rights in Colombia: Crimes of the Powerful, Corporate Complicity and the Paramilitary State', PhD Thesis (London: Middlesex University, 2005).
11. Vincenzo Ruggiero, *Organized and Corporate Crime in Europe: Offers that Can't Be Refused* (Aldershot: Dartmouth, 1996); R.T. Naylor, *Wages of Crime: Black Markets, Illegal Finance and the Underworld Economy* (Ithaca: Cornell University Press, 2002).
12. Francisco Thoumi, 'A Modest Proposal to Clarify the Status of Coca in the United Nations Conventions', *Crime, Law and Social Change*, 42 (2004), pp. 297–307.
13. Michael Woodiwiss, *Gangster Capitalism: The United States and the Global Rise of Organized Crime* (London: Constable, 2005); Mark Phythian, *The Business of Arms: Blurring the Boundaries of Legality* (London: Routledge, 2006).
14. Gruppo Abele, *Dalla mafia allo stato* (Turin: Gruppo Abele, 2005).
15. Vincenzo Ruggiero, *Crime and Markets: Essays in Anti-Criminology* (Oxford: Oxford University Press, 2000).

16. Samir Amin, *Accumulation on a World Scale: A Critique of the Theory of Underdevelopment* (New York: Monthly Review Press, 1974); Samir Amin, *Empire of Chaos* (New York: Monthly Review Press, 1992).

17. Giovanni Arrighi, *The Long Twentieth Century: Money, Power, and the Origins of Our Times* (London: Verso, 1994).

18. Ray Kiely, 'Globalization and Poverty, and the Poverty of Globalization Theory', *Current Sociology*, 53/6 (2005), pp. 895–914.

19. Vijay Prashad, *Fat Cats and Running Dogs: The Enron Stage of Capitalism* (London: Zed Books, 2002).

20. Marshall B. Clinard, *Corporate Ethics and Crime: The Role of Middle Management* (Beverly Hills: Sage, 1983).

21. Michel Foucault, *Discipline and Punish* (Harmondsworth: Penguin, 1977).

22. Prashad, *Fat Cats and Running Dogs*, pp. 72–3.

23. Lawrence E. Mitchell, *Corporate Irresponsibility: America's New Export* (New Haven: Yale University Press, 2001).

24. Nomi Prins, *Other People's Money: The Corporate Mugging of America* (New York: New Press, 2004).

25. Joel Bakan, *The Corporation: The Pathological Pursuit of Profit and Power* (New York: Free Press, 2004), p. 34.

26. Luciano Gallino, *L'impresa irresponsabile* (Turin: Einaudi, 2005).

27. Mitchell, *Corporate Irresponsibility*.

28. Prins, *Other People's Money*.

29. Gallino, *L'impresa irresponsabile*.

30. Doug Henwood, *Wall Street: How it Works and for Whom* (London: Verso, 1998); George Monbiot, *Captive State: The Corporate Takeover of Britain* (London: Pan Books, 2001); Henry N. Pontell, 'White-Collar Crime or Just Risky Business? The Role of Fraud in Major Financial Debacles', *Crime, Law and Social Change*, 42 (2004), pp. 309–24.

31. Jean Peyrelevade, *Le capitalisme total* (Paris: Seuil, 2005).

32. Terry Macalister, 'Shell Faces New Damages Claim', *Guardian*, 10 January 2006.

33. Robin Blackburn, 'Enron and the Pension Crisis', *New Left Review*, 14 (2002), pp. 26–52.

34. Prins, *Other People's Money*, p. 38.

35. Luigi Cavallaro, *Il modello mafioso e la società globale* (Rome: Il Manifesto, 2004).

36. Katherine Griffiths, 'Disgraced Black is Indicted for Fraud', *Independent*, 18 November 2005.

37. *Independent*, 26 June 2008.

38. Paolo Biondani and Giuseppe Guastella, 'Fiorani parla con i magistrati e fa nomi eccellenti', *Il Corriere della Sera*, 19 December 2005.

39. Alberto Statera, 'Antonio il pio: virtù private e vizi pubblici', *MicroMega*, 5 (2005), pp. 105–11.

40. Christopher Caldwell, 'Corruption at the Core of Congress', *Financial Times*, 3 December 2005.

41. Jacques Derrida, *Force de loi: Le fondement mystique de l'autorité* (Paris: Galilée, 1994).

42. Vincenzo Ruggiero, *Crime in Literature: Sociology of Deviance and Fiction* (London: Verso, 2003).

43. Terry Eagleton, *Holy Terror* (Oxford: Oxford University Press, 2005).

44. Ibid., p. 60.

45. Schumpeter, *The Theory of Economic Development*.

46. Merton, *Social Theory and Social Structure*.

7
Redefining Statehood in the Global Periphery

William Reno

Core global norms regarding the claims of armed groups to self-determination and sovereign statehood are changing.

At first glance, these norms seem to have operated with remarkable consistency since the end of the Second World War. Numerous international treaties assert that international recognition of new states and boundaries requires the consent of all affected parties. Secessionists or irredentists should not be able to gain recognition from an existing state as a new sovereign if they try to redefine the territorial basis of statehood through force. The failed attempt of Saddam Hussein in 1990–91 to force Kuwait to join Iraq made clear the global rejection of any right of conquest. Aside from a very few special cases, separatist groups have consistently failed to gain recognition from states or international organisations to back their claims to represent nascent sovereign states when this means the contentious breaking-apart of existing states.

These norms build on even older practice. The international boundaries of Africa remain little changed from the 1880s, despite the administrative weakness and internal turmoil besetting many of them. Most Latin American states have seen only minor adjustments of boundaries since they became independent in the 1820s – and especially since the end of the nineteenth century.

Changes in these core norms have accelerated since the start of the 1990s. These changes reflect political realities. In particular, separatist and irredentist group leaders are learning how to exploit new concerns among officials in the world's most powerful states. They manipulate fears among these officials that terrorists might set up bases in territories that existing states do not adequately control. They learn that new United States military doctrines that stress fighting counter-insurgency campaigns with expeditionary forces compels even the world's most capable army to seek out local proxies to fight effective campaigns. These groups observe that the record of international interventions since 1990 is one of escalating financial and political costs, and that diplomats are willing to engage indigenous groups in negotiations and include their interests in globally-recognised settlements if this will reduce their own countries' commitments.

The strategies of armed separatists and irredentists focus particularly on the inconsistencies between evolving new norms that insist on standards of sovereign state behaviour and older core norms that protect existing sovereigns against challengers. These non-sovereign groups often argue that they are more effective administrators, better observers of human rights and more reliable negotiating partners than their sovereign rivals. This development points to growing pressure to exhibit a 'civilised standard' in the internal organisation and behaviour of potential new sovereigns as they hasten to attract the approval of powerful actors. A few such, as, for example, among Kosovo and southern Sudanese separatists, succeeded in gaining diplomats' recognition of their rights to create their own new states, and in the case of the latter, potentially draw new boundaries. Kurdish groups in Iraq have gained a de facto separation from Iraq and now depend upon their usefulness to US military officers and politicians to gain eventual recognition of their sovereignty.

Separatists are better able than irredentists to combine old core norms with new norms, because they can limit their challenge to a single existing sovereign. Nonetheless, their successes raise the hopes of irredentists who would have to break apart multiple states to attain their goals. All of these groups learn from the experiences of others. They understand the obstacles and opportunities that global norms present. These developments point to the increasing probability that more existing states will fragment. They also may offer prospects for creating new states that are internally stable and better able to fulfil their international obligations. This promise of long-term internal order, however, poses the threat of disrupting a heretofore-remarkable stability in the external relations of even the world's weakest states.

THE CONSISTENCY OF CORE NORMS LIMITING THE DEFINITION OF STATEHOOD

International recognition of sovereignty customarily extends to the recipient regime the right to exercise its authority upon a piece of territory to the exclusion of any other state. Enshrined in such agreements as the 1933 Convention of Montevideo, this prerogative of exclusive competence relies upon the recognition of this sovereignty in relations between states. Mutual recognition stretches back at least to the Treaty of Westphalia of 1648, in which European rulers accepted the decisions of each ruler concerning his or her own realm's official religion.[1]

This principle is consistent with the idea of *uti possidetis* (as you possess) that declares that each sovereign is entitled to exercise control over the territory that the sovereign possesses. This idea does not rule out conquest, but it does recognise the exclusivity of sovereign authority within whatever borders come to be mutually recognised.

Nazi Germany's conquests and its attempt to create an empire in Europe rejected this Westphalian legacy. Hitler tried to reshape international society into a global system ordered according to a racial hierarchy. The parts of the German empire in which supposedly racially inferior people lived would be ruled to exploit most harshly those who were lowest in this racial hierarchy. Allied powers emphatically rejected this vision in their Atlantic Charter in August 1941, to clarify their aims in fighting Hitler's Germany. These included a desire to see no territorial changes that do not accord with the freely expressed wishes of the people concerned... respect the right of all peoples to choose the form of government under which they will live... to see sovereign rights and self government restored to those who have been forcibly deprived of them [and] a peace, after the final destruction of the Nazi tyranny, which will afford to all nations the means of dwelling in security within their own boundaries.[2]

Although the American and British leaders looked to a European audience, indigenous nationalists living under colonial rule applied the Atlantic Charter's call for the right for people to choose the form of government to their own situations. This expectation became a right entrenched in the charter of the United Nations in 1945. It reappeared in the UN General Assembly's Resolution 1514 of 1960, which stated:

All peoples have the right to self-determination... Inadequacy of political, economic, social or educational preparedness should never serve as a pretext for delaying independence.[3]

There was considerable discussion of pan-African unity among nationalist leaders in Africa in the 1950s and among rulers of newly-independent states in the early 1960s. But like their European counterparts, they were mindful of the dangers of self-determination outside the framework of existing boundaries. If colonial boundaries were contested, this would threaten peace, not to mention the continued existence of some of these newly-independent states. Even if boundary revisions could be agreed upon in specific cases, it would have been difficult to limit the application of this principle, given the ethnic complexities and competing pre-colonial historical claims across the African continent.

Accordingly, the 1963 Charter of the Organisation of African Unity (OAU) declared '[r]espect for the sovereignty and territorial integrity of each State and for its inalienable right to independent existence'.[4] All agreed to seek independence within the framework of existing territories and borders and 'pledge themselves to respect the frontiers existing on their achievement of national independence'.[5] Moreover, the organisation in 1965 adopted the Declaration on the Problem of Subversion, '[n]ot to create dissension within or among Member States by fomenting or aggravating racial, religious, linguistic, ethnic or other differences'.[6] By the mid 1960s, the world's newest, and geopolitically the weakest, states had effectively outlawed official support for secessionist and irredentist groups. The great majority of these states incorporated this prohibition in their own practice of international relations, at least in formal practice.

The mutual vulnerabilities of rulers to secessionist or irredentist challenges led to a remarkable formal respect for existing boundaries, even when states supported insurgents in neighbouring states to pressure those regimes. Moreover, rulers of independent states sought to ensure that the different armed liberation movements in remaining colonies would not pursue their own secessionist or irredentist programmes. Leaders such as Tanzania's Julius Nyerere and Guinea's Sekou Touré who provided rear bases for liberation movements insisted that different factions unify under a single banner and pledge to preserve the unity of their target state once it was liberated. To promote this outcome, the OAU organised a Liberation Committee that was charged with recognising only one liberation movement for each colony and provide it with funding so that it could organise itself as a government-in-waiting in liberated zones.[7]

The principle of recognising existing state boundaries was applied more extensively in a 1970 UN resolution. For the purposes of preserving peace, self-determination was mutually agreed to be limited to exclude anything that would 'dismember or impair, totally or in part, the territorial integrity or political unity of sovereign and independent States'.[8] This principle also guided the resolution of boundary disputes that did arise among the world's weakest states. The International Court of Justice in its ruling in 1986 on a border dispute between Mali and Burkina Faso provided the justification for this principle. 'The essential requirement of stability in order to survive, to develop and gradually to consolidate their independence in all fields,' the Court wrote, 'has induced African States judiciously to consent to the respecting of colonial frontiers, and to take account of it in the interpretation of the principle of self-determination of peoples.'[9] This principle was already an integral part of the Helsinki Final Act, which banned changes in European boundaries through force and declared that revisions required mutual consent.[10]

Colonial boundaries have survived essentially intact almost 50 years after the start of the final wave of decolonisation. Secessionist attempts attracted official recognition from few states: the Biafra split from Nigeria and Katanga from Congo, for example. The existing states that secessionists challenged received considerable diplomatic and material support. In a rare Cold War consensus, American and Soviet officials agreed that their shared interests in regional stability were best served if Congo and Nigeria remained intact. Those that succeeded in creating new states couched claims to self-determination in terms of respect for colonial boundaries. Eritrean independence in 1993 followed claims of the Eritrean People's Liberation Front (EPLF) that they simply wished to attain statehood within the borders of the Italian colony of Eritrea, which they argued was forced into a federation with Ethiopia after the Second World War under UN pressure.[11] The EPLF overthrew the Ethiopian government in 1991 with help from an allied liberation organisation that became the next government of Ethiopia. The new government's agreement ensured that the final separation was by mutual consent.

Events up to the end of the Cold War support the view of James Crawford that international law has played a growing role in regulating the creation of new states.[12] An anomaly appeared, however, in the case of the independence of Bangladesh from Pakistan in 1971. The Indian army supported Bengali separatists, which helped to force the Pakistani army to accept their declaration of independence. This violated the principle of mutual recognition of territorial integrity, since Pakistan's government fought to keep its Bengali portion under its sovereignty. India's government claimed that the extreme situation – 10 million refugees had fled to India – required a pragmatic solution. Since East Pakistan was an exclave, the ultimate settlement did not change existing international boundaries. Indian officials were careful to justify their intervention as part of an effort to maintain regional stability, arguing that supporting secession was a last resort.[13] Since then, however, separatists in places as diverse as Cyprus, Moldova, Georgia, Azerbaijan, Congo, Spain and Russia have consistently failed to gain recognition of their sovereignty from foreign states.

Nonetheless, India's intervention in pursuit of its own national interests raised an important ambiguity in the principle of self-determination. India's claim to be protecting refugees pointed to the deficiencies of Pakistani rule and portrayed secession as a remedy right. This, they argued, applied to cases of extreme persecution where there is no reasonable chance of amelioration inside the existing territorial framework of a state. India's actions raised the possibility that the obligation to protect human rights – in this case made easier by coinciding national interests – would supersede the protection of the territorial integrity of existing states. India's politicians were able to act because Pakistan failed to secure military help from other powerful states. Chinese and Soviet officials were wary of intervention, lest it worsen tensions over their mutual border dispute. American officials made it clear to their Pakistani counterparts that they would not lend support to counter the Indian move. Thus East Pakistan's secession took place in a rare Cold War instance in which a powerful state was relatively free to intervene in the affairs of its disintegrating neighbour without provoking further outside intervention.

Although international borders remained intact in South Asia, Pakistan's division raised the possibility that local insurgent groups could use the issue of human rights abuses and refugee flows to provoke the intervention of powerful states in favour of their interests. This dynamic became more important after the end of the Cold War, as constraints of superpower rivalries disappeared. Powerful states, especially the US, were left with more freedom to intervene in the affairs of states beset by internal turmoil. As a result, separatist and irredentist groups discovered that they had much more latitude to conduct their own 'international relations' with foreign states and their own sovereign rivals.

This external activity does not bestow juridical or diplomatic equality upon these groups, but it does equip them with important new tools that they can use to reshape the determination of statehood in the global periphery.

INCONSISTENT APPLICATIONS OF NORMS OF SELF-DETERMINATION

Since the Atlantic Charter, the recognition of people's right to change how they are ruled by an existing state has become a widely accepted principle of self-determination. For example, from 1961 the UN and many other international organisations provided diplomatic support to the African National Congress's right to change the relationship of black Africans to South Africa's apartheid regime. Until the 1990s, this support did not require a commitment from the armed group that it would govern in a particular way. Foreign governments often gave aid to these groups on the basis of shared commitment to a particular ideology – Soviets preferred Marxists and Americans preferred anti-Marxists, for example – but these groups had to promise their backers that they only wished to capture the capital city to form a new regime to assume the mantle of the existing state's sovereignty and not create their own new state.

Historically, powerful states have been able to impose conditions on weaker states regarding their internal administration in proportion to their hegemony. Stephen Krasner points out that, in the nineteenth century, core European states used their overwhelming power and consensus concerning the need to ensure regional stability to coerce or compel new Balkan states and what remained of the Ottoman Empire to offer legal protections to ethnic and religious minorities within their borders. This primarily took the form of treaty commitments by these states to extend full civil rights to members of minority groups. These reflected the concerns of leaders in Britain and in other European countries that mistreatment of minorities would lead to religious and ethnic strife, a reasonable fear, as later events demonstrated.[14]

Though Western European officials discovered that it was difficult to force Balkan rulers to respect these commitments, these measures legitimated a wider international interest in the affairs of these minority groups. They also provided incentives for groups that considered themselves oppressed minorities to petition foreign officials to provide them with protection. Armenian clergy, for example, took advantage of European intervention into Ottoman affairs in 1878 to ask that the negotiations for the Treaty of Berlin incorporate their demands. These included a request that police and courts be under Armenian control; and that Russia guarantee Armenian security and even offer the option of incorporating them as a province of Russia. Russian officials declared that protecting Armenians would promote regional stability. British and Austro-Hungarian officials, however, sought to weaken Russia's influence in Ottoman affairs, with the result that Armenian concerns were excluded from the overall settlement.[15] The affair showed though how secessionist and irredentist groups might use their status as oppressed minorities to engage in 'international relations' with powerful backers in a bid to re-draw international boundaries. The Armenian effort failed to achieve even its minimum objective of autonomy within the Ottoman Empire. But if Russian officials had been able to intervene without constraint from other European powers, the likely outcome would have been very different.

The concerns of officials in powerful states to maintain order and stability in weaker states appear in more recent agreements. The 1975 Helsinki Final Act directly incorporated UN provisions pledging respect for existing boundaries and committed the 35 signatory states to non-intervention in the affairs of each other. Like the nineteenth-century treaties, it obliged states to extend full civil rights to minorities. It recognised that 'all peoples always have the right, in full freedom, to determine, when and as they wish, their internal and external political status, without external interference, and to pursue as they wish their political, economic, social and cultural development'.[16] The 1990 Charter of Paris reinforced this commitment to minority rights among European and North American states. But these agreements lacked an enforcement mechanism.

Africa's OAU, for example, adopted an African Charter on Human and People's Rights with similar provisions. Mindful of the oppression in apartheid Africa, the agreement provided for a Commission to which states could refer violations of rights in other states. The agreement's lack of an enforcement mechanism and continued member state reluctance to formally intervene in the internal affairs of other states limited its application.

Even though these provisions were written to avoid conflict with existing rules concerning the territorial integrity of member states, they created arenas for political leaders who identified themselves as representatives of oppressed groups to press their claims against states. At first, these groups had no obvious leverage beyond their public campaigns, since these agreements were written with the assumption that state signatories could not be forced to comply with provisions. The Helsinki Agreement, for example, was signed during the height of the Cold War, when no state could coerce a signatory to comply with provisions protecting minority rights or recognise rights of self-determination against the will of its leadership without risking catastrophic war. In Africa in the 1980s, only Nigeria's and South Africa's armies possessed the capabilities to force other states to respect the rights guaranteed in their charter. But South Africa's apartheid system was a prime focus of the charter and Nigeria's rulers remained unwilling to systematically intervene in their neighbours' affairs (although in 1980, Nigeria's military claimed that its intervention in Chad was to restore stability and protect that country's citizens from turmoil, so that they would not become refugees in Nigeria). Moreover, Nigeria's lapse into military autocracy in 1983 increased observer complaints of violations of human rights.

The significance for statehood in the periphery at the end of the Cold War lay in the newfound capacity of powerful states to impose standards of behaviour on weaker states. No longer could the weak states threaten to side with a superpower's rival to ward off intervention. Now, if they had signed treaties that promised rights for potentially separatist minorities, they could be called to account for mistreatment. Powerful state officials found new freedoms to respond directly to the problems that oppressive rule and internal turmoil produced such as refugee crises. Moreover, the promise of democratic competition gave hope to nascent separatists that they would be free to press their claims for self-determination within an internationally sanctioned framework of internal politics. Now, if a government tried to repress separatist groups, what had been an internal affair became an active concern of foreign states. The repression of unpopular minorities, a common mobilising technique for incumbent leaders trying to survive in quasi-democratic and newly-democratising states, drew wider international concern.

Whether this was because officials in foreign states wanted to enforce treaty obligations or because they found that they could use these crises to solve other political problems is debatable. It was clear, however, that efforts on the part of states facing separatists were now likely to be defined as human rights violations and threatened to bring uninvited outside intervention into these states' domestic affairs.

This change appeared as Serbian political leaders tried to preserve what they considered to be the territorial integrity of what remained of their state during the collapse of Yugoslavia. The leaders in Belgrade believed that they were heirs to the Yugoslav state. Their government continued to occupy Yugoslavia's seat in the UN and in other international organisations. They retained recognition of their sovereignty from other states under the Helsinki Agreement's Conference on Security and Co-operation in Europe (CSCE). Nonetheless, the UN Security Council's Resolution 757 declared that 'the claim by the Federal Republic of

Yugoslavia (Serbia and Montenegro) to continue automatically the membership of the former Socialist Federal Republic of Yugoslavia in the United Nations has not been generally accepted'.[17] This action reversed the practice of continuing to recognise the sovereignty of parent states faced with partition, as occurred when Pakistan separated from India in 1947 and Bangladesh from Pakistan in 1971. The Serbian political leadership and the Yugoslav army committed, however, what now are widely viewed as grave human rights violations as they struggled to consolidate their control over what they considered to be the remains of their country.

The international 'decertification' of Yugoslavia's sovereignty meant that concerns to preserve its territorial integrity were moot. This opened the way for outside support for people invoking a right to self-determination that otherwise would have been contradictory to the territorial sovereignty norm. It also had become clear by mid 1991 that Yugoslav army efforts to prevent the secession of Slovenia would produce a refugee crisis. Fighting spread, as ethnic Serbian fighters in Croatia joined Yugoslav army units to resist Croatian separatist moves. This wider conflict also involved the use of paramilitaries and ethnic cleansing and other massive violations of human rights as specific strategies for war-fighting.[18] German officials argued that recognising these separatists as sovereigns would have the political impact of changing the conflict from an internal war to an inter-state war. This change would legitimate European political and military intervention into this conflict. The efforts of the Yugoslav army then could be defined as territorial conquest in neighbouring states and not an effort to resist secession. That view also meant that the sizeable ethnic Serb minorities in two of the new states were not free to accept military assistance from Yugoslav forces to redraw boundaries so that they could remain in Serbia.

The goals of separatists now coincided with the immediate political interests and capabilities of officials in powerful states. Once this became an inter-state war, those officials were freer to coerce Serbia's leaders and address the refugee crises, turmoil and human rights abuses that their policies fostered. The US intervention in Kurdish ethnic areas in northern Iraq in 1991 followed the same rationale. The UN resolution authorising humanitarian intervention highlighted concern about

> repression of the Iraqi civilian population in many parts of Iraq, including most recently in Kurdish populated areas, which led to a massive flow of refugees towards and across international frontiers and to cross-border incursions, which threaten international peace and security in the region.[19]

Like their Serb counterparts, the Iraqi regime's conduct resulted in massive violations of human rights and created threats to the security of neighbouring states. Like Pakistan's situation vis-à-vis India in 1971, the state that was to become the subject of intervention lacked a powerful backer or the military means to ward off intervention; and interveners could claim that their action solved a security threat to their own countries.

The claims of separatist groups struggling to split away from much more powerful states received different attention. Chechen separatist groups could not convince foreign officials to help them against Russia. Their struggle for statehood remained defined as an internal affair of this powerful parent state. Russia's military actions continued to be defined as an effort to maintain the territorial integrity of their state in spite of international criticisms of human rights violations. This political choice to treat Chechen separatism in this manner prevailed, despite the recourse to redefine administrative boundaries much like the ones that became international boundaries in Yugoslavia – indeed, the Yugoslav system of ethnically-defined administrative units was modelled on Russia.

Therefore, non-permissive secession has become more widely acceptable, but it requires the following three features. First, the state from which the secession occurs must be so militarily weak as to be unable to preserve control over its territory. Second, it must be diplomatically isolated to the extent that it cannot find a diplomatic or military ally strong enough to prevent secession. Related to this marginalisation of the parent state is the third factor: that secession will serve the security interests of powerful states. In the case of Yugoslavia and Iraq, ending refugee crises and ethnic cleansing served the interests of European and American officials. Among other secessionists, the separation of the Abkhaz ethnic region and South Ossetia from the Georgian Republic, for example, has served the regional strategic interests of Russia. So long as Russia's government continues to back those separatists and no ally helps Georgian leaders to defeat them, Georgia's government must take heed of Russian interests.

These three features were demonstrated in the case of the conflict between the Georgian Republic and the Russian Federation in August 2008. Georgian forces launched a military operation in what they regarded as a rebellious province. A Russian Federation counterattack pushed Georgian forces out. It soon became apparent that the Georgian Republic's president had miscalculated. Although in the habit of displaying the European Union flag alongside his own country's banner, he was unable to gain significant aid from European states or even from his American supporters to reverse the Russian counterattack. Moreover, Russian Federation officials justified their action as in defence of civilians in South Ossetia who suffered during the Georgian operation. On 26 August 2008 the Russian Federation announced its recognition of South Ossetian independence, the only United Nations member state to do so until Nicaragua joined it on 3 September 2008. Thus South Ossetia's separatists benefited from their powerful neighbouring state's support in addition to the Georgian Republic's weakness, and the Georgian Republic had to discover that it occupied a more marginal diplomatic and strategic position in world affairs than its leader had calculated.

In general, governments that commit massive human rights abuses are more likely to pose security threats to neighbours and attract negative attention for the behaviour of their armies and the consequences of internal disorder. These states become 'unpopular' in the eyes of a wide range of officials and the publics in other countries. All sorts of interests converge to the benefit of separatists. These interests range from hard-headed realist notions of military security; to considerations of historical justice; to idealist concerns to toughen the enforcement of human rights norms. Since the principle of the territorial integrity still applies to neighbouring states, irredentists are likely to become separatists instead and refrain from challenging existing borders. Note, for example, that South Ossetia's officials reversed a late August 2008 statement that their territory would be absorbed into the Russian Federation, a correction that Russian Federation officials endorsed. Once this coincidence of interests is recognised, leaders of these groups discover that they have a powerful new tool for pursuing their goals. They are able to claim that it is they who represent the continuity of principles in the international system and that it is their erstwhile rulers who are the rogues. This is a convergence that has become even more intense since the end of the 1990s.

RECENT POLITICAL CONSIDERATIONS IN WEAK STATE–STRONG STATE RELATIONS

The al-Qaeda attacks on New York and Washington, DC on 11 September 2001 ('9/11') brought to the fore a political issue in which the interests of armed separatists and strong states intersect. This conjuncture intensified the process of selectively retracting recognition for prerogatives of sovereignty. Outcomes have not always been as extreme as the extinguishing of sovereignty in Yugoslavia, but as in Yugoslavia, outsiders may regard the existing territorial definition of a state as threatening to their core interests.

Many officials in the US and in other powerful countries, for example, see a connection between terrorism and the failure of central governments in some states to control their national territory and monitor their populations. Terrorist groups exploit the turmoil that violent and repressive governments create in their own societies. Some armed separatists that fight these governments draw the attention of officials in strong states which appreciate their capacity to control local turf; provide access to outsiders like themselves; and deny refuge to terrorists. Counter-insurgency doctrine in the US – the Rumsfeld Doctrine – and similar developments in Europe reinforced these changes.

In emphasising the use of small, highly mobile units and contacts with friendly local groups to fight enemies in territories that sovereign states might not effectively control, operational features of the doctrine frequently come into conflict with established practices of international relations based upon recognition of sovereignty. Armed separatists in areas that are of strategic concern to these countries discover that they can exploit these changes – and their newfound importance – to extract diplomatic concessions and gain material aid from their new patrons.

Connections between failing states and security threats to the US were recognised before 9/11. George Tenet, the director of the Central Intelligence Agency (CIA), linked the 1998 terrorist attacks on the US embassies in Kenya and Tanzania, the failed 2000 Millennium plot to attack the Los Angeles airport, and the 2000 attack on the USS *Cole* warship in Yemen to the problem of failed states and governments that exploited conflict and disorder for their internal purposes. In his testimony before the US Senate, he said,

What we have in Afghanistan is a stark example of the potential dangers of allowing states – even those far from the US – to fail. The chaos there is providing an incubator for narcotics traffickers and militant Islamic groups operating in such places as Kashmir, Chechnya, and Central Asia. Meanwhile, Taliban shows no sign of relinquishing terrorist Usama bin Laden.[20]

Almost immediately after the attacks on New York and Washington, this link to Afghanistan became a matter of prime importance to US officials. Unlike in Yugoslavia, the turmoil in this instance affected states located well outside the immediate region. President George Bush declared a doctrine of 'pre-emptive self-defence' to justify US military actions.

> The events of September 11, 2001 taught us that weak states, like Afghanistan, can pose as great a danger to our national interest as strong states. Poverty does not make poor people into terrorists and murderers. Yet poverty, weak institutions, and corruption can make weak states vulnerable to terrorist networks and drug cartels within their borders.[21]

Britain's Foreign Secretary Jack Straw shared this view.

> After the mass murder in the heart of Manhattan, no one can doubt that a primary threat to our security is now posed by groups acting outside formal states, or from places where no state functions at all. It is no longer possible to ignore misgoverned parts of a world without borders, where chaos is a potential neighbour anywhere from Africa to Afghanistan.[22]

France's *Loi de Programmation Militaire, 2003–2008* also recognised threats that internal turmoil in failing states pose to even the strongest states and reserves the option of pre-emptive military action.[23]

Few failed states would become military targets after 9/11.[24] Those with compliant governments became candidates for increased military and economic aid instead. 'Aggression flowing from internal instability thus demands the actual transformation of an unstable or aggressive state into one which is both stable and willing to adhere to the norms of the international community', wrote Steven Metz and Raymond Millen.[25] But those like the Taliban regime in Afghanistan that incorporated violent transnational terrorist groups into their ruling cliques became prime candidates for removal. So, for example, US soldiers forced President Charles Taylor of Liberia into exile in 2003 after it became apparent that he relied upon criminal networks for resources and that his tyrannical rule was responsible for refugees and violence beyond his country's borders.[26] A key element of the US strategy in Liberia was to rely upon the efforts of the Liberians United for Reconciliation and Democracy, an armed group opposed to Taylor. Likewise, US forces in Afghanistan included the Northern Alliance, a largely ethnic Tajik armed group, in its campaign to overthrow the Taliban government after October 2001.

Neither proxy group demanded separation from existing states, but the changing international conditions that brought them powerful patrons made a big difference in their fortunes. They benefited from US backing because their interests in controlling territory coincided with the interests of the US government to remove local regimes. In essence, those regimes were 'decertified' for having collaborated with groups that threatened the security of other states and thus were denied the sovereign prerogative to exercise their rule in their own country's territory. These campaigns showed how using local armed groups as proxies greatly improved US access to information and mobilised motivated fighters toward the common goal of removing incumbent regimes. This collaboration enabled the US to minimise its political and military commitment to these campaigns since fewer of their soldiers were needed to fight and they did not have to administer these countries after the initial military campaign ended.

These challenges provide additional applications for a new US military doctrine under the guidance of Secretary of Defense Donald Rumsfeld, much of which has endured beyond his December 2006 resignation from his post. The Rumsfeld Doctrine aims to reduce military manpower needs and recognises the need to 'conduct war in countries we are not at war with (safe havens)' to fight enemies that are not members of regular military forces, including organised crime and extremist groups that are enablers of terrorism.[27] States that have hierarchically-organised armies and centralised authority structures can be defeated with relative ease. But where bureaucracies are fragmented in places like Afghanistan and Liberia, there was no single army leadership that could surrender. Fighters there were bound together by ties of kinship and culturally-contextualised obligations that were intensely confusing (to outsiders) and impervious to satellite surveillance or spy planes. This decentralised structure makes these kinds of societies exceedingly difficult to defeat and control on a long-term basis, even if the recognised government is friendly to US and European interests. In its final report, the US National Commission on Terrorist Attacks (the 9/11 Commission) identified these effectively-stateless areas as particularly susceptible to becoming terrorist sanctuaries because of these features.[28]

To avoid the heavy political and financial costs of controlling these places directly, the Rumsfeld Doctrine has evolved into a post-invasion search for local proxies to help isolate enemy groups. Many non-state armed groups, including separatists, share the decentralised features of 'terrorist enablers'. They also possess the local information needed to engage these foes outside the framework of customary laws of armed combat designed for conflicts involving bureaucratic militaries of states. They can easily identify people who are not locals and know how and when their opponents strain community tolerance. A major review of US military strategies observed that 'actions in 2001 in Afghanistan reinforced the principle of adaptability, speed of action, integrated joint operations, economy of force, and the value of working with and through indigenous forces to achieve common goals'.[29] Thus collaborations with non-state armed groups that share the same adversaries benefit both parties.

US official justifications for the harsh treatment of prisoners suspected of having information about terrorist activities further reinforces trends toward decertifying the sovereignty of some states to the benefit of cooperative armed groups. In explaining why he thought that the Geneva Conventions should not apply to members of the Taliban regime in Afghanistan, President George W. Bush's legal counsel argued that 'Afghanistan was a failed state because Taliban did not exercise full control over the territory and people…'[30] Since the Taliban regime did not really rule like a strong sovereign, it did not deserve international recognition. Since it was not really a state, combatants of this entity should not enjoy Geneva Convention protections, or so the argument went. This argument could, of course, apply to many other states;

but in reality, decertification is only sought selectively, on the basis of perceived threat that a regime poses. The President's lawyer also justified decertification in terms of the Rumsfeld Doctrine's premium on flexibility of military action. 'The nature of the new war places a high premium on other factors, such as the ability to quickly obtain information from captured terrorists and their sponsors in other to avoid further atrocities against American civilians.'[31] Of course this gives separatists and other groups incentives to convince outsiders that their foes are in league with terrorists.

STRATEGIES FOR NEW CLAIMS OF STATEHOOD IN THE GLOBAL PERIPHERY

The growing inequality in the application of sovereignty and rights of intervention has given new political resources to groups that want to change existing states' boundaries and gain international backing for their own state.

As already noted, separatists in East Pakistan benefited from India's overwhelming regional dominance and the interests of its politicians in seeing an independent Bangladesh. The break-away states formed out of Yugoslavia gained independence as European and American officials grew alarmed at the Serb leadership's behaviour and its impact on regional stability. Thus new states were recognised because this was in the interests of powerful states (or at least a less-bad outcome in the view of their officials) that could act unimpeded.

Is it possible for separatists to exploit these changes in the application of international norms concerning sovereignty? After all, separatists focus on encouraging others to strip away the prerogatives of sovereignty that their parent states previously enjoyed. They also exploit the interests of powerful states to recruit them to the aid of their goals. These strategies are outlined below for the cases of Kosovo's separation from Serbia; southern Sudan from the rest of that country; and the Kurdish Regional Government's claims of autonomy from the Baghdad government in Iraq.

Kosovo's separation from Serbia emerged as the first instance since Bangladesh's separation from western Pakistan in 1971 in which international recognition of separatists occurred at the expense of a multiparty democratic state. Instead of Pakistan's single foe, Serbia faced a coalition of powerful states in the Contact Group, formed in 1994 among non-Balkan states concerned about Serbia's repression in its province of Kosovo.[32] They 'recall that the character of the Kosovo problem, shaped by the disintegration of Yugoslavia and consequent conflicts, ethnic cleansing and the events of 1999...must be fully taken into account in settling Kosovo's status'.[33] Thus they considered recognising the independence of Kosovo, even though they acknowledged many deficiencies in Kosovo's preparation for self-rule.[34] The political decision to end negotiations for the final status of Kosovo gave the advantage to negotiators from Kosovo, regardless of preparation for self-rule in the eyes of outsiders. They could simply wear down diplomats and calculated that outsiders would see their Serbian counterparts as obstructionist if they used delaying tactics.

The decision of the Contact Group to declare a December 2006 deadline reflects the intersection of members' state interests. European members accept the principle that the past behaviour of Serbia's leaders has led to the loss of that country's right to rule what it considered to be a wayward province, even though Serbian voters had removed the Milosevic regime which many European governments held responsible for past abuses. This idea coincides with the UN General Assembly's November 2005 endorsement of the *Responsibility to Protect*, a report initiated in 2000 by the UN Secretary-General's suggestion to consider justifications for international intervention in conflicts. The report reinforces the notion of separation as a remedy principle for the abuses that Kosovo's inhabitants endured at the hands of Serbian government agents in its statement that 'state sovereignty implies responsibility, and the primary responsibility for the protection of its people lies with the state itself'.[35] Kosovo became a test case in which a state's mistreatment of its own citizens translated into a loss of the ultimate sovereign right to consider those people and their territory as part of that state. Kosovo declared its independence in February 2008, and by October of that year, over 50 UN member states had recognised this declaration.

The separatist Kosovo Liberation Army (KLA) and the associated civilian political leadership exploited the multiple interests of outside states. They offered NATO officials control over Kosovo society and offered cooperation to permit the US to withdraw its military contingent there in line with the Rumsfeld Doctrine of limiting post-conflict entanglements. For the US, this shifted costs of maintaining control in Kosovo – about $1.3 billion a year for the US since 1999 – to an 'EU Partnership' that was to take over the burdens of monitoring Kosovo's adherence to standards of governance.[36] Kosovo politicians recognise other interests of US and EU officials, catching their attention with periodic arrests of alleged 'Islamic radicals' and a mass demonstration to support the 2003 invasion of Iraq. Russian officials can equate the international community's acceptance of Kosovo's claims against a coercive and incompetent Serbia to the claims of Abkhaz separatists in Georgia Republic who receive Russian support for their autonomy.[37] Moreover, Russian officials cited the Kosovo example to justify their recognition of South Ossetia's independence in 2008.

Kosovo's local leaders also have a reasonable claim to be the only people who can control Kosovo's society and prevent its clans, illicit commercial networks and lightly-regulated economy from providing a haven for terrorists. The KLA gained this capacity when they drew Yugoslav forces out of their concealment to fight in 1999. This forced Yugoslav soldiers to expose themselves to NATO aerial attacks as the KLA consolidated its control on the ground. This group later gave tacit support for, if not direction, for attacks in March 2004, when 19 were killed and 4,500 displaced from ethnic Serb enclaves. Since then, foreign intervention has not been able to create a democratic and multi-ethnic Kosovo. Thus outsiders were forced to confront a choice: rule directly and oppose the KLA or grant them sovereignty, depart and declare victory. Some diplomats may even conclude that the expulsion of ethnic Serbs may reduce future flashpoints for political instability. An ethnically pure Kosovo will confront fewer complications in convincing the outside world that it can abide by democratic standards of governance. These incidents, together with the initial alliance between the KLA and NATO forces in 1999, may have convinced the separatist group that there are rewards for violence, provided their goals are compatible with the interests of powerful states.[38]

Members of the Sudan People's Liberation Army (SPLA) who aim to create an independent state in southern Sudan also benefit from the diminished sovereignty of their parent state. This separatist movement signed a US-mediated Comprehensive Peace Agreement with their foes in the government of Sudan in January 2005. This agreement provides for a referendum on independence in 2011, in return for recognition of the government's right to continue applying sharia (Islamic) law in areas that it controls. Sudan's government also won a commitment from US officials to reduce unilateral US sanctions against them. In any event, it appeared that Sudanese officials thought that they could divide and co-opt members of the SPLA to undermine the long-term implementation of the agreement.

Since August 1993, the US government has officially listed Sudan as a state sponsor of terrorism. The Clinton administration launched a missile attack on the country in August 1998 after the al-Qaeda bombings of US embassies in Kenya and Tanzania. This followed Sudan's hosting of Osama bin Laden until 1996 and its government's support for radical Islamist causes beyond Sudan's borders. By the late 1990s, US efforts to block Sudan's engagement with the IMF and World Bank hindered exploitation of new oilfield discoveries. Sudan's government needed to regularise its economic relations with the outside world if it was going to boost its domestic revenues, standing at only 7.4 per cent of GDP in 2002.[39] In October 2002, President George W. Bush signed the Sudan Peace Act, authorising the spending of up to $100 million in aid to Sudanese living in territory under SPLA control for 'preparing the population for peace and democratic governance, including support for civil administration'.[40]

To the extent that the US government blamed Sudan's government for human rights violations and state sponsorship of terrorism, it was determined to diminish its sovereign prerogatives vis-à-vis the SPLA. The Sudan government's campaign against insurgents in the Darfur region further complicated its position, especially after the US Congress declared that atrocities in Darfur, where up to 300,000 people had been killed by July 2004, amounted to genocide. In September 2004, the Bush administration reached the same conclusion.[41] The UN, however, disagreed. An international commission determined that the government had committed 'serious violations of international human rights and humanitarian law amounting to crimes under international law', but that the overriding aim of the government had been to carry out a counter-insurgency campaign against what it saw as anti-government rebels.[42] Though these abuses are lamentable – no matter what their label – the US decision to label them as 'genocide' aided the SPLA's argument that the extreme persecution of their community at the hands of Sudan's government meant that there was no reasonable chance of ameliorating their situation short of allowing them to form a new sovereign state.

Like the government of former Yugoslavia, Sudan's government faced an international audience that viewed its efforts to maintain control over its territory as a subject for international relations and not solely an internal matter. In this latter case, however, there was not a consensus among powerful states as to how to handle the situation. Moreover, officials in neighbouring African states have been reluctant to agree to secession against the wishes of a parent state that was a member of the African Union. The lack of agreement among factions of the SPLA did not reassure US and other foreign negotiators, but the SPLA was nonetheless able to benefit from the extremely poor international standing of their foes. Since independence is a highly salient issue for them, provisions that put off the referendum to 2011 conceded to them an important principle; preserved for Sudan's government the possibility of undermining its implementation; and for foreign diplomats and other officials, gave assurance that this issue would become the problem of new cadres of officials in a still-distant future.

In contrast, Kurdish separatists have benefited from their role in helping to solve the problems facing a troubled US occupation of Iraq and internal Iraqi turmoil, rather than from international condemnation of their parent state's government. The two main Kurdish separatist parties have benefited from the protection that they received in their position as administrators of the northern No Fly Zone in Iraq from 1991 as the Kurdish Regional Government (KRG). They control the *peshmerga* militia, an armed force capable of defending that territory. This armed group was powerful enough to secure and hand over the city of Kirkuk to US troops when they arrived in March 2003. More recently, they cooperated with US forces in counter-insurgency operations outside the territory of the KRG and have helped to staff Iraqi government security forces. Within the KRG, *peshmerga* are allowed to operate as an internal security and police force.

This capability and cooperation has ensured for the KRG a right to regional autonomy in the Iraqi constitution. But as Henry Kissinger opined, 'Kurds define self-government as only microscopically distinguishable from independence.'[43] Kissinger's suspicions received some support from the declaration of the head of the Kurdish Democratic Party, that 'the people of Kurdistan have a right to their own state'.[44] Like the KLA, the *peshmerga* have tried to force out people who they consider to be non-indigenes from places that they claim as part of the territory of their ethnic nation.[45]

Kurdish prospects for US support for their sovereignty depend on two factors. First, the secession has to avoid drawing the opposition of a blocking power. Turkish officials have expressed concern about the impact of an independent Kurdistan on their own ethnic Kurd population. Governments in other states with significant Kurd minorities, specifically in Iran and Syria, also would have ample reason to oppose the creation of a sovereign Kurdistan. Turkish efforts to gain entry into the EU might moderate their opposition to Kurdish secession from Iraq, if Turkish officials were convinced that EU membership would raise the value of Turkish citizenship to their own Kurdish population to the extent that they would reject calls to join the new Kurdish state. A second condition, the possible collapse of the US position in Iraq might counter-balance Turkish opposition. If public order broke down completely in core areas of Iraq, US officials might see some benefit to recognising greater autonomy for the KPG and eventual sovereignty if the remaining portions of Iraq broke apart.

UNEQUAL SOVEREIGNTY AND STATEHOOD IN THE PERIPHERY

The rise of US hegemonic power and the problems that disorder in the periphery poses to the US and other states, especially after 9/11, combine to generate a steeper hierarchy in degrees of sovereignty in international society. Weak and 'misbehaving' states are more likely to face limits on prerogatives associated with global recognition of their sovereignty. This occurs as officials in more powerful states solve political problems through intervening directly in those states' internal affairs. More frequently since the end of the Cold War, separatist groups can exploit the interests of constituencies in these powerful states. The most successful separatists are those that challenge the most internally-fragmented and violent states – enabling them to offer themselves as alternatives to the turmoil that they create – and whose separation does not seriously threaten the interests of another state capable of preventing this occurrence.

The environment for separatists is likely to improve so long as officials in powerful states consider the sovereignty of very weak or non-compliant states to be a threat to their own security. In many instances, this translates into greater aid for desperate regimes in these states. George W. Bush's famous statement, 'Over time it's going to be important for nations to know that they will be held accountable for inactivity', is as much an invitation to weak states as it is a threat. His proposition, 'You're either with us or against us in the fight against terror',[46] has translated into willing acceptance of military and security aid on the part of regimes eager to boost their own security and control. Aid of this sort creates proxy armies that can fight de-centralised non-state armed groups in situations where all sides either do not observe, or only selectively observe, conventional standards of behaviour in warfare.

But where regimes do not cooperate with this agenda, they risk losing the sovereign prerogative to remain unmolested in their internal affairs. The internal turmoil that usually accompanies this kind of situation also provides justification for decertification as a remedy to a government's severe abuses of human rights under the contractarian notion of international law that many human rights advocates support. This outside intervention is at the core of improved prospects for separatists. Recent developments continue to drive this structural change in international relations. The US refusal to recognise International Criminal Court (ICC) procedures reflects a Rumsfeld Doctrine effort to pursue unfettered intervention and to be able to attack non-state armed groups in the manner of their choosing. This reflects the idea that these enemy groups operate outside of international law, as do their erstwhile state backers, and that the US must be free to do so as well, in order to destroy these groups. Despite considerable international criticism of the US, some critics of US strategy seek the same exemptions to intervene. The UK, acting on behalf of 19 countries with peacekeepers in Afghanistan in 2002, negotiated an agreement with the interim government that peacekeepers 'may not be surrendered to, or otherwise transferred to, the custody of an international tribunal or any other entity or state without express consent of the contributing nation'.[47]

These measures and the multiple processes of intervention drive the creation of a steeper hierarchy of sovereignty. States that already exercised a lot of power in international society gain new powers to intervene in the affairs of the weak. The weakest states lose the greater degree of recognition of sovereign prerogatives, though not necessarily against the interest of incumbent regimes. But where regimes oppose this diminishment of autonomy in the international realm, and where separatists can convince powerful outsiders that they share interests, greater inequalities in the international recognition of sovereignty will be to the benefit of separatists and that is likely to result in the further fragmentation of some states.

This trend is likely to continue for the foreseeable future. It resembles conditions prior to the First World War when a similar consensus existed among powerful states in Europe. It is possible, however, that the current process of decertification of sovereignty and the promotion of alternative sovereigns will become more extreme in future. A second spectacular terrorist attack in the US or Europe and the fragmentation of Iraq into the violent competition of warring groups would give substantial boosts to this trend. Either of these events would also reinforce a consensus among officials in the US, EU, Russia and elsewhere about the necessity of redefining their recognition of statehood in the periphery.

NOTES

1. This evolution of exclusive competence is detailed in Daniel Philpott, *Revolutions in Sovereignty: How Ideas Shaped Modern International Relations* (Princeton: Princeton University Press, 2001).
2. Atlantic Charter, found at www.yale.edu/lawweb/avalon/wwii/atlantic.htm (last accessed 25 February 2006).
3. Declaration on the Granting of Independence to Colonial Countries and Peoples, UN General Assembly Resolution 1514 (XV), 14 December 1960, art. 2 and art. 3.
4. Charter of the Organisation of African Unity, art. III (3), in Ian Brownlie (ed.) *Basic Documents on African Affairs* (Oxford: Clarendon Press, 1971), p. 3.
5. OAU Resolution on Border Disputes, 21 July 1964, art. 2, in Ian Brownlie, *African Boundaries: A Legal and Diplomatic Encyclopædia* (London: C. Hurst, 1979), p. 11.
6. Declaration on the Problem of Subversion, art. 5(b), in Brownlie (ed.), *Basic Documents on African Affairs*, p. 17.
7. Emmanuel Dube, 'Relations between Liberation Movements and the O.A.U.' in N.M. Shamuyarira (ed.), *Essays on the Liberation of Southern Africa* (Dar es Salaam: Tanzania Publishing House, 1975), pp. 25–68.
8. Declaration on Principles of International Law Concerning Friendly Relations and Cooperation Among States in Accordance with the Charter of the United Nations, UN General Assembly Resolution 2625 (XXV), 24 October 1970, art. 1.
9. *Case Concerning the Frontier Dispute (Burkina Faso / Republic of Mali)*, ICJ Rep. 554, International Court of Justice, 22 December 1986, p. 567.
10. Conference on Security and Co-operation in Europe, Final Act, Helsinki, 1 August 1975, 14 ILM 1292, Principle III.
11. This theme recurs in the EPLF's journal *Liberation* (Beirut: EPLF Central Bureau of Foreign Relations).
12. James Crawford, *The Creation of States in International Law* (Oxford: Clarendon Press, 1979).
13. Viva Ona Bartkus, *The Dynamics of Secession* (New York: Cambridge University Press, 1999), pp. 154–8.
14. Stephen Krasner, *Sovereignty: Organized Hypocrisy* (Princeton: Princeton University Press, 1999), pp. 84–90.
15. Artem Ohandjanian, *Armenien: Der Verschwiegene Völkermord* (Vienna: Böhlau, 1989), pp. 9–17.

16. Helsinki Final Act, 1 August 1975, art. VIII.
17. United Nations Security Council Resolution 757 (Implementing Trade Embargo on Yugoslavia), Security Council Resolution 757, 30 May 1992.
18. On specific war-fighting strategies and human rights violations, see United Nations Security Council, *Final Report of the Commission of Experts Established Pursuant to Security Council Resolution 780 (1992)* (New York: UN S/1994/694, 27 May 1994).
19. United Nations Security Council, Resolution 688, 5 April 1991.
20. United States Senate, Armed Services Committee, 'Statement by Director of Central Intelligence: Worldwide Threat in 2001: National Security in a Changing World', 7 March 2001, p. 17.
21. George Bush, *National Security Strategy of the United States* (Falls Village, CT: Winterhouse Editions, 2002), p. 3.
22. Jack Straw, 'Order out of Chaos: The Challenge of Failed States', in Mark Leonard (ed.), *Re-Ordering the World: The Long-term Implications of September 11* (London: Foreign Policy Centre, 2002), p. 98.
23. LOI n° 2003–73 du 27 janvier 2003 relative à la programmation militaire pour les années 2003 à 2008 (1).
24. Keeping in mind that Iraq in 2003 was not a failed state, but it was considered an odious state (see below).
25. Steven Metz and Raymond Millen, 'Intervention, Stabilization, and Transformation Operations: The Role of Landpower in the New Strategic Environment', *Parameters*, 35 (Spring 2005), p. 42.
26. United Nations Security Council, *Report of the Panel of Experts pursuant to Security Council Resolution 1343 (2001)*, paragraph 19, concerning Liberia, S/2001/1015, 26 October 2001. See also Douglas Farah, *Blood from Stones: The Secret Financial Network of Terror* (New York: Broadway Books, 2004).
27. Department of Defense, *Quadrennial Defense Review Report*, 6 February 2006, p. vi.
28. *The 9/11 Commission Report: Final Report of the National Commission on Terrorist Attacks Upon the United States*, July 2004, sections 12–2, 365–7.
29. Department of Defense, *Quadrennial Defense Review Report*, pp. vi, 6.
30. Alberto R. Gonzales, 'Memorandum for the President: Decision Re Application of the Geneva Convention on Prisoners of War to the Conflict with Al-Qaeda and the Taliban', 25 January 2002, p. 1.
31. Ibid.
32. These are the US, Russia, the UK, France, Germany, and Italy.
33. 'Kosovo Contact Group Statement', London, 31 January 2006.
34. United Nations Security Council, *Report of the Secretary-General on the United Nations Interim Administration Mission in Kosovo*, S/2006/45, 25 January 2006, Annex I.
35. International Commission on Intervention and State Sovereignty, *The Responsibility to Protect* (Ottawa: International Development Research Centre, 2002), p. xi.
36. http://europa.eu.int/comm/enlargement/report_2005/pdf/package/sec_1423_final_en_pr ogress_report_ks.pdf (accessed 6 October 2006).
37. 'Abkhazia: Putin's Remark Sparks Debate on Self-Determination Question', 3 February 2006, www.unpo.org/news_detail.php?arg=03&par=3668 (accessed 6 October 2006). Thanks to Lee Seymour for this source.
38. For this interpretation of the KLA's calculations, see Michael Ignatieff, *Human Rights as Politics and Idolatry* (Princeton: Princeton University Press, 2003).
39. International Monetary Fund, *Sudan: Report on the Final Review of the 2003 Staff-Monitored Program and the 2004 Staff-Monitored Program* (Washington, DC: IMF, 8 June 2005), p. 7.
40. PL 107–245, 116 Statute 1504, in 'Enactment of the Sudan Peace Act', *American Journal of International Law*, 97/1 (January 2003), pp. 195–6.
41. Secretary of State Colin Powell, 'Testimony before the Senate Foreign Relations Committee', 9 September 2004.
42. *Report of the Commission of Inquiry on Darfur to the United Nations Secretary-General*, 25 January 2005.
43. Henry Kissinger, 'Reflections on a Sovereign Iraq', in *Kurdistan Observer* and other places, 8 February 2004.

44. Jackie Spinner, 'For a Proud Minority, a "Very Happy" Day', *Washington Post*, 31 January 2005, A15.

45. Human Rights Watch, *Claims in Conflict: Reversing Ethnic Cleansing in Northern Iraq*, August 2004.

46. Bush news conference with Chirac, November 2001.

47. Colum Lynch, 'European Countries Cut Deal to Protect Afghan Peacekeepers', *Washington Post*, 20 June 2002, A15.

Part II
Case Studies

8
The Sicilian Mafia:
Parastate and Adventure Capitalism

Henner Hess

Cambiare tutto per non cambiare nulla – change everything so that nothing is changed; change outward appearances to preserve the essence. This is how Giuseppe Tomasi di Lampedusa characterises the attitude of the Sicilians towards historical upheavals and changes in his famous novel *The Leopard*. Looking back over the developments of the last decades, this phrase also holds true in many ways for the 'mafia' phenomenon.

A SHORT LOOK BACK AT ORIGINS

The word 'mafia' may be derived from the Arabic (the Arabs ruled Palermo from 831 to 1072). In the Palermo dialect it had the meaning of 'boldness, ambition, arrogance'. A *mafioso* stood for a man *che non porta mosca sul naso*, who didn't have a fly dancing on his nose, who was always ready to defend his honour. In the first half of the nineteenth century the word took on a further meaning and was used in this sense for the first time in an official government document in 1865. It now described the private, and therefore criminal, violence of local strong-arm men and their clienteles. Gradually, the *delitto di mafia* came to mean more the offence of *manutengolo*, of being a fence or planner of crimes, and not so much the offence of *malandrino*, of banditry, of being an operational criminal. Eventually, the word 'mafia' was used, above all, for organised crime, until sensation-hungry journalists, confused Northern Italian jurists and foreign authors interpreted it as the name of an organisation. The emergence of the word was, then, linked with the emergence of a secret society and thus gave rise to fantastic speculations.[1]

Contrary to those speculations, however, the mafia phenomenon is neither very old, nor is it a centrally-organised secret society. 'Mafia' stands, in fact, for a plethora of independent clientelist groups around local strong-arm men; and the phenomenon did not come into existence before the nineteenth century. For centuries, even millennia, from the Greeks and Romans through Arabs, Normans, Hohenstauffens, Anjou, Spaniards and Neapolitans to the Italian nation-state, Sicily had been a colonised island with a population distrustful and inimical to the far-away central governments, the organs of which were usually impotent or even non-existent, especially in the countryside. The real rulers on the island were the land-owning barons, supported by their armed field guards, the *bravi*. At the end of the eighteenth century many of the barons moved to Palermo and Naples and leased their vast *latifundia* to lease-holders, the so-called *gabelloti*, who, in turn, farmed them out to numerous small tenants. In 1812, feudalism was abolished and the *latifundia* could be sold. Many were bought by the *gabelloti*, who often managed to intimidate any competition through threats and violence.

In many respects, especially as the 'real' power in the countryside, the new agrarian bourgeoisie of the *gabelloti* replaced the old aristocracy. Along with feudalism, a number of the traditional rights of the peasants on the *latifundia* were abolished, commons in the villages were privatised, and under the new liberal Italian government, the monasteries lost their vast agrarian territories in 1860 and became unable to support the poor. The situation of the peasants went from bad to worse and banditry developed from a sporadic phenomenon into a constant plague.

To control the unruly small tenants and farmhands, as well as to defend farms against cattle-raiders and the citrus plantations around Palermo against thieves, the owners and large lease-holders had to revert to private violence, the new Italian state being almost as weak as its predecessors. Now, however, this private violence was illegal, as the modern state claimed a monopoly on legitimate violence. An apparatus with the potential of violent enforcement at the service of its owners was also very useful when contracts were being negotiated with the tenants or when the crop was being divided. The class struggle in the countryside was thus very direct and not mediated by the state. The henchmen of the owners or large leaseholders, usually employed as field guards, in turn extorted from the tenants part of the crop as a tribute, called *u pizzu* (from '*fari vagnari u pizzu*', 'to wet one's beak'). In short, there was a specific 'opportunity structure' for local non-state strong-arm men, who came to be called *mafiosi*, or, when they had formed a group of henchmen around them, *capi-mafia*. This informal position could be filled by a landowner, a lease-holder, a field guard or whoever proved himself the most able.

This historical sketch makes it evident that mafia is – or at least, was – a phenomenon fundamentally different from banditry or common crime. The *mafioso* may have started out as a bandit or as a common criminal and, as such, may have gained a reputation as a reckless and violent person. However, while most bandits and common criminals remain what they are, some may follow a different career. Their reputation may help them to take over functions in the service of a landowner or of an established older *mafioso*. Gradually they become more and more independent of their employer or their *capo-mafia* – sometimes finally killing him and taking his place. Such functions as protection and mediation in all sorts of conflicts then legitimise their position as a patron in the eyes of the people. And since the early twentieth century, and the advent of political elections, supplying votes to politicians gave them very useful connections.[2]

Those connections form what is usually called *partito*, while *cosca* signifies the group of persons at the *mafioso*'s service, his closest male relatives and clients, what is sometimes called a 'mafia family'.[3] What is important to realise is that there were always many *cosche*, each with its own territory. These small clique-like associations are independent of each other, but maintain relations with one another, support each other, make arrangements with each other, at times take joint action, but on occasion can be at daggers-drawn. To describe the totality of these *cosche* as 'the Mafia' carries some dangers of misunderstanding (to which I will return later).

The *mafioso* was always an ambivalent figure. He was, of course, a dangerous criminal as far as the law of the state was concerned, but in the eyes of many Sicilians, that did not automatically discredit anybody. The state was considered by many as a foreign power that levied taxes and forced sons into military service, while it was incapable of running efficient administrations or protecting the people. Often enough, the servants of the state – coming from Italy, as many did – did not even understand the common people who, until the arrival of television, spoke only dialect. Besides the fear of reprisal at the hands of the *mafiosi*, the subcultural norms of *omertà* guaranteed almost total non-cooperation with the administration of justice. And without complaints, reports, depositions by witnesses and so on, the effectiveness of this administration was severely restricted.

The *mafioso*, on the other hand, was at least effective; and not only (even if foremost) in the service of the ruling class. When you were in trouble, you could turn to him and ask for help; when you needed protection; when you needed negotiation with cattle-thieves; when you needed a middle-man; when you needed a connection to the capital of the province, to Palermo or even to Rome, the *mafioso* was often ready to help. Months or years later, he would ask for some 'small favour', such as cutting down the olive trees of a land-owner who refused protection, or casting your vote for the candidate the *mafioso* had recommended. Gradually, you became his client, the patron–client relationship being the most important other than blood ties in all traditional societies. The *mafioso* was feared, to be sure, but he also commanded admiration as the quintessential *uomo di rispetto* or *uomo d'onore* in a society where respect and honour meant everything.

FROM POSTWAR TO THE 1980s: CHANGE AND CONTINUITY

Fascism persecuted and suppressed the mafia because it competed for local positions of power. The fascists took the repression of peasant movements, trade unions and left-wing parties into their own hands and thus supplanted the *mafiosi* in functions which had guaranteed their political connections and brought them the support of the Sicilian land-owning classes.[4] When the Americans occupied Sicily in 1943, the *mafiosi* were able to present themselves with some justification as antifascists and were made mayors and aldermen. Most importantly, they retrieved their old roles in the class struggles and political rivalries. At the end of the 1940s, private repressive violence and intimidation were employed again on a large scale to protect the big land-owners against the land-hungry peasants. Not until the 1950s and 1960s, when many Sicilians emigrated, first to northern Italy and then to central Europe, did the pressure in the villages abate.

Politically, many *mafiosi* initially favoured the separatist movement, which was very popular immediately after the war. In response to this danger, the Italian government granted Sicily broad administrative autonomy, transferring many responsibilities with regard to security, economy and culture to a regional government.

As a background to future developments, it is important to emphasise here that, for example, within this autonomous status, Sicilian banks were not controlled by the Italian Central Bank until 1982. Until then, they were merely placed under regional supervision. From 1947, many billion lire flowed into the region from the development funds of the Italian state as aid money intended for the modernisation of agriculture and the construction of airports, harbours, dams, water pipes, streets and housing. Access to these moneys, through the awarding and execution of public building contracts, became the most lucrative business in Sicily.

After the 1948 elections, the Christian Democrats dominated the region and had taken power in most districts. They owed their victory partly to the support of their mafia clientele. The *mafiosi* had promptly shifted their loyalty from the separatists to the Christian Democrats during the search for useful *partito* connections and, until recently, could count on the (frequently successful) efforts of a whole range of politicians to help them avoid criminal prosecution. In addition to these traditional reciprocal services came, above all, preferential treatment in the awarding of public contracts. With this, the network of corruption seems to have reached unprecedented proportions.

The politicians and their appointed followers from the district and regional administrations right up to the state ministries not only bought themselves electoral advantages in this way, but gained considerable financial advantage as well. The *mafiosi* used not only their access to votes but also the practice of intimidation and violence, with which they blackmailed politicians and officials and deterred competition. This served to the advantage of the businesses they 'protected', but increasingly was also to the advantage of their own firms. Because during the 1960s the phenomenon of the so-called 'entrepreneurial mafia' developed, mafia families who established themselves as construction, transport and business entrepreneurs, took public contracts for themselves and executed them or passed them to sub-contractors. In addition to the legal businesses of these entrepreneurs, sometimes conducted through illegal means, there were others which were entirely illegal: cigarette smuggling, since the 1950s, and drug trafficking, since the 1960s.

In the 1970s, drug dealing was to bring immense wealth. After the French Connection was cracked, Sicilian families (above all the Cuntrera and Caruana from Siculiana in Agrigento Province, with connections to South and North America, as well as the Inzerillo, Bontade, Badalamenti, Gambino and Spatola families from Palermo, with connections to New York) were able to control up to 30 per cent of the world's heroin trade and, at times, even process raw morphine into heroin in their own laboratories (with the help of hired experts from Marseille).[5] The Sicilian banks once again played a major role in the laundering and reinvestment of the profits, which were estimated at up to $1 billion per year. Mafia enterprises enjoyed a relatively undisturbed heyday until the beginning of the 1980s, particularly as public attention (and that of the Italian police and justice systems) was focused on another plague – that of leftist terrorism.

The great changes of this decade are obvious. The main focus of mafia activity has moved into urban areas of the economy, the range of business has multiplied, the whole type of *mafioso*, his social world and his technical apparatus seem to have fundamentally changed. This change has often been described as a change from *mafioso* to gangster, from man of honour to simple criminal.[6]

Even if this description is in general quite correct, we should nevertheless not underestimate the power of tradition and the continuity of structures and functions. Behind the changed appearance, if you look closely, much of the character of the traditional mafia has remained the same. Most importantly, mafia groups are still very much rooted in local ground and depend on local resources. Even today, the well-known *capi-mafia* are not sophisticated financiers, but simple people who speak the Sicilian dialect and uphold traditional values of family and religion and, above all, an otherwise amusing sense of honour (we will see later why this is). Their actual power is not a financial one, but one which grows continually from domination over a territory to which they cling, even if it means going underground. As previously stated, considerable continuity is to be found in the structures of mafia groups and in the functions of mafia behaviour.[7]

STRUCTURES: THE BASIS OF MAFIA POWER

> A mafioso is like a spider. He weaves networks of friendships, acquaintances and obligations.
>
> Antonino Calderone

The basic elements of traditional mafia structures were the *cosca* and the *partito* – the mafia 'family' and the network of connections to politically influential persons. These two elements correspond to the two resources on which the power of the mafia fed: on the one hand, the capability to use violence, manipulate public opinion, and so on; and, on the other, the ability to influence state authorities and neutralise the police in the process of justice. What was decisive was the optimal strategic position of the *mafioso* as provider of, and channel for, services, goods and information between members of the *cosca*, and the wide circle of clients, on the one hand, and members of the *partito*, on the other.

In general – and in principle – little has changed in this regard, even in the last decades. It seems that the *cosche* have become larger, in some instances even considerably larger. While previously the number of close followers of a *mafioso* seldom numbered more than 10 or 15 people, today, even if the average number may be similar, mafia groupings exist which are believed to number between 70 and 80 men. The *cosca* Bontade in Palermo is supposed to have had as many as 120 members during the 1970s and the *cosca* Santapaola in Catania at the start of the 1990s had more than 200.

The nucleus of the modern *cosche* consists, as it always has, of the biological family: the basic internal connection is blood ties. In this way, loyalty and mutual dependability are still best guaranteed. Through marriage or the establishment of ritual kinship links, such as a godparent relationship, the mafia still attempts to make use of this, the most strongly-binding force, weaving large circles of contacts with one another. A good example of this could be seen in Palermo in the 1970s, in the very powerful conglomerate of the Inzerillo–Di Maggio–Gambino–Spatola families, who were each related to the others by marriage.[8] Around this solid nucleus,

networks of friendships and clients are built up. There is, furthermore, the attempt
– through ceremonial induction rites into the *Cosa Nostra* ('our thing'), oaths of
loyalty and formal recognition as 'members' – to make use of the elements of
fascination and fear common to secret societies in order to foster mutual loyalty
(more on this subject to come). Also, mutual financial interests could be a binding
element. But mutual membership as *uomo d'onore* in the same *cosca*, and the
even weaker bond of the common membership in the *Cosa Nostra*, together with
common business interests, all remain secondary and precarious and do not prevent
changes of alliance.

The number of adult male relatives – the number of sons of a *mafioso*, the number
of brothers with their respective sons – is also the deciding factor of the military
strength of a *cosca*, or of the dominant strong man, or of the dominant family group
(from which the *cosca* usually takes its name). In addition, all *capi-mafia* are always
trying to further increase their means of force and may take bandits, field guards and
other promising young people into their service. This is often only done temporarily
and for particular tasks, but sometimes they also become long-term *bassa mafia*
clients, who have the opportunity to be co-opted into the inner echelons of the
cosca. The same mechanism is still functioning today, as we read in the statement
of the *pentito* (that is, a repentant former *mafioso* working together with the justice
system as a crown witness) Antonino Calderone from Catania:

> In the hazy circles of every reasonably influential uomo d'onore there are twenty
> or thirty young people moving around, who are nobody, but want to be somebody.
> These young people are at his disposal, always there to do him little favours,
> offering their services, asking if he needs them... willing to do anything and [who]
> like nothing more than an opportunity to prove themselves, and, if possible, be
> accepted into the Cosa Nostra.[9]

The supply of such criminal labour is plentiful everywhere where economic
misery and socio-cultural disintegration are particularly great, and in this regard
the poor, proletarian districts of the southern Italian cities of Palermo, Catania and
Naples strongly resemble those of the Third World. In these districts there are not
only higher levels of destructive, diffuse violence, but there is also a great potential
of military power which can be mustered by criminal organisations. However,
they must be capable of controlling this potential. And in this, the *mafiosi* are not
necessarily any more successful than the police, since the relationship is ambivalent
(just as it had previously been with the bandits in the provinces). The small criminals
provide not only a supply of new blood, they are also the plague against which the
mafia must defend the business people they 'protect'. They are partly even serious
competition for the dominance over territory. For example, for a time the *cosca*
of the Calderones had to withdraw from the centre of Catania to avoid large street
gangs.[10] The latest appearance, mainly in the provinces of Agrigento and Trapani, of
the so-called *stidde* (stars, criminal gangs which are not recognised by the *mafiosi* as
cosche or as *Cosa Nostra*) shows up such tensions. In addition, the wide availability
of these henchmen and their client-relationships with individual *mafiosi*, rather than

to the *cosca* as such, furthers potential divisions within the *cosca* as well as military clashes between *cosche*.

The other mainstay of *mafia* power is, as mentioned, the *partito*. Calderone also describes in detail the ways and functions of a modern *partito*. His *cosca*, led by his brother Giuseppe, had a strong connection to the Catanian entrepreneurial family, the Costanzo, on the basis of exchange of services. The Calderones protected the wealthy Costanzo family from kidnapping and blackmail and protected the firm's large construction sites and plants against extortion attempts. They obtained public contracts for them, often through their mafia contacts, mainly in Palermo. They conducted dealings with *mafiosi* from other territories when the Costanzos were carrying out building contracts in other provinces of Sicily. They intimidated workers who wanted to strike and carried out attacks on competing firms to throw them off balance. Although they were paid for these services, the protective screen against prosecution which the Costanzos could provide was much more important and more valued.

The Costanzos owned a hunting ground and a seaside hotel, where they entertained Carabinieri officers, judges and politicians and brought them together with *mafiosi*. A public prosecutor lived rent-free in one of their houses. One of their managers conducted an election campaign for the Christian Democrat candidate Milazzo with their money. Their money was used to bribe useful people (a secretary at police headquarters received 500,000 lire, a public prosecutor 30 million). As compensation, a politician would put in a good word to a judge, a Carabinieri colonel would organise the transfer of an overly diligent captain, a public prosecutor would strike certain names off the wanted list, a secretary would give warning of a planned arrest.[11]

It is the volume of such seemingly banal details which must be kept in mind to understand the power of the mafia phenomenon.

> To say it again, the Mafia is not a cancerous growth which by chance has begun to grow in a healthy body. It exists in complete symbiosis with the masses of protectors, collaborators, informants and debtors. That is the humus of the Cosa Nostra.[12]

And this humus reached up high, through many varying networks of power. Through the Socialist and Christian Democratic parties, in particular the Andreotti faction; through organisations as shrouded in mystery as the Knights of the Holy Sepulchre, Opus Dei, many Masonic Lodges and the most criminal of them all, the notorious secret Lodge, Propaganda Due,[13] through to the executives of a variety of power hierarchies in the state and in business associations. Even at the highest levels, the *mafiosi* were always concerned with neutralising the process of justice and with influencing legislation and the regulation of the economy. They have an interest in the loosening of currency regulations and currency-export restrictions and they attempt to prevent regulations which aim to make banking transactions and the awarding of construction contracts more transparent – or they must at least sabotage the application of such regulations.

In the last two decades, two new factors have been added to the existing ones: first, the enormous financial power of mafia entrepreneurs, which resulted from drug trafficking and made them independent of some connections; and, second, direct terrorist threats against members of the state apparatus, which had been very uncommon previously. These factors led to a greater autonomy of the mafia in dealings with political figures, but, as a result, also to a weakening of networks and ultimately to crisis.

THE RECIPROCAL INFLUENCE OF MYTH AND REALITY

> A Calabrian chicken decided to become a member of the mafia. He went to a mafia Minister to get a letter of recommendation, but was told that the mafia did not exist. He went to a mafia judge, but he also told him that the mafia did not exist. Finally he went to a mafia mayor, and he too told him that the mafia did not exist. So the chicken went back to the henhouse, and when the other chickens asked, he answered that the mafia did not exist. Then all the other chickens thought he had become a member of the mafia and became afraid of him.
>
> Luigi Malerba

In mentioning structures, one cannot avoid at least touching on the century-old debate about the theory of the mafia as one big secret society. The historical material seems clear to me: there are organisations, but not 'the organisation'.[14] In recent times, however, the confessions of so-called *pentiti* who have testified before examining magistrates suggest again more organisational formality. One must respect these testimonies, but, in so doing, neither discard definite knowledge about the past, nor abandon all scepticism with regard to the present day. First, as to the name of the organisation: earlier it was obvious that it was called 'mafia'. Today it seems equally clear that in reality it is known as *Cosa Nostra*. So far as this last name is concerned, one can confidently say that it was only recently imported from America, where it was misunderstood during the hearings of the McClellan Commission (1957–59) to be the proper name of an organisation. This was then propagated by the media.

The structure of the organisation is regularly presented as follows (and this corresponds broadly to schemata which have been set out for decades in American criminology textbooks and which appear in the press and on television). The *Cosa Nostra* consists of families which are autonomous in their respective territories. All members call themselves *uomini d'onore*, but the families are structured hierarchically. The basic members are known as *soldati*. From their own ranks they elect a *rappresentante*, a boss who represents the family. The chief appoints his deputy and *capi-decina* (heads of ten; that is, non-commissioned officers) and a *consigliere* (adviser). The *rappresentanti* represent the families in a provincial commission and representatives of the provincial commissions make up the most senior committee, the regional commission (*Regionale* or *Cupola*). New members are accepted in a ceremony marked by traditional initiation rites. Within the organisation, a strictly sanctioned system of norms is in place which commands, above all, absolute obedience to the *capi-decina* and the *rappresentante*, complete honesty and exchange of information on the inside and total secrecy on the outside and first loyalty to the organisation, before and above all other loyalties.[15]

Doubts about this exacting system are reasonable, particularly as the *pentiti* maintain, usually with regret, that they only came to know a deteriorated version of this old tradition – one with less formality; in which elections are decided in advance; in which initiation ceremonies no longer impress the hard-boiled new breed to whom violence is nothing new; and in which the only things that count are blood ties and the rights of the powerful.[16]

That is by no means an indication that all the abovementioned descriptions of the structure and inner life of a *Cosa Nostra* should be dismissed as pure fantasy. Rather, one can see here a circular interaction between mythology and reality. The media world (including judicial and criminological discourses, but above all novels, films and television) takes inspiration from real persons, cliques and events which it embellishes, idealises, condemns, and portrays so impressively that those who are depicted in turn attempt to stay true to the portrayal. Thus, *mafiosi* try to translate their portrayal in *The Godfather* into reality, or try to live out the reality of a secret society 'the way the judges who interrogated me defined it'.[17]

That can often bring tangible benefits. Gaining membership of the mafia or the *Cosa Nostra* through mutual recognition as *uomini d'onore*, which might sometimes be honoured in a more or less formal admission ceremony, offers not only a flattering image, but also considerable practical advantages, because each individual *mafioso*, in the performance of his function, profits from the fearful reputation of the organisation. The reciprocal recognition as 'legitimate' *cosche* restricts the operations of competing gangs which are regarded as non-*Cosa Nostra*. In addition, the portrayal of a central executive authority, as is constantly suggested in the media, has a certain attraction for the *mafiosi*.

In any case, there has always been a considerable need for regulation between the *cosche*, a need which has been constantly increasing since the 1950s because of increased mobility; the broader integration of the political and social life of Sicily; and as a result of commercial projects throughout the provinces.

Since the start of the 1970s, for example, Guiseppe Calderone, *capo* of a *cosca* from Catania, had been pushing for an inter-provincial body to avoid or reduce conflict and to facilitate cooperation. In 1975, the so-called Regional Commission brought together for the first time the chiefs of the leading *cosche* from six provinces and elected Calderone secretary. According to his brother's account, Guiseppe Calderone had far-reaching plans to create a *Cosa Nostra* according to the media image: the oligarchic leadership should be extended not only as an advisory and arbitration authority but also as a decision-making authority. They were to be able to enforce their decisions not by resorting to troops of the member *cosche*, but with the help of a special panel of 50 people chosen from all the *cosche* under the command of the secretary. Principles of organisational structure and standards of conduct for members were to be established in a statute. A standard which was particularly important – that no *cosca* could have more than two brothers as members or more than two blood relatives in the leadership – is symptomatic of the greatly desired intention: the creation of an effective modern organisation independent of traditional blood ties. The Regional Commission existed for a while and possibly still exists today, but obviously has not achieved its main purpose: internal pacification. Calderone's modernisation plans never had a chance against the needs of the local and provincial strong men for independence and against the power of traditional blood ties and clientele connections. Even so, the media for their part embellished these timid attempts at centralisation into an all-powerful *Cupola*.[18]

FUNCTIONS: MAFIA AS PARASTATE

> When you think closely about it, in character, the mafia is nothing other than the expression of a longing for order and thereby for government.
>
> Giovanni Falcone

In an ingenious essay, the American historian Charles Tilly described governments as protection rackets, as organised crime.[19] Taking the example of the formation of European states during early modern times, he analyses the functions which the introduction of organised force had (and in principle still has – even if modified and more latent): war as defence against rivals who pose a threat from outside the home territory, within which the ruler strives for a monopoly over force; the formation of states as the fulfilment of this monopoly against internal rivals; protection, above all, of economically powerful clients against the enemies within (for example, repression of social revolutions) or outside the territory (for example, trade wars); and finally, taxation levies to finance this monopoly. To understand the mafia phenomenon, it is useful to once again reverse the perspectives and, instead of seeing protection rackets in the process of government, to recognise government processes in protection rackets.

The central purpose of a *mafioso* or a *mafia cosca* is always to gain a monopoly of power and protection in a designated territory and to maintain it. Mafia murders and mafia wars are, above all, signs of the struggle for power in a territory or of arguments over territorial borders. Internal palace revolts and succession struggles are almost endemic, and alliances of civil war factions with rival external power groups are common. Wars of conquest are less common. The last major mafia war was fought between two alliances from 1981 to 1983: the large Palermo *cosche* Inzerillo and Bontade, with their allies in the provinces, on the one hand; and the *cosca* from Corleone (Luciano Liggio, Salvatore Riina, Bernardo Provenzano, and so on), the Greco family from Palermo, the *cosca* of Nitto Santapaola in Catania, and so on, on the other. From this war, which in 1982 alone had a toll of 300 dead and 150 missing, the Corleonesi, the men from the small agricultural town of Corleone south-east of Palermo, emerged as the dominant power. The 'dictatorship' of the Corleonesi in their attempt at centralisation during the 1980s resembled the attempt at an oligarchic trans-territorial authority of the Regional Commission or *Cupola* in the past. The ensuing events lead to the assumption that this attempt too came to nothing in the end. Under the particular circumstances of illegality, power monopolies seem to survive only in smaller territories.

Here, of course, 'monopoly' means only the exclusion of other *mafiosi*. The state remains as permanent competition for the supply of protection and the collection of relevant moneys. A good example of the functional equivalence of mafia and police is mentioned by Calderone:

> At the meeting with the other big developers Carmelo Costanzo constantly made it clear to everyone not to mess around with him, because the *mafia* was behind him... On the construction sites of the developer Rendo we caused a lot of damage in order to get money out of him and to subjugate him, to get him under our power... Also to do Costanzo a favour. But we didn't manage to subjugate him because he had police support. He was very big in the area of police and Justice.[20]

Competition is precisely the sore point for a convinced supporter of the powerful legal state like the judge Falcone. 'To say it again, the mafia does not have to be combated because of its values, which may seem warranted in a disintegrating society, but because of its very essence: there cannot be two systems of government in one society.'[21] The mafia system was only able to develop because the protective functions of a defective state were not put to adequate use. Once established, the mafia system cannot be removed just like that, even though the state could now do all its work. Economic and political life has adjusted to this system, and it has achieved its own strong momentum because not only the mafia protagonists, but also many others, profit from it.

The protective services the mafia provides for its clients comprise protection against criminal activities, negotiation and authoritative settlement of conflicts, the guarantee of contractual arrangements, and so on. It is difficult to assess the extent to which these services are genuine and appreciated by the recipients as a fair compensation for their payments, and to what extent the services are fictitious, in that protection is offered against a danger which is threatened by the protector himself, so that the payments are extortion money. While common discourse on the mafia stresses only the second scenario, it might well be that the extent of genuine exchange is underestimated. This is the central argument in Gambetta's *La mafia siciliana*, but the following sentence is already found in Max Weber's *Wirtschaft und Gesellschaft* (Economy and Society):

> The payments in practice often take on the character of subscriptions in return for which reciprocal services, namely guarantees of safety, are offered: The statement of a Neapolitan industrialist to me about 20 years ago reflecting on the effectiveness of the Camorra for businesses is relevant here: 'Signore, the Camorra takes X lire from me each month but guarantees security – the State takes ten times X lire and guarantees nothing.'[22]

There again, one could take the other perspective and see the blackmail factor in state income taxation. We are forced to pay taxes and have little to no influence on the way those taxes are used. Some of the purposes they are used for we might abhor. Other services for which we have paid are either withheld from us or of poor quality (for example, security) or we must struggle arduously to obtain them (one thinks of the often-difficult and expensive justice system). It would also be interesting to compare protection money with insurance premiums: here, also, we pay regularly, and in the majority of cases we receive no service in return, because we (fortunately) do not need it or because the insurer avoids payment.

Obviously, the protection money which is raised from small business people only makes up a small part of *mafiosi* income. When they demand protection money, therefore, it is mainly as a sign of subjugation, to signify recognition of their authority in a particular territory. As previously mentioned, these days the market for public contracts or European Union subsidies and some illegal markets, particularly the drug market, are financially much more significant.

It is in the context of these illegal markets that the mafia system achieves its greatest significance as a quasi-state. Illegality means that the trading in these markets is more uncertain and carries higher risks than in legal ones. Rights of ownership of goods are not documented anywhere and possession is precarious because of the constant threat of confiscation by the police and theft by rivals. Capital investment is also often very high. The quality of the goods varies greatly, is not standardised and is not subject to any official quality control. Contracts are entered into only verbally, are not confirmed in writing and are, therefore, always open to a variety of interpretations. The calibre of trading partners is difficult to scrutinise, as each reveals as little information as possible. Only physical persons serve as partners, not corporations, so that the enterprise disappears with the entrepreneur. Sources of mistrust, deception and conflict therefore abound, so that dealings in illegal markets are constantly characterised by pseudo-legal arguments about responsibilities and breaches of duty.[23] The illegality also means that the whole state legal system, with its arbitration and law enforcement apparatus, cannot be used. On the one hand, the need for a mechanism which in the broadest sense guarantees contracts is greater than in the legal economy. On the other hand, recourse to the state mechanism is almost completely impossible – I say 'almost', because the state mechanism can still be activated by informing and can thus be used to destroy competitors.

The two methods which in this scenario are employed in all illegal trades in order to reduce the high cost of transactions (procurement of information and secrecy, meeting of conditions, settlement of disputes and so on) are trust and violence. In providing trust, the bonds of solidarity groups with non-economic loyalties play an enormous role: family ties, mainly, but also local and regional ties, nationality, religion and political persuasion. The closer these ties, the more reliable the information about potential business partners and the more confident one can be that they will keep to arrangements and maintain confidentiality, because sanctions might include expulsion from the community – which often means not only economic, but also social, ruin. In illegal (and sometimes also in legal and quasi-legal) markets, this gives a great advantage to those people who are supported by a so-called trade diaspora, settlements of a community scattered by migration which, although geographically separated, feel connected (Jews, Armenians, southern Italians and Chinese are the best-known examples). The second method, as mentioned, is violence, or better, as the actual use of force is often costly and might even be counterproductive, the convincing threat of violence. *Mafiosi* employ both methods. To recognise one another as *uomo d'onore* initiates a bond of trust. And the knowledge that a *mafioso* will vouch for the soundness and honesty of a business partner or the security of a loan or an investment in a limited partnership (as often occurs in the drug trade) in word and, of course, if needed, in action, creates a certain reliability in a world where this is a rarity.

To fulfil this function, a *mafioso* must be seen as able to win through in conflict. His reputation gives him, today as before, a good deal of his strength, which would be exhausted fairly quickly if it had to be demonstrated in every situation by the use of violence. Here the previously-mentioned notoriety of the mystical *Cosa Nostra* helps, but a personal reputation which is beyond all doubt is essential. For the *mafioso* this means constant work on his reputation in regard to efficiency, precision in dealing, ruthless brutality, omniscience and omnipresence – but also in regard to facets of a very traditional honour such as male courage, keeping his word and leading a well-ordered family life (and most particularly in this most personal aspect he cannot afford any failures).[24]

FUNCTIONS: MAFIA AS ADVENTURE CAPITALISM

The attempt to monopolise illegal violence in a territory and to rule a territory is the special characteristic of a *mafioso* and the essence of any definition of 'mafia'. Mafia is a power structure and, as such, is of a quite different quality from what is commonly known as organised crime (which in most cases consists mainly of cooperation for the purpose of material profit). Psychologically, the deciding factor lies here too.

> The actual goal is power. The sinister passion of the *capi-mafia* is not the hunger for money, but the hunger for power. The fugitive bosses could live in luxury overseas until the end of their days. But instead they stay in Palermo – constantly hunted, ever in danger of being caught by the police or being killed by competitors – only to avoid losing control over their territory and falling from their pedestal. Marino Mannoia once said to me: 'It is often believed that people work with the Cosa Nostra for the money. But that is only partly true. Do you know why I became a *uomo d'onore*? Because before I had been a nobody in Palermo and then afterwards where I went, heads bowed. You can't value that in money.'[25]

To separate this political use of violence from the use of violence as an economic factor – not only for the benefit of clients of mafia services, but also for individual financial enrichment – is difficult and can only be done analytically. *Mafiosi* have always tried to use their positions of power in order to monopolise or at least improve certain opportunities for financial gains. In the 1970s, these efforts attained a new dimension with the spread of the so-called 'entrepreneurial mafia'.[26]

Since that time, unique hybrid phenomena have been noticeable in the economy of the Italian south (Sicily, Calabria and Campania): modern construction, trade and service enterprises which are technically up to date and which operate in expanding sectors of the economy, but which show traditional, or downright archaic, elements and which, above all, employ unscrupulous physical violence as a business method.

The great success and the extraordinary growth of such enterprises are based on competitive advantages which they gain simply through the use of violence or through other illegal activities. The most important competitive advantage lies in discouraging competitors through more or less explicit threats and, when necessary, through attacks on plant installations and staff. This mechanism functions above all in the competition for government contracts or in the allocation of subcontracts in the major industries of housing, harbour, motorway, and road construction, in tourist towns and in the transport sector.

A second competitive advantage is that mafia enterprises can count on reduced labour costs, in that they evade social security contributions, pay no overtime and prevent trade union activities; in short, they intimidate not only the competition, but also the workers.

A third advantage is the considerable financial resources at their disposal, which do not come from the accumulation of the usual profits or from bank loans for which interest would have to be paid, but from illegal activities outside the legal business sector (first from cigarette, and later from drug, smuggling).

In addition to the use of violence, a further traditional element which is foreign to modern capitalism, is the organisation of mafia enterprises on a basis of blood relationships, a type of 'family communism' with common ownership and without clear separation of the finances of the family and the business. The business relationship spans continents – efficiently reducing the cost of transactions – via family contacts.

Also characteristic of the mafia style of business is that the enterprising *mafioso* is only interested in fast wealth for which he does not have to work, but gains through a few speculative operations. He takes enormous risks and is constantly under the threat of death or prison. As quickly as he earns his fortune in these cases, he (and also the family) loses it.

Considering the mostly humble beginnings of the *mafiosi* of today, as of the past, the fascination with power and with money is understandable. One may presume, though, that with successful *mafiosi* we are taking a selection of personalities for whom risk has not only a functional, but also an expressive value, a very particular fascination. A sort of implicit existential philosophy is expressed in the answer to the question of a judge, whether the life of the *mafioso* Salvatore Inzerillo had been worthwhile, as he had to die so young:

Inzerillo dies at 37. That is true. But his 37 years are like 80 of any normal person. Inzerillo lived well. He got a lot out of life. Others will not even have one hundredth of these things. It's not a sin to die so young when one has done, experienced and had all that Inzerillo did, experienced and was able to have. He did not die weary of life or dissatisfied. He died satisfied. That is the difference.[27]

According to Max Weber's terminology, the *mafioso* is an adventure capitalist, occupied in the 'acquisition of capital as an adventure' and full of 'that ethos of adventure which scorns the barriers of ethics'. And the field of business in which the mafia entrepreneur is active, is that of adventure capitalism 'which is oriented around political opportunity and irrational speculation'.[28] Here, it is the construction and transport areas in which there are unusual financial opportunities for parasitic profits through particular political conditions, namely state and EC development funds and government contracts, and, of course, the drug market, in which prohibition pushes the risks and the profits into the realm of fantasy.

But I repeat that the economic activity of a *mafioso* is a secondary factor. His position and connections as a *mafioso* are very helpful in the process, but he does not carry on this financial activity as a *mafioso*. This is particularly clear in drug dealing. All the *pentiti* have stressed that the involvement in drug dealing is not a matter for *cosche* or for the *Cosa Nostra*, but rather a private matter of individual *uomini d'onore* in which they also regularly work with non-mafia people. The business of the *cosche* is, as mentioned, the power over a territory and, in that sense, mafia is something different and more than organised crime in the current sense (it is more the initial target of criminal prosecution to reduce it to that).

THE LAST 20 YEARS: MAFIA IN CRISIS?

The events of the past 20 or so years indicate success in weakening the power of the *mafiosi*. In this context, four points stand out: the rigorous criminal prosecution; the mafia's counterproductive reign of terror; the increasing number of *mafiosi* who break the *omertà* and give evidence; and, finally, the disintegration of the *partito* networks.

Criminal prosecution in the 1960s and 1970s presented a picture which was little different from the past. People under arrest had constantly to be released because the period of custody had expired; defendants were acquitted for lack of evidence or because judgments were quashed by higher authorities; and there were hardly any witnesses or confessed culprits.[29] The Antimafia Commission put out a voluminous report, the potential sharpness of much of which was blocked through the influence of Christian Democrats. Only the report of the minority group led by the Sicilian communist Member of Parliament, Pio La Torre, picked out the interweaving of mafia and politics as a central theme but, it being an era of anti-communism, this achieved no results.

In the early 1980s, several assassinations of police officers involved in drug investigations, the murder of La Torre and the bloody disputes between the *cosche* put pressure on the state to take action. In 1982, Carlo Alberto Dalla Chiesa, the Carabinieri general who had become a symbol of police efficiency through his successes against the Red Brigades, was appointed prefect of the province of Palermo. This appointment was probably only intended as a gesture, because the special powers initially granted to him were later withdrawn, and he felt increasingly hampered and isolated in his work.[30] However, he soon succeeded in becoming an embarrassment nevertheless, particularly because he immediately took on the dangerous subject of the mafia and had four dossiers put together: one on the allocation of public building contracts, by the mayors in the cities and towns in the province; a second about *cosche* disputes, by the police; a third about drug trafficking, by the Carabinieri; and fourth, from the *Guardie di Finanza* (Customs and Tax police), he ordered a dossier on the sources of wealth of 3,192 suspicious individuals and the business methods of newly-established banks that had sprung up in Sicily.

Moves in these directions were too threatening for the *mafiosi* and their collaborators. After 100 days in office, Dalla Chiesa was shot dead, together with his wife and a bodyguard. The public outrage was enormous. The government immediately appointed a 'High Commissioner for the fight against the mafia terror', with far-reaching special powers to bring together civil and police forces. In a few days, the Antimafia Law which Pio La Torre had introduced two years earlier was passed in parliament. It was aimed specifically at mafia organisations (and was the first time the word 'mafia' appeared in the Criminal Code); made the membership of such an organisation or the exploitation of advantages through cooperation with *mafiosi* a punishable offence; and allowed the confiscation of illegal earnings. Within a few years, numerous leading figures were arrested and hundreds of billions of lire confiscated under this law. In Palermo, a famous pool of judges was founded, among whom Rocco Chinici, Giovanni Falcone and Paolo Borsellino became well-known. This pool led the so-called Maxi-Trial in 1986 and 1987 against 187 *mafiosi*, which ended with their being sentenced to several thousand years' gaol. There were setbacks. The pool of judges was later disbanded, judges were transferred and the verdicts of the Maxi-Trial were quashed by the First Criminal Division of the Court of Appeals on technicalities (although later reaffirmed, in 1992). But, in general, the process of rigorous criminal prosecution was carried on and then intensified again after the murders of Judges Falcone and Borsellino (both in 1992). Special public prosecution authorities were established in the provinces, as well as a national prosecution centre, the *Direzione Nazionale Antimafia*, formed as a specialised police corps modelled on the FBI. The most recent successes of these forces are astounding and arrests have come thick and fast since the end of 1992. Among those arrested in 1993 were the victorious bosses of the 1981–83 mafia war, Salvatore Riina and Nitto Santapaola, who had both been untraceable for a decade (although apparently always present in their territory). Finally, in 2006, Bernardo Provenzano, the last of the great traditional *capi-mafia*, was arrested not far from his home-town of Corleone after more than 20 years of hiding right on 'his' territory.

The other points mentioned previously are closely connected to the rigorous prosecution. Thus, in the last decade the mafia terror against politicians who had become dangerous to them (for example, the regional president Piersanti Mattarella or the opposition politicians Reina and La Torre); or who obviously could no longer carry out their promises (for example, the Sicilian Christian Democrat and European Parliament MP Salvo Lima or the Christian Democrat financier Ignazio Salvo); and above all, against officials from the justice and police systems (such as Chinici, Falcone, Borsellino and other judges and public prosecutors, along with a whole range of police officers and their respective escorts), has increased in a way that would previously have been unimaginable. This terror can be partly explained by the fact that the state intervenes more efficiently and that the results of judicial intervention have become more serious. Very long gaol sentences are to be expected now, and in the process, a wide range of financial interests are seriously threatened. As the functioning of the state apparatus is dependent upon the employment of decisive and effective individuals, attempts are made to physically eliminate them and thereby to sabotage investigations and judicial proceedings (and at the same time, to deter others from effective work). Terror, however, is clearly a sign of weakness: what would previously have been manipulated through *partito* connections must these days be attempted with counterproductive violence.

Terror on the one hand, and state efficiency on the other, have led to the phenomenon of the so-called *pentitismo*, which formerly scarcely existed and which today takes place on an astounding scale. The first *pentiti* were members of *cosche* defeated in the mafia war, whose families were wiped out by the Corleonesi and who saw no way to save themselves other than to give themselves over to the protection of the state and collaborate (and in the process avoid the danger from that quarter of a long prison term). In the struggle against the leftist terrorism of the 1970s and 1980s the state had had positive experiences with crown witnesses, offering them reduction of sentences and protection; concessions to repentant *mafiosi* now went significantly further. The state granted not only considerably reduced sentences but a special department of the Interior Ministry also guaranteed the protection of the *pentito* and the members of his family, supporting them practically and financially to begin a new life with a new identity in new surroundings. More than 2,500 *mafiosi* and their family members profited from the protection and help programme of the Ministry of the Interior. The *pentiti* became an effective tool. The greatest number of state successes in recent years, hundreds of arrests and the confiscation of many thousand billion lire in the late 1990s, were all due to the skilful use of this tool.

Rigorous criminal prosecution, mafia terror and *pentitismo* led in turn to the disintegration of the *partiti*, the networks of *mafiosi* and their allies in politics and the state apparatus. Cooperation with *mafiosi* has become very dangerous for politicians, public servants and entrepreneurs. The Corleonesi have proven that they were not afraid to kill those who do not keep their promises. And keeping promises, influencing the state bureaucracies and law enforcement on behalf of the *mafiosi*, has become much more difficult since the Anti-Mafia Law has been enforced more rigorously and an increasing number of *pentiti* incriminate their former collaborators. In the 1990s, there were legal proceedings against more than 40 Sicilian politicians, among them a former minister, a senator, four members of the national parliament and a dozen members of regional parliaments, as well as mayors and aldermen, against judges like Domenico Signorino (who, after being incriminated in testimonies, committed suicide); against the former Palermo Police Commissioner Bruno Contrada, as well as a whole range of entrepreneurs, among them members of the abovementioned Costanzo family from Catania; and even against such a prominent figure like Giulio Andreotti, numerous times Prime Minister of the national government.

Various other factors have helped in the process of disintegration of the *partiti*. The involvement in drug trafficking, for instance, strengthened the financial power of the *mafiosi* but has undermined their traditional ideological legitimacy. Action groups such as the Sicilian Women Against the Mafia worked in the same direction. And with the end of the Soviet bloc and the communist threat, an essential legitimisation of ties with, and support of, powers which were not quite legal but at least anti-communist, was gone, as was a valuable excuse with which all criticism from the left could be dismissed as communist propaganda. Furthermore, for a while anti-mafia campaigns were connected with the broad anti-corruption movement *Operazione Mani Pulite* (Operation Clean Hands), which the Milan Public Prosecutor Di Pietro started with his investigations into cases of bribery and which has shaken and revolutionised the whole traditional political system.

With the rise of the Berlusconi government, the momentum of those changes has stopped or at least has taken directions which let the optimism of the early 1990s evaporate.[31] As far as the mafia phenomenon is concerned, the situation is unclear, and about the future one can only conjecture. Did the crisis of the 1990s really lead to the end of the mafia as a power structure and reduce it to simple organised crime? Or did the arrest of the leaders of the Corleonesi perhaps indicate that an internal opposition has gained the upper hand (and handed over its opponents)? Is there a trend inside the *cosche* which manoeuvres more carefully than the brutal Corleonesi, avoids provocation and wants to forge new *partito* networks with new people in the state apparatus? Will Italy split into three relatively independent regions and will the *cosche* in the south thereby gain more room to move in a less disturbing environment? Will Lampedusa, after all, be right in the end with his conviction that Sicilians always tend to *cambiare tutto per non cambiare nulla*?

NOTES

1. The early history of the myth of the secret society is documented in Henner Hess, *Mafia and Mafiosi: Origin, Power and Myth* (New York: New York University Press, 1998), pp. 99–107.
2. The typical career of a *mafioso* is described in detail in Hess, *Mafia and Mafiosi*, pp. 47–78.
3. The name *cosca* likens the *mafioso* to the trunk, and the men grouped around him to the leaves, of an artichoke. In addition to this term there are a number of others, such as *sodalizio, fratellanza, famiglia, compagnia, associazione, aggregato, cerchio* and *paracu*, but none of these is as good a visual simile of the true relationships and as much in use.
4. Cf. Christopher Duggan, *Fascism and the Mafia* (New Haven, London: Yale University Press, 1989), pp. 95–270.
5. In the early 1990s, the Sicilians' share is said to have declined to 5 per cent. Cf. Giovanni Falcone (with Marcelle Padovani), *Mafia intern* (München: Knaur 1993), pp. 126–34.
6. See, for example, Hess, *Mafia and Mafiosi*, Chapter 7.
7. For the entire section, see Alfonso Madeo (ed.), *Testo integrale della Relazione della Commissione d'inchiesta sul fenomeno della mafia* (Roma: Cooperativa scrittori, 1973); Werner Raith, *Die ehrenwerte Firma: Der Weg der italienischen* Mafia *vom 'Paten' zur Industrie* (Berlin: Wagenbach, 1983); Werner Raith, 'Postfazione', in Henner Hess, *Mafia* (Roma-Bari: Laterza 1984), pp. 251–86; Werner Raith, *Mafia – Ziel Deutschland: Vom Verfall der politischen Kultur zur Organisierten Kriminaliät* (Köln: Kösler, 1989); Pino Arlacchi, *Mafiose Ethik und der Geist des Kapitalismus: Die unternehmerische Mafia* (Frankfurt/Main: Cooperative Verlag, 1989); Werner Raith, *Parasiten und Patrone: Siziliens Mafia greift nach der Macht* (Frankfurt: Fischer Taschenbuch, 1992). Continuity in spite of all change is emphasised also in Diego Gambetta, *La mafia siciliana: Un'industria della protezione privata* (Torino: Einaudi, 1992) and Falcone, *Mafia intern*. Regarding mafia-like phenomena in Calabria and Puglia, see Pino Arlacchi, *Mafia, contadini e latifondo nella Calabria tradizionale: Le strutture elementari del sottosviluppo* (Bologna: Il mulino, 1980); James Walston, *See Naples and Die: Organized Crime in Campania*, in Robert J. Kelley (ed.), *Organized Crime: A Global Perspective* (Totowa, NJ: Rowman and Littlefield, 1986), pp. 134–58; Enzo Ciconte, *'Ndrangheta dall'unità a oggi* (Roma-Bari: Laterza, 1992). For developments in the United States, see Frances A.J. and Elisabeth A. Ianni, *Family Business* (London: Routledge and Kegan Paul, 1972); Dwight C. Smith Jr., *The Mafia Mystique* (New York: Basic Books, 1975); Peter Reuter, *Disorganized Crime: The Economics of the Invisible Hand* (Cambridge, MA: MIT Press, 1983); Alan A. Block, *East Side, West Side: Organized Crime in New York* (New Brunswick, NJ:

Transaction Publishers, 1983); Jay S. Albanese, *Organized Crime in America*, 2nd edn (Cincinatti: Anderson Publishing, 1989); James B. Jacobs, *Busting the Mob: United States vs. Cosa Nostra* (New York: New York University Press, 1994); James B. Jacobs, *Gotham Unbound: How New York City was Liberated from the Grip of Organized Crime* (New York: New York University Press, 1999); and James B. Jacobs, *Mobsters, Unions and Feds: The Mafia and the American Labor Movement* (New York: New York University Press, 2006).

8. Cf. Raith, *Postfazione*, pp. 271ff.; Arlacchi, *Mafiose Ethik und der Geist des Kapitalismus*, pp. 135–43, 197.

9. Pino Arlacchi, *Gli uomini del disonore: La mafia siciliana nella vita del grande pentito Antonino Calderone* (Milano: Mondadori, 1992), p. 149.

10. Cf. ibid., pp. 154ff., 215–32, 246.

11. Cf. ibid., pp. 175–214.

12. Falcone, *Mafia intern*, p. 88.

13. Cf. Luciano Violante, *La forza della mafia non è nella mafia*, in *Mafia: Anatomia di un regime*, Autori vari (Roma: Librerie associate, 1992), pp. 113–18, among others. At the end of 1992, charges were brought against 350 members of Freemason Lodges for supporting mafia organisations. Cf. Observatoire Géopolitique des Drogues, *La drogue – nouveau désordre mondial* (Paris: Hachette, 1993), p. 185. Incidentally, the Catholic Church played a most inglorious role in this humus in that it accepted the *mafiosi* as loyal servants and sponsors of religious celebrations and, thus, helped to legitimise the position of the *mafiosi*. This attitude has a long tradition, as from 1870 (the year of the conquest of Rome by the young kingdom of Italy) up until Mussolini's concordate with the Vatican in 1929, the Church was an adversary of the liberal state. And since the end of the Second World War, the Church was bound to the Christian Democrats who, in turn, relied on mafia connections. Only recently have the high clergy been able to make the decision to publicly pass judgement on the doings of the mafia. Cf. Gambetta, *La mafia siciliana*, pp. 52–61. On 'P2', see Ganser, this volume.

14. For this differentiation, see Donald Cressey, 'Foreword', in Hess, *Mafia and Mafiosi*. In *Fascism and the Mafia*, Duggan has again, with a great deal of material and strong arguments, dissected the theory of the mafia as one big secret society: Duggan, *Fascism and the Mafia*, particularly pp. 15–91. He has also analysed the functions of this theory: to simplify the interpretation of complicated courses of events on an island which was so difficult to govern; to stigmatise subcultural rival powers; to justify central state repression and to explain the failure of police, the justice system and government by reference to a sinister and perfectly-organised enemy.

15. Cf. Arlacchi, *Gli uomini del disonore*, pp. 21–7 and 52–61; Falcone, *Mafia intern*, pp. 94f.; Gambetta, *La mafia siciliana*, pp. 150f., 366–72.

16. Cf. only the numerous relevant statements of Calderone in Arlacchi, *Gli uomini del disonore*, pp. 22, 38, 57f., 105–7, 125f., 270f., and so on. Regarding the discrepancy between theory and reality in the organisational structure of the Red Brigades, a good parallel case, see Henner Hess, *La rivolta ambigua: Storia sociale del terrorismo italiano* (Firenze: Sansoni, 1991), pp. 113f.

17. '…come l'hanno definita i guidici che mi hanno interrogato', says Calderone. Arlacchi, *Gli uomini del disonore*, p. 83. Re. the popularity of *The Godfather*, see also pp. 23, 161. Re. whole argument, mainly Gambetta, *La mafia siciliana*, pp. 178–218.

18. Cf. Arlacchi, *Gli uomini del disonore*, pp. 122–37. In illegal circumstances, larger organisations generally cause larger difficulties and risks and the tendency towards smaller enterprises is encouraged. As to the problems and the downfall of the Neapolitan *Nuova Camorra Organizzata* under Cutolo, which grew too quickly and was too large, or the Bontade *cosca* in Palermo, two good examples of this theory, see Gambetta, *La mafia siciliana*, pp. 134, 341.

19. Cf. Charles Tilly, *War Making and State Making as Organized Crime*, in Peter P. Evans, Dietrich Rueschemeyer and Theda Skocpol (eds), *Bringing the State Back In* (Cambridge: Cambridge University Press, 1985), pp. 169–91.

20. Arlacchi, *Gli uomini del disonore*, pp. 187f.

21. Falcone, *Mafia intern*, p. 137.

22. Translated from Max Weber, *Wirtschaft und Gesellschaft: Grundriss der verstehenden Soziologie*, 5th edn (Tübingen: JCB Mohr, 1976), pp. 114f.

23. Cf. Reuter, *Disorganized Crime*, pp. 109–31, Arlacchi, *Mafiose Ethik und der Geist des Kapitalismus*, pp. 244f., Gambetta, *La mafia siciliana*, pp. 333–43.

24. The *mafioso* guards this reputation, is himself convinced of its veracity and sets it against, for instance, the dishonourable behaviour of politicians: 'It is hard for a politician to become an *uomo d'onore*. Within the Cosa Nostra there is a strong dislike of politicians because they cannot be trusted, because they do not keep their promises, because they constantly play the smart alec. They are false people without principles.' Calderone in Arlacchi, *Gli uomini del disonore*, pp. 208f.

25. Roberto Scarpinato, *Mafia et politica*, in *Mafia: Anatomia di un regime*, Autori vari (Roma: Librerie associate, 1992), pp. 89–112 at 94.

26. Cf. Arlacchi, *Mafiose Ethik und der Geist des Kapitalismus*.

27. Quoted in ibid., p. 132.

28. Quotations translated from Max Weber, *Die protestantische Ethik und der Geist des Kapitalismus*, in *Gesammelte Aufsätze zur Religionssoziologie*, 7th edn, Band 1 (Tübingen: JCB Mohr, 1978), pp. 17–206 at 43 and 61.

29. The percentage of murders resolved is extraordinarily low in Italy by comparison to all industrialised nations; it amounted to 51.8 per cent in 1986 and only 29.3 per cent in 1990 (in Germany in the same year it was 94 per cent). Unsolved acts of violence in southern Italy make up a significant proportion of these figures. Cf. *L'Espresso*, 25 October 1992, p. 45.

30. Cf. the book of his son, Nando Dalla Chiesa, *Der Palazzo und die Mafia: Die italienische Gesellschaft und die Ermordung des Präfekten Alberto Dalla Chiesa* (Köln: Förtner und Kroemer, 1985), an indictment of the Palazzo, the corrupt political caste. The case demonstrates in all clarity how differently the struggle against terrorism and the struggle against mafia are conducted.

31. Berlusconi himself, with all his manoeuvres, seems, for years now, only just one step ahead of the Public Prosecutor.

9
Drugs, Anti-communism and Extra-legal Repression in Mexico

Peter Dale Scott

The interaction between a government or society and a narcosystem[1] is an engagement between a known system and a relatively unknown one, between a well-defined entity and a relatively amorphous milieu. In such a situation, language is inevitably biased towards narrating the interaction from the perspective of the documented government or society. Thus in practice we tend to say that (for example) 'Mexico has a narcosystem (or narco-economy)'. But of course the verb 'has' here is misleading. There is also a sense in which one could say, 'the narcosystem has a government'. Here too the verb 'has' does not begin to capture the complexity of the interaction.

In the case of Mexico, a single narcosystem 'has' (in this misleading sense) two or more governments. It has been shown to be capable of influencing the United States government – at times notoriously, as when it proved impossible for Washington to act meaningfully against the drug bank, Bank of Credit and Commerce International (BCCI). By the 1980s, however, it can be argued that the narcosystem had come close to controlling the Mexican government, and that is the picture I shall present in this chapter.

THE PROBLEM OF DRUGS IN MEXICO

It is difficult in America to write authoritatively about Mexican politics. Even in the last decade, when it has become more fashionable to write about Mexico as a 'narco-democracy', few, if any, authors address the American share of responsibility for the staggering corruption that has afflicted Mexican politics.[2]

In this chapter, I shall attempt to describe how the US came to be allied with the drug traffic in Mexico in opposing left-wing political movements – much as it did in the same period in France and Italy. The key was a triarchic situation in which the Mexican drug traffic came to be partly managed and protected by the Mexican Federal Security Directorate (DFS); and the DFS in turn was partly managed and protected by its sister organisation, the Central Intelligence Agency (CIA).

173

I do not wish to suggest that Washington fully controlled this course of events. The DFS was not simply a CIA asset. However it could not have operated with impunity for as long as it did without ongoing CIA protection for its illegalities. And the CIA presence in the DFS became so dominant that some of its intelligence was seen only by American eyes, according to the famous Mexican journalist Manuel Buendía.[3]

Let me begin with a few facts not widely remembered. Mexican illegal drug traffic began around 1914 and grew out of three events, only one of which was Mexican. The first was the Mexican Revolution, which 'brought disorder and ungovernability to northern Mexico at about the same time that drug trafficking was outlawed in the United States'.[4] The second was the Chinese Revolution, in which one faction, the Kuomintang (KMT), was financed in part by global trafficking. This was done chiefly by Chinese secret societies, or *tongs*, in many nations, including Mexico and the United States.[5] The third, of course, was the passage of the Harrison Anti-Narcotics Act of 1914.

At first most of those involved in the Mexican drug traffic 'were Mexican residents of Chinese origin, although they were not the only ones'.[6] Their opium probably crossed the border in both directions. In 1931, a Mexican official reported his

> conclusion that the direction of the trafficking was more from the United States to Mexico than vice versa and that both he and [US] narcotics supervisor Harvey Smith thought that the large-scale traffickers resided north of the border.[7]

In the same year, a leader of a coast-to-coast Chinese *tong* in America, the Hip Sing, was arrested in a major drug bust that also netted the wife of Thomas Pennachio, Lucky Luciano's partner.[8]

Mexico was a traditional source of opium for medicines, American patent medicines, and eventually for supplementing shipments of illegal opium from Asia.[9] But Mexican production increased with the interruption of Chinese opium exports after 1937. At the same time, the KMT received more US protection and support from President Roosevelt. During and after the Second World War, the US consciously used drug lords like Lucky Luciano and their access to violence as assets, eventually to combat communism, especially communist China. We shall see that in Mexico too, the US used both the Mexican DFS and their drug traffickers as assets for violence against the Latin American left.

CIA protection for the DFS ended in 1985, after the DFS was implicated in the murder of a DEA agent. But the institutional arrangements of the drugs–DFS–CIA triarchy survived, at least into the administrations of Carlos Salinas de Gortari (1989–95) and his successor Ernest Zedillo (1995–2001). To this day, these sordid connections are still mostly unmentioned in America.[10]

THE LEGACY OF THE DFS AND EXTRA-LEGAL REPRESSION

Though the DFS was closed down in 1985, its legacy has survived. When Carlos Salinas de Gortari became President of Mexico in 1989, the American press was almost unanimous in praising him. However, one of the few dissenters, Andrew

Reding at the World Policy Institute, pointed to Salinas' appointment of Fernando Gutiérrez Barrios to the position of secretary of government (Mexico's Ministry of the Interior).

Gutiérrez's public career originated in the Federal Security Directorate (DFS), an intelligence agency of the Secretariat of Government, where he rose through the ranks to become director in 1964. He was thus in charge of the DFS at the time of the 1968 massacre of several hundred peaceful student protesters in the Plaza of the Three Cultures (Tlatelolco), an event as deeply seared in the Mexican national consciousness as the Tienanmen massacre in the Chinese psyche.[11]

Reding then described the 'variety of specialized police and intelligence agencies [that] emerged under the aegis of the Secretariat of Government'.

The most notorious of these agencies was the Federal Intelligence Directorate [Dirección Federal de Seguridad] (DFS), and its most notorious directors were Fernando Gutiérrez Barrios (1964–1970), Javier García Paniagua (1970–1976), and Miguel Nazar Haro (1976–1981). [...] The Gutiérrez–García–Nazar triumvirate was...the force behind the formation of the White Brigade, a clandestine paramilitary police unit that was responsible for the 'disappearance' of thousands of opponents of the regime between 1972 and 1980, of which more than 500 never reappeared.[12]

This is, all in all, a rather depressing insight into a country where the American FBI, army intelligence and CIA have exerted more influence (and for a long time maintained larger staffs) than anywhere else in the world. The CIA can be shown to have used its influence not to promote democracy and the public state, but to support and protect the countervailing, and largely extra-legal, 'deep state' of top-down repression. So, for example, Gutiérrez himself was, like other DFS officials, a high-level CIA asset, with the cryptonym LITEMPO-4.[13]

THE DFS, THE CIA AND DRUG TRAFFICKERS

From its beginnings in 1947, the DFS, set up with FBI assistance, developed a more and more institutional relationship with drug traffickers, whose own cadres supplied recruits for off-the-books governmental violence.[14] By the 1980s, possession of a DFS card was recognised by DEA agents as a 'license to traffic' in drugs.[15]

Using their DFS credentials as shields, agents regularly escorted narcotics shipments through Mexico and provided other services, frequently even selling seized narcotics to favored organizations. Later intelligence showed that the DFS embarked on an ambitious project to organize protection on a national scale, bringing as much of the nation as possible under a unified system.[16]

When DEA agent Enrique Camarena was murdered in Mexico in 1985, the subsequent investigation produced abundant testimony that the CIA, as well as the DFS, was protecting the top traffickers who were responsible.[17]

The DFS was nominally closed down in the wake of Camarena's murder and other drug scandals. The last two DFS Chiefs were both indicted and eventually convicted: Miguel Nazar Haro in San Diego, for smuggling stolen cars; and José Antonio Zorrilla Perez in Mexico, for the 1984 murder of the investigative journalist Manuel Buendía.[18] A new agency was created, the General Directorate of Political and Social Investigations, but it continued to issue protective badges to high-level traffickers.[19]

Both the FBI and CIA intervened to protest the 1981 indictment of Nazar Haro, claiming that Nazar was 'an essential repeat essential contact for CIA station in Mexico City', on matters of 'terrorism, intelligence, and counterintelligence'.[20] When Associate Attorney General Lowell Jensen refused to proceed with Nazar's indictment, the San Diego US Attorney, William Kennedy, publicly exposed their intervention and was promptly fired.[21]

A pilot, Werner Lotz, testified that Contras were being trained on a ranch near Veracruz that was owned by the DFS-protected kingpin Rafael Caro Quintero.[22] Lotz and other eyewitnesses also spoke of money passed to the Contras from Caro's partner Miguel Félix Gallardo.[23] Their associate in Honduras, Juan Ramón Matta Ballesteros, owned an airline, SETCO, which was picked by the CIA to be the main supply link to Contra camps on the Honduras–Nicaraguan border.[24]

In other words the CIA, as well as the Mexican government, was consciously drawing on Mexican drug-traffickers and their protectors as off-the-books assets, just as it was also doing in the 1980s in Afghanistan. Thus a hierarchy of untouchability was established, by which traffickers were protected and assisted by the DFS and both, in turn, were protected by elements in the CIA.

Mexican intelligence underwent a second reorganisation in the wake of the DFS scandals, out of which emerged the Center for Investigations and National Security (CISEN). Even after the fall of the PRI from power in 2000, CISEN's reputation was only a little less tarnished than that of its predecessor the DFS.[25] And the fact of continuing CISEN collaboration with the CIA and FBI was admitted in 2004, in connection with unpopular security procedures after 9/11.[26]

With the election of Vicente Fox in 2000, there were hopes that Mexico was beginning to emerge into a less corrupt and violent era. The presence of big drug cartels has, however, clearly survived the fall of the PRI, and some observers have predicted that 'Mexico is becoming the next Colombia.'[27] In 2006, there were reports that CISEN was fighting a 'dirty war' in Chiapas and Guerrero that was reminiscent of the 1960s.[28] Meanwhile, the *Los Angeles Times* reported

Hundreds of killings in Mexico in the last year are linked to the war between the Gulf cartel…and a Sinaloa-based group headed by Joaquin 'El Chapo' Guzman and Ismael 'El Mayo' Zambada… The country's brutal drug war has increasingly been marked by the use of hand grenades, large-caliber assault weapons and paramilitary-style attacks. Police and prosecutors are not simply killed, they are beheaded and put on public display.[29]

THE MEXICAN TRAFFIC, US ORGANISED CRIME AND THE CIA

The CIA's involvement with drug traffickers in Southeast Asia was largely disclosed in the 1970s, when the US disengaged from the region and the CIA distanced itself from its drug assets there.[30] Meanwhile in Mexico in the same period, drug trafficking, related state violence and CIA involvement all radically increased. There have been no comparable revelations of CIA involvement with drug traffickers in Mexico and Latin America,[31] but once again we can safely say that those at the very highest level of responsibility have been immune from prosecution.

After the Second World War, Mexico was a principal way-station in the smuggling of international opium and heroin into the US and Canada.[32] The Mexican traffic in the postwar years took place in a milieu that was from its outset dominated by important international players like the American Meyer Lansky, and they enjoyed a de facto immunity from the consequences of past collaborations with intelligence networks.[33]

Alfred W. McCoy, one of our best authorities on drug traffic, suggests a different picture. Describing Lansky's postwar entrance into the Mexican milieu through his Mexico City representative, Harold Meltzer, McCoy writes that 'Meltzer failed dismally in his bid to make Mexico a major supplier of opiates for American addicts.'[34] McCoy adds that Meltzer's group 'lacked Luciano's contacts...and Lansky's finances'.[35]

This is not what we learn from Meltzer's Federal Bureau of Narcotics (FBN) biographies and Alan A. Block. The former tell us that Meltzer was an associate of Meyer Lansky and 'a major figure in the organized underworld', who, outside the continental US, frequented 'Canada, Mexico, Cuba, Hong Kong, Japan, Hawaii and the Philippines'.[36] Block writes that Meltzer was 'reportedly bankrolled' by Lansky and Nig Rosen, in a wide-reaching syndicate stretching from Mexico City to Havana, New York and Los Angeles.[37] There are in fact numerous official references at this time to a coast-to-coast drug ring involving both Havana and representatives in Mexico City.[38]

McCoy's chief evidence that Meltzer failed is Meltzer's arrest (and subsequent conviction) in 1949, but in this period of violent syndicate reorganisation, there were many arrests, and even murders, of key players – notably that of Lansky's former intimate friend, Bugsy Siegel (an important figure in the postwar Mexican traffic who is overlooked by McCoy). Thus arrests by themselves tell us little. Luciano was arrested and jailed in 1936, but clearly remained a dominant figure in the international narcotics underworld until his death in Naples in 1962.[39]

The CIA regarded Meltzer, like Luciano earlier, as a potential off-the-books asset. Around 1960, CIA officer William Harvey, assembling a file of potential assets for a CIA assassination capacity (ZR/RIFLE), included Meltzer as a candidate.[40] At the time Meltzer was 'a longtime collaborator and sometime shooter for [John] Rosselli', the central figure in the CIA's mafia assassination plots against Fidel Castro.[41]

Like McCoy, Peter Lupsha once belittled the Mexican drug traffic in the 1940s. He depicted it as still controlled by regional *bandidos*, each dominating their local civic plaza, before 'the need for upper-world political connections increased'.[42] A diametrically opposed viewpoint is expressed by Luís Astorga – that 'high-ranking politicians' have been connected to the Mexican drug traffic since its origins over a century ago.[43]

Astorga claims further that, from the outset, 'the majority of influential traffickers who were not members of the political class were political protégés, not the politician's godfathers or controllers'.[44] It seems likely that before 1947, and the creation of the DFS, these relationships existed chiefly at the provincial level, especially in northern Mexico.[45]

Thus we can say that whereas in Asia the CIA helped to create and encourage the local intelligence–drug connections of the 1950s, in Mexico it largely inherited them.[46]

THE ORIGINS OF THE CIA–DFS–DRUGS TRIARCHY

There is general agreement, however, that with the US-assisted creation of the DFS in 1947

> a structural linkage was instituted between the ruling political class and the drug traffickers. Its work was to be twofold: on the one hand, it ensured that part of the profits was levied in exchange for protection; on the other, it served as a mechanism for containing violence and any political temptations on the part of the traffickers.[47]

The brains behind the creation of the DFS, President Alemán's friend and adviser Colonel Carlos I. Serrano, was himself connected to the drug traffic. As we learn from Professor Barry Carr, the prime purpose of the DFS was not to contain drug violence, but on the contrary to manage it and unleash violence against the pro-communist left:

> The most important of the new organizations created by Alemán was the National Security Directorate or Dirección Federal de Seguridad (DFS) which was the brainchild of one of the president's best known and most notorious advisors, Colonel Carlos Serrano. The DFS was modelled on the FBI, and 'engaged in telephone tapping with equipment provided with the assistance of the FBI'. In mid 1947 it employed FBI instructors in the training of nine recruits from the Military Academy attached to the new Security Police. The DFS retained a number of functions previously entrusted to other intelligence wings of the Ministry of the Interior, and one of its major responsibilities was to conduct surveillance of 'dissident' activities in the labor movement and on the Left, an activity which was well under way by the middle of 1947. It is no coincidence that the attack on the headquarters of the Mexican Railway Workers Union (STFRM) in October 1948, the first successful attempt to crush a powerful union, was carried out by elements of the DFS under the personal command of Carlos Serrano. The anti-communist campaign was personally directed by Senator Carlos A. Serrano, a friend of Alemán.[48]

The US Embassy in Mexico City became split over the use of the DFS and drug traffickers as anti-communist assets. The State Department and military attaché denounced the DFS for its drug involvement but the CIA did not.

The drug trafficking of Carlos Serrano was mentioned in a confidential State Department report of 4 September 1947, from the assistant military attaché. It listed Serrano, DFS Director Marcelino Inurreta and Deputy Director 'Lt. Col. Manuel Magoral' (Maj. Manuel Mayoral García) as being involved in drug trafficking.

> The report stated that Magoral controlled marijuana trafficking in Mexico City. It recorded the suspicion that these individuals requested information from the U.S. government and used it to get rid of their competition and control the business... The American military attaché [Maurice C. Holden] compared the DFS to the Gestapo because of the powers it had been given and the extremely dubious background of those persons recruited to form it.[49]

Holden's assessment was soon corroborated by events. In 1949, a self-exiled Mexican journalist in Los Angeles, Rafael García Travesi, reported in his newspaper that Col. Serrano's automobile had been seized in the United States while transporting a shipment of opiates.[50] The newly-formed DFS promptly arranged for the arrest and deportation of García Travesi to Mexico, where he was imprisoned on trumped-up bigamy charges until the end of the Alemán presidency.[51]

All this happened before the new CIA Mexico City station filed a secret CIA report in 1951 on the six intelligence services in Mexico. Of the six, the CIA report *preferred* the DFS, even though some of its personnel were recognised to have abused their power to conduct 'illegal activities such as the contraband of narcotics'. In a biographical annex, Serrano, who 'organized and controlled the DFS' was described as 'unscrupulous, involved in illegal activities, including narcotics'. Despite these concessions, the CIA report preferred the 'competent and capable' personnel of the DFS over competing agencies.[52]

Drug traffickers are of course notoriously 'competent and capable' at tasks which fall within the purview of the CIA, as opposed to the State Department. In the years to come, the CIA would oversee a range of covert activities, some of which were carried out by the DFS (wiretapping the Soviet and Cuban embassies), and some by the drug traffickers in Mexico themselves (such as José Egozi, a Cuban veteran of the Bay of Pigs who, in 1974, 'lined up CIA support for a right-wing plot to overthrow the Portuguese government').[53]

Between 1949 and 1985, the interdependence of the traffickers, DFS and CIA saw increasing power for all three, along with increasing political violence and increasing disparities of income (a matter to which we will return).

DID HOWARD HUNT COME TO MEXICO BECAUSE OF DRUGS?

A man widely reported to have been CIA Station Chief in 1950–51 is E. Howard Hunt, who later achieved notoriety for his role in the 1972 Watergate break-in. However the Rockefeller Commission Report, while confirming that Hunt served in the Mexico City CIA Station in 1950–51, denied that he had ever been Station Chief or Acting Station Chief. Nevertheless the CIA's favourable assessment of the drug traffickers raises the question of whether Hunt was the author. Along with Paul Helliwell, Hunt was a veteran of the Office of Strategic Services (OSS) in Kunming, China – a station that had made payments to its agents in opium. And by 1949, if not earlier, Helliwell, by now an Office of Policy Coordination (OPC) officer engaged in purchasing Civil Air Transport (the airline of General Claire Chennault, Chiang Kai-shek's ally) for the CIA, was counsel to the money-laundering bank of Meyer Lansky, mastermind of the US–Mexican drug connection.[54] Further research is needed to establish if Hunt was still part of the Helliwell cabal in government that in 1949–51 produced proprietaries for the OPC in Southeast Asia.[55]

Although Hunt had gone to Mexico on a Guggenheim Fellowship after the war, his prior government experience was not with Latin America, but with the KMT in Yunnan. It is thus perhaps relevant that the KMT was involved in the domestic Mexican opium traffic, through Chinese residents there. In 1946, the Federal Bureau of Narcotics (FBN) reported that '[i]n a recent Kuomintang Convention in Mexico City a wide solicitation of funds for the future operation of the opium trade was noted'.[56]

By the late 1940s, according to Douglas Valentine, KMT opium was again reaching the US via Mexico, thanks to the frequent trips to Mexico City of Bugsy Siegel's mistress, Virginia Hill. Hill ran a night club in Nuevo Laredo, directly across the border from Meltzer's base of operations in Laredo, Texas.[57] On her trips to Mexico, Hill travelled with Dr Margaret Chung, honorary member of the Hip Sing *tong* in San Francisco and physician to the pilots of Chennault's wartime Flying Tigers in China. Lansky, who had pre-war KMT connections, appears to have overseen this operation, since Virginia Hill moved to Mexico at Meyer Lansky's request and seduced a number of Mexico's 'top politicians, army officers, diplomats, and police officials'.[58] According to Harry Anslinger, Siegel and Virginia Hill also negotiated with Mexican politicians to finance poppy culture in the northwest part of the country.[59]

Hunt, after returning to Mexico City in 1953, created a Latin American branch there for the KMT's projected Anti-Communist League. Its first incarnation, the Asian People's Anti-Communist League (APACL), was only started in 1954 by the KMT, in alliance with South Korea and Yoshio Kodama, a Japanese war criminal and suspected drug trafficker released in 1950 to work with the CIA and US General Willoughby.[60] But Ting Tsuo-shou, an assistant to the KMT's drug-trafficking Gen. Li Mi in Burma, was trying as early as 1952 to recruit Burmese tribal delegations to the proposed League. (A Kachin contingent did eventually join.)[61]

Hunt in 1954 assembled in Mexico City a continental cast of Mexican and other Latin American right-wingers in a political coalition calling for the ouster of President Arbenz in Guatemala.[62] This group became a permanent participant in APACL conferences and, after 1966, in a larger World Anti-Communist League (WACL). Hunt's Mexican chapter in particular came under the control of a group of anti-Semitic neofascists, the Tecos, who in the 1970s developed liaisons with right-wing death squads and included DFS agents in their circle.[63]

HUNT, CLINE, SINGLAUB, HELLIWELL, LANSKY, DONOVAN: A META-GROUP?

OSS officers attached to the wartime station in Kunming (Helliwell, Hunt, Ray Cline, Lucien Conein, and Mitchell WerBell) cast a long shadow over both postwar intelligence–drug triarchies and WACL's history. In addition to Helliwell's support of the KMT drug-traffickers in Burma, and Hunt's contribution in Mexico, APACL's formation is said to have owed a large debt to Ray Cline.[64] In the late 1970s John Singlaub, another veteran of Kunming, took over WACL. Lucien Conein became a case officer of the Vietnamese officials overseeing anti-communist drug networks, first Ngo dinh Nhu and later police chief Nguyen Ngoc Loan.[65] Mitchell WerBell, who went on to develop small arms for intelligence services like the DFS, was also involved with WACL death squad patrons like Mario Sandoval Alarcón (see below) and was himself eventually indicted on drug charges.[66]

Both in Asia and in Latin America, WACL members have repeatedly been accused of drug trafficking and related activities. The most notorious of these was the so-called Bolivian 'cocaine coup' of 1980, in which a leading drug trafficker, with WACL help, briefly installed his cousin as Minister of the Interior.[67] Senate Counsel Jack Blum has described the role in the coup of the US and Argentina (using local WACL assets).

> During the Carter administration, when human rights became a public priority, we quietly encouraged other countries to act as our proxy. The Subcommittee took remarkable testimony from a former civilian employee of the Argentine military government, Leandro Sanchez-Reisse, who described their anti-communist efforts in detail. He told the Subcommittee that the Argentine military was responsible for the so called cocaine coup in Bolivia. He said the Argentine military intelligence people used the profits from their control of the Bolivian cocaine market to finance an anticommunist 'battalion' which operated all over the continent. He told the Subcommittee that he set up a money laundering operation in Fort Lauderdale to provide funds for the covert battalion. He claimed that our government assisted his efforts.[68]

A related drug bust in Florida, weeks before the coup, ended with the release of the alleged trafficker, José Roberto Gasser, without charges.[69]

Similarly WACL members in Latin America, most notoriously Mario Sandoval Alarcón of Guatemala and Roberto d'Aubuisson of El Salvador, were responsible for developing a network of death squads in Central America.[70] The former was rewarded with an invitation to Ronald Reagan's first Inaugural.

International drug trafficking becomes itself a form of social organisation, which WACL, especially in Latin America, exploited. But the use of off-the-books drug assets against the Left around the world dates back to covert US policy in the 1940s. In Marseilles in 1947, the American unionist Irving Brown worked with the Guérini brothers of the Corsican mafia to crush a communist dockers' strike, and thereby 'created the ideal environment for the growth of Marseilles' heroin laboratories'.[71] The strike-breaking tactics in Marseilles closely paralleled those of the DFS in the same year.

By 1951, if not earlier, Corsicans from Marseilles, notably Paul Mondolini (or Mondoloni) were using Mexico City as a way-station for their heroin to reach Montreal and New York.[72] Their chief Mexican contact, Jorge Moreno Chauvet (described as 'the most important Mexican trafficker' in 1964)[73] had in his network an officer of the DFS, Capt. Rafael Chavarri.[74]

Again in the same year 1947, William Donovan is said by an Italian authority to have financed the May Day massacre in Sicily, organised by the former Detroit Mafia figure Frank Coppola, in which eight people were killed and 33 wounded.[75] Frank Coppola had been recently deported to Italy, along with Lucky Luciano and more than 60 other American *mafiosi*, some of them allegedly on a US Army plane.[76] Most of them, including both Coppola and Luciano, became involved in high-level narcotics trafficking.[77] One of them, the drug trafficker Sylvestro Carolla of New Orleans, moved briefly to Acapulco in 1948 and is said to have helped Luciano establish 'criminal enterprises in Mexico'.[78]

By the 1950s there were thus triarchic power arrangements – connecting local security forces, the drug traffic and the CIA – in other countries besides Mexico, most notably Cuba, Thailand (under Phao Sriyanon), Vietnam (Ngo Dinh Nhu), Lebanon, Italy, and eventually Turkey and Pakistan.[79]

The activities of Donovan in Italy and Thailand, Helliwell in Thailand and the Bahamas, Lansky and Hunt in Southeast Asia and Mexico, and Brown in France, raise an important question. For years I assumed that these cliques and cabals were just separate projections of CIA or US parapolitical influence abroad. But now I see them as possibly something more: the first postwar meta-group, dominated by Lansky, Helliwell, and Donovan. This group was able to manipulate the resources of the drug traffic for its own ends, which were highly political, as well as (at least in Lansky's case) economic. At times, this meta-group seems to have had its own integrity and purpose, not reducible to the official goals of the US government.

DONOVAN AND THE WORLD COMMERCE CORPORATION

Many have described the private and often well-connected intelligence networks that filled the gap between the closing down of OSS in 1944 and the formation of the CIA in 1947. Alan Block writes of the uncontrollable subculture of intelligence evolving in this period, and 'the networks spinning from this subculture that were articulated by the extremely wealthy and well connected, and were not an intrinsic formal part of any government agency'.[80] Joseph Trento transmits the rumour at the time in Washington that Dulles 'was now running a private intelligence service out of an office at 44 Wall Street, using some of the biggest names in American business'.[81]

In this same postwar period, the FBI had Donovan under surveillance, suspecting 'that he had taken some steps toward formation of an anti-Communist intelligence service [on the model of] a private concern financed by oil and industries before the war'.[82] The FBI may have focused in particular on Donovan's World Commerce Corporation (WCC), an early transnational firm formed by Donovan with a number of OSS hands and backed by leading capitalists like John Keswick of Jardine Matheson, Nelson Rockefeller and John J. McCloy. Donovan's biographer describes the WCC, whose leaders included the legendary William Stephenson of British intelligence, as a 'commercial intelligence service'.[83] Undoubtedly it had its own agenda for promoting capitalism in the postwar era.[84]

The WCC also had links to the Kuomintang. Thus in early 1950, a Panama-based subsidiary of the WCC, Commerce International (China), was supplying military arms and training to Chiang Kai-shek on Taiwan, in a period when Secretary of State Acheson was not yet permitting official US support.[85] Bruce Cumings suspects that CI(C) 'may well have been a CIA proprietary company', in which case it is relevant that the CIA station responsible for Panama was Mexico City, where Hunt was stationed.[86]

Donovan, in addition, had his own personal links to the Kuomintang. In late 1949, he led a successful legal fight to prevent China's civil air fleet in Hong Kong from falling into the hands of the new Chinese People's Republic, largely because Chiang Kai-shek's ally, General Claire Chennault, wanted the planes on Taiwan 'as part of his arsenal for attacking the mainland'.[87] And in 1950, the WCC became involved in a complex manipulation of world soybean prices from which the KMT also profited.[88]

In the light of subsequent developments in the global drug traffic, particularly in the 1980s with the BCCI, I suspect we should think of the first postwar meta-group – the overlapping global operations of Hunt, Donovan, Helliwell and Lansky – as part of a historical succession of meta-groups shaping US governmental relations to the international drug traffic, often well before US government approval had been secured for these policies.

It is now generally acknowledged that the CIA, like the intelligence agencies of other great powers, has used drug traffickers as assets in virtually every continent of the globe. I once described this exploitation as an example of 'parapolitics', state covert actions and policies conducted 'not by rational debate and responsible decision-making but by indirection, collusion, and deceit'. Later I situated the role of deliberate governmental direction in the larger arena of 'deep politics', the entire field of political practices and relationships, deliberate or not, which are usually concealed rather than acknowledged.[89]

Recently I have suspected that the realm of shadows may be even more complicated. The drug collaborations of Howard Hunt and other Kunming OSS veterans – one of whom, Paul Helliwell, must be counted part of Meyer Lansky's milieu – suggests a third level, still deeper and even less documented, in which systematic conscious direction was coming from outside lawfully-constituted government. We can call this non-state parapolitics: actions and policies which are deliberate, but which are determined by groups and agencies beyond the reach of the domestic state.

Evidence for this hypothesis is very sketchy. One can, however, point to the arrival in Mexico of Mondoloni and Carolla, both associated with Luciano, shortly after an international 'roof' or protection for their activities had been established through various agencies, including the DFS.

THE MERGING OF ENFORCEMENT, TRAFFICKING AND COVERT OPS

The anti-left violence of the Mexican DFS continued after 1947. In the 1970s, DFS officials Miguel Nazar Haro and Esteban Guzman recruited and directed the Brigada Blanca, which was 'widely accused of torture and of being behind the disappearance of several thousand students and political opponents'.[90] At the same time, both men (according to a star US government witness) 'protected drug-smuggling operations and profited from the sale of seized narcotics', while serving in the DFS. Eyebrows were raised when Salinas appointed both men to the Mexico District police in 1989.[91]

The US also made use of Mexico's off-the-books drug assets. In the 1980s, the CIA, then headed by William Casey, helped protect the Mexican drug lord Miguel Félix Gallardo.[92] His pilot, Werner Lotz, told the DEA that Félix advanced him more than $150,000 to pass on to the Contras. Meanwhile Félix's Honduran supplier, Juan Ramón Matta Ballesteros, was officially estimated (according to *Newsweek*) to supply 'perhaps one-third of all the cocaine consumed in the United States'. But the CIA, and later the State Department, used Matta's airline, SETCO, to ferry supplies to the Contras, even after Matta came under investigation for his involvement in the 1985 torture and murder of DEA agent Enrique Camarena in Mexico. Both Félix and Matta were untouchable until after Congress closed down aid to the Contras in 1988.[93]

As the drug traffic proliferated under this protection, narco-corruption spread to other agencies of law enforcement, including the Mexican Federal Judicial Police (PJF or MJFP); its INTERPOL unit, which dealt with international drug trafficking; and the Federal District Police.[94] By the presidency of Carlos Salinas de Gortari in the 1990s, even 'the Attorney General's Office (PGR) [was at times] as much as 95 per cent...under narco-control. Thus, Mexico's justice agency was in reality an arm of drug trafficking, and organized crime's government intermediary.'[95]

The DFS has helped to institutionalise procedures whereby high-level drug busts are typically carried out with assistance from even higher-level traffickers. In this way Operation Condor, a Mexican anti-drug programme carried out with the help of a CIA airline, did the Guadalajara Cartel 'a great service by winnowing out the competition'.[96]

In Mexico the intelligence–drug connection continues, but no longer for the primary purpose of fighting communism. It has metastasised through many layers of society and it has become a major source of profits for the powerful, not just in Mexico, but also (as we shall see) in the US.

AN ECONOMIC OVERVIEW: INCREASING INCOME DISPARITY

There are many reasons for Mexico's colonial legacy of hopelessness, especially in the southern countryside. Of these, the chief is the gap between rich and poor, endemic for centuries in Latin America, where an over-class of Europeans destroyed native civilisations and enslaved their people.

> Latin America has always been the most unequal of the world's poorer regions. Even in 1978...the share of total income received by the poorest fifth of the population was lower than in any other region: 2.9 percent compared with 5 percent for southern Europe, 6.2 percent for East Asia, 5.3 percent for the Middle East and North Africa, and 6.2 percent for sub-Saharan Africa.[97]

American influence did not create this age-old problem, but recent decades of American capitalism have aggravated it. In Mexico, the share of the poor has been declining. The poorest 50 per cent received 20.7 per cent of national income in

1984, 18.7 per cent in 1989, 18.4 per cent in 1992 and 16 per cent in 1996.[98] The middle class also declined, from about 60 per cent of the population in the 1970s, to 35 per cent in 1995.[99]

Meanwhile the country in 1994 with the fourth-largest number of Forbes billionaires (after the US and Germany) 'was Mexico, with twenty-four. Their declared fortunes combined would represent nearly ten percent of Mexico's annual gross national product.'[100] (We shall see how a combination of drug trafficking, US market ideology and crony capitalism came to play a big role in the generation of those fortunes.)

United Nations and World Bank studies have confirmed that, outside of Africa, 'Mexico has the largest gap between rich and poor of all but six nations in the world.'[101] There is of course no way to keep this state of affairs confined within Mexico. Inevitably Mexico's dispossessed will continue to seek relief, often by immigrating illegally to the US.

MARKET FUNDAMENTALISM, CAPITAL FLIGHT AND INCREASING MEXICAN POVERTY

In the 1990s, Mexico, after a brief period of bubble prosperity, was forced to devalue its currency, resulting in income loss, rising unemployment and an increase in extreme poverty. This poverty both encourages drug production and becomes a factor ensuring that traditional economic policies for diminishing poverty will not work.

> Drug production is linked to poverty because it is driven in large measure by the failing agricultural economy and lack of reasonable alternatives for much of the impoverished rural populace; and second, the growing drug industry brings along with it a number of important 'negative externalities' such as violence, corruption, inter- and intra-community conflict, and a culture of operating outside the law and the formal economy which all work strongly against the creation of long-term, sustainable economic growth... Drug production and poverty are mutually reinforcing: poverty and the lack of economic alternatives motivate drug production, and drug production in turn perpetuates poverty and limits the creation of economic alternatives.[102]

Another factor in Mexican poverty is the economic 'liberalisation' pushed on Mexico and the rest of the world by the market fundamentalism of the so-called 'Washington Consensus'. This package of trade liberalisation, fiscal stability, privatisation and free capital flows is, in truth, hardly a consensus. As the *Wall Street Journal* once acknowledged, it derived from the Chicago School, 'an admittedly small minority in the economics profession'.[103]

In its empirical phase, the monetarist theory of Milton Friedman at the University of Chicago was a corrective to fiscal Keynesianism, which, when over-applied in inappropriate situations, had led to inflation.[104] But it was not long before the neo-liberalism of the Chicago School had become an over-applied ideology in turn. This was thanks to the intervention of the US government, anxious to use Friedman's doctrines to pry open foreign markets for US investment.

Today there is an increasing new consensus: that the ideas of market fundamentalism, far from solving the problems of developing countries, aggravated them.[105] Amy Chua, who once worked for a US bank on a Mexican privatisation project, is part of this new consensus. She has blamed the increase of poverty in the 1990s on this American promotion of what she called 'laissez-faire capitalism – a form of markets that the West abandoned long ago'.[106] She criticised the US and IMF campaign for freeing markets from government regulation, as a campaign that 'rarely includes any significant redistributive mechanisms',[107] despite the fact that, as Jorge Castañeda has commented, if 'democracy does not coincide with growth and with redistribution, in all likelihood it will not last in Latin America'.[108]

Actually 'laissez-faire' is too kind a term. 'Crony capitalism' would appear to better describe what we have usually seen: government-assisted globalisation that at home favours the cronies – such as Halliburton and Enron – of whatever government is in Washington, and also at the receiving end favours the cronies of the recipient government.

DRUGS, CAPITAL FLIGHT AND US BANKS

This is particularly true of Mexico, where twelve billionaires, the so-called 'Mexican twelve', were enriched by Salinas' programme (which was actually a product of the 'Washington Consensus') of 'directed' deregulation or 'selective liberalization'.[109] According to Elizabeth Carroll of the US State Department, some of the businesses privatised were 'snapped up by traffickers in order to launder and invest the profits from their drug operations'.[110]

The lack of controls over capital movements, another feature of the liberalisation pushed by the Washington Consensus, was a major factor in the impoverishment of the majority. In the case of Mexico, there was massive withdrawal of foreign and domestic capital in December 1994, leading to 'an estimated $70 billion loss in the stock-market value of Mexican corporations, an avalanche of bankruptcies, and nearly a million layoffs over the next twelve months'. Government figures confirmed that in the next 15 months the number of people living in extreme poverty increased by 5 million to 22 million.[111] In this context, 'the only part of the economy that was booming was…the drug trade'.[112]

The most reasonable explanation for this capital flight is that cronies – both inside and outside the country – are protecting their recent acquisitions in Mexico by translating them into secure dollar assets. Not just in Mexico, but all over the world, one sees this pattern. Too often US/IMF-enforced liberalisation benefits not the nation but a crony elite, those who, of all the elements in the local economy, are the most likely to recycle their earnings back to the US as soon as their crony status is threatened. It makes more sense to say that in such cases the effect of these liberalisation reforms is to strengthen US relations with crony elites through the world, rather than with market societies.

It also makes more sense to blame the outflows on US banks who continue to facilitate, indeed to encourage, massive movements of foreign flight capital into their own accounts. Often they do this by setting up private banks for this very purpose, sometimes in offshore tax havens. As the *Christian Science Monitor* reported in 1996:

> recently it was disclosed how Citibank helped Raul Salinas de Gortari (brother of the former Mexican president) hide a fortune in 'safe havens'. CBS's '60 Minutes' said on June 23 that the hidden assets could be worth more than $300 million.[113]

The Salinas–Citibank scandal attracted unusual attention, because almost certainly some of the funds involved were from payoffs by Mexican drug lords.[114]

The movement and concealment of Salinas' funds by Citibank was construed by some experts as conscious (or 'willfully blind') drug-money laundering.[115] An even more flagrant example was the frenzied activity of Lehman Brothers on behalf of the Mexican regional governor Mario Villanueva Madrid, as he fled into hiding after becoming the target of a drug and racketeering investigation. For this, a Lehman Brothers employee was indicted, but in the end the firm itself was not.[116]

Thus America's responsibility for income disparity abroad goes beyond enforcing the market fundamentalism of the 'Washington Consensus'. The case of Mexico is paradigmatic of how major US banks collude with criminals, like Raul Salinas, to spirit illicit profits, including drug profits, out of the country and often into the US. It is a symptom of their vigorous determination to stay in this business that they lobbied to gut US government proposals to regulate money-laundering scandals of the Salinas variety.

Congressional and Treasury documentations have led more than one journalist to conclude that US banks are 'collectively the world's largest financial beneficiaries of the drug trade'.[117] This estimated inflow of $250 billion a year to the US (which does not include real estate transfers) was of course a welcome offset to the US trade deficit, then in the order of $300 billion a year.

But the capital flight of oligarchic drug profits is only one of the ways in which drug trafficking weakened the incipient Mexican market society and contributed to misery. According to the French economist Guilhem Fabre,

> [s]tarting in the 1990s, Mexican drug dealers took charge of one half of the Colombian drug trade to the United States, and thereby repatriated some 3 to 8 billions dollars per year, which exceeded the value of Mexico's oil exports.... The hasty privatization initiated by Carlos Salinas also provided opportunities for recycling narco-profits, especially in the banking sector where the State sold a series of firms for $12 billion. After the crisis, these banks were saddled with debts in excess of $60 billion, which were subsequently assumed by the State.[118]

US banks are not the only beneficiaries of this recycling. For a half-century, laundered profits from drug trafficking have been recycled into American and Canadian real estate, notably in Florida and Nevada.[119] The US government has also benefited. Before the US offered an emergency bailout loan to Mexico in 1982 to forestall a default on payments to over-extended US banks, the CIA first verified that drug trafficking represented a significant source of the Mexican foreign exchange earnings that would be needed towards repayment.[120]

THE MEXICAN OLIGARCHS, THE DRUG TRAFFIC AND THE UNITED STATES

In country after country, crony capitalism and, in particular, the absence of currency controls, create super-rich tycoons who then proceed to plunder their country. In the case of Mexico, a new class of oligarchs, much like those in Yeltsin's Russia, emerged from the privatisations conducted under the presidency of Carlos Salinas.

One of the banks in the Salinas circle, Banamex, appears to have enjoyed American protection. In May 1998, two Banamex senior officials were indicted in the US as a result of Operation Casablanca, which US Treasury Secretary Robert Rubin called the 'largest, most comprehensive drug-money laundering case in the history of United States law enforcement'.[121] In a mock-Nevada casino that had, in fact, been specially created for a US Customs sting, they, and ten other senior Mexican bankers, had 'avidly discussed how to handle the latest half-billion dollars in drug proceeds already on hand'.[122] The Federal Reserve Board also seized $3.8 million from Banamex as a corporation. Citicorp subsequently purchased Banamex and the Casablanca prosecutions collapsed.[123]

One key to the Salinas fortunes was Carlos Hank González, 'considered by many to be the *éminence grise* of the 1990–94 Carlos Salinas presidency', and 'the compadre to successive Mexican heads of state, stretching back to Jose Lopez Portillo in the 1970s'.[124] In Congressional testimony, Andrew Reding reported the opinion of a top Mexican anti-narcotics investigator that Carlos Hank González was '*il capo di tutti capi*, the primary intermediary between the multinational drug trafficking enterprises and the Mexican political system'.[125] An article in *Insight* similarly said that tons of cocaine found their way to America in trucks, ships and planes linked to Hank González.[126] It said that TMM, a shipping company that investigators claim was controlled by him, was a favourite among Mexican and Colombian cartels.[127]

Mexican drug cartels continue to threaten public security, and the drug trade is a substantial part of the US–Mexican economy.[128] While a few cartel leaders have been killed or are now imprisoned, the numbers of drug-related murders – including beheadings of police officers – continues to rise, from 1,080 in 2001 to nearly 4,000 in the first ten months of 2008.[129]

NOTES

1. I use 'narcosystem' in place of the more widely-encountered 'narco-economy' because it is important to recognise that what is involved is more than an economy. Narcosystems have undeveloped forms of features associated with the state: notably enforcement powers and mediation processes. They are thus worthy of being termed 'partial states' or 'undeveloped states'. In addition, as they develop, narcosystems enlarge into related criminal activities: other forms of smuggling (notably arms, humans and stolen cars) and money-laundering. For this reason I would prefer 'kryptosystem', except that this term has the disadvantage of being less self-explanatory.

2. The term 'narco-democracy' received currency in 1995 with the publication of Eduardo Valle's *El Segundo disparo: la narcodemocracia mexicana* (*The Second Shot: The Mexican Narco-*

democracy) (Mexico: Oceano, 1995). Cf. Leonardo Curzio, 'Organized Crime and Political Campaign Finance in Mexico', in John Bailey and Roy Godson (eds), *Organized Crime and Democratic Governability: Mexico and the U.S.–Mexican Borderlands* (Pittsburgh: University of Pittsburgh Press, 2000), p. 85.

3. Manuel Buendía, *La CIA en Mexico* (Mexico City: Oceano, 1983), p. 24.
4. John Bailey and Roy Godson, 'Introduction', in Bailey and Godson, *Organized Crime*, p. 24.
5. Peter Dale Scott, *Drugs, Oil, and War: The United States in Afghanistan, Colombia, and Indochina* (Lanham, MD: Rowman & Littlefield, 2003), p. 62.
6. Luís Astorga, 'Organized Crime and the Organization of Crime', in Bailey and Godson, *Organized Crime*, p. 61. Cf. pp. 67–8.
7. Ibid., p. 63.
8. Scott, *Drugs, Oil, and War*, p. 193.
9. Elias Castillo, in Bailey and Godson, *Organized Crime*, p. 200.
10. Also rarely mentioned in the US until recently were two major Mexican drug traffickers who emerged from the CIA-protected Cuban émigré community. Cf. Peter Dale Scott and Jonathan Marshall, *Cocaine Politics: Drugs, Armies, and the CIA in Central America* (Berkeley: University of California Press, 1998), pp. 33–4, etc.
11. Andrew Reding, 'Mexico Under Salinas: A Façade of Reform', *World Policy Journal*, Fall 1989, www.worldpolicy.org/globalrights/mexico/1989-fall-WPJ-Salinas.html (accessed 29 December 2006).
12. Ibid. Ten years after Reding's essay, Gutiérrez Barrios was still an *éminence grise*. In November 1999 he organised the come-from-behind PRI primary victory of Francisco Labastida.
13. Jefferson Morley, 'LITEMPO: Los ojos de la CIA en Tlatelolco', *Proceso*, 1 October 2006; in English as 'LITEMPO: The CIA's Eyes on Tlatelolco', National Security Archive, www.gwu.edu/~nsarchiv/NSAEBB/NSAEBB204/index.htm (accessed 29 December 2006).
14. Sergio Aguayo Quezada, *La Charola: Una Historia de los Servicios de Inteligencia en México* (Mexico City: Grijalbo, 2001), pp. 74–5, 84; Peter Dale Scott, *Deep Politics and the Death of JFK* (Berkeley and Los Angeles: University of California Press, 1996), pp. 104–5.
15. Scott, *Deep Politics and the Death of JFK*, p. 105, quoting from Elaine Shannon, *Desperados* (New York: Viking, 1988), p. 179.
16. Terrence E. Poppa, *Drug Lord: The Life and Death of a Mexican Kingpin* (Seattle: Demand Publications, 1990), p. 165.
17. Institute of Policy Studies, 'A Tangled Web: A History of CIA Complicity in Drug International Trafficking', *Congressional Record*, 7 May 1998, H2956, www.fas.org/irp/congress/1998_cr/980507-l.htm (accessed 29 December 2006). Cf. Aguayo Quezada, *La Charola*, p. 241.
18. Scott and Marshall, *Cocaine Politics*, p. 36; Aguayo Quezada, *La Charola*, p. 247; Peter Dale Scott, *Minding the Darkness* (New York: New Directions, 2000), p. 136.
19. Poppa, *Drug Lord*, pp. 74, 166. A photo of one of these badges is reproduced at p. 74.
20. Cables from Mexico City FBI Legal Attaché Gordon McGinley to Justice Department, in Scott and Marshall, *Cocaine Politics*, p. 36.
21. Scott, *Deep Politics and the Death of JFK*, p. 105; quoting from *San Diego Union*, 26 March 1982.
22. Cf. Scott and Marshall, *Cocaine Politics*, p. 41. 'The CIA ran the facility, he told DEA agents at one point, using DFS "as a cover".' Cf. Charles Bowden, *Down by the River* (New York: Simon & Schuster, 2002), p. 148: 'When he dies, Buendía is rumored to be looking into the links between the drug business, the CIA, and the contra war in Nicaragua.'
23. Scott and Marshall, *Cocaine Politics*, p. 41.
24. Ibid., pp. 10, 42, 56–8, 98–100.
25. 'CISEN has far to go before it sheds its dark past: It was formed in the mid-1980s from the ashes of the despised Federal Security Department... In CISEN's ranks of former agents is the late master spy Fernando Gutierrez Barrios, known as the former ruling party's keeper of dark secrets. Another original CISEN agent was Jorge Carrillo Olea, who later became governor of Morelos state.' Ricardo Sandoval, *Dallas Morning News*, 27 May 2003, www.thestate.com/mld/thestate/news/world/5951462.htm (accessed 29 December 2006).

26. Mexico, *Milenio*, 7 January 2004. Barnard R. Thompson, 'Mexico is collaborating with the CIA and FBI', Mexidata.Info, 12 January 2004, www.mexidata.info/id117.html (accessed 29 December 2006).

27. Ted Galen Carpenter, 'Mexico Is Becoming the Next Colombia', Cato Institute, Foreign Policy Briefing no. 87, 15 November 2005, www.cato.org/pub_display.php?pub_id=5149 (accessed 29 December 2006). Cf. Ted Galen Carpenter, *Bad Neighbor Policy: Washington's Futile War on Drugs in Latin America* (New York: Palgrave Macmillan, 2003).

28. Carlos Montemayor, *La Jornada*, 13 May 2006. Cf. *The Eyeopener*, Ryerson's Independent Newspaper, 18 January 2005.

29. *Los Angeles Times*, 17 August 2006.

30. A key event of course was the publication of Alfred W. McCoy's *The Politics of Heroin in Southeast Asia* (New York: Harper & Row, 1972). McCoy's copious footnotes make it clear that he interviewed such important US CIA officers as Lucien Conein and William Young. My own book, *The War Conspiracy*, published shortly before McCoy's, was able to reveal further details of the drug traffic (including the key role of Paul Helliwell, not mentioned by McCoy until 1991). I too was helped in part by conversations with an author and former CIA officer whom I met accidentally (as I then believed) in the library at UC Berkeley.

31. The best essay is by Jonathan Marshall, 'CIA Assets and the Rise of the Guadalajara Connection', in Alfred W. McCoy and Alan A. Block, *War on Drugs: Studies in the Failure of U.S. Narcotics Policy* (Boulder, CO: Westview Press, 1992), pp. 197–208.

32. Testimony of George Gaffney, US Congress, Senate, Committee on Government Operations, *Organized Crime and Illicit Traffic in Narcotics*, Hearings, 88th Cong., 2nd Sess. (Washington: Government Printing Office, 1964; henceforward cited as Narcotics Hearings), p. 899. Cf. Jean-Pierre Charbonneau, *The Canadian Connection* (Ottawa: Optimum, 1976).

33. Lansky had been a major player in the so-called Operation Underworld conducted by the OSS and ONI during the Second World War to use information from Lucky Luciano in operations on the New York waterfront and later in Sicily (Scott, *Deep Politics and the Death of JFK*, pp. 100, 145, 165). His opposite number in Mexico, the Corsican Paul Mondoloni, was likewise protected by the French government: Douglas Valentine, *The Strength of the Wolf: The Secret History of America's War on Drugs* (London: Verso, 2004), p. 323.

34. McCoy, *The Politics of Heroin in Southeast Asia*, p. 44.

35. Ibid., p. 443.

36. Narcotics Hearings, pp. 781, 989. Lansky was an unindicted co-conspirator (and conceivably even an informant) in the case that convicted Meltzer: Valentine, *The Strength of the Wolf*, p. 95.

37. Alan A. Block, *Perspectives on Organizing Crime* (Dordrecht: Kluwer Academic Publishers, 1991), pp. 230–1.

38. Scott, *Deep Politics and the Death of JFK*, pp. 140–1. One syndicate representative in Mexico City was Paul Roland Jones, who opened a casino there. Jones was later convicted in a major drug bust that involved both Jack Ruby (the future killer of Lee Harvey Oswald) and his brother Hymie (Scott, *Deep Politics and the Death of JFK*, pp. 138–41). A Dallas detective, Lt. George Butler, taped Jones discussing how the US government had stopped his activities in Mexico City, 'at least until Aleman gets in': Butler notes, in records of Senate Commerce Committee. Cf. House Select Committee on Assassinations, Appendix to Hearings, Vol. IX, p. 516.

39. Thirty minutes after Luciano's death from a massive heart attack, FBN Deputy Commissioner Henry Giordano announced that the FBN 'had been on the point of arresting the powerful Mafioso for having introduced $150 million worth of heroin to American territory over the previous ten years': Charbonneau, *The Canadian Connection*, p. 168; quoted in Valentine, *The Strength of the Wolf*, p. 247. It is clear that arrest does not necessarily prove dismal failure.

40. CIA 'Review of ZRRIFLE File', October 1976, NARA #104-10308-10287.

41. Richard D. Mahoney, *Sons and Brothers: The Days of Jack and Bobby Kennedy* (New York: Arcade Publishing, 1999), p. 269; citing Mason Cargill Memorandum to the File, Subject: Project ZR/RIFLE and QJ/WIN, 30 April 1975, HSCA.

42. Peter Lupsha, 'Drug Lords and Narco-Corruption: The Players Change but the Game Continues', in McCoy and Block, *War on Drugs*, pp. 177–9, 181.

43. Luís Astorga, 'Drug Trafficking in Mexico: A First General Assessment', Management of Social Transformations – MOST, Discussion Paper No. 36, UNESCO, www.unesco.org/most/astorga. htm (accessed 29 December 2006).

44. Ibid., p. 63.

45. Ibid., pp. 62–5, 72.

46. So, for example, Mexican Minister of Gobernación [Interior] back in 1931, Carlos Riva Palacio, resigned because of his alleged complicity in an international drug smuggling operation transiting Mexico: Scott, *Deep Politics and the Death of JFK*, p. 104.

47. Luís Astorga, 'The Limits of Anti-drug Policy in Mexico', *International Social Science Journal*, 53/169 (2001), pp. 427–33 at 428, and also at www.justiceblind.com/drugwar/mexicolimits.pdf (accessed 29 December 2006).

48. Barry Carr, 'The United States and Mexican Unions in the Early Cold War 1946–1955', La Trobe University, http://www.yale.edu/las/coldwar/papers/Carr.doc (accessed 29 December 2006). When E. Howard Hunt opened the first CIA office in Mexico City in 1950, he took over (in his own words) 'from the slash-and-burn remnants of the FBI office': Interview, www.gwu. edu/~nsarchiv/coldwar/interviews/episode-18/hunt1.html (accessed 29 December 2006).

49. Luís Astorga, 'Organized Crime and the Organization of Crime', p. 72, citing US State Department, Confidential Report No. 4543 of the Assistant Military Attaché on the National Security Police of Mexico, 7 September 1947; NARA Record Group 59, 812.105/9–447.

50. *El Angelino*, edición especial, 16 December 1949. Aguayo Quezada, *La Charola*, p. 84. The driver was the nephew of Juan Ramón Gurrola, the number two official and eventual head of the DFS: Luís Astorga, *Drogas sin Fronteras* (Miguel Hidalgo, Mexico, D.F.: Grijalbo, 2003), p. 285. Cf. Drew Pearson, *Washington Post*, 29 February 1948.

51. Aguayo Quezada, *La Charola*, pp. 84–6.

52. Ibid., pp. 74–5, quoting (in translation) from CIA, 'Mexico', SR-18, 24 January 1951, pp. 57–8, 69.

53. Marshall, 'CIA Assets and the Rise of the Guadalajara Connection', pp. 198, 200. Cf. Scott and Marshall, *Cocaine Politics*, pp, 34, 86; James Mills, *The Underground Empire: Where Crime and Governments Embrace* (New York: Dell, 1986), pp. 360–3.

54. As we shall see, six of the known OSS officers in Kunming – Paul Helliwell, Howard Hunt, Ray Cline, Lou Conein, John Singlaub and Mitchell WerBell – went on to develop postwar drug-linked activities for the CIA. See Scott, *Drugs, Oil, and War*, pp. 20, 207.

55. See Scott, *Drugs, Oil, and War*, pp. 61–2, 198.

56. Valentine, *The Strength of the Wolf*, p. 73.

57. Ibid., p. 71. Both Hill and Chung were under FBN surveillance, but no case was ever made against either woman.

58. Ed Reid, *The Mistress and the Mafia: The Virginia Hill Story* (New York: Bantam, 1972), p. 42.

59. *Novedades*, 14 May 1962; Astorga, 'Organized Crime and the Organization of Crime', p. 65.

60. Scott Anderson and Jon Lee Anderson, *Inside the League* (New York: Dodd, Mead, 1986), pp. 46–7. For Kodama and drugs, see David Kaplan and Alec Dubro, *Yakuza* (Reading, MA: Addison-Wesley, 1986), p. 66.

61. Bertil Lintner, *Burma in Revolt* (Boulder, CO: Westview Press, 1994), p. 134. Cf. p. 234.

62. Jorge Prieto Laurens was one of the politicians whose telephone was tapped by the DFS: Aguayo Quezado, *La Charola*, p. 308.

63. Anderson and Anderson, *Inside the League*, p. 79; Rogelio Hernandez, *Zorrilla: el Imperio del Crimen* (Mexico City: Editorial Planeta Mexicana, 1989), p. 26.

64. Anderson and Anderson, *Inside the League*, pp. 54–5; Jonathan Marshall, Peter Dale Scott and Jane Hunter, *The Iran–Contra Connection: Secret Teams and Covert Operations in the Reagan Era* (Boston: South End Press, 1987), p. 65; Thomas Bodenheimer and Robert Gould, *Rollback: Right-wing Power in U.S. Foreign Policy* (Boston: South End Press, 1989), www.thirdworldtraveler. com/Foreign_Policy/GlobalRollbackNetwork.html (accessed 29 December 2006).

65. Cf. McCoy, *The Politics of Heroin in Southeast Asia*, pp. 203, 210.

66. Marshall, Scott and Hunter, *The Iran–Contra Connection*, pp. 62–4.

67. Anderson and Anderson, *Inside the League*, p. 204; Scott and Marshall, *Cocaine Politics*, pp. 45–6, 109. In April 1971, the chief Laotian delegate to WACL, Prince Sopsaisana, was caught in Paris with 60 kg of high-grade heroin, worth $13.5 million on the streets of New York: Scott, *Drugs, Oil, and War*, p. 163; McCoy, *The Politics of Heroin in Southeast Asia*, p. 379.

68. Testimony of Special Counsel Jack A. Blum, Senate Intelligence Hearing on Drug Trafficking and the Contra War, 23 October 1996; *Washington Weekly*, 28 October 1996.

69. Mike Levine, *The Big White Lie* (New York: Thunder's Mouth Press, 1993), pp. 35–6.

70. Scott and Marshall, *Cocaine Politics*, p. 46; Marshall, Scott and Hunter, *The Iran–Contra Connection*, pp. 20–5; Loretta Napoleoni, *Terror Incorporated: Tracing the Dollars Behind the Terror Networks* (New York: Seven Stories Press, 2005), pp. 19, 247.

71. McCoy, *The Politics of Heroin in Southeast Asia*, pp. 59–60. Through the Guérinis of the Corsican mafia, Brown also made 'contact with the mafia in Italy': Valentine, *Strength of the Wolf*, p. 112. Valentine confirms allegations that Brown himself came under FBN investigation in the 1960s, because of his unexplained travels in the company of Corsican drug trafficker Maurice Castellani: pp. 362–3. Cf. pp. 270–4. See also Douglas Valentine, 'The French Connection Revisited: The CIA, Irving Brown, and Drug Smuggling as Political Warfare', *Covert Action*, www.covertaction. org/content/view/99/75/ (accessed 29 December 2006).

72. Charbonneau, *The Canadian Connection*, pp. 69, 75; Valentine, *The Strength of the Wolf*, pp. 328, 331.

73. Charbonneau, *The Canadian Connection*, p. 209.

74. *Proceso*, 5 August 1985, p. 30; Lupsha, 'Drug Lords and Narco-Corruption', p. 180. Chavarri was described by Lupsha as a founder of the DFS. But *La Charola* (pp. 65–6) gives a list of the founding officers; there is a Fernando Rocha Chavarri, but no Rafael Chavarri.

75. Gaia Servadio, *Mafioso* (New York: Dell, 1976), pp. 125–8; Scott, *Deep Politics and the Death of JFK*, p. 174.

76. Scott, *Deep Politics and the Death of JFK*, p. 174.

77. Ibid., pp. 174–7.

78. Wikipedia, 'Sylvestro Carolla', citing Jay Robert Nash, *The Encyclopedia of World Crime*, i (A–C) (Wilmette: CrimeBooks Inc., 1990).

79. Alfred W. McCoy, *The Politics of Heroin in Southeast Asia* (Chicago: Lawrence Hill Books/ Chicago Review Press, 2001), p. 39 (Lebanon), p. 162ss (Thailand), p. 197 (Vietnam), pp. 476–7 (Pakistan), etc.; Jeffrey M. Bale, 'The "Black" Terrorist International: Neo-Fascist Paramilitary Networks and the "Strategy of Tension" in Italy, 1968–1974', Ph.D. dissertation (University of California, Berkeley), p. 170, etc. (Italy); Warren Hinckle and William Turner, *The Fish Is Red* (New York: Harper & Row, 1981), p. 314, etc. (Cuba); Daniele Ganser, *NATO's Secret Armies: Operation Gladio and Terrorism in Western Europe* (London: Frank Cass Publishers, 2005), pp. 240–3 (Turkey). Ganser also presents evidence of a CIA–local security–drugs triarchy involving Spanish intelligence (pp. 106–7) and the French OAS (p. 100). By the 1980s, such triarchic arrangements were widespread in Latin America: Scott and Marshall, *Cocaine Politics*, pp. vii–xii, 79–85, etc.

80. Alan A. Block and Constance A. Weaver, *All Is Clouded by Desire: Global Banking, Money Laundering, and International Organized Crime* (Westport, CT: Praeger, 2004), p. 28.

81. Joseph J. Trento, *Prelude to Terror: The Rogue CIA and the Legacy of America's Private Intelligence Network* (New York: Carroll & Graf, 2005), p. 1. I have not found documentation for this claim. The closest might be Dulles' overseas work in 1949 as legal adviser to Overseas Consultants, Inc., whose 'most promising venture was the design of a long-range development program [for] Mohammed Reza Pahlavi, shah of Iran': Peter Grose, *Gentleman Spy: The Life of Allen Dulles* (Boston: Richard Todd/Houghton Mifflin, 1994), p. 295.

82. Anthony Cave Brown, *The Last Hero: Wild Bill Donovan* (New York: Times Books, 1982), pp. 821–2.

83. Ibid., pp. 795–800.

84. Bruce Cumings, *The Origins of the Korean War*, ii (Princeton: Princeton University Press, 1990), pp. 509–12; Scott, *Drugs, Oil, and War*, pp. 109–10, 197.

85. Cumings, *The Origins of the Korean War*, ii, p. 511; Scott, *Drugs, Oil, and War*, pp. 109–10, 197. Satiris 'Sonny' Fassoulis, accused of passing bribes as the vice-president of Commerce

International, was under indictment ten years later when he surfaced in the syndicate-linked Guterma scandals.

86. Cumings, *The Origins of the Korean War*, ii, p. 511.

87. Ibid., p. 513. Cf. William M. Leary, *Perilous Missions: Civil Air Transport and CIA Covert Operations in Asia* (University, AL: University of Alabama Press, 1984), p. 102.

88. Scott, *Drugs, Oil, and War*, pp. 109–10, 197; *New York Times*, 23 May 1950, p. 34.

89. Scott, *Drugs, Oil, and War*, p. xx. The term 'parapolitics' has now expanded to include academic study of these phenomena: see Cribb, this volume.

90. *St. Louis Post-Dispatch*, 8 January 1989.

91. *Washington Post*, 6 February 1989.

92. Scott and Marshall, *Cocaine Politics*, p. 37. Cf. pp. 41–2.

93. Ibid., pp. 41–2 and passim, quoting *Newsweek*, 13 May 1985.

94. Lupsha, 'Drug Lords and Narco-Corruption', pp. 185–7.

95. Peter Lupsha, 'Transnational Narco-Corruption and Narco Investment: A Focus on Mexico', excerpted from Peter Lupsha, 'Under the Volcano: Narco Investment in Mexico', *Transnational Organized Crime Journal* (Spring 1995); posted originally on the Internet by PBS/Frontline, 8 April 1997, www.eco.utexas.edu/~archive/chiapas95/1997.04/msg00066.html (accessed 29 December 2006).

96. Elaine Shannon, *Desperados* (New York: Viking, 1988), p. 67; quoted in Scott and Marshall, *Cocaine Politics*, pp. 38–9.

97. Jorge Castañeda, *The Mexican Shock: Its Meaning for the United States* (New York: New Press, 1995), p. 222.

98. Ibid., p. 215; *New York Times*, 20 July 1996.

99. Clyde Prestowitz, *Rogue Nation: American Unilateralism and the Failure of Good Intentions* (New York: Basic Books, 2003), p. 78.

100. Castañeda, *The Mexican Shock*, p. 37.

101. Anthony DePalma, 'Gap Between Mexico's Rich and Poor Is Widening', *New York Times*, 20 July 1996: 'Today the richest 10 percent of Mexicans control 41 percent of the country's wealth, while the bottom half of the population receives only 16 percent of all national income. The government admits that the number of Mexicans living in extreme poverty has grown to 22 million, an increase over just the last 15 months of 5 million people, roughly equal to the population of Scotland.'

102. Chris Humphrey, 'Narcotic, Economics, and Drug Production in the Southern States', http://wbln0018.worldbank.org/lac/lacinfoclient.nsf/d29684951174975c85256735007fef12/63a3f4e71ce14d2385256dc500661aaf/$FILE/Mexico%20SouthStates%20Narcotics%20and%20Poverty.pdf (accessed 29 December 2006).

103. *Wall Street Journal*, 30 September 1998.

104. George Soros, *The Crisis of Global Capitalism* (New York: Public Affairs, 1998), p. 117.

105. See, for example, Pedro-Pablo Kuczynski and John Williamson, *After the Washington Consensus: Restoring Growth and Reform in Latin America* (Washington: Institute for International Economics, 2003). Williamson originally coined the phrase 'Washington consensus' in 1990.

106. Amy Chua, *World on Fire: How Exporting Free Market Democracy Breeds Ethnic Hatred and Global Instability* (New York: Doubleday, 2003), p. 14.

107. Ibid., p. 195.

108. Castañeda, *The Mexican Shock*, p. 239.

109. Andres Oppenheimer, *Bordering on Chaos: Mexico's Roller-Coaster Journey Toward Prosperity* (Boston: Little Brown, 1998), pp. 90–3: 'Mexico in the early nineties was similar to American capitalism in the late 1870s... Like the American "Robber Barons" of their time, the Mexico Twelve were making a fortune from their close partnership with the government.' What Oppenheimer writes of the Mexico Twelve in Mexico could be said also of Halliburton and Enron in Washington.

110. Tom Barry, Harry Browne and Beth Sims, *The Great Divide: The Challenge of U.S.–Mexico Relations in the 1990s* (New York: Grove Press, 1994), p. 69.

111. *New York Times*, 20 July 1996.

112. Oppenheimer, *Bordering on Chaos*, pp. 5, 164.

113. *Christian Science Monitor*, 15 July 1996.

114. Cf. Oppenheimer, *Bordering on Chaos*, pp. 306–7.
115. Arguments for this can be found in 1996 issues of *Money Laundering Alert*, www.pbs.org/wgbh/pages/frontline/shows/mexico/family/citibankaffair.html (accessed 29 December 2006). Cf. Stephen Bender, 'American Banks and the War on Drugs', *Z Magazine* (March 2001), www.zmag.org/ZMag/articles/mar01bender.htm (accessed 29 December 2006)
116. Busca AAAFlash, 12 November 2002. http://support.casals.com/aaaflash1/busca.asp?ID_AAAControl=8392 (accessed 29 December 2006).
117. Bender, 'American Banks and the War on Drugs'. The Minority Staff Report is at http://govt-aff.senate.gov/110999_report.htm (accessed 29 December 2006).
118. Guilhem Fabre, 'Prospering on Crime: Money Laundering and Financial Crises', www.mamacoca.org/FSMT_sept_2003/en/doc/fabre_prospering_on_crime_en.htm (accessed 29 December 2006). Details in Guilhem Fabre, *Criminal Prosperity: Drug Trafficking, Money Laundering and Financial Crises after the Cold War* (London: Routledge/Curzon, 2001), Chapter 5.
119. Scott, *Drugs, Oil, and War*, pp. 198, 207.
120. Before the first loan was issued in 1982, the US government had already ascertained from DEA and CIA that the profits from drug exports for Colombia and Mexico 'probably represent 75 percent of source-country export earnings': Mills, *The Underground Empire*, pp. 1135, 1181.
121. CNN, 18 May 1998.
122. Sally Denton and Roger Morris, 'Prologue', in *The Money and the Power: The Making of Las Vegas and Its Hold on America, 1947–2000* (New York: Knopf, 2001). Denton later enlarged on the details: 'When it became clear 70 United States, American, banks were involved, had the complicity, knew about every single one of the wire-transfers and transactions – banks including Chemical Bank, Bank of New York, CitiBank, American Express – ... President Clinton and Madeline Albright stepped in and intervened and stopped the entire investigation and closed all of the cases.' Discussion at Taos Community Auditorium on 12 October 2002, www.taosplaza.com/taosplaza/2003/pages/tmff_drugs.php (accessed 29 December 2006).
123. Interview with Al Giordano, *Multinational Monitor*, April 2002; http://multinationalmonitor.org/mm2002/02april/april02interviewgiordano.html (accessed 29 December 2006).
124. Jamie Dettmer, 'Family Affairs', *Insight Magazine*, www.insightmag.com/main.cfm?include=detail&storyid=208995 (accessed 29 December 2006).
125. Andrew Reding, 'Political Corruption and Drug Trafficking in Mexico', Senate Committee on Foreign Relations, 'The Drug Trade in Mexico and U.S. Policy Implications', 8 August 1995; www.worldpolicy.org/globalrights/mexico/1995-0808-Senate.html (accessed 29 December 2006).
126. A federal US official from South Texas has confirmed to me that tractor-trailers loaded with drugs come across the border; and if detected are likely to result in prosecutions of the driver only.
127. Jamie Dettmer, 'Family Affairs', *Insight Magazine*, www.insightmag.com/main.cfm?include=detail&storyid=208995 (accessed 29 December 2006).
128. According to US sources in 1998, 'The Mexican federation of [drug] cartels alone is believed to earn between $17 and $30 billion each year': Richard Parker, 'U.S. Fickle on Anti-Narcotics Aid', ABQjournal (Albuquerque Journal), www.abqjournal.com/news/drugs/2drug3-5.htm (accessed 29 December 2006). These estimates seem consistent with official estimates of drug consumption in the US, in the order of $64 billion a year: Prestowitz, *Rogue Nation*, p. 259. To put the Mexican estimates in perspective, consider that the total of US–Mexican trade in both directions, for the first nine months of 1996, was $94 billion.
129. Alma Guillermoprieto, 'Days of the Dead: Letter from Mexico', *New Yorker*, 10 November 2008, p. 46.

10
Parapolitics and Afghanistan

Rensselaer W. Lee III

The term 'parapolitics' generally connotes a pattern of purposive state activity in collaboration with international organised crime. Classic parapolitics envisages such complicity as an attribute of statecraft, in which a nation's security and intelligence services (as opposed to the visible authorities) tend to assume a dominant role. Parapolitics can be distinguished from conventional modalities of corruption, which link criminal funds to the exercise of state functions. While some of its practitioners may be corrupt, their activities relate to a nation's vital interests and transcendent policy goals. In what is essentially a goal-directed exchange of values, state agencies acquire additional covert capability for operations outside normal channels, providing in return a measure of protection for criminals' illegal businesses as well as such benefits as money, arms and logistical support.

Parapolitics, thus defined, has been deeply embedded in national and global systems of conflict management. The US government, for instance, has used criminal groups as intelligence assets and proxy fighters in various small wars over the past half-century – the CIA's dalliances with Southeast Asian and Afghan drug lords are prominent cases in point. Similarly understandings or liaisons with criminal actors have been survival strategies for countries mired in life-or-death internal conflicts. Criminal organisations can provide financing, tactical intelligence and even armed support for counter-insurgency operations, as recent histories of Colombia, Peru, and other war-torn countries attest.

Yet parapolitics also shades into official tolerance or accommodation of criminal activity, qualitatively different from collusion for specific state ends. The central idea here is that governments may simply choose to acquiesce in extant criminal complexes or place a low priority on combating them. Flourishing criminal enclaves such as the notorious Tri-Border region of South America, the so-called 'garrison communities' in downtown Kingston, Jamaica, much of modern-day Afghanistan (an evolving narco-state) and certain coca-growing zones in the Andes come to mind as modern-day examples. The reasons for accommodation vary. States may be too weak to impose their writ on these intractable regions; alternatively they may be reluctant to wage war against a lucrative criminal status-quo, fearing a loss of income, jobs and other benefits. Additionally, counter-crime strategies pose the

195

risk of pushing criminals into a collective self-defence posture with enemies of the state – a continuing concern in chronically unstable countries such as Colombia and Afghanistan.

Parapolitics connotes 'systemic clandestinity' in the affairs of government and it functions on a different level from the world of conventional visible politics. Parapolitical complexes can engage in activities at odds with human rights and democratic processes (such as the CIA–American mafia conspiracy to assassinate Cuban leader Fidel Castro in the 1960s and the Colombian army's sordid collaboration with cocaine-funded paramilitaries to target suspected guerrilla sympathisers). Practitioners of parapolitics doubtless would argue that their efforts served the larger purpose of fighting against profoundly undemocratic movements and regimes – whether driven by Soviet power, Marxist ideology or radical Islamic fundamentalism. Yet parapolitics, which necessarily involves assumptions about threats and priorities, can shape policy outcomes in ways that detract from a nation's stability and wellbeing.

Afghanistan – the subject of this chapter – represents a case study of what Robert Cribb calls 'the tripartite relationship between security and intelligence organisations, international criminal networks and quasi-states'.[1] Whether, or to what extent, the continuing failure of nation-building in that country represents a legacy of parapolitics is an issue of theoretical and practical concern, to be taken up in the following pages.

AFGHANISTAN'S OPIUM DILEMMA

Afghanistan, a land-locked country the size of Texas, is the world's preeminent opiate producer, accounting for more than 90 per cent of global output, according to the UN Office on Drugs and Crime (UNODC). In 2007 UNODC estimated Afghan production to be 8,200 tons, a more than forty-fold increase over the 200 tons recorded in 1980. Moreover, the Afghan national economy is hooked on drugs to an extent unparalleled in any other country. Revenue from opium and its derivatives in 2007 was calculated at approximately $4 billion, about one-third of the country's total (legal plus illegal) GDP. According to UNODC, some 3.3 million people, or 14.3 per cent of the total Afghan population, are directly employed in opium cultivation.[2] Yet the full employment impact is more extensive, since the opium-heroin industry stimulates the supply of goods and services to the legal economy – for example, tools and fertiliser for farmers; chemicals for converting opium to morphine and heroin; and luxury housing for major drug kingpins.

While the full dimensions of the opium economy cannot be ascertained with certainty, available information suggests that it penetrates and influences most spheres of Afghan life. Afghanistan and its international sponsors face an agonising dilemma. A frontal assault against the illicit drug industry will entail substantial risks in terms of lost income and jobs, and disrupt rural livelihoods. Escalating political tensions and armed conflict with producers and traffickers are likely outcomes. On the other hand, eradication of the industry is a prerequisite for successful nation-building in Afghanistan, a country fragmented by diverse ethnic, tribal and political loyalties. Drug profits represent a significant centrifugal force in Afghan politics, underwriting the military forces of local power-holders and preventing the post-Taliban Afghan government from extending its control. Conversely, a resurgent 'neo-Taliban' (a loose alliance of former Taliban, anti-Western warlords, Nationalist-Islamist Pashtuns, and assorted foreign fighters, including al Qaeda) is extending its influence over southern Afghanistan, encouraging farmers to grow poppy, and taxing the proceeds to pay new fighters for its cause. 'Either Afghanistan destroys opium, or opium will destroy Afghanistan', Afghan president Hamid Karzai has warned.[3]

The surge of opium cultivation over the past quarter century coincides with a period of protracted internal strife that began with the 1979 Soviet invasion and persists today. The mujaheddin resistance against the Soviet occupation, the warlord groupings that took shape in the 1990s, the neo-Taliban insurgency against the Afghan government and the foreign coalition forces all have exploited the drug trade to advance their respective military and political agendas. These different factions have encouraged farmers to grow opium poppy but farmers' choices have, to a great extent, been determined by a lack of viable agricultural alternatives. Former CIA analyst Michael Scheuer has eloquently described the ravages inflicted by the Soviet occupiers on traditional farming ways of life.

> The centuries-old and indispensable irrigation and agricultural terracing systems were ruined during the war by natural deterioration after farmers were driven abroad, and more tellingly, by deliberate destruction by the Soviets in their efforts to depopulate areas supporting the insurgency. Afghanistan's limited road system was likewise destroyed and the penury produced by years of war spurred a lucrative crop substitution program, saw farmers abandon grains and fruits for poppies to feed the expanding heroin industry.[4]

Yet Afghanistan's mounting drug crisis also coincided with episodes of US covert support for its major perpetrators – warlords who sponsored or engaged in the traffic in opiates, while advancing US strategic objectives regionally. As Alfred McCoy has noted, the Afghan mujaheddin's largest recipient of CIA military aid during the anti-Soviet campaign, Gulbuddin Hekmatyar, also was the country's leading drug lord.[5] Following the Soviet withdrawal in 1989 and the collapse of the USSR in 1991, US interest in Afghanistan ebbed. It only reawakened in the late 1990s, following the radical Taliban's accession to power, the relocation of Osama bin Laden from Sudan to Afghanistan and the appearance of jihadist training camps there. At this time, capturing or killing bin Laden became the top US priority. To this end, the CIA formed an intelligence collection liaison with another heroin-tainted warlord, Ahmed Shah Massoud, the leader of an anti-Taliban assemblage of commanders known as the Northern Alliance. This relationship stopped short of outright military assistance to the Alliance, until the US-led coalition forces swept the Taliban from power in late 2001.[6] Meanwhile, opium production climbed steadily from 200 tons in 1980, to 1,600 tons in 1990 and to 3,100 tons in 2000.[7]

Afghan warlords doubtless would have pressed their peasant supporters to expand cultivation of opium regardless of outside assistance levels (indeed, the CIA had largely terminated covert operations in Afghanistan during most of the 1990s, leaving rival warlord factions to jockey for power among themselves). Nevertheless, CIA sponsorship of men such as Hekmatyar and Massoud may have emboldened and even legitimised smuggling schemes. *Washington Post* writer Steve Coll observed in his book *Ghost Wars* that while the CIA's Counter Terrorism Center was aggressively touting Massoud's strategic importance to the US, the Agency's Counter-Narcotics Center reported that Massoud's men 'continued to smuggle large amounts of opium and heroin into Europe'.[8]

Controlling such traffic was simply not a priority for the US at this time. Only after the fall of the Taliban in 2001 did drug control become a functional part of the US–Afghan agenda. Even then, however, it was hedged with other priorities, such as fostering economic stability and pursuing the 'war on terror'. Moreover, by this time the US may have let pass an historic opportunity to rid Afghanistan of the opium scourge, as will be discussed below.

THE TALIBAN AND DRUGS

In the late 1990s, the American government seemed to be of two minds on how to deal with the Taliban regime. The CIA, or, at any rate, its Counter-Terrorism Center, leaned towards an outright military alliance with Massoud's forces (beyond mere intelligence cooperation) on the grounds that replacing the Taliban was the only way to exert serious pressure on Osama bin Laden. On the other hand, ranking officials in the Clinton State Department held out the hope of a grand bargain with the Taliban, by which Washington would trade diplomatic recognition and economic benefits for delivery of bin Laden to US custody.[9]

Events in 2000 and 2001 created an opportunity for Washington to engage the Taliban on these various issues and possibly to extract major concessions. The occasion was the regime's surprising decision to attack the entrenched opium trade beginning with the 2000–01 poppy-growing season. Calling drug cultivation 'un-Islamic', Taliban leader Mullah Mohammed Omar issued a religious decree in July 2000 completely outlawing the practice (early partial prohibitions had been announced by the Taliban in 1997 and 1999, with little apparent effect). The 2000 ban was strictly enforced: Taliban authorities reportedly imprisoned violators and uprooted or incinerated their crops. As a result, the poppy cultivated area in Afghanistan shrank overall by more than 90 per cent according to UN figures.[10] Opium production declined even more drastically, falling to the 1980 level of 200 tons. A notable exception to the pattern was Badakhstan province in the northeast, dominated by warlords of the Northern Alliance, where cultivation increased by almost 4,000 hectares between 2000 and 2001.[11]

The Taliban's initiative received mixed international reaction. 'We have to recognise it as a major result', said Bernard Frahi, a regional director for the UN Drug Control Program. Then-Secretary of State, Colin Powell, described the poppy ban as 'a decision by the Taliban that we welcome'. A less enthusiastic response came from then-National Security Advisor Condoleezza Rice, who reportedly told Pakistan's ambassador to Washington, referring to the crackdown, 'Yeah, Stalin also got a lot of things done.'[12]

Yet the Taliban's sudden up-ending of the opium economy had harsh, and possibly destabilising, consequences. 'Success was achieved through draconian enforcement action with no concern for poor farmers' welfare', said the State Department's International Narcotics Control Strategy Report of 2001.[13] The multiplier effects in the agricultural sector were apparently devastating. 'The bad side of the ban is that it is bringing their country – or certain regions of the country – to economic ruin', said an observer from the US Drug Enforcement Administration, who visited the country in the spring of 2001.[14] Tens of thousands of farmers and other agricultural workers, unable to earn a living from lower-value staples such as wheat and cotton, simply abandoned poppy-growing zones, swelling the ranks of Afghanistan's refugee population and exacerbating the country's economic crisis.[15] As one British opium expert concluded in a paper written in August 2001, 'There is certainly little sense that the Taliban have considered the full implications of the ban and what is required to address the resource gap that the rural population is currently enduring due to the loss of opium.'[16]

By mid 2001, the situation in Afghanistan had grown desperate. It was apparent that the opium ban could not be sustained without substantial external assistance. In June, the Taliban itself petitioned the UN for aid to displaced poppy farmers, saying in a statement to UN Secretary General Kofi Annan that 'eradication of drugs cannot be [the] work of any one country'.[17]

At this juncture the West might have intervened to stabilise Afghanistan's economic situation, assist desperate rural dwellers and help keep the lid on opium cultivation. The US, in fact, announced a $43 million aid package on 21 May, ostensibly aimed at Afghan farmers affected by drought; but a much larger commitment was needed to rebuild infrastructure, create alternative income opportunities and reorient the rural economy away from drugs.[18] The Taliban may have calculated that banning opium would win international recognition and support, but doubtless had its own domestic reasons for the crackdown, such as consolidating power and containing drug abuse – reportedly rampant in opium-growing areas and major cities at the time.[19] In any case, the Taliban – faced with the catastrophic consequences of drug prohibition – might have been induced to accommodate Western demands, especially on the all-important bin Laden issue. Western acceptance of an Islamist regime in Kabul, divorced from its al Qaeda patron and strongly committed to drug control, would have been essential ingredients of a new grand bargain, could one have been reached. Furthermore, a sustained Western economic presence in Afghanistan might have nudged the regime to adopt less repressive and more moderate and outward-looking policies, though such a judgement is speculative.

Yet whatever the international response to Afghanistan's economic plight might have been in the offing was overtaken by events – or put on hold – following the terrorist attacks of 11 September 2001 and ensuing coalition military action. Moreover, according to UN officials, the Taliban effectively lifted its ban in late September, telling the farmers that they could once again produce opium if the US launched an attack on Afghanistan.[20] Farmers responded by sowing opium in droves, taking advantage of the extreme price escalation resulting from the ban. From mid 2000 to mid 2001, the price of opium increased 600 per cent from $100 to $700 per kilogram and, correspondingly, opium production rebounded to 3,400 tons in 2002.[21]

In the post-9/11 period Washington continued to compromise with political forces which – while definitely opposed to the Taliban – had a history of profiting from the opium-heroin trade. The US-backed Northern Alliance dominated the cabinet of the new Afghan interim administration (AIA) formed in December 2001, though it held slightly less than half of the seats in the Transitional Islamic State of Afghanistan (TISA) which succeeded the AIA in June. A State Department cable of November 2002 states:

> Given the way in which many senior officials rose to power, it is more difficult to say categorically that no senior official of TISA engages in, encourages, or facilitates the illicit production or distribution of such drugs or substances, or is the beneficiary of proceeds from illicit drug transactions.[22]

Other commentary was more explicit. For instance in October 2002 the *Boston Globe*, citing international drug control officials, noted that 'Every major warlord and every provincial government in northern Afghanistan is involved in the drug business.'[23] An article in the London *Guardian* made the point in polemical fashion. 'By using the heroin-financed gangsters of the Northern Alliance to overthrow the Taliban regime and pursue al Qaeda remnants ever since, the US has handed over most of the country to the same war criminals that devastated Afghanistan in the early 1990s.'[24]

THE CURRENT MORASS

Modern-day Afghanistan is in a precarious state, its virulent opium-heroin business having reached almost unmanageable proportions. An aggressive onslaught against the traffic could destabilise Afghan society and also aggravate the country's ongoing authority crisis – provoking resistance from regional warlords now loosely aligned with the central government and pushing farmers into the arms of the resurgent Taliban. At the same time, continued access to drug-related funds by regional power-holders jeopardises political and economic reconstruction and places the survival of the Afghan government at risk. As one US military commander put it, 'Local terrorist and criminal leaders have a vested interest in using the profits from narcotics to oppose the central government and undermine the security and stability of Afghanistan.'[25]

To its credit, the Afghan government and its international backers have taken some modest drug control measures: issuing decrees banning drug cultivation and trafficking, adopting a national drug control strategy, creating a counter-narcotics ministry and police department and establishing a centralised poppy-eradication force.[26] Yet the government's enforcement powers do not extend far beyond the city limits of Kabul. Despite some eradication in the provinces, assisted by foreign military forces, the opium cultivated area reached an all-time high of 193,000 hectares in 2007, 260 per cent above the first post-Taliban extension of 74,000 hectares.[27] Despite US urging, the Afghan authorities have refused to implement aerial spraying of poppy, fearing its consequences for the rural economy. Allied military units operating around the country have perceived their main mission as counter-terrorism – defined as rooting out remnants of al Qaeda and Taliban loyalists. Hence, they may have mostly avoided becoming entangled in downstream counter-narcotics operations: destroying heroin labs, disrupting open opium markets, attacking opium convoys and bringing major traffickers to justice.[28] A *New York Times* article of 22 October 2006 states, '...the Americans have more or less turned a blind eye to the drug-trade spree of their warlord allies...'[29]

Afghanistan's national drug strategy states that '[i]n carrying out law enforcement interventions, it will be important to balance the political risk caused by counter-narcotics measures with the political desirability of extending central authority over the entire country'.[30] The requisite balance has not been struck. Permissiveness toward drugs in the name of fighting terror, broadly defined, has bequeathed Afghanistan more of both. Vast opium harvests, especially in southern Afghanistan, have provided neo-Taliban insurgents with the means to acquire modern weapons, attract new recruits and launch devastating attacks (Taliban fighters are paid a daily wage four times higher than the Afghan army or police, according to a *Financial Times* report).[31] The Taliban have been able to convert the government's feeble eradication effort into a propaganda advantage – now posing (ironically) as staunch defenders of the opium economy and of poor farmers' rights to grow poppy.

The unrelenting expansion of cultivation, in turn, correlates with escalating casualties among non-allied forces, from 68 in 2002 to 232 in 2007[32] as Iraq-style tactics such as suicide bombings and use of improvised explosive devices, almost unknown in 2001–02, have become commonplace. The US-backed government in Kabul is increasingly viewed by Afghans as weak and corrupt – unable to deliver economic benefits, exercise its authority or stem the rising Taliban attacks. At this point only a significantly larger commitment of US and NATO forces to take on the Taliban, massive investments in rural reconstruction and alternative livelihoods and aggressive targeting of the narcotics-trafficking infrastructure might save Afghanistan from disintegrating again into rival armed factions.[33]

Many observers see little near-term prospect of eradicating illicit drugs in Afghanistan. For now, they argue, the focus should be on region-wide containment, particularly on strengthening the border interdiction capabilities of neighbouring states. An effective regional strategy might disrupt the market for Afghan opium and increase the relative attractiveness of farming licit crops. Washington already provides some counter-narcotics and law enforcement assistance to central Asian countries and to Pakistan, and this might be increased. However, Iran, which the United States accuses of nuclear ambitions and sponsorship of terrorism, is the principal transit country of choice for Afghan drug kingpins – an estimated 60 per cent of the flow of opiates from Afghanistan moves through that country. Iran is said to have the highest rate of opiate abuse in the world, its addicts numbering an estimated 3 million, or roughly 4 to 5 per cent of the national population.[34] Also, (Shi'ite) Iran cannot help but feel apprehensive of a resurgent (Sunni) Taliban, historically an inimical group. Such concerns would appear to jibe with Washington's drug-control, counter-terror and nation-building agendas in Afghanistan.

Engagement with Iran on drugs, including development of a joint interdiction strategy, thus makes eminent sense. Yet, as of this writing, the leadership in Washington refuses to cooperate with the Iranians on this and other outstanding issues, until Iran suspends enrichment of uranium. Hence the prospect of an encompassing drug interdiction strategy seems a forlorn hope at present.

CONCLUSION

Afghanistan offers a classic – and tragic – illustration of Cribb's 'tripartite alliance' of clandestine operatives, criminal entrepreneurs and failed or failing states. Admittedly, the responsibility of parapolitics *per se* for Afghanistan's current ills remains somewhat murky. Certainly the CIA's activities conformed generally to the US strategic agenda in that country, which was to fight Soviet expansionism and, later, international terrorism. In this sense, the machinations of parapolitics simply equate to the preferences of the visible state authorities applied in the field. Additionally, CIA officers doubtless would justify their collaboration with men such as Hekmatyar and Massoud as based on the latters' perceived brilliance as military commanders, not their ties to drugs (indeed, one wonders if any prominent military players in Afghanistan during the period of CIA involvement were free of such ties). Finally, as Scheuer has noted, growth of the opium trade clearly signified farmers' reduced opportunities to earn a living from traditional crops.

Yet parapolitics may have subtly shaped US policy to the detriment of Afghanistan's future. Policy makers' mindsets may well have reflected what McCoy calls 'a growing tolerance of narcotics as an informal weapon in the arsenal of covert warfare'.[35] Hence for many years drug control barely figured in US priorities *vis-à-vis* Afghanistan. It is increasingly apparent that successful management of the drug problem is what matters most in determining Afghanistan's nation-building process; yet the problem now has metastasised to an advanced and potentially fatal stage.

NOTES

1. Cribb, this volume. On this general subject, see also essays in Roy Godson (ed.), *Menace to Society: Political-Criminal Collaboration around the World* (New Brunswick, NJ: Transaction Publishers, 2003).
2. United Nations Office on Drugs and Crime (UNODC), *Afghanistan Opium Survey 2007*, Executive Summary (Vienna, 2007), p. 5. UNODC, *Afghanistan Opium Survey 2006*, Executive Summary (Vienna, 2006), pp. iv, v, 1.
3. UNODC, *Afghanistan Opium Survey 2006*, p. 1. See also Senlis Council, *Afghanistan Five Years Later: The Return of the Taliban* (Spring–Summer 2005), p. 53. Pashtuns, who represent the principal ethnic-base of the Taliban, account for roughly 42 per cent of the Afghan population. Leaders of the old Taliban are believed to reside in Pakistan's border regions.
4. Michael Scheuer, *Imperial Hubris: Why the West is Losing the War on Terror* (Washington, DC: Brassey's, 2004), p. 27.
5. Alfred McCoy, *The Politics of Heroin: CIA Complicity in the Global Drug Trade* (Brooklyn, NY: Lawrence Hill Books, 1991), p. 450.
6. See discussion in Steve Coll's excellent study, *Ghost Wars: The Secret History of the CIA, Afghanistan, and Bin Laden, from the Soviet Invasion to September 10, 2001* (New York: Penguin, 2004), pp. 416–584.
7. UNODC, *Afghanistan Opium Survey 2006*, p. 12.

8. Coll, *Ghost Wars*, p. 524.

9. Ibid., pp. 431, 454, 468, 529.

10. UNODC, *Afghanistan Opium Survey 2006*, p. 2.

11. *State Department International Narcotics Control Strategy Report (INCSR)* (Washington, DC: March 1992), pp. vii–3. UN Office of Drug Control and Crime Prevention, *Afghan Opium Survey 2002* (Vienna, 2002), pp. 4, 49.

12. Scott Baldauf, 'Afghans Try Opium-Free Economy', *Christian Science Monitor*, 7 April 2001, p. 1. State Department, 'Humanitarian Assistance to Afghanistan', *eMediamillWorks*, 17 May 2001, p. 1. Coll, *Ghost Wars*, p. 512.

13. United States Department of State, International Narcotics Control Strategy Report (INCSR), March 2002, pp. vii–3.

14. Barbara Crossette, 'Taliban's Ban on Poppy a Success, U.S. Aides Say', *New York Times*, 20 May 2001, p. 7.

15. Julian West and Philip Sherwell, 'Afghanistan's Heroin Ploy', *Sunday Telegraph*, London, 18 February 2001, p. D10.

16. David Mansfield, 'Alternative Development in Afghanistan: The Failure of Quid-Pro-Quo', unpublished paper, August 2001, p. 1.

17. 'Taliban Calls for Help in Anti-Drugs Drive', *Associated Press*, Kabul, 26 June 2001, p. 1.

18. 'Humanitarian Assistance'. Even this modest aid package was criticised by some as incongruous with overall US policy of isolating the Taliban. As *Newsday* wrote, 'The Bush Administration, intent on fighting illegal drug production abroad, is so delighted at the opium ban that it is willing to overlook America's differences with the Taliban – such as its barbaric treatment of women, and trampling on the rights of religious minorities, its destruction of religious statues, even its protection of bin Laden.' See 'Afghanistan's Taliban Regime is Brutal and Harsh – So Why Does Washington Give It Aid?', Editorial, 29 May 2001.

19. Rensselaer Lee, *Afghanistan: Prospects for Opium Eradication*, Congressional Research Service Report 31710, 24 January 2003, p. CRS-11.

20. John Donnelly, 'America Prepares Overseas Development: Kabul Drops Opium Ban, Boom Feared', *Boston Globe*, 26 September 2001, p. A1.

21. UNODC, *Afghanistan Opium Survey 2006*, pp. 2, 12, 23.

22. State Department cable, 'International Narcotics Control Strategy Report: Part One', Kabul, 7 November 2002, p. 4.

23. David Filipov, 'Drug Trade Flourishes Again in Afghanistan. Critics Want the US to Target Production', *Boston Globe*, 21 October 2002, pp. 1–3.

24. Seumas Milne, 'Comment and Analysis: A war that can't be won: the west isn't just losing the fight against terrorism – it is fuelling it around the globe', *Guardian*, 21 November 2002.

25. Cited in Senlis Council, *Afghanistan Five Years Later*, p. 51.

26. Government Accountability Office, *Afghanistan Reconstruction: Despite Some Progress, Deteriorating and Other Obstacles Continue to Threaten Achievement of US Goals*, GAO-05-742 (Washington, DC: July 2005), pp. 84–5.

27. UNODC, *Afghanistan Opium Survey 2007*, p. 1.

28. 'That's not our mission', General Tommy Franks, then-Commander of the US forces in Afghanistan, was quoted as saying in March 2002. Some 'mission creep' has been apparent in recent years, with US forces sometimes attacking trafficking facilities that they find in the course of counter-terror operations. An unusual case of deliberate targeting of 'Taliban' heroin labs by a US Special Forces team was reported in *Soldier of Fortune* in February 2004, but the raconteur noted that 'our mission in Afghanistan was not anti-drug – just the opposite – we were directed not to interfere with the opium and heroin trade'; but they did so anyway. See Bill Geertz, 'Military Opposes Spraying Poppies, Bush Seeks to Hit Afghan Crop', *Washington Times*, 26 March 2002, p. A1. Author interview, State Department official, 23 October 2006. Paul Avellone, 'Striking at the Heroin Trade', *Soldier of Fortune*, February 2004, p. 75.

29. Elizabeth Rubin, 'In the Land of the Taliban', *New York Times Magazine*, 22 October 2006, p. 92.

30. Government of Afghanistan, *National Drug Control Strategy* (Kabul, 2001), p. 14.

31. Rachel Morarjee, 'Poppy Wars and Unpopularity: Why Afghanistan Looks on Course to Fail', *Financial Times*, 5 September 2005, p. 15.
32. Operation Enduring Freedom Coalition Military Casualties by Year (www.icasualties.org/oef).
33. Elizabeth Rubin, 'Taking the Fight to the Taliban', *New York Times Magazine*, 29 October 2006, p. 60. Rubin notes that Western troops in Afghanistan number only 42,000 in a country one-third larger than Iraq, where there are about 150,000.
34. United States Department of State, International Narcotics Control Strategy Report (INCSR), March 2006, Africa and the Middle East: Iran, www.state.gov, 4 December, 2006.
35. McCoy, *The Politics of Heroin*, p. 492.

11

From Drug Lords to Warlords: Illegal Drugs and the 'Unintended' Consequences of Drug Policies in Colombia

Francisco E. Thoumi

The illegal drugs industry has been a feature of Colombia since the early 1970s.[1] Since then the industry has evolved in complex and frequently unpredictable ways. Illegal industries evolve in response to market forces and to Colombian and foreign governments' anti-drug policies. These policies have been repressive, respond to a simple police model of organised crime and most often not only fail to achieve their desired goals but also result in nasty 'unintended' consequences.

The first section of this chapter summarises a theory of competitive advantage in plant-based illegal drugs. The second section explores some policy consequences derived from that theory. The third section highlights some of the characteristics of Colombia that made it a fertile ground for the development of the illicit industry. The development of the country's illegal drug industry through the mid 1990s is sketched in the fourth section. The fifth section shows the evolution of the illicit industry during the last ten years. In this period the warlords gained control of the illegal industry from drug-trafficking organisations. The chapter ends with a short set of conclusions.

THE COMPETITIVE ADVANTAGE IN PLANT-BASED ILLEGAL DRUGS

Plant-based illegal drugs are easy to produce. They require little capital, their technology is widely known, and they use labour skills that are relatively abundant. Yet, with the exception of marijuana, their production does not take place in many countries; indeed, it is, and has been, remarkably concentrated in a few countries. Furthermore, several countries that were important producers in the past, when those drugs were legal, do not produce illegal drugs now, despite their profitability. During the last 45 years, since the Single Convention of the United Nations made coca and cocaine illegal, coca production has been concentrated in Bolivia, Colombia and Peru. The shares of coca production of these three countries have varied through time but their total has accounted for over 95 per cent of global coca production throughout this period.[2] Interestingly, during the first 40 years of the twentieth century, while cocaine was legal, the largest coca suppliers to the cocaine industry were Indonesia, Malaysia and Taiwan.[3] Beginning in the early 1970s, Colombia concentrated illegal cocaine manufacturing and since then it has remained the largest cocaine producer in the world. By the late 1990s it had also become the largest coca grower in the world.

Opium poppies can grow in a larger number of countries than coca but production is also concentrated in a few countries. In 2003, three countries (Afghanistan, Laos and Myanmar) accounted for 91.5 per cent of the world's illegal acreage of poppy and 95 per cent of the potential opium output.[4] Adding Mexico and Colombia, the two next largest producers that supply the American market, these shares increase to 96.8 and 97.9 per cent respectively. Today Colombia produces over 60 per cent of the coca and cocaine and Afghanistan over 80 per cent of the opium poppy and heroin of the world. In 1970, Colombia was not known for its production of illegal drugs and Afghanistan had been a minor producer of opium for a long time; opium was not really a 'traditional' crop in Afghanistan, where it was not cultivated in most parts of the country until the 1990s.[5] Unlike most countries in the region, Afghanistan did not have much of an 'opium culture'. Thus opium consumption, until recently, remained relatively low.[6] At that time, neither of those two countries was a large producer of opium poppy or coca nor a significant player in international drug markets.

The high concentration of the production of illegal drugs stands in stark contradiction with commonly-held beliefs about the reasons why a country produces them. The most commonly-held belief in producing countries is that production is driven by international demand, which generates the very high profits that drive the illegal industry. 'When there is demand there is supply' is a frequent justificatory assertion that 'explains' why drugs are produced. It is obvious that if nobody used drugs, there would not be production. This, however, is a simplistic and trivial assertion because the converse – 'if nobody produced drugs, nobody would use them' – is equally valid. As is explained in the most elementary economics textbooks, supply and demand are like the two blades of scissors: they are both necessary to cut. There is no question that profitability is a necessary condition for illicit drug production, but it is certainly not a sufficient one. Indeed, if profitability were a sufficient condition for production, illicit drugs would be produced in all countries and regions where they could be produced and Afghanistan and Colombia would today be only minor players in the illegal drug business.[7]

Legal and illegal economic activities require different skills. In contrast to the legal economy, producing illicit opium-heroin and coca-cocaine requires the performance of a series of illegal activities: purchasing illegal inputs, which are frequently controlled substances and have to be smuggled and/or obtained on an underground market; cultivating illicit crops; creating clandestine manufacturing facilities; developing domestic and international criminal distribution networks to sell at home, to smuggle and distribute drugs and to launder illegal revenues; transporting illegally obtained currency across international borders and exchanging these funds from one currency to another without revealing their origin; laundering and investing illegally obtained funds; and managing portfolios of illegally obtained capital. The need to minimise risks in performing these illicit activities determines the location of the illegal industry. The successful performance of these tasks requires special 'illegal skills' used to develop illegal business organisations, social support networks to protect the industry from law enforcement efforts; to provide contract enforcement and conflict resolution systems within the criminal organisations; and to have the will to break economic laws and regulations and to use violence if necessary.[8]

Human compliance with norms and laws depends on the state's ability to enforce its laws, the degree to which social institutions like family, peer groups and religion sanction or condone norm-breaking behaviours, and on the internal controls that individuals develop during their socialisation processes. Illegal economic activities flourish in societies with weak states and lax social controls. These factors determine whether illegal economic activities become important in a country. Indeed, it can be asserted that international norms that make illegal the production and trafficking of goods like cocaine and heroin, that have known production technologies and do not require large amounts of capital and particularly scarce labour skills, create strong competitive advantages in countries where the state is weak or fails to control large sections of its territory and where social norms are lax and tolerate illegal economic activities.

All illegal economic activities require social support networks to operate. These include civilians who cooperate with or condone the illegal activities and government officials who help them or allow them to go on. The social networks that develop in each country depend on specific factors and characteristics of each society. Some of these are related to geography: availability of natural resources needed to produce illegal goods, location near large consumption and production areas or in transit routes. Others are related to each country's history, structure, institutions and culture. These factors are diverse and specific to each society. Several examples come to mind. One is the existence of social groups that have traditionally used mind-altering drugs or practised and profited from contraband and are not part of the social mainstream. These groups would be more likely to break the government's laws than those that are integrated into the mainstream.

The role of the armed forces in politics and in the control of the territory is also a factor. Countries with large, isolated areas outside state control are also more vulnerable to the development of illegal economic activities. Location on a trafficking route or possible route is also important. Country size is another element to take into account, as it influences who should be bribed to operate illegally. In large countries illegal organisations can operate in coordination with local authorities only; the smaller the country, the more they have to make alliances with high-ranking national political figures. In authoritarian countries there is a greater need to get the nod of the dictator or dominant political figure. These factors, among others, determine the role that the country plays in the illegal industry and the nature of the illegal activities developed: the actual size of the illegal industry, whether they develop large trafficking 'cartels', large plantings, or participate in money laundering, etc.

Involvement in illegal drugs is more likely to be socially tolerated when it is limited to production and trafficking but excludes local consumption. Non-state actors frequently justify their involvement in drug production and trafficking as actions directed towards evil imperialists or infidel foreign consumers. Such is the case with Colombian guerrillas and some Afghani tribes who have strong prohibitions against drug consumption but see exports as a way to weaken imperialist or infidel societies. These organisations are very authoritarian and such governments or organisations tend to be strongly prohibitionist regarding consumption.

The dynamics of the illegal industry are also important. Illegal economic activities continuously adapt to law enforcement tactics, seek to lower the risks of production and trafficking, and are continuously searching for safe locations for their activities, new trafficking routes, markets and money-laundering systems. These changes require the development of new support networks and the adaptation of established ones. Law enforcement agencies respond to these changes, adapt their tactics and strategies and search for new ones. It may be argued that the illegal industry is in continuous disequilibrium: some members hiding from the law, others seeking new routes and markets, others in gaol and seeking ways to get out, and so on.

The sustained presence of the illegal drugs industry generates large structural, institutional and cultural changes in the societies where it is established. After some time, the presence of illegal drugs activities causes social institutions and cultures to change. This makes it difficult to estimate the effects of the illegal drugs industry on a country. On the one hand, the growth of this industry generates income and may increase the supply of foreign exchange. This can have some positive economic consequences. In the cases of Bolivia and Peru, for instance, the illegal drugs industry played an important role in facilitating the structural macroeconomic adjustments of the late 1980s and early 1990s. On the other hand, the industry influences and corrupts politics; changes social attitudes towards law compliance, weakening the rule of law; increases expectations of quick profits which can easily lead to speculative investments; increases criminality and violence; requires shifts in the government budget from investment and social expenditures to law enforcement; increases the risk of expanding local drug consumption; and strengthens some social groups (overtly criminal and otherwise), while weakening others. These negative changes are cumulative through time and produce changes in institutions and culture. While positive economic effects may be felt in the short run, in the long run the industry brings negative social and economic consequences. These do not depend directly on current illegal production or income but on the history and trajectory of the illegal industry in a country; its government's past policy responses to it; and the social and economic changes it has generated.

The Andean countries are a clear example of those processes. All estimates of the size of the illegal drugs industry in Bolivia, Colombia and Peru show that the current drug-generated income is a much lower share of GDP than in 1980. Yet the consequences of having a drug industry are felt more dramatically today than almost three decades ago. Until about 2000, the share of GDP generated by the illegal industry in Colombia was significantly lower than in Bolivia and Peru, yet the negative effects of the industry were much greater.

It should be pointed out, however, that some of the important consequences of the development of the illegal drugs industry may not be classified as either positive or negative. Because the illegal industry is instrumental in changes in institutions and culture, the evaluation of these changes requires strong value judgements. For example, the illegal industry and the government responses to it in Bolivia have resulted in great political changes and the rise of a strong *cocalero* movement with deep Indian roots and the election of Evo Morales, a *cocalero* leader, to the presidency of Bolivia. This development may be seen as positive from the point of view of the long-suppressed Indian population but raises fears and distrust among the country's elite and foreign investors.

To conclude, the development of the illegal drugs industry is not a purely exogenous event that falls on a society because of bad luck or destiny. It establishes itself in countries that are vulnerable to it, that is, that have a particular set of institutions, productive structure and culture that make them fertile grounds for the industry. Once established, the industry changes the economic structure of the society, its institutions and culture. Therefore, to understand the illegal drugs industry it is necessary to study the processes that lead to its development and evolution in each society. These are society-specific and their understanding requires knowledge of the society's history, structure, institutions and culture.

POLICY IMPLICATIONS OF THE 'COMPETITIVE ADVANTAGE' THEORY OF DRUG PRODUCTION

Most anti-drug policies attack drug profits. These policies aim to lower profits for producers and to increase risks and costs for all actors in the illegal industry. An important basic question is: what results can be achieved by going after contributing and necessary, but not sufficient, conditions for the development of an illegal activity? A simple answer is that results depend on the policies' ability to eliminate that necessary condition. Unfortunately, current repressive policies do not have this capacity and some anti-drug policies work at cross-purposes in this respect: they seek to lower the revenues received by peasants and increase the retail prices of cocaine and heroin, thus raising profits at the retail end of the market. Policies aiming to achieve these goals can succeed only if they eliminate market incentives for production in every location where drugs can be produced. To do so, it is necessary to establish and maintain indefinitely a very high level of repression in the presence of increased potential retail profits – an impossible task for most governments with the resources and technology available today.

Repressive policies are promoted by the United States, but prohibitionism is supported by an overwhelming majority of the countries and societies in the world. Indeed, it can be said that the world is prohibitionist. A list of current prohibition- ist countries includes: the US, Sweden, all Eastern European countries and those of the former Soviet Union, all Islamic nations, China, Japan and other Southeast Asian countries, all South Saharan African countries and many Latin American and Caribbean Nations. A relatively minor deviation from this pattern is found among several Western European countries that want to deepen their experiments with harm-reduction policies on the consumption side; and a few drug-producing countries that have suffered the negative consequences of the increased influence of the illegal economy and organised crime. The deviance of the Western European countries is quite mild. Their efforts are in the direction toward a public health approach to drug consumption problems but none of those countries advocate liberalising drug production, much less a free, unregulated drug market. In this sense they support a less drastic form of prohibitionism.

Colombia must face the fact that illegal drug profitability will continue for the foreseeable future. To produce drugs there are other necessary factors besides profitability, such as an appropriate institutional environment and a culture that encourages individuals to take advantage of illegal market opportunities. This presents an interesting policy problem. In order to succeed through repressive policies, Colombia must eliminate illicit drug profitability within its borders in the presence of external profitability. To achieve this goal, the level of repression necessary would be extremely high, so much so that it will be socially and politically unacceptable.[9] Indeed, the level of repression required to achieve a particular goal is inversely proportional to the extent of the rule of law. Since the illegal industry locates itself in the countries and regions where the rule of law is weakest, it is precisely in those societies where repressive policies would have to be the strongest in order to achieve any result.[10] Even in this case, it would also be necessary to have uncorruptable law enforcement officials, otherwise the stronger the pressure, the more opportunities for corruption and the lower the chances of success. Not surprisingly, for drug policy to succeed by repressive means in Colombia would require large sacrifices in human rights and other government policy goals such as the environment, the strengthening of government legitimacy in illegal crop zones and long-term stable governability.

An important lesson from the analysis of the competitive advantage in illegal activities is that as long as the rule of law in drug-producing societies remains low, repressive policies will have to be very strong and will, at best, achieve short-term successes, unless extreme repression is maintained indefinitely, a very unlikely scenario. This is why to guarantee long-term success it is necessary to establish the rule of law. In other words, the 'drug problem' in plant-based drug-producing countries is structural, institutional and cultural, not a simple policy problem to be tackled with traditional policy prescriptions. The current policy debate is framed as a confrontation between 'legalisers' and 'criminalisers'. From the point of view of Colombia, the real long-term issue is how to develop social behavioural controls and how to strengthen the state's capacity to enforce its own laws. Without these, it will not achieve a long-term solution to its 'drug problem'.

The role of traditional repressive policies raises other important issues; first, to what extent current policies complement or conflict with each other or generate 'unintended consequences' that neutralise the effects of other policies; and second, whether these policies are complementary or will conflict with the social changes needed to achieve long-term success. An important issue is whether policies designed to produce certain short-run results will be obstacles to achieving the deeper changes required for long-term success.

Current policies frequently conflict with each other and generate 'unintended consequences'. For example, forced eradication tends to displace plantings to new areas. This so-called 'balloon effect' means that policy success remains local; globally, eradication may have little or no long-term effect. Furthermore, if a 'balloon effect' does occur, forced eradication results in a significant 'unintended' environmental damage as more old native forest is destroyed to plant new illegal crops; and in some cases, it causes large migrations to other rural and urban areas where uprooted peasants settle. Forced eradication also has the 'unintended' effect of weakening community loyalty to the state; and the displacement of peasants might increase the willingness of young people to join armed groups like the Revolutionary Armed Forces of Colombia (FARC). Both of these are obstacles to achieving long-term solutions.

Common a-historic and non-institutional economic analyses, based on models that have direct and clear causality of the 'if X then Y' type, fail to understand these processes and may lead to misleading results. For example, economists' general equilibrium analyses assume static institutions and culture. In the case of Colombia, they would conclude that the effects of the illegal industry were greater in 1980 than at present and they would fail to realise that in 1980 the illegal income contributed to wealth creation, while currently it is the main source of subversive and counter-subversive guerrilla funding and now contributes to wealth destruction. These analyses also present problems when they are used for cross-country comparisons, because in each country the impact of the illegal industry on institutions and culture vary and are cumulative through time, and thus, they differ, depending on the initial structure and institutions, their evolution and the time elapsed between the moment of the analysis and the onset of the industry.

The work of other economists recognises the catalytic effects of the development of the illicit drugs industry but fails to explain why they develop in a particular country. For example, in 2000 Gaviria showed how the growth of the illegal drugs industry in Colombia triggered increased criminality and an explosion in the homicide rate.[11] To be able to model the drug industry, Gaviria treats the growth of the industry as an 'external shock', similar to an increase in coffee or oil prices. This approach can be explained by the modelling difficulties common in formal economic studies, but it fails to consider domestic factors leading to the development of the industry in Colombia. Indeed, Gaviria does not explain why this 'external shock' affected Colombia but not other countries. Furthermore, once the problem is defined as being caused by an 'external shock' the policy recommendation that follows would focus on the 'external shock', rather than domestic issues.

WHY COLOMBIA?[12]

Before examining the development of the illegal drugs industry in Colombia it is important to understand the reasons why this country has a competitive advantage in the production of illegal goods. The main problem has been persistent difficulty in generating strong communities, bridging social capital and creating a national identity for which people are willing to make sacrifices. Indeed, Colombia is an extremely individualistic society in which social and state controls on individual behaviour are very weak.[13]

The reasons for the peculiar Colombian societal development are many but the country's geography has been a key determinant. For centuries the Colombian central state was the poorest in Latin America. Until the 1920s coffee boom, Colombia had the lowest exports per capita of any Latin American and Caribbean country and, of those, the lowest taxes per capita. Because of its geography, the country was faced with the poorest state and the greatest challenge to integrate markets and form a true nation. The result was a set of relatively isolated settlements with very little trade and communication among them. These were poor, but quite autonomous from Bogotá, the capital. These regions developed their own loyalties, accents and cultural traits and many had little to do with the central state. This was also true of the native communities that existed before the Conquest. Indeed, in contrast with the communities in Mexico, Guatemala, Ecuador, Peru, Bolivia and Paraguay that were part of strong central states, Colombian Indians were settled but were only a collection of chiefdoms that frequently fought each other.

These problems were compounded by Simón Bolívar's debt-funded campaign to free Ecuador, Peru and Bolivia, which saddled Colombia with an unpayable foreign debt and blocked its access to fresh international funds until the 1920s.

In this environment the two traditional parties, Liberal and Conservative, became the source of personal identities that are normally associated with a nation. During the 1940s and 1950s, they fought an ambiguous war known as 'La Violencia' that killed about 200,000 people out of a population of some 11 million and in which local warlords were key figures. Warring factions had ideological discourses but a main purpose of the war in many regions was to capture land, displacing opponents. 'La Violencia' and the population explosion generated a significant peasant migration both to cities and other rural areas. Any map of the country taken at ten-year intervals shows a very significant expansion of the rural frontier as many peasants migrated to unsettled areas. Most of the rural–rural migration was spontaneous and in most new settlements state presence was precarious. Many of these lands were distant and unconnected from the main markets. Worse yet, part of this migration was made up of people who had been displaced by groups associated with the establishment and for whom, therefore, the state was viewed with great distrust. Colombian migrants differ from most others in Latin America because many of them have been displaced by violence and have lost their roots.

After 'La Violencia', some former left-leaning fighters settled in isolated areas and developed their own protection systems. These peasants formed the original FARC core. Other guerrilla groups like ELN, M-19 and EPL also developed and sought haven in areas with little or no state control.

The Colombian military is atypical in Latin America. It has traditionally supported civilian governments and its members do not come from the upper classes. The armed forces status is relatively low. One may argue that military service is the most evaded tax among the upper classes. The military's role in society is quite limited and its members relatively anonymous. It is remarkable that in Congress there are several former guerrillas but only one former police sergeant has been elected in recent years. The armed forces have not been able, as in other countries, to generate a sense of belonging to the nation.

In summary, in Colombia there have been many factors that have prevented the development of strong communities, the rule of law and the bridging of social capital. The result has been the development of a very individualistic society in which a significant part of the population is willing to break legal and social norms and where illicit economic activities are accepted as normal. Not surprisingly, when the demand for illegal drugs increased sharply in the late 1960s, Bolivia and Peru – where coca was a traditional consumption item – expanded their plantings but it was in Colombia where the cocaine refining and trafficking organisations developed.

During the second half of the twentieth century, infrastructure developed and the country became more integrated. Still, the central state had great difficulty providing conflict resolution systems and guaranteeing property rights, particularly in many rural areas.

It can be argued that a large part of the Colombian territory is a white elephant for the economic and political establishment. The large eastern half of the country has been sparsely populated and quite unproductive. It is true that there are some oil wells and cattle ranches in the eastern *llanos*, but most of the land is not productive in the sense of providing goods and services for the modern economy. The jungle areas, including some of the tropical lowlands of the western Pacific coast and in a few other regions, are more difficult to exploit productively. Though these jungles should be preserved as a long-term carbon sink, for many people their felling brings more immediate financial return. This is a clear case of 'market failure' that leads to misuse of these resources. A basic problem confronted by the Colombian government is that establishing a strong presence in a large part of the country has a cost that exceeds what it can afford, what it can collect in taxes and the income the private sector can generate in those areas. It is not surprising that throughout the last two centuries Colombia has tried to protect its territory through strict adherence to international treaties, rather than by establishing and maintaining a significant state presence in those territories.[14]

The impossibility of sustainable and profitable crops or industries in many areas and the difficulty in exploiting other possible resources means that those who control the central state have very little incentive to invest in social and physical infrastructure in those regions. Indeed, were it to do so, the state might end up spending a large chunk of its resources in rather unproductive places. This is why FARC and other guerrilla groups have been able to survive unchallenged for many years in some isolated areas.

The lack of permanent state presence in many areas does not pose an important problem, so long as there is no population settled there. When settlement occurs – and because of its cost, the state has only a meagre or token presence – a power vacuum results that is filled by parastatal groups. In reality, the ideology of those groups is largely irrelevant and in Colombia both left- and right-wing parastatal groups have filled such power vacuums. Ironically, while legal production is unprofitable in many of these areas, illegal production is not. The parastatal groups can exploit illegal activities while the state may not. What happens then is that parastatal organisations have an absolute competitive advantage in those regions because they can produce illegal goods.

THE DEVELOPMENT OF THE ILLEGAL DRUGS INDUSTRY IN COLOMBIA UP TO THE MID TO LATE 1990s

The illegal drugs industry started around 1970 with the planting of marijuana in the snow-capped Santa Marta Sierra on the northwest Caribbean coast. This was a 'balloon effect' of the aerial spraying of marijuana in Mexico and Jamaica with the herbicide paraquat, a highly toxic and carcinogenic chemical compound. In the beginning, Colombian farmers were responding to the foreign traffickers' demand for marijuana, but Colombians very soon developed their own export trafficking networks. The marijuana boom did not last very long, however, as the more potent *sin semilla* variety was developed in the US and Colombian marijuana lost market share. The experience with marijuana led Colombians to seek other profitable illegal drugs and start to purchase and import coca paste and cocaine base from Bolivia and Peru to process into cocaine to be exported. Colombians organised distribution networks abroad and a cocaine boom appeared. Trafficking organisations were complex, although many parts of them were decentralised. Two large, loose organisations emerged: the so-called 'cartels' based in the cities of Medellín and Cali. Other significant trafficking groups developed in Bogotá and on the Caribbean coast. These organisations brought coca paste and cocaine base from abroad, processed and exported it. This business gave rise to the establishment of coca plantings that sprouted as a 'backward linkage' of the cocaine manufacturing and trafficking industry.

The two large cartels developed armed branches to protect their leaders and their investments, to enforce deals and to intimidate the government, the press and others who opposed them. These were used in the 1980s to fight extradition to the US. This was the 'narco-terrorism' period, during which traffickers killed a large number of politicians, journalists, law enforcement personnel and others who opposed the illegal drugs industry. The government reacted with the support of the US, other governments and multilateral agencies and a war against narco-terrorism followed. By 1993, most members of the Medellín cartel were dead or in gaol. The fight against the Medellín traffickers was supported by the Cali cartel, which provided the government with intelligence about their competitors.

All trafficking organisations have been instrumental in corrupting government organisations. Indeed, all criminal organisations require social support networks to operate and seek to develop links with national institutions. The Medellín cartel had invested heavily in rural land that had to be protected against guerrilla groups. To do so, it developed links with the military and organised its own armed branch, which became one of the roots of the paramilitary movement. This group fought the national police, which was trying to destroy the cartel. The Cali trafficking organisation invested mainly in urban areas and developed strong links with Cali police. Both groups also developed support networks with politicians.

In the mid 1990s, the government turned its attention to the Cali cartel and succeeded in eliminating some of its leaders and gaoling the rest. The policies against the large cartels were part of the 'kingpin' strategy promoted by the US government aiming to eliminate the leadership of the cartels and, as seen below, it generated significant 'unintended consequences'. Indeed, the illicit drugs industry that had been controlled by large trafficking organisations evolved to a point where it became ruled by warlords. These were also aided by other important policy changes during this period.

RECENT DEVELOPMENTS: FROM DRUG LORDS TO WARLORDS

After the capture of the main leaders of the Cali cartel the Colombian illegal drugs industry experienced a substantial restructuring. The two large cartels lost their market dominance and a large number of small '*cartelitos*' and a few mid-sized ones emerged. Their number is uncertain but several DEA documents suggest that there have been some 200 to 300 smaller trafficking organisations.[15]

Another development related to this structural market change has been the growth of coca and poppy plantings, as small trafficking organisations have strong incentives to purchase opium, coca paste, cocaine base and cocaine locally. This was also a factor in the development of opium poppy plantings and the heroin trade. Heroin trafficking is also more attractive to small crime syndicates because of its higher price per unit of weight and volume. There have been other important changes as paramilitary warlords and left-wing guerrillas became increasingly involved in the illicit industry. These changes in the illegal drug industry have had a dramatic impact on the political structure of the country.

In the early 1990s, coca plantings began to expand in Colombia. Official data, both from the United Nations and the US Department of State, show the expansion beginning in 1995 and attribute this to the success of Peru's 'Air bridge denial strategy' whereby suspicious aeroplanes were captured on the ground, forced to land or even shot down.[16] Official data provided by the Peruvian Air Force shows that it 'neutralised' three planes in 1990, eleven in 1991, twelve in 1992, 25 in 1993 and 15 in 1994; while UN data shows that coca prices in the Upper Huallaga Valley, the main coca-growing area, remained stable. The official government version is that after 20 planes were neutralised in 1995, coca prices in that region collapsed and remained low. However, only three planes were neutralised in 1996, ten in 1997, none in 1998 and 1999, two in 2000 and one in 2001. These data show that in 1995 Colombian buyers simply stopped purchasing.

United Nations data[17] show that coca prices per kilo in the Upper Huallaga (in constant 2000 US dollars) were very low in 1992 ($0.92), when the Colombian government was fighting the war against narco-terrorism. These prices increased in the following years and remained in the $2–$3 range until 1995, when they fell to $1.24. Coca prices bottomed out in 1996 at $0.66, and in 1997 at $0.77. They recovered in the following years, reaching $2.70 in 2000.[18] These data are consistent with a different set of explanations for the decline in coca prices and the ensuing fall in the coca acreage in Peru.

First, every illegal industry requires a social support network to operate successfully. In the 1980s and early 1990s, the Shining Path guerrillas provided that support in Peru. After the Fujimori regime neutralised that guerrilla organisation, support was provided by government agencies that controlled the territories where the illegal industry operated. Indeed, some government personnel became directly involved in drug trafficking.[19] This was the time when the infamous Vladimiro Montesinos, the head of intelligence (SIN) for the regime, controlled the illegal trade and charged a fee for each planeload of drugs that left Peru. This practice had existed before Fujimori took office. Pablo Escobar's brother[20] confirms that Montesinos, a lawyer, frequently defended drug traffickers including Evaristo Porras, a well-known Colombian trafficker from Leticia, the Colombian port in the Amazon. He also claims to have met Montesinos at Hacienda Nápoles, Pablo's famous farm, where Pablo agreed to pay Montesinos $300 per kilogram from Peru that arrived safely in Colombia.[21]

Fujimori's main goal for the coca-growing areas in the early 1990s was to wrest territorial control from the guerrillas. To achieve this goal, he needed support from peasant communities. He stopped eradication programmes and the involvement of the army in the war against the guerrillas in those regions made the army very vulnerable to corruption. This problem became more pressing after Fujimori closed Congress in 1992 and promoted the 1993 constitutional reform that strengthened the executive power and the armed forces. After the constitutional reform, corruption in the coca-growing areas was exacerbated.[22]

Second, the fall in coca prices in the Upper Huallaga coincides with events in Colombia. Official data of the United Nations and US Department of State show that coca plantings in Colombia began to expand in 1995, when the Peruvian acreage began to decline. However, independent research[23] shows that the area under coca cultivation in 1994 was already 83,500 hectares – about twice the official figure. In the late 1970s, Colombian peasants began to grow coca in distant isolated jungle regions. In these areas the state failed to provide effective law and order and conflict resolution services. Guerrilla and paramilitary organisations took advantage of this power vacuum and saw in it an opportunity to profit from the illegal business. These groups collected 'taxes' from coca growers, cocaine manufacturers and traffickers. Paramilitary groups also benefited from these sources, and their links with drug-trafficking organisations facilitated their involvement in cocaine refining and trafficking. The interest of both types of armed organisations led to a large expansion in coca cultivation and the beginning of opium poppy plantings. By 1994, Colombia was already the world's second largest coca producer.[24]

The fragmentation of the cocaine syndicates encouraged local coca production because small trafficking groups, as noted earlier, have a strong preference for buying their inputs locally. Left-wing guerrillas lost Soviet and Cuban economic support and found coca and poppy plantings and drug trafficking to be excellent sources of 'taxes'. The growth of the paramilitary movement also required funding, and illegal crops and cocaine and heroin processing provided a good share of it. The confrontation between guerrillas and paramilitaries displaced a large number of peasants, many of whom settled in illicit crop producing areas. During the last ten years of ambiguous internal war the guerrillas and paramilitary have clashed directly very few times. Their strategy has been to attack civilians who they suspect are helping or may help their opponents. As a result, most victims of this war have been civilians: after Sudan, Colombia is the country with the second largest number of displaced citizens in the world.

Other important policy changes generated 'unintended consequences'. In 1990, Colombia implemented a strong policy of opening the economy, which substantially increased competition in the market for agricultural products. A rural crisis ensued in parts of the country, generating a willing labour force for coca production. Indeed, many peasants migrated from coffee, rice and other farms to unsettled areas, where they started coca and poppy fields.

The persistent internal conflicts in the country led to a Constitutional Assembly that produced the 1991 Constitution, aiming to establish a more democratic society. The new constitution 'guaranteed' important economic rights to education, health and housing and established systems to transfer funds from the central government to local governments.[25] These attempts to deepen democracy meant that, for the first time, poor municipalities (the equivalent of county governments) in isolated regions had significant revenues. These municipalities did not have administrative capabilities or accountability systems and became bounties for guerrilla and paramilitary organisations.

These changes created a premium on territorial control. Guerrilla and paramilitary groups realised that they could profit from controlling coca- and poppy-growing areas and municipalities. Today these groups obtain revenues from municipal budgets, illicit drugs, extortion (protection services) and ransoms from kidnappings. They also conduct licit business to complement their income and launder some of their illicit profits.

The fragmentation of the drug industry increased the power of left- and right-wing guerrillas and their involvement in the drug trade. The large Cali and Medellín 'cartels' had security organisations to protect their businesses. Small *cartelitos* do not have the size or resources to do so. They started hiring guerrillas and paramilitary groups for protection. Guerrillas provide protection and gained control mostly over coca and poppy planting regions. The paramilitary tend to do so in the more advanced stages of the productive chain.

The expansion of illicit plantings multiplied the number of peasants involved and they became politically organised, although their capacity to act independently from the violent actors of the Colombian conflict is limited. In 1996 there were very large organised marches of peasant protestors in response to the eradication efforts of the government. Guerrilla groups took advantage of this situation and encouraged these protests.[26]

In 1994 Ernesto Samper was elected president with significant funding from the Cali cartel. When this was uncovered his administration had to devote almost all its energy to responding to the drug funding accusations and it failed to confront the growing social and political problems of the country. During his administration, both guerrillas and paramilitaries gained power and control over larger areas of the country. The subsequent administration of Andrés Pastrana (1998–2002) was elected on a peace platform. Pastrana met with the main guerrilla leaders before the election and projected the image of the person who could and would negotiate peace with them. One of the first measures taken by Pastrana's government was the granting of a 'distension' zone to the FARC, the largest guerrilla group. The purpose of this measure was to provide an area where peace discussions could take place. The distension zone had a size of 42,000 square kilometres, included large coca-growing areas and was out of bounds to the Colombian police and armed forces. FARC was supposed to have respected local governments but it became a de facto government that imposed its own laws and a primitive justice system.

Not surprisingly, FARC used this area to deepen its participation in the illegal drug industry. It first established minimum prices for coca and then proceeded to control coca buyers and control or eliminate other intermediaries. In effect, it granted franchises to cocaine laboratories. The distension zone also allowed FARC to build and control landing strips from where the illegal trade could be conducted. One issue raised by these actions is whether FARC is a drug 'cartel'. There is no question that all non-governmental violent actors benefit from the illegal drug trade. They all tax coca and poppy growing peasants and control the manufacturing and local marketing of illicit drugs. However, it is unlikely that the old Marxist guerrilla groups (FARC and ELN) could have developed significant international distribution networks of their own. On the other hand, the paramilitaries have deep roots in drug-trafficking organisations and, indeed, their very creation was promoted by the cartels.[27] Because of their opposition to left-wing guerrillas, they also attracted many former military officers and soldiers with ties to the Colombian establishment. There is no question that paramilitary organisations provide a service to some groups of the Colombian social and economic mainstream, particularly in regions where agriculture and husbandry are important.

FARC's main presence is in the south and the paramilitary groups have gained control of other parts of the country, mainly in the Atlantic coastal departments. In some of these their control is clear. For example, in a couple of departments and a significant number of towns they have allowed only one candidate in recent elections. In these places they have threatened or eliminated their opponents.[28]

The paramilitary began in part as a movement by landlords who were victims of guerrilla extortions and kidnappings. Armed branches of the drug cartels joined them to protect drug traffickers' investments. In the past, they have fought guerrillas for control of coca-producing areas and trafficking corridors. In the last few years, however, there are increasing signs that – at least in some regions – guerrilla and paramilitary fronts collude to profit from the illegal drugs industry.[29] In some regions those groups divide coca- and poppy-growing regions, manufacture cocaine and heroin, and sell to the same trafficking networks. In other locations, FARC oversees coca production and sells coca to the paramilitary, which refines and sells the cocaine to traffickers or exports it itself. According to police reports there have been cases in which large seizures included cocaine from FARC, paramilitary groups and traffickers.

A decline in the income of the peasants growing coca and poppy is another significant effect of control of territory by guerrillas and paramilitaries, which set coca and opium prices and also control the markets of staples, which are sold at very high nominal prices. In those regions, guerrillas and paramilitaries act as monopsonists and monopolists who exploit the peasants twice: fixing low prices for peasants' products and high prices for what peasants purchase.[30] Similarly, their military power has put drug traffickers at a disadvantage, since they now have to buy cocaine from those armed groups.

President Pastrana realised that it was imperative for the Colombian state to develop a strong military force, to establish its presence in, and control, the country's territory and to fight the growth of illegal crops. In late 1998, with the collaboration of the US administration, its government formulated 'Plan Colombia' to achieve these goals. The US provided a significant amount of resources but limited them to fighting drugs, preventing the Colombian government from using them against guerrilla and paramilitary organisations. Plan Colombia has been instrumental in expanding government control over the national territory. After 11 September 2001, FARC and paramilitary groups were declared terrorists by the US government and the Colombian government could then combat those organisations using Plan Colombia funds.

During the Pastrana administration, the 'Peace Process' with FARC floundered. Indeed, it was never a 'process'. There were dialogues between the government and FARC but they did not develop an agenda of the issues to be discussed. FARC realised that it was gaining military strength while confronting a weak state and had strong incentives to delay negotiations indefinitely or at least until it had a stronger position from which to bargain. After more than three years of frustrations, the Pastrana administration cancelled the 'distension' zone in early 2002.

The failure of the peace process with FARC created disillusion among many Colombians about the likelihood of achieving peace though negotiations. It facilitated the election of Álvaro Uribe in 2002 on a platform of heavy-handedness against FARC. Uribe's agenda emphasised state control over the territory and the establishment of 'democratic security', that is, the ability of citizens to reclaim their rights to move freely around the country without fear of kidnapping or extortion. Uribe's hard hand has forced FARC into a more passive position. It has also been applied to drug traffickers. Indeed, by April 2006 Uribe had extradited almost 400 traffickers – about four times the number extradited between 1984 and 2002.

In 2004, President Uribe started negotiations with paramilitary groups and introduced a bill in Congress to pass a law on 'Peace, Justice and Reparation'. He agreed to give a safe haven to paramilitary leaders in Ralito, a small town in the north coast region where negotiations have taken place. These have resulted in a massive demobilisation of approximately 37,000 paramilitary fighters – a far greater number than the 14,000 that had been expected.[31] The negotiations have, however, resulted in a law of 'Peace and Justice', in which reparation is highly doubtful. Drug traffickers have taken advantage of this situation to pass as paramilitary members and attempt to cleanse their assets. In some cases, rich drug traffickers have 'purchased' paramilitary battalions or 'franchises' so that they can be part of the negotiation. Also, they have accumulated very large amounts of land. Some of it was purchased from owners of large plots but a significant proportion was obtained by threatening peasants who owned small plots.[32] Worse yet, in many cases paramilitary groups have accused peasants of being guerrilla supporters and thus forced them to flee their lands. This has resulted in a significant 'counter land reform' and increased land tenancy concentration. It is feared that government negotiations with the paramilitary may lead to the legalisation of titles in a large quantity of illegally-obtained land and other assets. Indeed, the peace process of the Uribe administration may produce the largest episode of drug money-laundering in the country's history.

In late 2003, the Uribe administration formulated 'Plan Patriota' aiming to establish control and state presence over large parts of the territory. This is a military programme that has had support from the US and is part of the process of strengthening the Colombian armed forces. It may be argued that this action is also designed to combat FARC. This guerrilla group appears to have been retreating into jungle areas which the government has extreme difficulty entering and controlling.

The government has claimed several victories in gaining control over some areas but FARC has not suffered any hard blows. In fact, none of the members of the FARC secretariat have been captured and the two highest-ranking guerrillas imprisoned were captured in Venezuela and Ecuador.

Aerial spraying of illicit crops was practised in Colombia in the 1980s. During the Samper administration this practice was reinforced and, since 2002, spraying with glifosate has been massive. In the last four years, interdiction has also been important and the amount of drugs seized has ballooned. However, alternative development programmes have been relatively marginal in the broad scheme of anti-drug policies. At face value, aerial spraying is presented as a success. Depending on which sources are used, total illicit crop acreage declined from over 160,000 (or 125,000) hectares in 2000 to 114,000 (or 86,000) hectares in 2004.[33] The reality, however, is more complex. In 2003, 2004 and 2005 the government sprayed over 130,000 hectares per year. In addition, in 2005 over 32,000 coca hectares were eradicated manually. In 2003, the government achieved an apparently significant reduction but in 2004 it did not. Furthermore, retail prices of cocaine on the main markets did not increase significantly, if at all. Official explanations have it that, while cocaine supply declined, traffickers still had large stocks that they were selling. There were several variants of this version. One is that traffickers in Ralito wanted to sell out before signing an agreement with the government, so that they would not be accused of trafficking afterwards. Another is that FARC had been cornered and was also selling to get rid of hard-to-protect stocks. A third was that traffickers in Northern Mexico had accumulated stocks that they were now getting rid of. None of these versions explain why stocks were accumulated in the first place. Indeed, it is hard to find another product line in which entrepreneurs would have less incentive to accumulate stocks. Even if there is oversupply in one year, the high risks of the business and the large number of actors discourage stock accumulation. Furthermore, even if they had accumulated large stocks, why were they selling before prices rose? If there were stocks, it is remarkable that the traffickers behaved as though they were managing a commodity price-stabilisation fund rather than as successful speculators.

The success claims and the retail price data were so inconsistent that when the 2005 International Narcotics Control Strategy Report was published in March 2006, it did not have any estimates of the size of the area under illegal cultivation in Colombia. Finally, on Good Friday 2006, the US Office of National Drug Control Policy (ONDCP) gave a figure of 144,000 coca hectares, or a 26 per cent increase above the 2004 figure. They qualify this figure, explaining that the rise was due to coverage of a higher area and that only 106,000 hectares of the 114,000 cultivated in 2004 were under cultivation in 2005. These figures appear to be an attempt to put a good face on a bad situation. Reporting the figures on Good Friday, ahead of a long weekend, also suggests that the Colombian government wanted to have low news coverage of this report.

Intensive aerial spraying has produced several 'unintended consequences'. First, it has spread illicit crops across the country. Second, plantings are now a lot smaller, making spraying difficult. Third, peasants have devised methods of protecting their plants. Coca plants are now heavily pruned immediately after being sprayed to prevent the herbicide from reaching the plant roots. Coca leaves are then processed into cocaine. Government officials now say off-the-record that they need to spray the same planting four times a year to ensure that peasants desist from cultivating coca. Fourth, spraying contributes to the displacement of people and plantings and increases the supply of labour available to illegal armed groups.

A FEW CONCLUSIONS

The economic, social and political effects of the illicit drug industry in Colombia have evolved through time. Illegal drugs produced regional booms and a welcome influx of foreign exchange in the 1970s, but by the 1990s they became a main funding source for both left-wing guerrillas and right-wing paramilitary forces. The illegal drugs industry has contributed to the persistence and deepening of the armed conflict experienced by Colombia; has been a significant factor in the de-politicisation of the guerrillas; has played a significant role in the development of paramilitary groups; has corrupted the country's polity and the state; and its funding of armed actors has been a main cause of violence, as their presence is the main explanatory variable of the extremely high murder rates that prevail in some regions of the country.[34]

The cocaine and heroin industry became principal funding sources for political campaigns and a main source of political corruption. There is no doubt that a significant group of politicians have been, and are, dependent on the industry. Paramilitary leaders have publicly asserted recently that 35 per cent of Members of Congress are their 'friends'. Both paramilitary and guerrillas control and fight for control of many municipal governments, particularly in rural areas where illicit crops are grown, where drugs are manufactured and where there are drug and chemical precursor trafficking routes. Many of the frequent massacres suffered in the countryside are the result of these fights.

In the 1970s and 1980s, most Colombians perceived the illicit drug industry as beneficial. It provided channels of upward mobility and generated large amounts of needed foreign exchange and a real estate boom. By the late 1990s, the negative effects of such developments were obvious to the majority of the population. Indeed, the effects of the industry evolved from an illegal economic boom into the principal cause of a deep social and political crisis.[35] Illegal drugs used to fund contraband of foreign goods and real estate. Today, they still fund contraband and some real estate investments but they also fund subversive and counter-subversive organisations. Illegal drugs were perceived as offering opportunities for quick enrichment and wealth accumulation; today they are used to fund wealth destruction.

The illegal drugs industry internationalised the long-running domestic armed conflict. It led to the involvement of foreign governments and international agencies in Colombian policy-making functions and has limited the country's policy options. Today, left-wing guerrillas and paramilitary groups are internationally branded as terrorists. The external meddling in the country's affairs and the revenues provided to those groups by the illegal industry have frustrated possible solutions to the country's internal conflict. Drugs and armed conflict have become intertwined, making potential solutions to the problem more complex and inter-dependent.

A main implication of the growth of the illegal drug industry in Colombia has been its catalytic effect on a process of institutional weakening and de-legitimation of the state. The illicit drug industry flourished in Colombia because its institutions and the rule of law had become very weak. Once the industry became established, it accelerated and aggravated this weakening process.

Both FARC and the paramilitary have the same need for territorial control in order to operate, even though their goals are radically different. FARC wants to overthrow the regime and establish a new government. While some of its commanders may have accumulated some capital from the illicit trade, most of the illegal profits go to support their armies and war machine. The paramilitary does not want to change the regime but to be accepted as part of it. Their leaders accumulate large fortunes, many from rural lands that need protection. They have gained a strong influence in Congress and politics, and their power is such that some of the leaders who participated in the Ralito negotiations want to become politicians.

Decentralisation is a goal of the new constitution, and a decentralised expenditure system based on the transfer of funds from central to local government was established. This resulted in large budgetary increases in many locations with very weak bureaucracies, authoritarian traditions and absolutely no accountability. Not surprisingly, municipal budgets became the target of both guerrilla and paramilitary organisations. Ironically, the central state has become a funding source for those groups that now have stronger incentives to gain territorial control of areas of the country where they can exploit local budgets.

Territorial control by the illegal armed groups today has several goals: protection of illicit plantings and refining labs; control over trafficking corridors, airports and ports; and control over local budgets and other sources of funds (protection and extortion). This has been so important that in some departments and municipalities the paramilitary threatened all candidates that did not have their blessing and in a couple of departments there was only one candidate in the last election. In guerrilla-controlled areas they also veto candidates who are not their de facto accomplices.

The Colombian central government has been making strong efforts to control the territory and has made significant advances in some regions. These efforts, however, have been mostly on the military front and aspects such as providing social and physical infrastructure have been slow to develop or remain wanting. Again, the state is confronting a shortage of funds and excessive needs. While these efforts should be acknowledged and encouraged, the magnitude of the task is such that one should raise serious questions about the possibility of lasting success.

One of the unintended consequences of the destruction of the large trafficking organisations coupled with the growth of illegal crop plantings in Colombia has been the empowerment of warlords and guerrillas in large parts of the country. Some argue that drug traffickers are now subordinated to warlords and guerrillas while others may argue that there has been a symbiosis between them. In any case, the illegal drugs industry has evolved – from traditional trafficking groups interested in drug profits needed to influence politicians to protect their investments and avoid extradition and gaol, to current organisations that seek territorial control, have strong armed groups and profit from several other illegal activities, including corruption.

The current negotiations with paramilitary groups are very illustrative of this development. In the negotiations the government distinguishes paramilitary groups that traffic in drugs from 'full-blooded' drug traffickers and negotiates with the former but not with the latter. The former have strong armies and have not been defeated in battle, while the latter appear weak. Not surprisingly, some drug traffickers have purchased paramilitary 'franchises' that would allow them to negotiate the legalisation of their wealth and the length of their possible sentences, which may end up being paid in house arrest or rural farms. These negotiations are producing a situation in which paramilitary leaders who might be responsible for massacres, tortures, peasant displacements and drug trafficking get mild sentences, while 'full-blooded' traffickers are extradited and 'sent to the slammer' for a very long time.

One interesting issue raised in recent research is why some traffickers could not join or develop large war machines, while others did. A plausible explanation has to do with the nature of the region and local governments near their area of operation.[36] In the most primitive areas with weaker local administrations, warlords could control the region and the governments, while in areas where there were larger cities and more sophisticated populations, drug traffickers had to remain drug traffickers. The importance of warlordship has become quite clear as the old 'full-blooded' traffickers, leaders of the Cali 'cartel' like the Rodríguez-Orejuela brothers, were extradited while the current paramilitary leaders might end up in Congress.

NOTES

1. A detailed analysis of the development of the illegal drugs industry in Colombia and other Andean countries is found in Francisco E. Thoumi, *Illegal Drugs, Economy and Society in the Andes* (Baltimore, MD: Johns Hopkins University Press, 2003).
2. The United Nations data show that currently only these three countries grow coca. United Nations Office on Drugs and Crime (UNODC), *World Drug Report 2004* (New York: United Nations, 2004).
3. Joseph Gagliano, *Coca Prohibition in Peru: The Historical Debates* (Tucson: University of Arizona Press, 1994); Paul Gootenberg, 'Reluctance or Resistance? Constructing Cocaine (Prohibitions) in Peru, 1910–1950', in idem (ed.), *Cocaine: Global Histories* (London and New York: Routledge, 1999). Indeed, Peruvians complained bitterly of not being able to export coca until the 'Japanese occupation of the Netherlands East Indies (Indonesia) and the British coca outlets in Asia closed important supply sources for the United States and its wartime allies. Peruvian coca was sought to fill the need.' Gagliano, *Coca Prohibition in Peru*, p. 147.
4. UNODC, *World Drug Report 2004*, vol. II, p. 205.
5. For a detailed comparison of the development of the illegal drugs industry in these two countries, see Francisco E. Thoumi, 'The Rise of Two Drug Tigers: The Development of the Illegal Drugs Industry and Drug Policy Failure in Afghanistan and Colombia', in Frank Bovenkerk and Michael Levi (eds), *The Organized Crime Community: Essays in Honor of Alan A. Block* (vol. vi of *Studies of Organized Crime*) (New York: Springer, 2006).
6. UNODC, *The Opium Economy in Afghanistan: An International Problem* (New York: United Nations, 2003), pp. 87–8.
7. Thoumi, *Illegal Drugs, Economy and Society in the Andes*, Chapter 3, develops a model of the competitive advantage in illegal drugs to explain this phenomenon.
8. Ibid., p. 56.
9. This is why in Colombia some people clamour for international 'legalisation', that is, for an external solution to their policy problem.
10. Putting this in simple terms, the level of repression required to control an illegal market in Norway is much lower than in Colombia.

11. Alejandro Gaviria, 'Increasing Returns and the Evolution of Violent Crime: The Case of Colombia', *Journal of Development Economics*, 61 (2000), pp. 1–25.
12. The issue of why the illegal drugs industry has concentrated in Colombia has been treated at length in Francisco E. Thoumi, 'The Role of the State, Social Institutions, and Social Capital in Determining Competitive Advantage in Illegal Drugs in the Andes', *Transnational Organized Crime*, 5/1 (Spring 1999); Thoumi, *Illegal Drugs, Economy and Society in the Andes*; Francisco E. Thoumi, 'The Colombian Competitive Advantage in Illegal Drugs: The Role of Policies and Institutional Changes', *Journal of Drug Issues* (Winter 2005).
13. Colombian intellectuals have frequently referred to these issues: María Teresa Herrán, *La Sociedad de la Mentira*, 2nd edn (Bogotá: Fondo Editorial CEREC – Editorial la Oveja Negra, 1987); Salomón Kalmanovitz, *La Encrucijada de la Sinrazón y otros Ensayos* (Bogotá: Tercer Mundo Editores, 1989); Hernando Gómez-Buendía, 'La Hipótesis del Almendrón', in idem (ed.), *¿Para Dónde Va Colombia?* (Bogotá: TM Editores-Colciencias, 1999); Emilio Yunis, *¿Por Qué Somos Así? ¿Qué pasó en Colombia? Análisis del mestizaje* (Bogotá: Editorial Temis, 2003).
14. Rodrigo Pardo, 'La Política Exterior', in Fernando Cepeda (ed.), *Fortalezas de Colombia* (Bogotá: Editorial Planeta Colombiana, 2004). A former foreign minister, Pardo argues that the main historical constant in Colombia's foreign policy has been respect for, and trust in, international treaties.
15. See for example, Sid Zabludoff, 'Colombian Narcotics Organizations', *Transnational Organized Crime*, 2/2 (Autumn 1996).
16. This strategy is analysed and criticised in Theo Ronken, Kathryn Ledebur and Tom Kruse, 'The Drug War in the Skies: The U.S. "Air Bridge Denial" Strategy: The Success of a Failure' (Cochabamba: Acción Andina- Transnational Institute, May 1999).
17. United Nations Office for Drug Control and Crime Prevention (UNODCCP), *Global Illicit Drug Trends 2001* (New York, 2001), p. 73.
18. Ibid.
19. Fernando Rospigliosi, *Montesinos y las fuerzas armadas. Cómo controló durante una década las instituciones militares* (Lima: Instituto de Estudios Peruanos, 2001); Manuel Dammert Ego-Aguirre, *Fujimori-Montesinos: el Estado Mafioso* (Lima: Ediciones El Virrey, 2001).
20. Pablo Escobar Gaviria, *Mi hermano Pablo: los secretos de Pablo Escobar* (Quintero Editores Ltda., 2002), pp. 7–11.
21. Ibid., p. 136.
22. Pablo G. Dreyfus, 'When All the Evils Come Together: Cocaine, Corruption, and Shining Path in Peru's Upper Huallaga Valley, 1980 to 1995', *Journal of Contemporary Criminal Justice*, 15/4 (November 1999), pp. 387–8.
23. Sergio Uribe, 'Los cultivos ilícitos en Colombia. Evaluación: extensión, técnicas y tecnologías para la producción y rendimientos y magnitud de la industria', in Francisco Thoumi (ed.), *Drogas Ilícitas en Colombia: su impacto económico, político y social* (Dirección Nacional de Estupefacientes y PNUD) (Bogotá: Editorial Planeta, 1997), p. 127.
24. Uribe, 'Los cultivos ilícitos en Colombia'.
25. I use 'guaranteed' in inverted commas, because the constitution did not establish a credible funding mechanism to pay for the rights it granted the citizenry.
26. An elaborate analysis of this development is presented in: María Clemencia Ramírez, *Entre el estado y la guerrilla: identidad y ciudadanía en el movimiento de los campesinos cocaleros del Putumayo* (Bogotá: Instituto Colombiano de Antropología e Historia, 2001); see also María Clemencia Ramírez, 'Construction and Contestation of Criminal Identities: The Case of "Cocaleros" in the Colombian Western Amazon', *Journal of Drug Issues*, 35/1 (Winter 2005).
27. Thoumi, *Illegal Drugs, Economy and Society in the Andes*.
28. The growth of paramilitary power and the role of the illegal industry in the armed conflict have been studied recently in Alfredo Rangel (ed.), *El poder parmilitar* (Bogotá: Editorial Planeta Colombiana, 2005); Ricardo Vargas, *Narcotráfico, guerra y política antidrogas: una perspectiva sobre las drogas en el conflicto armado colombiano* (Bogotá: Ricardo vargas Meza- Acción Andina Colombia, 2005); Ricardo Vargas, 'Cultivos ilícitos en Colombia: elementos para un balance', in Alfredo Rangel (ed.), *Narcotráfico en Colombia: Economía y Violencia* (Bogotá: Fundación Seguridad y Democracia, 2005); Gustavo Duncan, 'Narcotraficantes, mafiosos y guerreros. Historia de una subordinación', in Rangel (ed.), *Narcotráfico en Colombia*.

29. Duncan, 'Narcotraficantes, mafiosos y guerreros'.
30. Ibid.
31. According to the government, the large figure is the result of non-combat personnel turning themselves in. This might be partially true but it is also true that others have taken the opportunity to 'demobilise' and obtain some of the benefits granted by the government, including a small monthly paycheque.
32. For example, a peasant who does not have his land for sale is approached by a buyer who offers a very low price and tells him that if he does not agree to a sale, his widow will.
33. The higher figures are from the US State Department and the lower ones from UNODC.
34. Mauricio Rubio, *Crimen e Impunidad: Precisiones Sobre la Violencia* (Bogotá: TM Editores-CEDE, 1999).
35. Thoumi, *Illegal Drugs, Economy and Society in the Andes*.
36. Duncan, 'Narcotraficantes, mafiosos y guerreros'.

12

Covert Netherworld: Clandestine Services and Criminal Syndicates in Shaping the Philippine State

Alfred W. McCoy

At the cusp of the twenty-first century, a succession of spectacular crises breached an invisible barrier between the formal and informal, civil and criminal facets of the Philippine polity, exposing the pervasive influence of a 'covert netherworld' on the country's politics. In January 2001, after the impeachment of President Joseph Estrada for taking bribes from an illegal lottery called 'jueteng' failed on a technicality, a quarter-million protestors mobilised for days of demonstrations, dubbed 'People Power II', that soon forced him from office. When his successor Gloria Arroyo then jailed Estrada on corruption charges, nearly a half-million of his supporters rallied round-the-clock in a violent reprise called 'People Power III'. After days of impassioned speeches, a hard-core of 50,000 slum dwellers, led by rogue police commanders and drug gangs pumped up on illegal methamphetamines, stormed the palace for seven hours of street fighting that left four dead and the Arroyo government badly shaken. Finally, in May 2005 accusations that President Arroyo's husband had taken jueteng bribes to fund her election campaign plunged the country into protracted instability marked by abortive coups, mass demonstrations, and attempted impeachment. Looking back on these events, it seems both surprising and significant that an illegal lottery could rise from the country's slums to spark a crisis of legitimacy at the highest levels of the Philippine state.

If scholars had focused on police and crime as they have on peasants or parties, then these unexpected developments might have seemed less so. In the back alleys of sprawling squatter settlements, hidden from public scrutiny and academic analysis, illegal jueteng gambling has become one of the Philippines' largest industries, generating much of the cash to sustain the country's costly election campaigns.

A 1999 survey found that 28 per cent of all adult Filipinos bet on jueteng. A parallel legislative study estimated the annual gross of all jueteng syndicates on the main Philippine island of Luzon at US\$918 million and bribes to police and politicians at US\$180 million. This illegal lottery has become one of the country's largest employers, with an estimated 400,000 workers – far more than the 280,000 then employed in the country's largest export industry, silicon chip manufacturing. With an illicit income equal to 10 per cent of all tax revenues and larger than the entire budget for law enforcement, jueteng had commensurate power to corrupt both police and politicians. If we add this $1 billion in illegal gambling to the $5 billion from illicit drug sales, then their sum was a vast underground vice economy whose revenues equalled nearly half the government's annual budget.[1]

Grasping the sheer size of this illicit enterprise is the first step to unlocking a central mystery of modern Philippine politics and discovering the mechanism that allows a vast electoral superstructure to stand on such feeble economic foundations. How, we might ask, can such a poor society sustain such costly elections?

Over the span of a century, the slow decline of patronage politics and relentless rise of illegal gambling combined to make jueteng a key source of finance for campaigns whose costs have risen relentlessly.[2] Just as big city 'bosses' in Boston and New York once rewarded ward heelers with patronage and voters with social services, so a 1970 survey of 4,000 village *liders*, or precinct organisers, in Camarines Norte Province found that cash and patronage jobs determined which candidate voters would support.[3]

In the half-century since independence in 1946, campaign costs have risen to unsustainable levels. Indeed, between 1953 and 1961, presidential campaign expenses increased ten-fold.[4] To win reelection in 1969, President Marcos emptied the national treasury to spend an unprecedented $50 million on his campaign – far more than the $34 million Richard Nixon had needed to capture the US presidency in 1968.[5] In 1992, the next full presidential campaign after Marcos's martial rule, election costs resumed their relentless rise, reaching some P6 billion (US$240 million) for all candidates.[6] Although they alone are large enough to distort the nation's budgetary process, these presidential campaigns are just one facet of a costly electoral cycle for thousands of village, municipal, provincial and legislative offices.

Apart from tracking government pork barrel, none of the many studies of Philippine politics has probed for the source of these vast campaign funds. If we look beneath the visible political process, we can find the answer to this mystery in the country's vice economy. Throughout the twentieth century, jueteng closed the gap between the country's pervasive poverty and the high costs of what one columnist called 'one of the most expensive elections among the democracies of the free world'.[7] In Luzon and the Visayas, political patronage, police corruption and jueteng gambling have served, for nearly a century, as interlocking gears in the machinery of provincial politics.

Commercially, jueteng's gendering, probabilities and mystique have made it an extraordinarily lucrative enterprise. From obscure origins in China, this distinctive lottery came to Southeast Asia with migrants who made 'the 37 beasts' a popular illegal game in colonial cities. In Saigon during the early 1950s, for example, a local Sino-Vietnamese mafia, the Binh Xuyen bandits, ran a daily lottery that sent 'thousands of salesmen…through all the alleys of all the quarters while crying out, "Thirty-six beasts, thirty-six beasts"'.[8] In the Philippines, jueteng's popularity and persistence, despite its legal prohibition for nearly a century, rests upon the peculiar probabilities of betting on just two numbers from 1 to 37 that foster an illusion of easy winnings – simultaneously attracting bettors and assuring profits for payoffs to police and politicians. In contrast to the male-only domain of the Philippine cockpit, jueteng has, since the 1920s, incorporated women as bettors, clerks and operators, effectively doubling its clientele.[9] Among 1,200 adults surveyed in September 1999, exactly 20 per cent of both males and females had bet on illegal jueteng – in marked contrast to the 13.7 per cent of males and just 0.6 per cent of females who gambled at legal cockfights.[10]

With its chimera of easy jackpots and popularity across the gender divide, jueteng's mystique has somehow tapped into a deep Filipino folk belief in 'suerte', or fate. Marginalised by their relentless poverty, lower-class Filipinos have made jueteng a vehicle for their hopes and dreams, transforming this illegal lottery into a populist futures exchange where they can invest with only their spiritual destiny as collateral. Intertwined with fantasy and reality, police and politics, jueteng has grown from a few local networks in the early twentieth century into a lower-class Filipino obsession, a vast illicit industry, and a central feature of modern Philippine life.

COVERT NETHERWORLD

As these stunning statistics on illegal gaming indicate, the study of crime, police and political crisis can take us beyond the conventional approach to Philippine politics. To learn something of the causality underlying this or any country's recurring crises, we need to look beneath the surface formalities of elections and administration into a netherworld where secret services and criminal syndicates play a defining, yet unexamined, role in contemporary political life – in effect, probing that murky interstice between the formal and informal, or licit and illicit, that we call, for want of better words, the 'covert netherworld'. Other terms, recently coined, fail to capture the analytical import and robust multi-disciplinary reach implicit in this phrase. The term 'parapolitics', for example, denotes a narrow, synchronic sub-field that masks its actual agenda – a wide-ranging inquiry with well-developed diachronic dimensions. Similarly, the term 'deep politics', though more evocative, is freighted with undertones of conspiracy theory from Peter Dale Scott's book, *Deep Politics and the Death of JFK*, and its association with Oliver Stone's controversial film *JFK* that distract from a significant scholarly inquiry encompassing covert operations, criminal syndicates, and global commodities.[11]

By contrast, the term covert netherworld conjoins the contemporary term 'covert', signifying state security, and the classical 'netherworld', connoting the parallel subterranean kingdom of the dead, to signify a similarly spectral clandestine realm intersecting with and influencing the visible surface of society in ways that elude existing models of politics or political economy. Indeed, this term and the analytical approach it entails can open us to a changing modern world in all its complexity, allowing new perceptions of politics, entire polities, and the global system that encompasses both. Just as exploration of the covert netherworld offers a powerful prism for understanding Philippine politics, so a close-grained case study of a single country shows the potential of this paradigm to open new perspectives on entire national polities, in first world and third.

At its core, this covert netherworld is an invisible interstice, within both individual nations and the international system, inhabited by criminal and clandestine actors with both the means and need to operate outside conventional channels. Among all the institutions of modern society, only intelligence agencies and crime syndicates can carry out complex financial or political operations without leaving any visible trace. Just as legal imperatives force syndicates into elaborate concealment of membership, criminal activities and illicit profits, so political necessity dictates that secret services practise a parallel tradecraft of anonymous membership, off-the-shelf financial transactions and covert operations. In sum, both are practitioners of what one CIA operative, Lucien Conein, has called 'the clandestine arts' – that is, the essential skill of operating outside the normal channels of civil society.[12]

Throughout much of the twentieth century, there have been recurring signs of a surprising affinity between these two clandestine actors. Since the 1920s when global drug prohibition amplified the scale and scope of the illicit economy, state security services around the globe have found drug traffickers useful covert-action assets – from Nationalist China's reliance on Shanghai's Green Gang to fight the communists in the 1930s through the Gaullist regime's use of Marseilles' *milieu* against military terrorists in the 1960s. As our knowledge of the Cold War grows, the list of drug traffickers who served the CIA lengthens to include Corsican syndicates, Nationalist Chinese irregulars, Lao generals, Afghan warlords, Haitian colonels, Panamanian generals, Honduran smugglers and Nicaraguan Contra commanders.[13] The sum of these *sub rosa* alliances is a political symbiosis that amplifies the reach of state security services and provides informal protection for criminal syndicates.

After the Cold War's blocs of rival states collapsed, the international community was suddenly forced to confront an extraordinary array of non-state actors who threatened the stability of global governance. As an organisation that engages the world as it is rather than one imagined by political theorists, the United Nations General Assembly adopted the Convention Against Transnational Organized Crime in 1998 allowing states 'legal force to deprive drug traffickers of ill-gotten financial gains and freedom of movement'. To give force to this convention, the UN established the Office of Drugs and Crime to tame 'highly centralised' transnational crime groups with some 3.3 million members worldwide who traffic in drugs, arms, artefacts, humans and endangered species.[14]

At the dawn of the twenty-first century, the UN thus discovered both the scale and significance of this supra-national netherworld where criminal syndicates and clandestine services coexist and collaborate. As an index of scale, consider illicit drug trafficking which, according to the 1997 edition of the UN's *World Drugs Report*, is a $400 billion industry with 180 million users and 8 per cent of world trade – larger than textiles, steel or automobiles.[15] As an index of significance, consider contemporary Afghanistan where the 2004 opium harvest comprised 60 per cent of GDP, generating some $2 billion in illicit income to sustain local warlords and Taliban commanders who defy and may yet defeat NATO efforts to restore stability to this war-torn nation.[16] Even though the transnational drug traffic is larger than the legal trade for textiles, one of three human essentials, surprisingly few among the thousands of historians who populate university faculties across the globe have studied this illicit economy and the social forces that sustain it.

This social interstice that we call the covert netherworld is a vast, complex and uncharted terrain operating at three distinct yet intersecting levels: the transnational, the national, and the local. Taking a leaf from recent UN documents, its *transnational dimension* is an elusive, non-territorial, even invisible sector of the global economy created by international or national prohibitions and sustained by a contraband commerce. Though its clandestine character usually denies it any spatial manifestation, this illicit international commerce occasionally touches ground, thereby creating a *local dimension* of free ports or outlaw zones that are simultaneously detached from nation-state controls, sustained as epicentres of transnational contraband circuits, and demarcated by evocative vernacular place-names such as the Golden Triangle, Golden Crescent or Tri-border area. Inside *individual nations* the interaction between the state's lawful secret services and its outlaw fragments, whether rural warlords or urban gangsters, can define the character of an entire polity. During volatile periods in their respective national histories, nominally non-state actors such as Italian *mafia*, Indonesian *preman* or Japanese *yakuza* have become levers of social control integral to the functioning of the legitimate state. Just as E.H. Norman and Maruyama Masao argued that a *sub rosa* alliance of military factions and urban crime syndicates was central to the pre-war Japanese empire and Tim Lindsey has recently reached parallel conclusions about the contemporary Indonesian state, so we need to explore how similar influences at transnational, national and local levels might have shaped the modern Philippine polity.[17]

At the transnational level, the Philippines has remained, for the past five centuries, an archipelago incompletely incorporated within any single state structure and thus pulled by strong centrifugal forces from neighbouring power centres – the Chinese empire to the northwest, the Malay trading world to the southwest, and European influences from westward across the Pacific. Tugging constantly at the integrity of the Philippine polity, these three zones of culture and power inject alien actors, criminal or clandestine, and pull the nation apart at its historical stitches in the Muslim south. From the sixteenth to eighteenth centuries, Spain made Manila its fortified entrepot for the China trade but failed to conquer and Christianise the Moluccas after a half-century of warfare in the sixteenth century, forcing its retreat to a fortress at Zamboanga that left the Sulu archipelago and its window on the Malay maritime world unsealed. During the century-long high tide of European empire that ended in 1941, reinvigorated Spanish and then American colonial states mobilised military forces on land and sea that finally, after three centuries, circumscribed the Philippine archipelago within formal nation-state boundaries, reducing Chinese and Malay influences to faint impulses mediated through Manila. Since independence in 1946, however, the pull of centrifugal forces revived – with China transmitting capital and commerce, both legal and criminal; the Malay zone drawing the Muslim south towards armed secessionist struggle via arms, trade and radical religion; and America maintaining its post-colonial influence through markets, migration and military protection whose sum serves, at least momentarily, to keep China and its navy at bay.

Within the Philippine archipelago, these centrifugal forces have created, over the last two centuries, a quasi-autonomous outlaw territory called the Sulu Zone. Starting in the late eighteenth century, a 'triangular trade' boomed between Calcutta,

Canton and Liverpool comprising, by the 1820s, £22 million worth of Indian opium and cotton to China; next, £20 million in Chinese tea to Britain; and, finally, £24 million in British textiles and machinery back to India.[18] As the flow of opium and tea surged along the Calcutta to Canton route in the early nineteenth century, the Sulu sultanate grew rapidly into a strong state through its entrepot role in a secondary trade-triangle – sending fleets of its Muslim fighters to raid Filipino Christian villages for slaves, using these legions of coerced labourers to harvest exotic products from the seabed for the China market, and bartering these goods for firearms to supply future raids. For a full century after 1870, however, Sulu was subdued under a succession of policy regimes imposed from Manila – Spain's naval marauding, US military massacres and the Philippine Republic's patronage politics.[19]

After the Philippines won independence in 1946, the centrifugal pull of the Malay world was soon felt at Sulu through the de-centring impact of regional smuggling, radical Islam and secessionist revolt. When a bankrupt Republic imposed import duties to break Filipino addiction to American cigarette brands like 'Camel' in 1949 and the new Indonesian Republic punished exporters by overvaluing its currency, two once-legal commodities, imported tobacco and export coconuts, entered international contraband circuits. Driven by the rhythms of this vast, illicit commerce, new entrepreneurs emerged along an arc of islands from Sulawesi to Luzon, seizing profits and power at each strategic point. Starting with small shipments in the mid 1950s, cigarette smuggling grew steadily until, within a decade, a poor Filipino fisherman from Cavite had been transformed into the smuggler-king and political king-maker Lino Bocalan.[20] During these same years, farmers on Indonesia's sprawling Sulawesi Island sold their copra at world-market prices to local rebels who financed their secessionist struggle by smuggling cargoes across the Sulawesi Sea to the port of Sandakan in nearby North Borneo.[21] By 1957, the convergence of these illicit circuits at Sandakan – copra out, tobacco in – made this tiny north Borneo port 'the largest importer of American cigarettes in the world' and may well have provided the balanced trade that fuelled an explosive expansion of cigarette smuggling into the Philippines.[22] After this massive tobacco trade breached the country's southern sea frontier and allowed unfettered contact with the wider Malay world, localised smuggling, radical Islam and arms trafficking introduced the prime ingredients for a secessionist revolt by the Moro National Liberation Front in the early 1970s.[23]

In searching for appropriate analysis of the Philippine state we can peel the academic onion, stripping away the scholarly layers to reach this distinctive polity's core characteristics. For decades, historians and political scientists have studied how the Philippines adapted formal structures of electoral democracy, developed under US colonial rule, with extra-systemic elements such as clientelism, bossism and social protest. But this literature did not explore the influence of the coercive apparatus and its invisible netherworld. Comparing American colonial policing in the Philippines to the Dutch panopticon on Java, for example, the distinguished historian Theodore Friend dismissed US political surveillance as 'inexact and unsystematic' and its Constabulary as 'light-fingered with others' possessions, heavy-handed with their liberties, and sometimes trigger-happy'.[24] Though useful for formalities of elections and debates, such superficial political history cannot explain the country's recurring extra-systemic crises marked, most recently, by martial law in 1972 and the succession of people-power protests in the decades since.

Among the American specialists in Philippine politics, only one, John Sidel has fused the formal and informal to produce a corpus that approximates the elusive reality of the country's political culture. In his study of bossism, Sidel argues that the Philippine state is a 'complex set of predatory mechanisms for private exploitation and accumulation of the archipelago's human, natural, and monetary resources', mediated by an incessant electoral competition, that makes the Philippine state 'essentially a multi-tiered racket'.[25] Beyond the formal bureaucracy, regular elections foster a system of 'bossism' that rests, say Sidel and Eva-Lotta Hedman, on 'an impoverished, insecure, and economically dependent electorate susceptible to clientelist, coercive, and monetary inducements and pressures'.[26]

If we shift perspective from elite to mass, then mobilisation of these voters and their social control between elections rests upon a diverse range of actors including, elected officials, warlords, militia chiefs and crime bosses. With insight and innovative research, Sidel shows how Manila's use of informal immunities shapes the character of the provincial periphery, creating this array of nominally non-state actors and their localised systems of social control. In his blood-stained biographies of two Cebuano criminals, Sidel argues that the state used them 'as subcontracted law enforcement agents' to control the poor of a major city, 'bearing witness not to the state's supposed weakness but to its strength' and thus raising, for Sidel, serious questions about the reigning view of the Philippine state as 'chronically "weak,"…besieged by "lawlessness" and "unrest"'.[27]

In another instance of the state's power to structure its criminal periphery, Sidel shows how the Marcos regime transformed Don Jose 'Pepe' Oyson from a petty criminal into a powerful syndicate boss. Under the protection of Marcos's security chief, General Fabian Ver, petty smuggler Jose soon became the crime boss 'Don Pepe' with a Roxas Boulevard nightclub, a large Manila cockpit, and impunity to smuggle. With the regime's protection, he took control of the illegal importation of methamphetamine hydrochloride (*shabu*), a drug whose energy surge initially appealed to an expanding clientele among Manila's nocturnal working class – taxi drivers, casino workers and nightclub hostesses.[28] Apart from its impact on a single syndicate, the regime's alliance with Don Pepe impacted significantly upon Filipino society by introducing an illicit drug, *shabu*, whose pricing and pharmacology would soon make it a pandemic in the country's impoverished slums – with profound implications for the country's political culture.

From the perspective of the covert netherworld, however, even Sidel fails to fulfil the potential of his project by inverting his analytical frame to show, not just the centre's influence on its criminal and provincial peripheries, but the periphery's role in shaping the centre, both its political process and actual administration. If we reverse this analytical telescope and use it as a microscope to scrutinise the state apparatus through the study of crime, police and political crisis, we can move beyond formal structures to see the Philippine polity as a fusion of centre and periphery, formal and informal, licit and illicit.

At the epicentre of the Philippine polity, Manila's nation-state apparatus exercises a supple strength despite seemingly weak central controls. Struggling to contain the centrifugal pull of transnational forces, the Republic has deputised a panoply of parastatal elements – bandits, warlords, smugglers, gambling bosses, militia chiefs and rebel commanders. Though many are at best quasi-legal and some are outright outlaws, these fragments of the state are not mere aberrations but are instead integral facets of an administration whose sum, in fusion with constitutional elements, defines the Philippine polity. Instead of relying solely on the formal coercive instruments of bureaucracy, military and police, Manila controls its disparate archipelago by delegating informal authority to an array of agents awarded legal immunity and political autonomy. Beneath a seemingly untidy, even chaotic spectacle of episodic political violence, rural revolt and secessionist struggles, the state apparatus might stretch and even strain but it never breaks and thus retains, through these deputies, ad hoc control of even its most remote and troubled regions.

As the state's key mechanism for ordering both provincial and criminal peripheries, police can serve as an apt point of entry, an Archimedean fulcrum, for study of this otherwise invisible political interstice. In modern societies police are not simply guardians of an impregnable social frontier that keeps moral outcasts at a safe remove from society. Since modern states began applying the force of law to govern personal behaviour in the mid nineteenth century, police have served as regulators of parallel social systems, the licit and illicit, civil society and criminal netherworld. This *demi-monde* of commercial vice – gambling, prostitution and illegal drugs – is not simply the realm of derelicts and deviants. It is the meeting ground of high and low, a levelling marketplace where the privileged and underprivileged exchange goods and services otherwise prohibited by moral and legal sanctions. Breaking through this social barrier and merging these separate realms – police and politics, scandal and legitimacy, sordid and sublime – allows us, for the first time, a fuller, three-dimensional view of the past and its politics.

SYNDICATED VICE

In thinking about such syndicated vice, it is important to treat it not in isolation, as if a simple moral dereliction, but instead place it at the intersection of politics and police, supply and demand. Most importantly, morality, at least as it takes form in law, plays a paramount role by prohibiting specific goods and services, thus moving them from the legal to the illicit economy. Indeed, legal prohibitions are the necessary precondition for a vice economy and all it entails – criminal syndicates, police corruption and political collusion.

Once banned, illegal goods and services, such as gaming or commercial sex, are no longer the object of the usual taxation and market regulation but are instead subjected to police control, both legal and extra-legal. Instead of eradicating such activity, law enforcement often acts an informal regulator, controlling the volume of vice trading and shaping the level of syndication. Aggressive, uncorrupted enforcement can, in theory, crush powerful syndicates and curb such illegality. At the opposite end of the spectrum, a symbiosis of politicians, police and vice entrepreneurs can foster powerful syndicates and a high volume of illicit activity. Wherever a particular vice sector might fall on this scale, any analysis of this criminal netherworld must be mindful of four strategic roles: that of law in setting the parameters of the illicit market; police in regulating both the volume and level of syndication; political leadership in either protecting or attacking such collusion; and criminal entrepreneurs in exploiting both legal immunities and market opportunities.

In the case of the Philippines, the US colonial regime, with the support of the Filipino political elite, banned opium and most forms of gambling between 1906 and 1908, creating, in retrospect, a regulatory framework for the later rise of a thriving vice economy. Though the opium ban was moderately effective, similar gambling restrictions were an ill-advised attempt to transform popular culture through police coercion. Police could raid gambling dens endlessly, but mere physical force could not change a political culture that made betting, as indicated by the statistics cited above, an abiding Filipino passion. As Manila grew into a metropolis and the Philippines prospered through free trade with America, illegal gambling generated a rising surplus that sustained the high cost of pre-war political campaigns. After independence in 1946, a conservative moral consensus preserved these prohibitions, making illegal gambling a significant source of campaign funds under the postwar Republic. Apart from a periodic recurrence of illegal drugs – heroin in the 1960s and amphetamines since the 1980s – illegal gambling has shaped the vice economy through its resilience, sheer size and political articulation.

Ignoring the significant, even seminal role of police and crime in modern political life, the academy, in particular its history faculties, has long relegated them to the realm of entertainment or vocational education. Such conventional history requires both inclusions and exclusions. Inclusion entails predictable narratives of national triumph as the sum of individual and collective destiny. Exclusion is, however, more complex than mere excision. Soldiers and conventional warfare, in all their heroics, are integral to national narratives; prison guards, syndicate bosses and spies, with their repellant brutality and duplicity, much less so. Workers who strike are included, but the private detectives and secret services who plot their defeat or even death receive, at best, brief mention. In effect, historians have encircled the state with a sacral barrier that bars cognizance of its profane margins – systemic violence, institutional corruption, extra-legal state security, illegal social controls and, most importantly, syndicated vice.

It is both unfortunate and understandable that historians have so long ignored a topic of such importance, one that looms so large in popular concerns, leaving a void in our understanding of contemporary politics. In contrast to the heroic grandeur and accessible archives that fill academic journals and library shelves with military history, police, with their sordid aura and sealed dossiers, remain the subject for a lower order of intellectual discourse via popular film, pulp fiction or tabloid exposé. Yet uniformed police, omnipresent on streets and highways, remain for many citizens the most visible symbols of state power. Under the right circumstances, seemingly mundane matters of crime, corruption, and policing can cast new light on the character of modern state, particularly the vexing problem of political legitimacy.

PROBLEM OF LEGITIMACY

In our thinking about the Philippines and its police, Max Weber's axiom about a state's monopoly of violence seems an apt starting point. 'What is a "state"?' he asked an audience at Munich University in 1918. 'Today,' Weber answered, punctuating carefully to accent his axiom, 'we have to say that a state is a human community that (successfully) claims the *monopoly of the legitimate use of physical force* within a given territory.'[29]

But Weber does not explore the converse of this proposition. What happens when a state fails to win a monopoly over physical force? Alternatively, what happens when it achieves such a monopoly but fails to use its coercive powers in a legitimate manner? Weber seems to hint that a state loses legitimacy if it fails in this critical area of coercion. By contrast, Ben Anderson argues that, in twentieth-century Indonesia, violence 'has never been a legitimate monopoly of the State', in large part from 'the absence of a Law by which the monopoly could be justified'.[30] If Anderson's implicit critique is correct, then conventional political theory seems somehow less relevant in the Third World where regimes are unstable and legitimacy is both fluid and bitterly, even violently, contested.

Instead of a rigid concept enshrined in constitution and refined by legal precedent, the Philippines has fashioned multiple overlapping, and often conflicting, arenas of legitimacy, particularly over illegal gambling. Although 63 per cent of 1,200 adults surveyed in 1999 said that 'gambling is always bad', 64 per cent admitted to some gambling in the past year – including a majority of those who disapproved.[31] For the third of Filipino adults who bet regularly on illegal lotteries, the syndicate operators and their protectors among local officials are, in a certain sense, legitimate if they comply with the game's outlaw ethics. Among the half-million who work in this illegal industry, there are operators, financiers and official protectors who earn loyalty, even legitimacy, through fair exchange according to the rules of the game. Similarly, local officials who break the law by taking bribes from jueteng legitimate their deviance by passing on a share of illicit proceeds to the poor as patronage and social welfare. Adding to this ambiguity, by the 1990s the Philippines had five state gambling agencies that were its third largest source of tax revenue.[32]

Confronted with this omnipresent gaming culture, the Catholic clergy and their devout, often of the middle and upper classes, equate legitimacy with strict morality and thus reject both illegal gaming and the corruption that sustains it. By contrast, jueteng, apart from offering what we might call, albeit somewhat hypothetically, a legitimating link between poor bettors and local officials, allows the poorest of the poor dreams to salve an otherwise unsustainable desperation, thus fostering a limited loyalty among impoverished masses towards a state that otherwise does little to alleviate their misery. In effect, there is an elusive, even ambiguous moral economy surrounding jueteng, making participation a moral right for the poor but any protection or profit a moral failing for the nation's political elite. As James C. Scott argued in his seminal study of moral economy, 'any class system, no matter how legitimate, promotes a certain cultural differentiation', producing a 'dissonant subculture of a subordinate group' that expresses itself not just in revolt but in 'deviant values' manifest in 'myths, jokes, songs, linguistic usage' or, in this case, illegal gambling.[33]

Such contradictions seem to rise at each successive level within the Philippine state. Municipal mayors can lose office from blatant corruption, but are still expected to distribute kickbacks from illegal gambling as patronage for the poor. Though provincial governors should be more discreet, involvement in illegal jueteng is not uncommon. But for the nation's chief executive, standards are strict, even unbending. As head of state and the embodiment of its majesty, a president must manoeuvre skilfully, through countless compromises, to maintain moral ascendancy. Yet as both head of government and party, presidents lead coalitions that win votes through violence, cash and patronage – creating endless pressures for compromise and even corruption. In this tension between the substance and symbolism of office, a chief executive must balance carefully. When the public perceives that a president has erred towards compromise, a storm over legitimacy can build with surprising speed. Among the many issues that stoke popular outrage, poor economic performance might cost a president votes, but problems of police and public order seem to arouse popular outrage in ways that more complex, nuanced issues cannot.

'In the Philippines,' observed police general Cicero Campos, 'police...corruption is chronic; scandals are discovered perennially.'[34] Most of these are unremarkable, a passing flurry of newspaper headlines that produce, at best, pressure for internal investigation. If provincial officials are implicated in a serious dereliction, Manila can intervene to remove a mayor or governor – a matter of local import but usually little more. But those scandals that somehow implicate national officials can convince key social sectors to withdraw their obedience and create a *grande scandale d'état*.

GOVERNOR ARROYO'S JUETENG SCANDAL

If we juxtapose two gambling scandals, one provincial from 1930 and another national in 2005, we can see revealing elements of both continuity and change in jueteng's role within Philippine politics. In 1929, the leading newspaper in Iloilo City, *El Tiempo*, launched a crusade against a local jueteng syndicate that soon forced Governor Mariano Arroyo from office, eclipsing his powerful political dynasty for two generations and elevating a rival clan, the Lopezes, to national prominence. Then some three generations later in 2005, the nation's 'first gentleman' Miguel Arroyo, the grandson of Governor Arroyo's brother, was accused of taking bribes from jueteng syndicates, sparking a protracted political crisis that nearly precipitated the resignation of his wife, President Gloria Arroyo.

Despite the 75 years of political change separating these two scandals, there are some striking similarities. Both arise, at base, from the political decline of entrenched local landlords like the Arroyos and the rise of national machines led by professionals and driven by cash. In the first years of US rule, the colonial regime fostered an elaborate electoral system with mass suffrage whose costs, with each successive election, seemed to strain society's resources to breaking point, creating a widening gap between society's underlying poverty and its costly political campaigns.[35]

As we will see in the two case studies that follow, jueteng has filled that void and fuelled the machinery of local politics – initially by contributions, and more recently by providing both cash and campaign workers. During the daily betting, jueteng *cobradores*, or runners, emerge from a maze of urban slums with hundreds of small bets whose sum is a billion-dollar industry. Reversing this process during elections, jueteng runners move back down these same nameless alleys to numberless squatter shacks collecting intelligence and mobilising otherwise faceless voters.

In the last years of US colonial rule, this intersection of politics and illegal gambling led to a succession of scandals. But few could equal the sensationalism and significance of Iloilo City's spectacular, year-long controversy that, apart from its impact on local elite families, provides our earliest evidence of a synergy among illegal gambling, provincial politics and police corruption.

In June 1929, two rising young media magnates, Eugenio and Fernando Lopez, launched their first newspaper, the Spanish language *El Tiempo*, with a crusade against urban vice, branding Iloilo's leading Chinese gambler Luis 'Sualoy' Sane as the city's 'Emperor of *jueteng*'. Even though this powerful criminal had been operating in Iloilo for at least five years and been the subject of periodic police raids, the paper's drum-beat coverage made his presence somehow seem an immediate threat. By September, every edition of the Lopez paper was carrying the illegal lottery's winning number in a boldface box on page one – a stark accusation of political protection and police corruption.[36]

By October, *El Tiempo* had moved beyond the lottery's Chinese 'banker', hinting, with increasing bluntness, that Governor Mariano Arroyo and his ally, Iloilo City's Police Chief Marcelo Buenaflor, were protecting illegal gambling through 'corruption and bribes'.[37] Indeed, the Constabulary's provincial commander, Captain Ramon Gaviola, later found these politicians had shared a monthly payment of P1,000 (US$500) from 'Emperor Sualoy'.[38]

The object of this attack, the Arroyo family, had enjoyed a meteoric political rise since 1916 when Governor Mariano's brother, Jose Ma. Pidal Arroyo, ran for the legislature from Iloilo's second district. With the backing of his father Ignacio, a Spanish mestizo and 'one of the richest men in the province', he scored an impressive win that launched his political career. In the years that followed, Jose Arroyo consolidated his control over the entire Western Visayas region through three successful races for the Seventh Senate District.[39] By the mid 1920s, Arroyo had become the trusted regional leader of the colony's dominant party led by Senator Manuel Quezon with the authority, as first vice-president of his Partido Nacionalista-Collectivista, to award patronage in an arbitrary even capricious manner.[40]

As the region's party boss, Senator Arroyo soon discovered the invisible market forces making jueteng a force in provincial politics. In January 1925, he wrote his leader Senator Quezon that the 'famous smuggler' Luis 'Sualoy' Sane, a Manila-Chinese criminal who had first earned notoriety in 1908 as the 'terror of Chinatown', had recently arrived in Iloilo to become 'impresario of a game called *jueteng* which is the ruin of many poor Filipino families'.[41]

This Sualoy is allied with local authorities and many have informed me in a reliable way that he is secretly paying a thousand pesos a month to the current

Municipal Mayor of Iloilo, who is a Democrata…and thus has the advantage of this monthly support from Sualoy along with other means that are not licit. We can catch him at this in a flagrant way if the Constabulary in Manila will send secret agents in disguise who are not known in Iloilo, since no other means will work. By doing this, we can save the poor from this terrible game of *jueteng*, which has made a millionaire out of its organizer through these illicit gains, and we can block the advantage of a Democrata mayor, a candidate for reelection who has a gold mine while our own candidates have empty pockets.[42]

After the senator's sudden death in March 1927, his brother Dr Mariano Arroyo, then director of Iloilo's St Paul's Hospital, inherited the leadership of the local Nacionalista Party and was elected provincial governor in October 1928.[43] Lacking his brother's strong Manila backing, Governor Arroyo instead compensated by forging local alliances with Representative Tomas Buenaflor and the powerful opposition leader, Democrata Party boss Ruperto Montinola. These moves apparently concerned Senator Quezon, who was, as his party's national leader, zealous in defence of its dominance.[44]

To finance this bid for autonomy, Governor Arroyo began taking bribes from 'Emperor' Sualoy's jueteng racket and, ironically, exposing himself to the same political attack his brother had suggested to Senator Quezon three years before. In addition to publishing the Emperor's winning numbers on page one, an implicit indictment of official protection, *El Tiempo* also charged that an illegal casino was operating in the Mahinay Building on Ortiz Street, protected by 'grease money' to city police.[45]

In October 1929, PC Captain Gaviola responded to rising public pressure by raiding a gambling and opium den on Iznart Street, arresting 15 Chinese smokers and two lottery runners. With a brazenness that hinted at protection, the 'Emperor' quickly posted bail for the runners and sent them home in his flashy automobile.[46] When the city's press bannered these arrests, Governor Arroyo issued a statement denying the lottery's existence: 'I am in complete agreement with…a strong campaign against the supposed jueteng gaming in Iloilo, if it really exists.'[47] In its response, *El Tiempo* hinted at his corruption, asking: 'What mysterious hold has the "Jueteng Boss" over some of our officials that he seems immune?'[48]

At this sensitive juncture, the gambling syndicate miscalculated by trying to crush this controversy with violence. On 10 October, the paper's editor, Jose Magalona, was entering the Wing Kee Restaurant on Plazoleta Gay when he was badly beaten by a notorious local thug named Luis 'Toldo' Elipio.[49] 'Jueteng alone is responsible for this brutal aggression', *El Tiempo* editorialised in its declaration of war on the governor. 'Several persons, one of them Governor Arroyo himself, directly or by indirections had made the members of editorial staff of this paper understand that there were people who were determined to club some of the *El Tiempo* personnel if the paper did not stop bothering the jueteng "interests."'[50]

Through this moral crusade, *El Tiempo*'s publisher, Eugenio Lopez, skilfully courted support from the antipodes of colonial society. By charging corruption, Lopez assured the intervention of the US colonial executive, long opposed to illegal gambling and its social costs. Moreover, by bundling illegal gambling, Chinese criminality, and political corruption in a single scandal, the paper stirred strong popular emotions. As the news spread through the vernacular press, particularly in the respected *Makinaugalingon*, the city's workers responded with angry letters-to-the-editor that offer us, in an era before opinion polls, a rare sampling of popular attitudes. 'Arrest and imprison the operators for at least one month, but on each Sunday afternoon march them around every turn in the road so we can scream at them', raged Ramon Quimsing who signed himself 'a poor man from Molo'.[51] Such a strong public response soon forced the Constabulary to intervene.

After weeks of careful preparation, the colonial police finally moved against the Emperor's lottery in March 1930. Recently assigned to Iloilo, PC Lieutenant Gregorio Balbuena launched a lightning raid, crashing through a concealed entrance at 75 Iznart Street to catch the Emperor 'red handed' with gambling paraphernalia and arrest him along with 14 of his runners. In June, Iloilo's Court of First Instance sentenced Sane to five months in prison and a fine of P500. Significantly, all involved in this prosecution, the provincial fiscal and presiding judge, were outsiders only recently assigned to Iloilo and thus untainted by the Emperor's generosity.[52]

Two months later, controversy flared anew when *El Tiempo* published a confidential Constabulary report about Iloilo's gambling problem. This sensational document cited Chief Buenaflor's admission that he had conspired with Governor Arroyo and Representative Tomas Buenaflor, his brother, in the operation of an illegal *monte* game to fund their faction's campaign in the 1931 elections.[53] Within days, the governor retaliated by filing a criminal libel case against *El Tiempo*'s entire staff, including its publisher Eugenio Lopez.[54]

With exceptional speed, the Justice Department dispatched a distinguished Manila judge, Manuel V. Moran. After weighing both sides in this bitterly contested case, the judge found that, in an effort to amass P100,000 (US$50,000) in anticipated election expenses, 'Governor Arroyo and Representative Buenaflor operated a gambling den...from March 3rd to April 13th, 1929, and...Governor Arroyo received P1,000 [US$500] per month as his share of the gambling proceeds.' Given this evidence, the judge exonerated *El Tiempo* on all libel charges, asserting that 'a newspaper has reason to publish this excess so that the society can correct itself'.[55]

In the subsequent administrative hearings initiated by *El Tiempo*, Governor Arroyo fared even worse before special investigator, Judge Marceliano R. Montemayor.[56] Exemplifying the damaging testimony before this inquiry, Attorney Pio Sian Melliza, a close ally of Governor Arroyo, recalled their conversations about the illegal gambling racket earlier that year.[57]

I kept going back to see him four or five times in February with the aim of reminding him why he still had not arrested the jueteng runners, not even a surprise police raid... In March I went again...and he said to me the following: '*Compadre*,...why are you so determined to get rid of jueteng gambling? Isn't it clear to you that most of the jueteng runners and sellers are our own political *liders* [precinct organisers]? The elections are close and I am running for reelection. Not including the money they are giving us for election expenses, they can hurt us in this election because there are many of these jueteng runners in this province.'

In his report to the governor-general, Judge Montemayor found Governor Arroyo guilty of blatant corruption, stating that jueteng 'had been played rather scandalously in the city of Iloilo and...the respondent...knowingly tolerated it so as not to incur the displeasure and animosity of friends and political leaders'. Citing the court's decision in the earlier libel case, Judge Montemayor also found the governor had received bribes of P1,000 per month (US$500) from *monte* gambling.[58]

On 7 October, the US governor-general ordered Arroyo's removal from office 'for the good of the service' and replaced him with an apolitical figure generally considered a 'close friend of the Lopezes'. Pending completion of Constabulary investigations, Arroyo's closest allies, Iloilo's Mayor Eulogio Garganera and Police Chief Buenaflor, were suspended.[59] Despite a strong outpouring of local support and later announcements of plans for future campaigns, Governor Arroyo's political career was over.[60]

This high-stakes Iloilo scandal allows rare insight into the underside of pre-war Philippine politics. Most significantly, the governor's target of P100,000 (US$50,000) in illicit revenues indicates, for the first time, the extraordinary cost of these early elections. In a poor colonial economy, with carefully audited government accounts, jueteng was the only possible source of cash to sustain such a costly patronage system. This controversy reveals, moreover, that boundaries between the legal and illegal had already blurred – with the city's police chief protecting syndicates, political *liders* doubling as jueteng runners, kickbacks financing campaigns, and officials at all levels colluding in corruption.

Of equal import, this incident also shows that the period's dominant national leader, Senator Quezon, kept a judicious distance from a scandal that tarred all who touched it. Even though the controversy represented a devastating blow to his own party in the country's second city, Quezon remained aloof and ignored increasingly desperate communications from Governor Arroyo.[61] With the senate president uninvolved, the governor-general impartial, and the Constabulary apolitical, this spectacular instance of police corruption lacked the national linkages to spark a legitimation crisis for the colony's leading Filipino party.

While Quezon survived this spectacular scandal and the Lopez brothers used it to launch their rise to national power, the Arroyo family suffered a complete political eclipse, virtually disappearing from politics for the remainder of the twentieth century. With their aspirations to provincial dominance destroyed, the family retreated to second-tier membership in Manila society until, through the mysteries of mutual attraction, Senator Arroyo's grandson would marry President Diosdado Macapagal's daughter in 1968, making her bearer of the family name as Gloria Macapagal Arroyo.[62]

POLITICS BY SCANDAL

In the restored democracy that followed President Ferdinand Marcos's fall in 1986, jueteng emerged from the margins of provincial politics to become, for the first time, a major force in national elections and a potent source of political scandal. The extension of jueteng's reach from provincial to national politics is most evident in a quick succession of gambling scandals that forced one president from office and nearly ousted another. At the time, president Estrada's jueteng corruption might have been dismissed as an individual aberration, but a second, similar incident just four years later involving his successor, Gloria Macapagal Arroyo, indicates the need to probe for more fundamental factors.

After independence in 1946, a complex of changes, spun out over the span of a half-century, made illegal jueteng gambling a central, controversial force in the country's electoral politics. Most fundamentally, rapid social change created an electorate of millions and overwhelmed the older, personalised forms of patronage and political mobilisation, producing a new system of mass politics mediated by cash and celebrity.[63] Indicative of this expanded electorate, the number of voters in Cavite Province rose from just 7,000 in 1912 to 400,000 in 1992.[64]

During the 1950s, therefore, rival political machines used systematic cash payments to replace social reciprocity as the main mechanism for mobilising voters.[65] By the early 1970s, rapid urbanisation and rising poverty were overwhelming the old political machines in major cities. As evidenced by the 'dramatic rise in violent and mass urban activities', one study found the lower classes were 'becoming increasingly vulnerable to market forces that weak machines cannot assuage'.[66] The country's rapid postwar urbanisation was reflected in Manila's explosive growth from a modest colonial port of 200,000 in 1902 and 623,000 in 1938 into a mega-city of 11 million that was, by 2000, the core of a metropolitan region of 22 million with 30 per cent of the country's population, most of its economic activity, and much of its crime.[67]

The full force of these changes was blunted by the sudden declaration of martial rule in 1972, postponing its impact until Marcos's regime fell from power 14 years later. Although long an important source of support for provincial campaigns, jueteng became a major national force after the resumption of regular elections in 1987. Instead of bartering votes for patronage through personal, primarily rural networks, post-Marcos politicians relied upon mass media, business contributions and jueteng cash for voter mobilisation. Instead of trading their votes for real material resources as they had once done, the poor were now investing themselves in an illegal lottery that fed their dreams of a better future. As politics and fantasy thus merged in a latter-day moral economy, parties courted a floating mass of predominantly urban voters with cash handouts and celebrity candidates – film stars, television personalities and sports heroes.

Through four successive administrations over 20 years, 1986 to 2006, jueteng's grip on the country's politics tightened. Confronted with a succession of military coups after taking office, members of the Aquino administration (1986–92), desperate for cash to build a private army and fund a bloc of loyal legislators, reputedly forged the first explicit alliance between the national executive and provincial jueteng bosses. Under the Estrada administration (1998–2001), this invisible alliance suddenly erupted into public view and forced him from office. Although his successor, Vice President Gloria Macapagal Arroyo, took her oath of office before a crowd that cheered her promises of reform, she too was soon mired in a strikingly similar jueteng scandal.

Demonstrating the deep alliance between gambling and politics, later allegations that President Arroyo's husband had collected bribes from jueteng syndicates to fund her 2004 campaign sparked a crisis that nearly forced her from office. Instead of responding with jaded resignation at yet another jueteng scandal, the electorate was outraged by these charges – in part because they lent credence to long-running rumours of an alliance between the president and the country's top gambling boss, Rodolfo 'Bong' Pineda. At a more immediate level, however, this controversy had its origins in a political vendetta between President Arroyo and her chief political rival, Panfilo 'Ping' Lacson – starting with her dismissal of him as national police director after 'People Power II' and deepening with his leadership of an abortive mob attack on the palace in May 2001. In the months following these landmark events, President Arroyo used the state security apparatus to harass Lacson with charges arising from his troubled tenure as chief of the Philippine National Police (PNP) – including illegal wiretapping, expatriation of illicit drug income in overseas bank accounts, the mass murder of the Kuratong Baleleng bank-robbery gang and, above all, the killing of publicist Salvador 'Bubby' Dacer. In turn, Lacson, first as senator and later as presidential candidate, fought back with scandal by targeting the president's controversial consort, First Gentleman Jose Miguel 'Mike' Arroyo. After winning an upper-house seat in the May 2001 elections, Senator Lacson would draw on sources inside the PNP and FBI for attacks on corrupt fund-raising by the first family.

To check his rise, the president set a supercop to catch a supercop, investing Lacson's blood enemy, PNP Superintendent Reynaldo Berroya, with special powers and direct access to her office.[68] In just three months, this covert campaign culminated in a high-stakes showdown between Senator Lacson and the palace's top intelligence officers – the street-tough supercop Berroya who headed PNP intelligence; the taciturn police professional Reynaldo Wycoco who led the NBI, or National Bureau of Investigation; and the idealistic ex-communist Victor Corpus who commanded ISAFP, or the Intelligence Service Armed Forces of the Philippines.

In their pursuit of Ping Lacson, these operatives used a shotgun approach, blasting away with a pump-action succession of sensational allegations. First, they charged that he had controlled the illicit amphetamines traffic as PNP director – dealing drugs, kidnapping Chinese suppliers and laundering profits through US banks. When these accusations failed, they revived cold-cases against his police crew for murders old (the 1995 Kuratong Baleleng massacre) and murders new (the 2000 Bubby Dacer rub-out). But by the end of this three-year battle, the elusive Lacson bested them all, checking their criminal charges with his media counter-charges. With uncommon insight into the country's political culture, Lacson seemed to understand, first, that the scurrilous only became scandalous if it touched the executive and, second, some corruptions, such as jueteng, resonated more deeply than others.

Significantly, this bitter rivalry revolved, in its first rounds, around charges and counter-charges over illicit drugs instead of jueteng. After a decade of rising amphetamine abuse in the country's slums, the traffic had finally gained sufficient scale to erupt from the back alleys onto the front pages. And instead of jueteng's blatant bribes to police and politicians, long accepted within the country's folk culture, drug trafficking brought new, disconcerting dimensions to Philippine politics – notably, kidnapping, cold-blooded rub-outs, and mass murder. In their pursuit of Lacson, these intelligence mandarins – Corpus, Berroya and Wycoco – would charge him, in effect, with a rationalisation of the vice economy that had transformed his elite police squad, the PAOCTF, into a lethal criminal syndicate. Instead of taking a cut from the old jueteng lottery, Lacson's supercops had, during the tumultuous 1990s, focused on the more lucrative drug traffic, allegedly maximising profits by kidnapping overseas Chinese suppliers, draining their bank accounts, and dumping their bodies. Alone among these three top cops, Colonel Victor Corpus seemed to understand the deeper implications of this general shift from jueteng to *shabu*, warning that the country could become 'a narco-state like Colombia'.[69]

During the Arroyo administration's first weeks in February and March of 2001, the former PNP operative Mary Ong, code-named 'Rosebud', launched the hunt for Lacson with public allegations, widely reported in the Manila press, that his disbanded police squad, the PAOCTF or Police Anti-Organized Crime Task Force, had kidnapped 21 Chinese, many of them drug traffickers, and summarily executed at least six after collecting substantial ransoms. Specifically, she accused police of killing Chinese drug lord Calvin Wong in 1998 after extracting information about a *shabu* factory in Quezon City; and later, in May 2000, arranging the 'disappearance' of their own Filipino-Chinese agent, Angelito M. Sy, when he learned of a drug shipment from Hong Kong.[70]

Only days after taking office in January 2001, the new NBI director Wycoco promised he would leave 'no stone unturned' to find Dacer's killers. Within weeks, the NBI filed criminal charges against seven PAOCTF agents, all subordinates of Senior Superintendent Cesar Mancao – the very officer Lacson had once assigned to head the original investigation into Dacer's death. Threatened with jail, the accused patrolmen proved 'willing to squeal'. Then, during a dawn raid on 28 March, NBI agents arrested two farmers at Indang, Cavite who admitted witnessing Dacer's grisly execution cum immolation on the day of his abduction. Confronted with body parts and eyewitnesses, the four arrested police soon cracked, claiming that President Estrada had ordered Dacer's killing through PNP Superintendent Glenn Dumlao – a sensational revelation slammed across the front pages under the headline, 'Erap Named Brains in Dacer Murders'.[71]

After the Justice Department indicted eleven PAOCTF police for the Dacer murder, Berroya, now head of the PNP Intelligence Group, moved deftly to round them up. On 4 June, his men scored a coup by snatching the most senior, Superintendent Dumlao, from Manila's Victory Liner bus terminal. Just eight days later, Dumlao confessed he had, as PAOCTF's deputy operations chief, interrogated Dacer right after his kidnapping at the direction of Lacson's trusted lieutenants, Cesar Mancao and Michael Ray Aquino. Within weeks, both Mancao and Aquino, Lacson's closest protégés, had slipped through Cebu's airport on fake passports and disappeared into the United States.[72]

Throughout August and September of 2001, the showdown shifted to Congress as Colonel Corpus unleashed a series of sensational, ultimately unsustained allegations against Lacson for drug trafficking, money laundering, and murder. On the eve of these hearings, Colonel Corpus released an intelligence report stating Senator Lacson and ex-president Estrada had laundered $728 million from drugs and kidnapping through foreign banks – charges that stunned the nation and held television audiences spell-bound for weeks.[73] When the Senate inquiry opened in

August, however, Colonel Corpus could only confirm a single San Francisco account with $24 million – far from the $211 million he had first alleged.[74]

Instead of responding, Senator Lacson, in a brilliant use of scandal, spoke from the Senate floor on 3 October, charging that First Gentleman Mike Arroyo had made the Philippine Charity Sweepstakes Office his 'cash cow' by diverting some P250 million (US$6.3 million) into private accounts.[75] A month later, as the Senate closed its inquiry into his own crimes, Lacson cited PNP intelligence reports to accuse top NBI and police with splitting an annual 'jueteng payola' of P16.5 billion (US$412 million). Lacson alleged that the president had proved 'helpless in the last eight months before the jueteng lords' whose collections were 'back with a vengeance' – notably, Bong Pineda himself who controlled most of the P13 million (US$325,000) daily gross from four Central Luzon provinces. To protect their operations, the gambling syndicates were, the senator charged, bribing Arroyo's top police, paying P3 million (US$75,000) monthly to PNP Central Luzon director Berroya and P2 million (US$50,000) more to NBI director Wycoco.[76]

As the Senate committee investigating Lacson adjourned to write a report that would take years to appear, the Arroyo administration shifted its get-Lacson effort to the Kuratong Baleleng massacre, making this cold case central to the nation's political future. Investigators turned up four new eye-witnesses among the hundreds of police involved in the slaughter. But in late August, just as the government was moving to arrest Lacson, the Court of Appeals issued a permanent injunction against any further prosecution, saying the maximum period had lapsed since an earlier pre-trial dismissal of these murder charges.[77]

On balance, President Arroyo's pursuit of Lacson via her three intelligence czars produced results that, at best, can be styled mixed. On the debit side, Colonel Victor Corpus's sensational allegations of billion-dollar deposits were not corroborated. On the credit side, NBI director Wycoco had pursued the Dacer murder deep into the senator's entourage, getting so close that the two prime suspects, both Lacson protégés, fled to America. On balance, Lacson had, through a mix of media and legal manoeuvres, eluded all three of his netherworld rivals to win a senate seat and establish himself as a viable presidential candidate.

PRESIDENTIAL ELECTIONS 2004

For the next two years, Senator Lacson, while preparing the ground for his 2004 presidential bid, relied on a deft mix of scandal and legal manoeuvre to avoid trial for the brutal Kuratong massacre. In August, 2003, he scored a decisive blow against the president with a privilege speech accusing the First Gentleman Mike Arroyo of heading a corrupt coterie that, first, diverted over P270 million (US$6.1 million) of campaign contributions into private accounts and, then, used these funds to bribe his chief accusers. Critically, Lacson documented his allegations with verifiable details of banking transactions – notably, accounts at Union Bank and Morgan Stanley with deposits of P36.6 million (US$832,000) under the name of 'Jose Pidal', a fictional persona who, the senator charged, shared a Makati office address at the LTA Building with Mike Arroyo. Initially, the First Gentleman dismissed the senator's allegation by announcing 'I don't know any Pidal.' But with superb timing, Lacson countered, in a second senate speech, by disclosing the details of recent deposits totalling P260 million (US$5.9 million) into a dozen bank accounts in the name of 'Jose Pidal'. Then, in a stunning revelation, the ABS-CBN television network, owned ironically by grandchildren of the original Arroyo nemesis Eugenio Lopez, revealed that Mike Arroyo's great-grandmother was, in fact, Maria Pidal, an uncommon surname that had disappeared from the Philippine census rolls for over 50 years. To defuse this explosive revelation, the First Gentleman's younger brother, Representative Ignacio Tuason Arroyo, Jr., announced, unconvincingly, 'I am actually Jose Pidal.'[78]

In retrospect, Lacson's 'Jose Pidal' revelations were superbly timed to frame, or re-frame, key issues at the start of the presidential campaign, shifting the focus of public concern from unsustained allegations about his past drug dealing to more recent and better documented charges about the president's illegal campaign funding. In the weeks following revelations about the Pidal accounts in August 2003, the president's approval rating fell sharply from 51 to 41 per cent. By contrast, Ping Lacson's main negative, mass murder charges from the Kuratong killings, had long lost its shock value and now seemed, in comparison with the stunning Pidal revelations, lighter electoral baggage.[79]

Nonetheless, memory of the Kuratong massacre did in fact tarnish Lacson's lustre as a national leader, and his low poll numbers, never higher than 10 per cent of voters, weakened as the campaign ground on to election day in May 2004. While the mass of Filipino voters viewed him guardedly, the Manila Chinese, seeing him as a guardian against a resurgence of lethal kidnappings, were enthusiastic backers and donated P11 million (US$220,000) to his campaign at a single luncheon. Despite lavish campaign spending, Lacson finished a distant third, with a dismal 8 per cent of votes behind a victorious President Arroyo. Even so, issues of order and justice loom so large for ordinary voters in this post-colonial society that even Lacson's third-place showing marked him as a viable presidential candidate, in the strong-man mould of his hero Marcos, for 2010 or beyond.[80]

FIRST GENTLEMAN ARROYO'S JUETENG SCANDAL

In the electoral aftermath, Senator Lacson emerged as one of the opposition's key leaders and used his access to intelligence files inside the FBI and PNP for new attacks on Arroyo.[81] In May 2005, the first anniversary of his presidential defeat, Senator Lacson announced that he would hold hearings with 'very explosive testimony' that people in 'high places' were taking a cut from jueteng gambling. Through the senator's good offices, the *Philippine Daily Inquirer* interviewed these witnesses who 'claimed to have given or collected protection money' for First Gentleman Mike Arroyo and first son Representative Juan Miguel 'Mikey' Arroyo. In a sworn affidavit, a bagman from Legazpi City stated that he had collected P500,000 (US$9,800) from three of the Bikol region's top jueteng bosses on behalf of a presidential aide. A second bagman, from Central Luzon, showed a ledger with payments of P1.93 million (US$37,840) monthly from 24 jueteng operators, including Bong Pineda, to top PNP officials, including Director General Arturo Lomibao. All the appointments of these corrupt cops had been, the paper asserted, 'made by Mike Arroyo'. Within hours, the president ordered officials to investigate these charges against her son and husband.[82]

The controversy soon focused on President Arroyo's long alliance with Luzon's top jueteng boss, Bong Pineda, that reached back to shared roots in the same small town, Lubao, Pampanga. Ironically, after the earlier jueteng scandal that had ousted Estrada, Bong Pineda was able, according to journalist Sheila Coronel, 'to expand and consolidate illegal gambling operations', earning an unprecedented P2 billion annually (US$39.2 million). At the start of these Senate hearings in August, political insider Michaelangelo Zulce testified that the gambling boss's wife, Lubao mayor Lilia Pineda, had handed out fat envelopes with P30,000 (US$600) to all 27 Mindanao election officials at the Arroyos' Quezon City home just before the 2004 voting – an alleged generosity that, if accurate, may explain this region's lopsided tally for the president.[83]

Midst escalating controversy, the scandal suddenly became a full-blown crisis on 7 June 2005 when the opposition released a short 'Hello Garci' tape of the president asking Virgilio 'Garci' Garcillano, elections commissioner and veteran vote rigger, 'So I will still lead by 1 million overall?' – apparent orders for a million-vote margin in the presidential count. In a desperate effort to defuse this explosive scandal, the president made an extraordinary act of contrition on national television, admitting that it was her voice on the 'Hello Garci' tapes and announcing, two days later, that she was sending her husband into political exile.[84] In effect, President Arroyo had confessed to a lesser crime within the country's political culture, vote rigging, but resolutely denied any personal involvement in jueteng corruption, apparently sensing, with the keen instincts that assured her ultimate survival, that admitting any direct tie to this illegal lottery would prove politically fatal.

As her cabinet resigned en masse and the opposition announced impeachment proceedings, Arroyo's government teetered on the brink of collapse until former president Fidel V. Ramos made a dramatic call, on 8 July, for the opposition to set aside partisan charges in favour of fundamental constitutional change. Two weeks later, President Arroyo survived the opposition's bungled impeachment attempt, which garnered little more than half the needed votes for trial in the Senate. Signalling the collapse of the opposition's impeachment effort, in early August one of its key witnesses, jueteng bagman Richard Garcia, appeared weeping at a press conference to retract his senate testimony and beg the president for forgiveness, claiming that Senator Lacson 'insisted on linking the First Family when I didn't have any information about it'. Through its own deft manoeuvres and the opposition's inherent weakness, the Arroyo administration clung to power, albeit with greatly diminished prestige and capacity for effective executive leadership, leaving the country to wallow in an endless, unresolved crisis.[85]

CONCLUSION

Comparison of these two scandals separated by 75 years, 1930 and 2005, indicates both continuity and change illustrative of jueteng's persistent role in Philippine politics. First, some obvious continuities. In their reach for extraordinary political power, provincial and then national, two generations of the same elite family, separated by seven decades of turbulent change, relied on illegal campaign finance from the same gambling racket. At the dawn of the twenty-first century, two succeeding presidents, the arriviste Estrada and the aristocratic Arroyo, were plunged into protracted political crises sparked by allegations of bribes from gambling racketeers. Moreover, jueteng's passage from provincial to national acceptance in this same period reveals much about the changing character of Philippine politics, particularly the shift from tight rural patronage ties to a more impersonal urban electoral mobilisation by cash and celebrity.

In both cases, 1930 and 2005, allegations about alliances with syndicate bosses aroused public anger and destroyed the legitimacy of politicians so caught, whether a lowly provincial governor or president of the Republic. In these and similar political crises involving jueteng, provincial and national administrations either reformed or faced a long, painful erosion of legitimacy that usually culminated in a dramatic denouement – electoral upset or mass protests. Though the immediate conflict has usually been resolved, at the national level, by a loss of power and change in administration, these legitimation crises, as Jurgen Habermas argues, seemed to produce a political denouement of either repression or reform.[86]

Next, some troubling changes. Clearly, if we juxtapose Senator Quezon's careful distancing from the 1930 scandal with the calculating, even cynical complicity of President Arroyo's closest confidantes – husband, son and brother-in-law – the country's political elites had shed ethical restraints, extending the corrupting influence of illegal gaming to the country's highest echelons. Paralleling this extension of gambling corruption, the scale of the racket's profits and alleged political payoffs have expanded exponentially by a factor of 500 – from Governor Arroyo's monthly gambling kick-backs of P1,000 (US$500) and his P100,000 (US$50,000) goal in illegal campaign collections in 1930 to First Gentleman Arroyo's P500,000 (US$9,800) in alleged monthly payments from Bikol alone and the P260 million (US$5.9 million) in the 'Pidal' political slush fund allegedly under his control.

Similarly, both police corruption and Chinese criminality have expanded substantially in the past century. After independence in 1946 breached the bilateral isolation of colonial rule, the Philippines was again open to unfiltered contacts with the vast Chinese cultural imperium to its northwest. At first the Taiwanese and overseas Chinese influence was limited, but south China's capitalist transformation after the Cold War opened the Philippines to an intensified incursion by nascent Chinese crime syndicates and their chief export, methamphetamines. This sudden surge in Chinese capital, criminal and commercial, made the Manila community both principals and victim's in the city's flourishing criminality. During the 1990s, the Chinese presence was suddenly an omnipresent feature of Manila's crime scene through kidnappings, community protests, drug dealing and gangland killings. The scale of this change is evident in the striking contrast between Emperor Sualoy's provincial jueteng operations with its thousand-peso bribes in the 1920s versus the billions of pesos in the South China drug circuits of the late 1990s. In a related yet somewhat different trend, the debut of the Manila-Chinese as a significant factor in presidential politics during the 2004 elections reflects their response to countless kidnappings and a perception of Senator Lacson as the community's protector against crime syndicates, allowing him to draw campaign finance from the Manila-Chinese to challenge an established political dynasty, the Arroyos.

In equal measure, the limited, localised police corruption of 1930 had given way to widespread complicity by the PNP hierarchy in 2005. As guardian of Manila's criminal netherworld, police have experienced a parallel expansion in the scale and scope of their corruption. Although Iloilo's municipal police took small bribes to protect the city's jueteng racket in 1930, the national police, then called the Philippines Constabulary, were still free from such systemic corruption and thus symbolised the legitimacy of the colonial state. Four decades after independence, the new national police, or PNP, exhibit a pervasive corruption as protectors of regional jueteng syndicates and principals in the nation's drug traffic. Reflecting, moreover, its role as a quasi-autonomous power-centre within the Philippine state, the national police have produced candidates for each of the presidential elections over the past 20 years. In 2004, the most recent of these police candidates, Senator Lacson, led a law-and-order campaign that combined PNP veterans as staffers, and political use of police intelligence, arousing enough popular support to split the opposition and position himself as a potential contender in 2010. More broadly, through their fusion of legitimate force with control over the illicit economy, the national police have emerged as a quasi-autonomous power centre within the Philippine state.

Turning this analytic microscope back into a telescope to glimpse the future, this four-year confrontation between President Arroyo and Senator Lacson may be a bellwether of longer-term changes in the relationship between the formal and informal sectors with profound implications for the character of the Philippine polity. If, as their critics have alleged, the national police had ties to overseas Chinese drug syndicates and Arroyo's presidential campaign was financed by jueteng bosses, then illicit drugs may be replacing illegal gambling as the dominant form of political funding and police corruption. Though it has been illegal for nearly a century, jueteng enjoys a certain legitimacy within the moral economy of Filipino popular culture. Its massive cash transactions are conducted without violence, and its political bribes fund both electoral campaigns and an informal social welfare system. More importantly, jueteng binds a potentially disaffected mass to the Philippine polity. Its syndicates' role in election-day turn out assures political participation by the very poor, just as daily dreams of jueteng jackpots allows aspirations midst squatter desperation, lending legitimacy to an otherwise unsustainable social contract. By contrast, drug use is universally condemned, its traffic is marked by lurid violence, and its bribes, lacking the legitimacy for socially recognised uses, seem to fund amoral, individual acquisition.

If these subterranean rackets indeed have the power to shape the political super-structure, then drug trafficking's displacement of jueteng as the dominant force in the country's covert netherworld has the potential to rend the moral fabric of Philippine politics, introducing a more brutal violence, a self-aggrandising corruption, escalating police brutality and amoral actors. These changes in the vice trades may thus have a profound impact on the moral economy of political life, superseding a social system that fosters bonds across the class divide and a legitimating linkage, through the medium of dreams and aspirations, between the poorest Filipinos and the national polity. In its place, a violent, demoralised drug milieu is emerging that offers neither the political mobilisation nor ideological legitimation, leading to the possibility that the supple character of the Philippine state may delegate police and political power to an illegitimate criminal sector, attenuating invisible social ties and eroding the state's moral authority, allowing a painful spiral downward into violence, class-based insurgency and regional revolts.

At the risk of overburdening a single election, the 2004 presidential campaign may seem, in retrospect, a turning point in Philippine politics when entrenched elite families like the Arroyos, rooted in provincial landholdings and ruling through familial reputation, were displaced by a new kind of national politician sustained by more heterogeneous forces. If the old provincial politicians under the pre-Marcos Republic relied on the 'three Gs' of guns, goons and gold, then we can describe the new forces that emerged after his fall as the 'three Cs' of celebrity, criminality and Chinese. Just as movie and basketball stars have played upon their celebrity to win seats in a reconstituted senate, once a body of elder, aristocratic statesmen, so Lacson's campaign allegedly fused the latter two forces, criminality and Chinese, in a serious challenge to an incumbent president with a more established profile of educational achievement, aristocratic lineage and jueteng finance. If this electoral cameo is indicative of larger trends, then rural landed patrons with their armed peasant militia, agricultural export profits, familial prestige and illegal gambling networks are giving way to a new-model urban politician supported by slum gangs, Chinese capital, mass-media advertising and illicit drug profits. In this mix of complex social forces, changes in criminality seem to be playing a seminal, even central role.

In sum, the study of an obscure illegal lottery casts some new light on the overall character of the Philippine polity and the history of its political crises, showing how an illicit industry has emerged from the social margins to become a major force in the country's politics. Ultimately, the persistent role of a criminal racket and its syndicate bosses in both provincial politics and presidential succession shows the significance of the covert netherworld as a frame for academic analysis of the Philippine polity. If this study of a single country has broader implications, then ignoring the influence of the covert netherworld upon this or any other modern state may well produce a picture that is not only incomplete but inaccurate.

NOTES

This chapter has countless intellectual debts to transnational scholarly communities that work on the Philippines and, separately, the covert netherworld. I am grateful to Tim Lindsey and Eric Wilson, of the University of Melbourne and Monash University law schools respectively, for organising an exemplary conference in August 2006 to establish the study of 'parapolitics' and 'deep politics', or what I call here the 'covert netherworld', as a coherent academic field – in effect, elevating this inquiry beyond the elementary empirical level by investing it with both methodology and theory. Closer to home, at the University of Wisconsin-Madison where I teach, this chapter benefited from comments by fellow Philippine specialists Michael Cullinane, Dan Doeppers and Paul Hutchcroft.

1. For various press reports on the gross revenues for jueteng, see, *Manila Bulletin*, 18 September 2000; *Philippine Daily Inquirer*, 22 March 2000, 6 October 2000, 9 October 2000; Wilfredo R. Reotutar, *So the People May Know: All About Gambling in the Philippines* (Quezon City: Programs Enterprises, 1999), pp. 113–17. For sources on employment in jueteng, see *Manila Bulletin*, 18 September 2000, 11 October 2000, 21 November 2000; *Philippine Daily Inquirer*,

6 October 2000. For jueteng's popularity, see, Social Weather Stations, SWS Media Release: 8 December 1999, 'Moral Attitudes Against Gambling Hardly Affect Gambling Behavior – SWS Survey', www.sws.org.ph/pr120899.htm (accessed 5 June 2001). For sources on the gross sales of illicit drugs, see, US Department of State, Bureau of International Narcotics and Law Enforcement Affairs, *International Narcotics Control Strategy Report 2001, Philippines*, www.state.gov/g/inl/rls/nrcrpt/2001/rpt/8483.html (accessed 28 March 2002). In 2000, the US$6 billion gross for gambling and drugs was equivalent to P300 billion, or 46 per cent of P651 billion in total government expenditures for that year. For budgetary statistics, see, Republic of the Philippines, National Statistical Coordination Board, *2000 Philippine Statistical Yearbook* (Manila: National Statistical Coordination Board, 2000), Tables 15.2, 15.4, 15.5. For employment in the Philippine electronics industry, see, Steven C. McKay, 'Securing Commitment in an Insecure World: Power and the Social Regulation of Labor in the Philippine Electronics Industry' (doctoral dissertation, University of Wisconsin-Madison, 2001), Figure 8, Chapter 2; and, Steven C. McKay, *Satanic Mills or Silicon Islands? The Politics of High-Tech Production in the Philippines* (Ithaca: Cornell University Press, 2006), pp. 46–7.

2. Brian Fegan, 'Entrepreneurs in Votes and Violence: Three Generations of a Peasant Political Family', in Alfred W. McCoy (ed.), *An Anarchy of Families: State and Family in the Philippines* (Quezon City: Ateneo de Manila University Press, 1994), pp. 73–6, 82–102; Brian Fegan, 'The Social History of a Central Luzon Barrio', in Alfred McCoy and Ed. C. de Jesus (eds), *Philippine Social History* (Honolulu: University of Hawaii Press, 1982), pp. 106–7, 118–23; Benedict J. Kerkvliet, *The Huk Rebellion: A Study of Peasant Revolt in the Philippines* (Berkeley: University of California Press, 1977), pp. 6–7.

3. Louis Paul Benson, 'Changing Political Alliance Patterns in the Rural Philippines: A Case Study from Camarines Norte', in Benedict J. Kerkvliet (ed.), *Political Change in the Philippines: Studies of Local Politics Preceding Martial Law* (Honolulu: University of Hawaii, Asian Studies Program, 1974), pp. 133–42.

4. David Wurfel, *Filipino Politics: Development and Decay* (Ithaca: Cornell University Press, 1988), pp. 98–100.

5. Ray Bonner, *Waltzing with a Dictator: The Marcoses and the Making of American Policy* (New York: Times Books, 1987), pp. 76–7; Conrado de Quiros, *Dead Aim: How Marcos Ambushed Philippine Democracy* (Pasig City: Foundation for Worldwide People's Power, 1997), pp. 65–6, 221.

6. Carl H. Landé, *Post-Marcos Politics: A Geographical and Statistical Analysis of the 1992 Presidential Election* (Singapore: Institute of Southeast Asian Studies, 1996), pp. 108–12, 133–4.

7. *Philippine Daily Inquirer*, 10 November 1995.

8. Lucien Bodard, *La Guerre d'Indochine: L'Humiliation* (Paris: Gallimard, 1965), pp. 110–11; Bernard B. Fall, 'The Political-Religious Sects of Viet-Nam', *Pacific Affairs*, 28/3 (1955), pp. 235–53; A.M. Savani, 'Notes sur les Binh Xuyen' (ms., December 1945), pp. 188–90, 215–16.

9. Major Emanuel A. Baja, *Philippine Police System and Its Problems* (Manila: Pobre's Press, 1933), pp. 349, 350–4.

10. SWS Media Release, 'Moral Attitudes Against Gambling Hardly Affect Gambling Behavior'.

11. For a definition of both 'parapolitics' and 'deep politics' as used by Peter Dale Scott, see the entry for 'Deep Politics' in Internet encyclopedia Wikipedia, http://en.wikipedia.org/wiki/Deep_politics (accessed 20 December 2006). In assessing Scott's considerable scholarly achievements, the Wikipedia entry under his name comments: 'Scott has researched and written several investigative books that critics dismiss as conspiracy theories. However, Scott rejects this label and has used the phrase "deep politics" to describe his heavily-footnoted political writing.' (See, http://en.wikipedia.org/wiki/Peter_Dale_Scott#Investigator [accessed 20 December 2006]). In a section of his own webpage for his book *Deep Politics and the Death of JFK*, Peter Dale Scott lists a promotional blurb from Oliver Stone, reading; 'Oliver Stone, director, *JFK*: "A book that will become part of our alternate history – to be read and studied by future generations."' (See, http://socrates.berkeley.edu/~pdscott/revDP.html [accessed 20 December 2006].)

12. Interview with Lieutenant Colonel Lucien Conein, former CIA operative in Saigon, McLean, Virginia, 18 June 1971.

13. Frederic Wakeman, Jr., *Policing Shanghai, 1927–1937* (Berkeley: University of California Press, 1995), pp. 116–31; Alfred W. McCoy, *The Politics of Heroin: CIA Complicity in the Global Drug Trade* (New York: Lawrence Hill Books, 2003), pp. 53–63, 331–4, 470–500.

14. United Nations, United Nations Office for Drug Control and Crime Prevention, *World Drug Report 2000* (Oxford: Oxford University Press, 2000), pp. 5, 13–14, 143–8; United Nations, United Nations International Drug Control Programme, *World Drug Report* (Oxford: Oxford University Press, 1997), pp. 132, 162–3.

15. *New York Times*, 26 June 1997; United Nations International Drug Control Programme, *World Drug Report*, pp. 31, 32, 124; United Nations Office for Drug Control and Crime Prevention, *World Drug Report 2000*, p. 70.

16. United Nations Office on Drug and Crime, *Afghanistan: Opium Survey 2004* (United Nations, 2005), pp. 75–6, www.unodc.org/pdf/afg/afghanistan_opium_survey_2004.pdf (accessed 5 October 2006).

17. Tim Lindsey, 'Law, Violence and Corruption in the *Preman* State' (Melbourne: Conference on Government of the Shadows, 10–12 August 2006); Maruyama Masao, *Thought and Behaviour in Modern Japanese Politics* (London: Oxford University Press, 1963), pp. 84–131; E.H. Norman, 'The Genyosha: A Study in the Origins of Japanese Imperialism', in John Livingston et al. (eds), *The Japan Reader I* (New York: Random House, 1978), pp. 355–67.

18. Tan Chung, 'The Britain–China–India Trade Triangle 1771–1840', in Sabyasachi Bhattacharya (ed.), *Essays in Modern Indian Economic History* (New Delhi: Munshiram Manoharlal Publishers, 1987), pp. 114–30; J.F. Richards, 'The Indian Empire and Peasant Production of Opium in the Nineteenth Century', *Modern Asian Studies*, 15/1 (1981), pp. 67–9.

19. James Warren, 'Slavery and the Impact of External Trade: The Sulu Sultanate in the 19th Century', in Alfred W. McCoy and Ed. C. de Jesus, *Philippine Social History: Global Trade and Local Transformations* (Quezon City: Ateneo de Manila University Press, 1982), pp. 415–34.

20. Under Executive Order No. 193, effective 1 January 1949, 'nonessential' and 'luxury' imports were controlled, quickly cutting tobacco imports by nearly half. Under Republic Act No. 698 of May 1952, the government reduced all tobacco imports. Finally, in July 1954, the government established the Philippine Tobacco Administration to promote local cultivation and, under this protectionist legislation, effectively banned tobacco imports. Under these laws, tobacco imports dropped from P45.1 million in 1946 to P28.2 million in 1955 and only P1.4 million in 1957. As legal imports declined, cigarette smuggling grew. See, Robert R. Reed, 'The Tobacco Economy', in Robert E. Huke (ed.), *Shadows on the Land: An Economic Geography of the Philippines* (Manila: Bookmark, 1963), pp. 353–6; Frank H. Golay, *The Philippines: Public Policy and National Economic Development* (Ithaca: Cornell University Press, 1961), pp. 163–6, 336; *Daily Mirror*, 12 March 1963.

21. For the way that Indonesian fiscal policies encouraged smuggling and the role of copra in financing Sulawesi's regional revolts in the 1950s and early 1960s, see, Barbara Harvey, 'Tradition, Islam and Rebellion: South Sulawesi, 1905–1965' (doctoral dissertation, Cornell University, 1974), pp. 264, 322; Kathryn M. Robinson, *Stepchildren of Progress: The Political Economy of Development in an Indonesia Mining Town* (Albany: State University of New York Press, 1986), pp. 85–6; Herbert Feith, *The Decline of Constitutional Democracy in Indonesia* (Ithaca: Cornell University Press, 1962), pp. 488–94.

22. A.V.H. Hartendorp, *History of Industry and Trade of the Philippines: The Magsaysay Administration* (Manila: Philippine Education Company, 1961), pp. 273–4; Thomas M. McKenna, 'The Defiant Periphery: Routes of Iranun Resistance in the Philippines', *Social Analysis*, 35 (April 1994), p. 21.

23. Eva-Lotta E. Hedman and John T. Sidel, *Philippine Politics and Society in the Twentieth Century: Colonial Legacies, Post-Colonial Trajectories* (London: Routledge, 2000), pp. 166–73.

24. Theodore Friend, *The Blue-Eyed Enemy: Japan Against the West in Java and Luzon, 1942–1945* (Princeton: Princeton University Press, 1988), pp. 34–48.

25. John T. Sidel, *Capital, Coercion, and Crime: Bossism in the Philippines* (Stanford: Stanford University Press, 1999), pp. 146–7.

26. Hedman and Sidel, *Philippine Politics and Society in the Twentieth Century*, pp. 108, 172–3.

27. John Sidel, 'Filipino Gangsters in Film, Legend, and History: Two Biographical Case Studies from Cebu', in Alfred W. McCoy (ed.), *Lives at the Margin: Biography of Filipinos Obscure, Ordinary, and Heroic* (Quezon City: Ateneo de Manila University Press, 2000), pp. 149–80.

28. John Sidel, 'The Usual Suspects: Nardong Putik, Don Pep Oyson, and Robin Hood', in Vicente L. Rafael (ed.), *Figures of Criminality in Indonesia, the Philippines, and Colonial Vietnam* (Ithaca: Southeast Asia Program, Cornell University, 1999), pp. 70–90.

29. H.H. Gerth and C. Wright Mills, *From Max Weber: Essays in Sociology* (New York: Oxford University Press, 1946), pp. 77–8.

30. Benedict Anderson, 'Introduction', in Vicente L. Rafael (ed.), *Figures of Criminality in Indonesia, the Philippines, and Colonial Vietnam* (Ithaca: Southeast Asia Program, Cornell University, 1999), pp. 18–19.

31. SWS Media Release, 'Moral Attitudes Against Gambling Hardly Affect Gambling Behavior'.

32. This contradiction between social practice and formal sanctions, both legal and religious, has parallels elsewhere – notably in Quebec City where police, who accepted its inevitability, and Church, which insisted on its immorality, created a political stalemate over prostitution that allowed a notorious 'red light' district to operate illegally from 1880 to 1940. (See, Jean Paul Brodeur, 'Legitimizing Police Deviance', in Clifford D. Shearing [ed.], *Organizational Police Deviance: Its Structure and Control* [Toronto: Butterworths, 1981], pp. 148–9). Reotutar, *So the People May Know*, pp. 6–7.

33. E.P. Thompson, 'The Moral Economy of the English Crowd in the Eighteenth Century', *Past and Present*, 50 (1971), pp. 76–136; James C. Scott, *Moral Economy of the Peasant* (New Haven: Yale University Press, 1976), pp. 1–12, 225–40.

34. Cicero C. Campos, 'The Role of Police in the Philippines: A Case Study from the Third World' (doctoral dissertation, Michigan State University, 1983), p. 346.

35. Willem Wolters, *Politics, Patronage, and Class Conflict in Central Luzon* (The Hague: Institute of Social Studies, Research Report No. 14, 1983), pp. 166–7; US War Department, *Report of the Governor General of the Philippine Islands to the Secretary of War 1919* (Washington: Government Printing Office, 1920), p. 5.

36. *Makinaugalingon*, 10 September 1929.

37. *El Tiempo*, 2 October 1929.

38. Baja, *Philippine Police System and Its Problems*, pp. 353–6, 372–4, 423–5, 428–9, 432–3, 467–8.

39. Newspaper clipping titled 'Ignacio Arroyo Dies of Heart Failure in Residence in Iloilo', enclosed in letter from Dr Mariano Arroyo to Manuel Quezon, 19 January 1935, Box 65, File: Arroyo, Ignacio, Manuel Quezon Papers, Philippine National Library; Fernando Ma. Guerrero, *Directorio Oficial del Senado de Filipinas* (Manila: Bureau of Printing, 1921), pp. 34–5; Fernando Ma. Guerrero, *Directorio Oficial del Senado y de la Camara de Representatives* (Manila: Bureau of Printing, 1917), pp. 157–8; Republic of the Philippines, Supreme Court, *Beaterio del Santisimo Rosario de Molo* vs. *Court of Appeals, Jose Arroyo, et al.*, G.R. No. L 44204, 11 July 1985, www.lawphil. net/juduris/juri1985/jul1985/gr_144204_1985.html (accessed 6 June 2006); Jet Damazo, 'The Pidal Connection', *Newsbreak* (Manila), 15 September 2003; Inquirer News Service, 20 August 2003, www.inq7.net/nat/2003/aug/20/text/n at_5–1p.htm (accessed 13 June 2006); T. Villavert, 'FG Arroyo to Continue "Arroyo tradition"', PIA Information Service, 'PIA Press Release 05/05/2005', www.pia.gov.ph/news.asp?fi=p050505.htm&no=1 (accessed 6 June 2006).

40. Letter from Jose Ma. Arroyo to Manuel Quezon, 27 December 1924, Box 182, File: Iloilo 1921–23, Manuel A. Quezon Papers, Philippine National Library; Damazo, 'The Pidal Connection'.

41. It seems likely that this Luis Sane who appeared at Iloilo in 1925 was the same as the 'Luey Sane' notorious in the Manila press as the 'terror of Chinatown' for leading notorious Gee Hock Tong in a series of murder and extortion attempts in 1908. A year later in 1909, the same member of the Gee Hock group, with the spelling of his name changed to 'Luis Sane', also played an active role in opposing the deportation of alleged Chinese gangsters. (See, *Cablenews American*, 1 August 1908, 22 August 1909.) Letter from Jose Ma. Arroyo to Manuel Quezon, 24 January 1925, Box 182, File: Iloilo 1921–23, Manuel A. Quezon Papers, Philippine National Library; Baja, *Philippine Police System and Its Problems*, p. 356; letter from J. Harding to Executive Secretary, 4 September 1909, No. 370–234 Entry 5, RG-350, National Archives & Records Administration.

42. Letter from Jose Ma. Arroyo to Manuel Quezon, 24 January 1925, Box 182, File: Iloilo 1921–23, Manuel A. Quezon Papers, Philippine National Library.

43. Letter from Dr. Mariano Arroyo to Senate President Manuel A. Quezon, 15 August 1927; letter from Manuel A. Quezon to Dr. Mariano Arroyo, 23 August 1927, Box 182, File: Iloilo 1926–29, Manuel A. Quezon Papers, Philippine National Library.

44. Letter from Jose B. Ledesma to Manuel A. Quezon, 23 February 1929, and letter from Manuel Quezon to Senator Jose B. Ledesma, 29 May 1929, Box 182, File: Iloilo 1929; letter from Dr. Mariano Arroyo to Manuel Quezon, 5 January 1929 and letter from Manuel Quezon to Dr. Mariano Arroyo, 10 January 1929, Box 182, File: Iloilo 1929, Manuel A. Quezon Papers, Philippine National Library.

45. *El Tiempo*, 2 October 1929; Godofredo Grageda, 'The El Tiempo and Iloilo Times' (ms, 15 November 1976), pp. 1–5. pp. 8–10.

46. *El Tiempo*, 5 October 1929.

47. *El Tiempo*, 5 October 1929.

48. *El Tiempo*, 7 October 1929.

49. *Makinaugalingon*, 11 October 1929.

50. *El Tiempo*, 11 October 1929.

51. *Makinaugalingon*, 11 October 1929, 22 October 1929, 29 October 1929, 1 November 1929.

52. *Philippines Free Press*, 28 June 1930, pp. 4, 44; *Makinaugalingon*, 20 June 1930. Although he advertised in *El Tiempo* as an import-export dealer who 'buys and sells all classes of local products' (*El Tiempo*, 3 October 1929), Sane could not withstand this pressure on his illegal operations. In October 1930, he sailed for China (*El Tiempo*, 14 November 1930). After he later returned to Iloilo, the Constabulary raided his house on Iznart Street in March 1933, seizing a notebook showing income from jueteng in January amounting to P2,175.60 and seven payments to police ranging from five to thirty pesos (*Makinaugalingon*, 21 April 1933). In October 1937, a Manila court convicted Sane for possession of false bank notes and ordered him deported to China (*El Tiempo*, 31 March 1937). According to an obituary, he appealed the decision to the Philippine Supreme Court and fled to China where he died at Kinchang, Chingkang, of heart disease on 3 August 1940 (*Makinaugalingon*, 24 August 1940).

53. *Makinaugalingon*, 6 August 1930.

54. *Makinaugalingon*, 11 August 1930.

55. *Makinaugalingon*, 22 September 1930.

56. *Manila Times*, 27 September 1930.

57. *Makinaugalingon*, 24 September 1930. The original Hiligaynon text of Arroyo's alleged statement reads: 'Kumpare, ang siling niya, ngaa buut ka gid nga madula ang sugal nga hueteng? Wala ka makasayud nga ang kalabanan sang mga Wakha kag mga magulibud sa pagpapatad mga lider natun? Malapit na lamang ang piniliay kag magapasulpu aku kag ina sila makagdaut sa atun gani madamu sila sa sini nga probinsia, wala'y labut nga ginahatagan kita nila sing pilak nga galastohon sa piniliay.'

58. *El Tiempo*, 15 November 1930; *Makinaugalingon*, 3 October 1930.

59. *El Tiempo*, 24 October 1930, 15 November 1930; Grageda, 'The El Tiempo and Iloilo Times', pp. 8–10; *Makinaugalingon*, 3 October 1930.

60. *El Tiempo*, 14 October 1930; letter from Manuel Quezon to Mariano Arroyo, 31 May 1932, Box 65, File: Arroyo, Ignacio, Manuel A. Quezon Papers, Philippine National Library.

61. Letter from Manuel Quezon to Mariano Arroyo, 13 June 1929, Box 65, File: Arroyo, Ignacio, Manuel A. Quezon Papers, Philippine National Library. After Judge Montemayor recommended his dismissal, the governor himself telegrammed Quezon pleading: 'Our enemies moved heaven earth to destroy Collectivism Iloilo. We ask justice. Please wire Governor General recommending acquittal. Reply prepaid.' Despite his extraordinary gesture of paying P11.60 for a reply, there was no response. (See, telegram from Buenaflor/Arroyo to Manuel Quezon, 26 September 1930, Box 65, File: Arroyo, Ignacio, Manuel A. Quezon Papers, Philippine National Library.)

62. After the death of Senator Jose Ma. Pidal Arroyo on 8 March 1927, his widow, Jesusa Lacson vda. de Arroyo, moved to Negros Occidental where she raised her seven children, including her fourth son, Ignacio Lacson Arroyo (born 25 April 1917). In turn, Ignacio Arroyo married Lourdes Tuason (born 10 August 1907), a daughter of a wealthy, well-connected Manila family whose first husband

had died in 1939. Their marriage produced two sons, Jose Miguel Tuason Arroyo (born 27 June 1946) and Ignacio Tuason Arroyo, Jr. (born 24 October 1950). On 2 August 1968, Jose Miguel, known as 'Mike', married Gloria Macaraeg Macapagal (born 5 April 1947), the eldest child of Diosdado Macapagal, then president of the Philippines. (See, Curriculum Vitae, Gloria Macapagal Arroyo, www.macapagal.com/gma/bio/main/html [accessed 6 June 2006]); The Descendants of Teresa de la Paz, 'The Family Tree of Doña Teresa de la Paz', in *Teresa de la Paz and Her Two Husbands: A Gathering of Four Families* (Manila: The Descendants of Teresa de la Paz, 1996).

63. Wolters, *Politics, Patronage, and Class Conflict in Central Luzon*, pp. 166–7; Republic of the Philippines, Bureau of Census and Statistics, *1971 Philippine Yearbook* (Manila: Bureau of Census and Statistics, 1973), p. 73.

64. Sidel, *Capital, Coercion, and Crime*, p. 79.

65. Mary R. Hollnsteiner, 'Reciprocity in the Lowland Philippines', in Frank Lynch and Alfonso de Guzman II (eds), *Four Readings on Philippine Values* (Quezon City: Ateneo de Manila University Press, 1973), pp. 69–92; Mary R. Hollnsteiner, *The Dynamics of Power in a Philippine Municipality* (Quezon City: Community Development Research Council, University of the Philippines, 1963), pp. 86–109; Carl H. Landé, *Southern Tagalog Voting, 1946–1963: Political Behavior in a Philippine Region* (DeKalb: Northern Illinois University, Center for Southeast Asian Studies, 1973), pp. 99–100; K.G. Machado, 'From Traditional Faction to Machine: Changing Patterns of Political Leadership and Organization in the Rural Philippines', *Journal of Asian Studies*, 33/4 (August 1974), pp. 523–8, 537–45; Howard M. Leichter, *Political Regime and Public Policy in the Philippines: A Comparison of Bacolod and Iloilo Cities* (DeKalb: Northern Illinois University, Center for Southeast Asian Studies, 1975), pp. 55–9, 107–10; Carl H. Landé, *Leader, Factions and Parties: The Structure of Philippine Politics* (New Haven: Southeast Asia Studies, Yale University, Monograph Series No. 6, 1965), pp. 60–4.

66. Thomas C. Nowak and Kay A. Snyder, 'Economic Concentration and Political Change in the Philippines', in Kerkvliet, *Political Change in the Philippines*, pp. 185–6, 225–9.

67. Philippine Commission, *Census of the Philippine Islands: Volume II* (Washington, DC: US Bureau of the Census, 1905), p. 130; *1971 Philippine Yearbook* (Manila: Bureau of Census and Statistics, 1973), p. 82; Aprodicio A. Laquian, *The City in Nation Building* (Manila: School of Public Administration, University of the Philippines, 1966), pp. 47–8; Republic of the Philippines, National Statistical Coordination Board, *2000 Philippine Statistical Yearbook* (Manila: National Statistical Coordination Board, 2000), Table 1.1.

68. A year later, a reputable columnist described Berroya as 'close to First Gentleman Mike Arroyo and the First Family'. (See, *Philippine Daily Inquirer*, 8 July 2002.)

69. *Philippine Daily Inquirer*, 8 August 2001.

70. *Philippine Daily Inquirer*, 10 February 2001, 9 March 2001, 10 March 2001, 20 March 2001, 11 August 2001, 7 June 2002; *Philippine Star*, 13 March 2001.

71. *Philippine Daily Inquirer*, 26 January 2001, 21 February 2001, 22 February 2001, 27 February 2001, 7 March 2001, 12 March 2001, 13 March 2001, 28 March 2001, 28 March 2001, 29 March 2001, 30 March 2001, 4 April 2001, 17 April 2001, 19 April 2001, 21 April 2001, 22 April 2001, 25 April 2001, 12 May 2001, 18 May 2001; *Philippine Star*, 30 March 2001, 31 March 2001, 5 April 2001, 19 April 2001, 18 May 2001.

72. *Philippine Daily Inquirer*, 12 April 2001, 18 April 2001, 22 April 2001, 30 May 2001, 5 June 2001, 8 June 2001, 22 June 2001, 23 June 2001, 24 June 2001, 3 August 2001, 4 August 2001, 8 August 2001, 19 May 2002, 12 February 2003; *Philippine Star*, 15 April 2001, 18 April 2001, 19 April 2001, 21 April 2001.

73. *Philippine Daily Inquirer*, 5 August 2001, 6 August 2001, 7 August 2001, 8 August 2001, 10 August 2001, 11 August 2001, 12 August 2001; *Manila Bulletin*, 7 August 2001.

74. *Philippine Daily Inquirer*, 20 August 2001, 24 August 2001, 16 June 2002, 5 August 2003; *Philippines Free Press*, 25 August 2001, pp. 3–6.

75. *Philippine Daily Inquirer*, 4 October 2001, 28 October 2001.

76. *Philippine Daily Inquirer*, 4 October 2001, 6 October 2001, 14 November 2001, 15 November 2001, 16 November 2001; *Filipinas*, October 2001, p. 39.

77. *Philippine Daily Inquirer*, 2 July 2001, 7 August 2001, 16 February 2002, 10 March 2002, 5 April 2003; *Philippine Star*, 30 March 2001, 25 August 2001.

78. *Philippine Daily Inquirer*, 19 August 2003, 20 August 2003, 27 August 2003; *Time Asia Magazine*, 15 September 2003; *Inquirer News Service*, 20 May 2005; Miriam Grace A. Go, 'Mike's Companies', *Newsbreak*, 15 September 2003; Miriam Grace A. Go, 'Ping's Coup', *Newsbreak*, 15 September 2003; Miriam Grace A. Go and Jet Damazo, 'Who is Victoria Toh?' *Newsbreak*, 15 September 2003; Miriam Grace A. Go, 'Shadow President?' *Newsbreak*, 10 November 2003; Senator Panfilo M. Lacson, 'The Incredible Hulk: Chapter One, Privilege Speech on the Floor of the Senate', 18 August 2003, www.pl.888ph/speeches/Incredible%20Hulk.htm (accessed 6 June 2006); Senator Panfilo M. Lacson, 'The Incredible Hulk: Chapter Two, Privilege Speech on the Floor of the Senate', 1 September 2003, www.pl.888ph/speeches/Incredible%20Hulk%202.htm (accessed, 6 June 2006); Senator Panfilo M. Lacson, 'The Incredible Hulk: Chapter Three, Privilege Speech on the Floor of the Senate', 14 October 2003, www.pl.888ph/speeches/Incredible%20Hulk%203. htm (accessed 6 June 2006).

79. Concepcion Paez, 'Run, Gloria, Run', *Newsbreak*, 10 November 2003; Aries C. Rufo, 'It's Make or Break for Ping', *Newsbreak*, 10 November 2003.

80. *Philippine Daily Inquirer*, 7 August 2001, 24 April 2003, 16 November 2003, 22 November 2003, 27 November 2003, 3 December 2003, 5 December 2003, 11 February 2004, 22 February 2004, 5 March 2004, 9 March 2004, 10 March 2004, 13 March 2004, 14 March 2004, 17 March 2004, 23 March 2004, 24 March 2004, 25 March 2004, 1 April 2004, 18 April 2004, 1 May 2004, 2 May 2004, 7 May 2004, 10 May 2004, 12 May 2004, 14 May 2004, 20 May 2004, June 7, 2004, 22 June 2004.

81. *Philippine Daily Inquirer*, 12 April 2001, 18 April 2001, 22 April 2001, 30 May 2001, 5 June 2001, 8 June 2001, 22 June 2001, 23 June 2001, 24 June 2001, 3 August 2001, 4 August 2001, 8 August 2001, 1 October 2001, 6 October 2001, 19 May 2002, 12 February 2003; *Philippine Star*, 15 April 2001, 18 April 2001, 19 April 2001, 21 April 2001.

82. *Inquirer News Service*, 19 May 2005, 20 May 2005; *Sunstar*, 20 May 2005; *Philippine Daily Inquirer*, 21 May 2005, 14 June 2005.

83. *Sunstar*, 26 May 2005; *Inquirer News Service*, 20 May 2005; Sheila S. Coronel, 'Anak ng Jueteng', *I Report* (Manila), September 2005, pp. 2–5; Yvonne T. Chua, 'Jekyll-and-Hyde Campaign', *I Report*, September 2005, p. 7.

84. *Philippine Daily Inquirer*, 1 June 2005, 8 June 2005, 9 June 2005, 25 June 2005; *International Herald Tribune*, 30 June 2005; *New York Times*, 22 July 2005; *Manila Times*, 25 August 2005, 13 January 2006; Sheila S. Coronel, 'The Unmaking of a President', *I Report*, special edition, 'The Queens' Gambits' (2005), pp. 3–6; Sheila S. Coronel, 'System Under Stress', *I Report*, September 2005, pp. 20–3; Sheila S. Coronel, 'Master Operator', *I Report*, special edition, 'The Queens' Gambits' (2005), pp. 18–21; 'Shame and Scandal in the Family', *I Report*, special edition, 'The Queens' Gambits' (2005), pp. 28–9; 'Hello, Garci? Transcript of Three-Hour Tape', *I Report*, special edition, 'The Queens' Gambits' (2005), pp. 39–51.

85. *Manila Times*, 5 August 2005, 7 August 2005, 25 August 2005, 13 January 2006; *Manila Standard*, 8 November 2005; Coronel, 'The Unmaking of a President'; Luz Rimban, 'Despite Susan, the Opposition is Not Quite Smelling Like Roses', *I Report*, special edition, 'The Queens' Gambits' (2005), pp. 9–11.

86. Jurgen Habermas, *Legitimation Crisis* (Boston: Beacon Press, 1975), pp. 69, 73, 95–6.

13
Beyond Democratic Checks and Balances: The 'Propaganda Due' Masonic Lodge and the CIA in Italy's First Republic

Daniele Ganser

During the Cold War (1947–91), the European continent was divided into two blocs: a bloc of communist countries in Eastern Europe and a bloc of capitalist countries in Western Europe. From the very beginning of the Cold War, the capitalist countries in Western Europe cultivated a transatlantic friendship with the United States of America and together created the North Atlantic Treaty Organisation (NATO) in 1949. NATO, which remains the world's largest military alliance, guaranteed mutual military assistance, as the member countries agreed that a military attack on any single NATO country would be regarded as an attack on all of them.

On the other side of the 'Iron Curtain' which divided the European continent, the communist countries of Eastern Europe fell into the sphere of influence of the Soviet Union. Countering the perceived threat from the NATO alliance, the Russians, together with the countries of Eastern Europe, in 1955 formed the so-called 'Treaty of Friendship, Cooperation and Mutual Assistance', often referred to as the 'Warsaw Pact'. Like the NATO alliance, the Warsaw alliance was a military organisation in which the members pledged to defend each other if one or more of them were attacked. With the end of the Cold War following the collapse of the Soviet Union, the Warsaw Pact was dissolved in June 1991 and many of its former member states in Eastern Europe have since joined NATO.

Historical analysis of the recent history of the European continent has correctly pointed out that during the Cold War the countries in Eastern Europe were not governed according to the principles of democratic transparency, the rule of law and political accountability. The Soviet Union, having suffered a very high death toll during the German attacks on Russia in both the First and Second World Wars, made it clear that the Warsaw Pact served as a security belt for the USSR and political independence for Warsaw Pact countries was therefore not an option. The human security of citizens in the Warsaw Pact countries was thus violated repeatedly and consistently, most famously during the anti-Soviet revolt in Hungary in 1956, which was suppressed by Soviet troops and led to thousands of deaths, and during the 'Prague Spring' of 1968, when the struggle for greater political freedoms by Czechoslovakia was ended by a Warsaw Pact invasion labelled 'fraternal assistance against the counter-revolution'.

While historical analysis of the recent history of Eastern Europe has been successful in pointing out the numerous democratic deficits of the Warsaw Pact countries, the same rigour has not yet been applied to the history of Western Europe. On a very superficial level of analysis, the myth has been cherished that all countries of Eastern Europe were dark and brutal dictatorships, while all countries of Western Europe were shining examples of transparent democracies, where power was at all times controlled by the rule of law and an intelligent system of checks and balances which prevented abuse and crime.

A closer look at the historical data, of course, quickly reveals this to be a myth. Spain, Portugal, Greece and Turkey during the Cold War all suffered from either military dictatorship or military coups d'état which destroyed the democratic rule of law in these countries and led to torture and abuse of power in NATO-controlled Western Europe. Furthermore, new historical research by the author has revealed in 2005 that secret military structures existed, under the designation 'stay-behind armies' in most countries of Western Europe, including Germany, Switzerland, Belgium, France, the Netherlands, Greece, Spain, Portugal, Turkey, Sweden, Finland, Austria, Luxembourg, Norway and Denmark. These secret armies operated beyond checks and balances and for many years remained unknown to parliamentarians and the public at large.[1] A detailed examination of the historical data also shows that checks and balances and constitutionalism did not, in fact, rule supreme at all times in the democracies of the West.

All of this sheds a completely new light on our understanding of the recent history of the European continent. But it goes further still, for in addition to military dictatorships, secret armies and clandestine operations by intelligence services, the rule of law and political accountability in Western Europe suffered a further heavy blow from so-called 'secret societies', the most well-known example of which in Europe today is the Masonic Lodge 'Propaganda Due' (P2), discovered in Italy in 1981. P2 was literally a state within the state and operated beyond any democratic controls.

Large differences exist among Western European countries – for example, Turkey and Denmark – and hence the data must be studied independently for each country specifically. Accordingly, in this chapter I will deal with one country only, and show how Italy has been affected by such secret structures and clandestine operations by looking at the relationships between the United States Central Intelligence Agency (CIA), the P2 and NATO's stay-behind army.

THE CIA AND THE ELECTIONS OF 1948

The US foreign secret service, the Central Intelligence Agency, was founded in 1947. The first covert action operation ever carried out by the CIA targeted not a country in Latin America or Southeast Asia, but a European country: Italy – specifically, the then strong Italian Communist Party.

US President Harry Truman, together with all other members of the US National Security Council (NSC) in Washington, feared that in Italy's first postwar election scheduled for spring 1948 the Communists might win an overwhelming victory. The Italian Communists' popularity rested on their prominent role in the resistance against the Italian fascists and the German Nazis during the First World War.

The NSC, consisting of the US President, Vice President, Defense Minister, Foreign Minister and the Director of the CIA as well as a number of other high-ranking members of the US administration, was founded together with the CIA in 1947. Meeting in the White House, the NSC has been responsible for directing secret operations for six decades and during this period it has repeatedly operated at, or across, the borderline of legality. This led US historian Kathryn Olmsted of the University of California to remark that the NSC and the intelligence services it controls represented a form of 'secret government'. The NSC was investigated following the Watergate scandal, but according to Olmsted, these investigations were terminated without much success. 'After starting the investigations,' Olmsted asked in 1996, 'why did most members of the press and Congress back away from challenging the secret government?'[2]

With the introduction of the Internet in the 1990s, a larger audience has become interested in covert action operations and the business of both the NSC and the CIA. 'Who decides when CIA [sic] should participate in covert actions, and why?' one of the frequently asked questions (FAQ) on the official CIA homepage inquires. 'Only the President can direct the CIA to undertake a covert action', the CIA answers.

Such actions usually are recommended by the National Security Council (NSC). Covert actions are considered when the NSC judges that US foreign policy objectives may not be fully realized by normal diplomatic means and when military action is deemed to be too extreme an option. Therefore, the Agency may be directed to conduct a special activity abroad in support of foreign policy where the role of the US Government is neither apparent nor publicly acknowledged.[3]

The first of these NSC operations targeted Italy. The NSC issued a document, NSC 1/1 of 14 November 1947, which read: 'The Italian Government, ideologically inclined toward Western democracy, is weak and is being subjected to continuous attack by a strong Communist Party.'[4] Thereafter the NSC, on 19 December 1947, adopted the top secret directive NSC 4-A, which ordered CIA Director Roscoe Hillenkoetter to undertake a broad range of covert activities to prevent a communist victory in the first national postwar Italian election scheduled for 16 April 1948. Within the CIA, Director Hillenkoetter gave the task of manipulating the Italian election to the CIA's covert action department, 'Office of Policy Coordination' (OPC), headed by Frank Wisner.

Targeting liberated Europe with secret covert action operations was a highly sensitive strategy, as the NSC members knew. If uncovered, European trust in the US could be severely damaged. The highest standards of secrecy were therefore applied. There were only three copies of NSC 4-A, one of which Hillenkoetter had 'closely guarded in the Director's office, where members of his own staff who did not "need to know" could gain no access to it'. A second copy was with George F. Kennan at the State Department.[5]

In order to guarantee plausible denial, the majority of the transcripts of NSC meetings, as well as the majority of NSC assessments, decisions and orders to the CIA, remain inaccessible to researchers until today. Also, US special parliamentary investigations only rarely publish top secret NSC documents. However, exceptions do exist. In the aftermath of the Watergate scandal, the select US Senate committee under Senator Frank Church critically investigated the CIA and the NSC and discovered during the investigation that the CIA had carried out covert action operations in Europe.

> The national elections in Europe in 1948 [in Italy] had been a primary motivation in the establishment of OPC. By channellng funds to center parties and developing media assets, OPC attempted to influence the election results – with considerable success. These activities formed the basis for covert political action for the next twenty years.[6]

Most Italians were unaware that the CIA manipulated their elections in 1948. The Italian Communist Party (PCI) – the largest in Western Europe – and the Italian Socialist Party (PSI) had united for the elections, forming the Popular Democratic Front (FDP). They competed with the Christian Democratic Party (DCI), which had been newly created after the Second World War with US assistance. In municipal elections preceding the national vote the FDP had shown its muscle, assigning only second rank to the DCI.

Most observers expected the FDP to gain the majority in the Italian parliament. But CIA covert action successfully manipulated the outcome so that of a total of 574 seats in the Italian parliament the majority, at least 287 seats, would go to the CIA-supported DCI. The strategy was simple: the DCI would be strengthened by the pumping of $10 million into its campaign,[7] while the communist–socialist coalition would be weakened through a smear campaign. The CIA issued 'anonymous pamphlets which defamed PCI candidates' sex and personal lives' and 'smear[ed] them with the Fascist and/or anti-Church brush'.[8] This tactic of targeting specific seats to give control to the DCI rather than going for a complete sweep 'was successful in all but two of the two hundred plus seats selected'.[9] In the final election the DCI won 307 seats – 48 per cent of the vote – with the leftist coalition unexpectedly polling only 31 per cent and thus not even winning 200 seats.

President Truman was so impressed by the CIA's Italian operation that he saw to it that covert action was institutionalised as an instrument of US statecraft. Only two months after the Italian election, on 18 June 1948, the National Security Council passed directive NSC 10/2 to replace NSC 4-A. While NSC 4-A had authorised the CIA to carry out covert action operations in Italy only, NSC 10/2 gave the CIA the task to carry out covert actions across the world. The documents stated:

> 'covert operations' are understood to be all activities…which are conducted or sponsored by this government against hostile foreign states or groups or in support of friendly foreign states or groups but which are so planned and

conducted that any US Government responsibility for them is not evident to unauthorized persons and that if uncovered the US Government can plausibly disclaim any responsibility for them. Specifically, such operations shall include any covert activities related to: propaganda; economic warfare; preventive direct action, including sabotage, anti-sabotage, demolition, and evacuation measures; subversion against hostile states, including assistance to underground resistance movements, guerrillas and refugee liberation groups, and support of indigenous anti-communist elements in threatened countries of the free world.[10]

By creating the CIA and passing NSC 10/2 Truman had unleashed US covert action, secret warfare and dirty tricks on a grand scale. 'During his twenty-year retirement Truman sometimes seemed amazed, even somewhat appalled, at the size and power of the intelligence community he had brought into being', British historian Christopher Andrew commented.[11] Retired and fragile, Truman himself claimed, 'I never had any thought when I set up the CIA that it would be injected into peacetime cloak and dagger operations.'[12] In 1964, eight years before his death, Truman had moral doubts about what he had done and declared that he had never intended the CIA 'to operate as an international agency engaged in strange activities'.[13]

PROPAGANDA DUE (P2)

Until as recently as a quarter of a century ago the official political history of Italy's First Republic (1945–93) did not mention the influence of the international society of the Freemasons on the country. Italy, to many, was a normal democracy in Western Europe, governed by the rule of law and a system of transparent checks and balances.

This noble image changed abruptly in April 1981, when Milan magistrates investigating the crimes of US Italian Mafia banker Michele Sindona broke into the villa of a certain Licio Gelli near Arezzo in Italy's Tuscany region. Gelli, until then, had been almost completely unknown to a larger public in Italy, let alone on the stage of world history. The people in his village Arezzo knew him as a friendly businessman and the owner of a company named Permaflex which produced mattresses.

In Gelli's villa, the Italian police came across documents which were to forever change the political history of Italy's First Republic. Due to the extraordinary nature of these documents, historians are still struggling today to integrate them into a larger international interpretation of the Cold War. The documents confirmed the reality of an entire Italian parallel state named 'P2' and headed by Licio Gelli, revealing that 962 Italians belonged to Gelli's secret P2 Lodge at the time of its discovery. The member list – and this was of particular political relevance – included some of the most powerful members of Italian society and read like a 'Who's Who' of Italy.

While the French *philosophe* Montesquieu (1689–1755) had insisted that for a state to be democratic it must feature a clear division of power between the legislative, the executive and the judicature, P2 literally destroyed this principle of checks and balances. Its members came from all three branches of the state, a mechanism which subverted the original democratic idea according to which the three branches of the state are designed to control and balance each other. P2 members, instead of controlling each other, cooperated in secrecy and operated beyond all accountability. Fifty-two were high-ranking officers of the Carabinieri paramilitary police; 50 were high-ranking officers of the Italian army; 37 were high-ranking officers of the Finance Police; 29 were high-ranking officers of the Italian navy; 11 were Presidents of the police; 70 were influential and wealthy industrialists; 10 were presidents of banks; 3 were acting ministers; 2 were former ministers; 1 was the president of a political party; 38 were members of parliament; and 14 were high-ranking judges. Others were mayors, directors of hospitals, lawyers, notaries and journalists.

Next to Licio Gelli, the most prominent person on the P2 list was Silvio Berlusconi. The exposure of Berlusconi as a P2 member did not end his career. On the contrary, he later entered politics and rose to become Prime Minister of Italy, while his business operations enabled him to become Italy's richest man; according to *Forbes* magazine 2005, his €12 billion placed him among the 50 richest persons in the world.

When P2 was discovered, the spotlight was not on Berlusconi but on Licio Gelli, a veteran of the Italian political right who had spent most of his life fighting communism across the world. Born in 1919 and only semi-educated, having been expelled from school at the age of 13 for striking the headmaster, Gelli aged 17 had travelled to Spain and had enrolled as a volunteer in the Black Shirts of Franco to fight on the side of the fascists in the Spanish civil war. During the Second World War, Gelli was a sergeant major and supported the fascist German SS division of Hermann Goering. The Italian communists, who fought both Hitler and Mussolini during the Second World War, hated Gelli. When they captured him at the end of the war his death came close, but Gelli managed to flee to the US army in Italy, which protected him from the Italian left and helped him to reach a position of great influence as a leading anti-communist in postwar Italy.

As a sign of trust and respect, Gelli was regularly invited to the White House in Washington. Gelli's most influential decade was the 1970s. In 1974, he was a guest at Gerald Ford's presidential inauguration ceremony and in 1977 he was present again at Jimmy Carter's. And when Ronald Reagan was inaugurated in 1981, Gelli sat in the first row. P2 member Colonel Antonio Viezzer later confirmed that in the 1970s Gelli was 'the most powerful man in Italy beyond whom nobody else stood'.[14] P2 member Federico Umberto D'Amato, head of the Italian political police from 1972 to 1974, also had vivid memories of Gelli's political power and related one of his meetings with Gelli:

While he [Gelli] was standing in front of me a politician called who right then was about to become Prime Minister. He [the politician] said to him [Gelli]: 'Licio, see, if you say that I should not accept then I will not accept [the position of Prime Minister]'.[15]

An enigmatic symbol of extra-constitutional power, Gelli never had any qualms about illegal operations outside the framework of democratic checks and balances because he was convinced that he was doing the right thing, namely, saving Italy from communism. 'I deserve a medal', he once remarked.[16]

In order to escape the Italian police following the discovery of the P2 in 1981, Gelli fled to South America. A year later he was seen in Switzerland, seeking to withdraw $120 million from an anonymous Swiss number account in a UBS bank in Geneva. The Swiss police arrested him on 13 September 1982 and locked him up in the Champs Dollon prison. For almost a year, Gelli was Switzerland's most prominent prisoner. However, on 10 August 1983, he escaped under mysterious circumstances and made his way to France, whereupon both the Swiss and French authorities, like their Italian colleagues, issued an international search warrant. In 1989 the Swiss were able to arrest Gelli again. They handed him over to Italy, where he was charged and sentenced but released seven months later 'for reasons of ill health'.

Legal battles aiming to imprison 'Cold Warrior' Gelli continued, however, into the 1990s. He was charged with conspiracy against the state and subversion and sentenced by Italian magistrates for having been involved in the Bologna terror attack of 2 August 1980, which had killed 85 and injured or maimed 200. When the Bologna verdict had to be dropped due to lack of proof, Gelli was accused in the context of another sinister affair: the Banco Ambrosiano scandal. The bank had allegedly recycled illegal mafia money and sponsored Italian right-wing terrorists in their battle against the Italian communists. The judges concluded in 1992 that just before the bank had gone bankrupt in the early 1980s, Gelli had moved part of the Ambrosiano millions to a Swiss bank account, an offence for which he was sentenced to 18 years and 6 months imprisonment. Gelli appealed the verdict, but the highest Italian court in Milan confirmed on 22 April 1998 that Gelli was guilty, whereupon the 79-year-old man fled to France. In Cannes, in the south of France, Gelli was arrested on 10 September 1998. When the French police seized him he broke his glasses and unsuccessfully tried to commit suicide by cutting an artery.[17]

Interpretation and contextualisation of the phenomenon of the P2 parallel state and its leader, Licio Gelli, is very difficult for historians and academics who work in the fields of law and political science. Most have chosen either to ignore the topic, or to touch on it only briefly. British historian Paul Ginsborg, who arguably wrote the standard English-language work on the political history of postwar Italy (*A History of Contemporary Italy: Society and Politics 1943–1988*), uses 400 pages to introduce his subject to the interested reader, yet offers only three sentences on the P2. He notes that in 1981

the existence of a subversive Masonic lodge, the P2, was discovered. Its members included prominent figures in the armed forces, in business and in the world of politics. The precise objectives of the lodge have remained obscure, but there is little doubt that its head, Licio Gelli, was seeking to construct an anti-communist network within the highest echelons of the Italian state.[18]

Ginsborg was right. Gelli had never made any secrets about the fact that he hated the communists, and that everybody else in the P2 was also strictly anti-communist. 'I can tell you that we [in the P2 lodge] were always anti-communist', he told journalists.[19] Aware of the fact that in Italy the fight between the political right and the political left had led to numerous deaths in the 1960s, 1970s and 1980s, pushing the country to the brink of civil war, the journalists wanted to know whether Gelli had also been involved in operations which killed other Italians on the political left. 'How far would you have gone in your campaign against communism?' Gelli was asked, to which he replied evasively: 'Ah, number one enemy was communism [silence] – We were an association of believers – We did not admit non believers – We wanted to stop communism in its track, eliminate communism, fight communism.'[20]

From a political perspective, this secret fight of the P2 against the Italian communists represented a constitutional problem because roughly one-third of the Italian population regularly voted for PCI, the communist party, which therefore was very strong in the Italian parliament.[21] When the Italian parliament discovered in 1981 that the secretive P2 had formed a parallel state, beyond checks and balances and with the aim to fight the PCI, it decided that such shadow governance represented a threat to the state, was illegal, and had to be closed down and investigated in detail. In 1981, a Parliamentary Commission was created with the task of investigating P2's shadow government. Headed by a courageous woman, Tina Anselmi, the P2 Commission shed some light on the international network of Freemasons and, above all, on the Italian P2 Masonic Lodge and secret politics in Italy. Three years later, after having heard hundreds of witnesses, including many Freemasons, and having looked through thousands of pages of documents, the Anselmi Commission presented its final report on the P2, on 3 July 1984.[22] The Commission left 115 volumes for future historical research in which the details of its investigations, the protocols of interrogations and debates and confiscated documents and expert judgements were contained.

Based on the documents available, the Anselmi Commission judged that the 962 P2 members mentioned on the lists found in Gelli's villa were only the tip of the iceberg. The total number of P2 members in Italy, according to the Commission's estimate, was 2,500. Yet, signalling its limited strength, the Anselmi Commission was unable to identify the remaining 1,500 members.

Among the Italian communists ranked with the best understanding of the parallel state and shadow politics was parliamentarian Sergio Flamigni. He represented the PCI in the Italian legislature for more than 20 years and was a member of both the Anselmi Commission investigating the P2, as well as of the commission which investigated the 1978 death of Italian Prime Minister Aldo Moro. Few knew the secrets of the P2 anti-communist campaigns as well as Flamigni, who published a book on the P2 in which he explained that the 1981 discovery and the subsequent investigation and scandal 'gravely hurt' the P2 but did not end this form of secret government. 'The P2 Lodge remains active, in Italy and abroad', Flamigni concluded in his book in 1995.[23]

Freemasonry is a worldwide metaphysical brotherhood with ancient historical roots and organised according to rigid hierarchical structures. To the public at large in Italy and beyond it has remained, however, either unknown, mysterious or suspect. According to the *Encyclopaedia Britannica*, Freemasonry is 'the largest world-wide secret society'. It evolved from the guilds of stonemasons and cathedral-builders of the Middle Ages, when some masons, unlike fellow artisans such as carpenters and blacksmiths who continued to be organised in guilds, left the guilds and as 'freemasons' travelled from town to town setting up their tents, which they called 'lodges', wherever they worked.

Freemasons exclude women and keep a very low profile, and the aims, structures and strategies of Freemasonry, incompatible with the democratic principle of transparency, are hardly ever the subject of international media or political science debates. In fact, Freemasonry is not a phenomenon studied at all at universities. In order to become a Freemason one must be male and above a minimum age of around 21 years, and have references from current Masons. Freemasons use an initiatory system of different degrees, similar to the ranks used in military service, where senior Freemasons support junior Freemasons to progressively explore political, economic and philosophical issues.

Unlike the Catholic Church, with its rigid hierarchical global structure headed by the Pope in Rome, Freemasons recognise no central global Masonic organisational structure, nor a specific Freemason who serves as the highest global authority. While the first centre of Freemasonry – the Grand Lodge of England, founded in 1717 – represents a centre of gravity, several Grand Lodges exist across the world, with each being a self-governing entity. No single authority exists above the Grand Lodges or over the whole of Freemasonry. Fearing both the influence of the secret society and its tolerance of different religions, Pope Clemente XII condemned Freemasonry in 1738, only five years after the first Italian Lodge had been set up in Florence.

Masonic practices vary greatly from country to country and within each country are determined by Lodge custom, the Lodge being the basic organisation of Freemasonry. Every new Lodge must be warranted by a Grand Lodge. A Master Freemason is generally entitled to visit a number of different Lodges in different countries, as long as these Lodges among each other have agreed on a certain set of principles. Lodge buildings have for many years been known as 'Temples', and, indeed, several different Lodges often use the same premises – each on published dates.

The P2 Masonic Lodge, the Anselmi Commission found, was a very particular and arguably very powerful Lodge, while other Lodges usually united men with much less political influence. Of the latter, more than 1,200 Lodges existed in the 1980s in Italy alone, with a total of 35,000 members. Masonic Lodges existed also in Germany, Spain, France, Australia, Switzerland, Argentina, Uruguay, Ireland, Greece, Indonesia and many other countries of the world. With an estimated 5 million members, the United States allegedly ranked as the country with the highest density of Lodges and Freemasons.[24]

Communist parliamentarians in the Anselmi Commission, including Antonio Bellocchio, considered the P2 Masonic Lodge as a threat to democracy, due to its explicit political plan to fight communism. 'We have come to the definite conclusion that Italy is a country of limited sovereignty because of the interference of the American secret service and international freemasonry', Bellocchio later recalled and remembered how he had wanted to enlarge the investigation and look beyond the borders of Italy in order to research similar structures of shadow governance in the US. 'If the majority of the commission had been prepared to follow us in this analysis they would have had to admit that they are puppets of the United States of America, and they don't intend to admit that, ever.'[25]

While Italian communists insisted that the P2 had used dirty tricks and even criminal methods to fight the communists during the Cold War, other members of the Anselmi Commission were concerned with the reality of shadow governments and their implications.

> If democracy is a system of rules and procedures which define the parameters within which political action can take place, what happens when alongside this system there is another one whose rules are mysterious, its procedures unknown, its power immense and which is able to protect itself against the formal institutions of democracy by a wall of secrecy?[26]

Clearly, from a democratic perspective, such powerful groups were, in theory at least, unacceptable. 'This is the dangerous side of extra-parliamentary activity', the Anselmi Commission concluded.[27]

Six years after the publication of the final report of the Anselmi Commission on the P2 an anonymous source labelled 'Zero One', later revealed to be former CIA agent Richard (Dick) Brennecke, claimed on Italian state television RAI 1 in summer 1990, 'I knew the P2 ever since 1969 and have dealt with it until the beginning of the 1980s. The government of the United States financed the P2 with up to $10 million per month [sic].' This was an incredible statement, as it suggested that the US had supported an Italian shadow government with $120 million per year, and implied that the White House had secretly controlled crucial parts of the Italian political process, making the idea of a sovereign Italian democracy look childish. Adding fuel to the fire, Brennecke claimed that the US, through the P2, had sponsored terrorism in Italy.

> We have used the P2 to create tensions which led to the explosion of terrorism in Italy and other countries during the 1970s... The P2 is still active and is still being used for the same purpose as in the beginning of the 1970s. One of its most common names now is P7... In some cases I met terrorists. They were seen as people who helped the cause of the United States.[28]

The Brennecke testimony hit both Italy and the government of George Bush Senior in the US like a bomb. The CIA immediately denied the claim as 'absolute nonsense', while the Bush administration focused on Kuwait, which in the following month (August 1990) was invaded by Saddam Hussein, and thereafter attracted much media attention.[29] Licio Gelli sued Italian state television for £5 million in damages, and Italian Prime Minister Andreotti strongly denied that the CIA had ever backed terrorism in Italy, making a stinging attack on state television for broadcasting the reports. 'It is totally nonsensical to imagine that the US Congress could have authorised or even tacitly supported an operation of destabilisation conducted against a friendly and allied country like Italy', Andreotti claimed in front of an excited Italian parliament.[30]

Italian President Francesco Cossiga ordered that the Brennecke television tapes be brought to him at the Quirinal Palace at once, and on 3 July 1990 he wrote to Prime Minister Andreotti, 'If these allegations are true, then a full legal investigation must follow', adding, 'If the allegations are untrue and this is "creative journalism", then the situation is no less serious and the courts must intervene.'[31] According to Licio Gelli's mistress, Nara Lazzerini, Giulio Andreotti had himself been a member of the P2 and allegedly one of great influence. 'Gelli told me that Andreotti was also a member of his Lodge... I remember that within the P2 there was the rumour that Andreotti and not Gelli was the real boss.'[32]

As rumours and speculations as to the 'true nature' of the P2 and the involvement of the US spread in subsequent months and years, President Cossiga confirmed in 1993 that the P2 had been 'an American import', designed by US hard-liners in order to fight their worst fears 'concerning a potential alliance of DC–PSI–PCI', that is, the Italian communists into the government in coalition with the US-supported Democrazia Italiana (DC) and the Italian Socialist Party (PSI).[33] Cossiga said that it was obvious that American anti-communists were in charge of the P2 and that Gelli was their trusted man in Italy. 'There is no doubt that Gelli was not the real boss of the Lodge. Do you think military Generals of the highest ranks could have followed the orders of somebody like Gelli? He was a point of reference, who distributed key positions of power to those Generals who were friends of the US.'[34]

According to German journalist Regine Igel, it was Frank Gigliotti, a high-ranking US Freemason, who came to Italy in the 1950s and personally recruited Licio Gelli, giving him financial assistance and the task of building up an Italian network to fight communism.[35] Gigliotti was a powerful man, as Gelli knew, who had served in Italy as a member of the American secret service OSS (the predecessor of the CIA) during the Second World War, and who later advised US President Truman in the field of security policy and secret politics.[36] After his meeting with Gigliotti, Gelli had allegedly chosen the P2, which had existed for more than a century, to function as the centre of this anti-communist battle. Gelli became the director of the P2 in 1961 and enlarged the Lodge in subsequent years.[37]

Allegedly, Gelli repeatedly flew to the US for further instructions. Among other things, Washington informed him that the CIA had cooperated closely with the Italian intelligence service, SIFAR, whose director, Giovanni De Lorenzo, had begun to compile secret files in 1956 on over 157,000 Italian personalities. The existence of the secret SIFAR files was discovered in 1962, leading to a national scandal and a Parliamentary Commission. The files, containing information on abnormal habits or extramarital sexual relationships, were a powerful weapon of coercion. General Aldo Beolchini, President of the Parliamentary Commission, stated that through the files De Lorenzo had held most of the political class in his hand and that they were intimidated by his threats.[38] The parliamentary investigation was stunned at the level of interference and intrusion.

The persons were spied upon with cameras making close up pictures from afar, secret systems with which their correspondence was controlled, recordings of what they had said in their phone calls, documentation with pictures of their extramarital relationships or sexual habits.[39]

In front of the parliamentarians investigating the scandal, SIFAR director De Lorenzo was forced to admit that the US and NATO had ordered him to set up the files as part of the larger task of fighting the Italian communists, as NATO feared that the PCI might weaken the transatlantic defence alliance from within.[40] Thereafter De Lorenzo was forced to resign and ordered to destroy the secret files. Clandestinely, however, he handed a copy over to his successor, General Giovanni Allavena, who in 1967 was recruited by Licio Gelli into the new and secretive P2 Lodge. Allavena gave Gelli a complete copy of the 157,000 'pressure files', thus adding greatly to the political influence of the P2 shadow government.

According to the anti-terror office of the Italian intelligence service SISMI, P2 grew steadily, as Gelli was given orders by representatives of the administration of US President Richard Nixon. In 1969, Gelli met with US General Alexander Haig, who had just returned from the war in Vietnam and from 1974 to 1979 served as the Supreme Allied Commander of NATO in Europe. Haig ordered Gelli to include selected NATO officers as members of the secretive P2. The SISMI report of 16 April 1983 read:

[i]t was Ted Shackley, director of all covert actions of the CIA in Italy in the 1970s, who presented the chief of the Masonic Lodge [Licio Gelli] to Alexander Haig. Haig and Kissinger authorised Gelli in the fall of 1969 to recruit 400 high ranking Italian and NATO officers into his Lodge.[41]

More than a quarter of a century after the discovery of the P2 it is still not possible to write a conclusive history of this Italian shadow government, its ideology, its strategy, the operations it carried out and the exact links it cultivated with the White House in Washington. Much more research is needed. A provisional conclusion on shadow governments must be that the historical data on the P2 proves that shadow governments do exist at times, that they operate beyond checks and balances and can lead to destruction of the democratic process. 'The damage that the P2 had caused to Italy has been compared to a wooden wardrobe attacked by an army of woodworms', Regine Igel commented. 'The wardrobe – the society – from the outside looks unchanged and stands on its four legs. While in reality the worms have eaten up everything and only a skeleton remains.'[42]

STAY-BEHIND

Licio Gelli, the Venerable Master of the P2, confirmed in the early 1990s that a secret anti-communist army, run by the Italian military secret service SIFAR and supplied by the CIA, had existed in Italy during the Cold War under the code-name 'Gladio' ('the sword'). In case of a Soviet invasion of Western Europe, the secret Gladio soldiers were trained to operate as a guerrilla force behind enemy lines. In the absence of an invasion, their task was to fight the communists through clandestine warfare. 'The aim of Gladio and other similar organisations which existed in all countries of Western Europe was to counter the invasion of the Red Army or the coming to power by coup d'état of the communist parties', Gelli explained. 'That the PCI, during all those years, has never come to power, although they have tried to do so repeatedly, is [to] the merit of the Gladio organisation.'[43]

In 1992, Gelli explained to the British newspaper the *Observer* that many Gladiators had been recruited on the political right. 'Many came from the ranks of mercenaries who had fought in the Spanish Civil War and many came from the fascist republic of Salo', Gelli said.

> They chose individuals who were proven anti-communists. I know it was a well constructed organisation. Had communist strength grown in Italy, America would have assisted us, we would have unleashed another war and we would have been generously supplied with arms from the air.[44]

William Colby, Director of the CIA from 1973 to 1976, emphasised that this was 'a major program' of the CIA, designed to have top secret armed soldiers in Western Europe 'ready to be called into action as sabotage and espionage forces when the time came'.[45] And British intelligence scholar Nigel West confirmed that the Americans had carried out the operation in very close cooperation with British experts. 'We were heavily involved and still are…in these networks… The people who inspired it were the British and American intelligence agencies.'[46] According to Gelli, the US paid the bill. 'The Americans pay them [the Gladiators] large sums of money, the equivalent of an excellent salary. And they guaranteed the financial support of the families in case the Gladiator was killed.'[47]

Clandestine, anti-communist stay-behind armies existed in the NATO countries Germany, France, Italy, Greece, Spain, Portugal, Turkey, Belgium, Luxembourg, the Netherlands, Denmark and Norway, as well as in countries that were officially neutral, including Sweden, Switzerland, Finland and Austria. For many years the CIA and the MI6 closely cooperated with European military and civilian intelligence services including, among others, SIFAR (Italy), UNA (Switzerland), MIT (Turkey), SGR (Belgium), BVD (Netherlands), BND (Germany), DGSE (France), NIS (Norway), KYP (Greece) and PIDE (Portugal).[48]

Within the CIA, the Covert Action Department Office of Policy Coordination (OPC) under Frank Wisner was responsible for setting up the stay-behind network after the Second World War, as William Colby recalled in his memoirs.

> Thus, the OPC had undertaken a major program of building, throughout those Western European countries that seemed likely targets for Soviet attack, what in the parlance of the intelligence trade were known as 'stay-behind nets', clandestine infrastructures of leaders and equipment trained and ready to be called into action as sabotage and espionage forces when the time came.[49]

According to Italian sources familiar with Gladio, the CIA also used the secret soldiers – in the total absence of a Soviet invasion – to influence European politics through covert action operations. General Gerardo Serravalle, commander of the Italian stay-behind within the Italian military intelligence service from 1971 to 1974, recalled how one day the CIA, which had long supplied secret soldiers across Western Europe with cash, guns and explosives, had stopped sending money and weapons for his Gladio unit. Serravalle was angry and called for a meeting with the chief of the CIA station in Italy, Howard Stone, whereupon Stone agreed to meet the Italian commander at the clandestine Gladio training centre, Saboteur's Training Camp (Centro Adestramento Guastatori, CAG) in Sardinia, on 15 December 1972.

> Stone had come over because I asked him to. When I took over command, I noticed that the American financing, agreed in bilateral accords and in particular the shipping of material and armaments to us, had stopped. I did not understand why and they wouldn't give me an explanation. So I called this meeting in order to find out why they had stopped sending us the supplies,

Serravalle recalled,

> So, after months of manoeuvring on both diplomatic and military fronts, I could finally invite Mr Stone and Mr [Mike] Sednaoui to the base in Sardinia. I said to them: 'This is our training centre etc., you could help us achieve our full potential. So why cut your aid? If this is your government's position, we accept it. But you owe us an explanation.'[50]

Serravalle reveals he only then started to understand that the CIA wanted to use the clandestine forces against domestic political enemies, that is, the Italian Communist Party, and not the Red Army.

> I realised that the CIA interests, as represented by these officials, weren't really concerned with the level we had reached in training but rather with the subject of internal control. That is, our level of readiness to counter street disturbances, handling nation-wide strikes and above all any eventual rise of the Communist Party.[51]

Serravalle got a very clear impression of what the CIA and the US government wanted. 'Mr Stone stated, quite clearly, that the financial support of the CIA was wholly dependent on our willingness to put into action, to programme and plan these other – shall we call them – internal measures.'[52] Greatly disturbed members of the Italian parliament investigated the secret CIA army in the 1990s and came to the sensitive conclusion that members of the CIA network had linked up with Italian right-wing extremists in covert action operations and had supported them in a top secret campaign, which included terrorist attacks against civilians – attacks that were wrongly blamed on the Italian communists in order to discredit them at the polls. When Stanfield Turner, CIA Director from 1977 to 1981, was questioned on this dark side of the stay-behind operation in an interview in December 1990, he angrily ripped off his microphone and shouted, 'I said, no questions about Gladio!'[53]

Members of the Italian intelligence community have now gone on the record with claims that CIA covert action in Europe included the sponsoring of terrorism. In March 2001, General Gianadelio Maletti, the former head of Italian counter-intelligence, had to testify on the Piazza Fontana case. Shortly before Christmas 1969, four bombs had exploded in public places in Rome and Milan, killing 16 and maiming or wounding 80, most of them in the Piazza Fontana in Milan. After the massacre, the Italian intelligence service planted bomb parts in the villa of well-known leftist editor Giangiacomo Feltrinelli, in order to blame the terror on the communists and the extreme left.

'The CIA, following the directives of its government, wanted to create an Italian nationalism capable of halting what it saw as a slide to the left, and, for this purpose, it may have made use of right-wing terrorism', Maletti testified in the Piazza Fontana trial. 'The impression was that the Americans would do anything to stop Italy from sliding to the left', the 79-year-old General explained, and added: 'Don't forget that Nixon was in charge and Nixon was a strange man, a very intelligent politician, but a man of rather unorthodox initiatives.'[54]

The European network of clandestine stay-behind armies was coordinated by NATO, because in the event of an invasion of Western Europe it would have been NATO's task to coordinate military manoeuvres and re-establish European independence. Within NATO, two clandestine committees – the so-called 'Clandestine Planning Committee' (CPC) and the 'Allied Clandestine Committee' (ACC), both linked to NATO's SHAPE (Supreme Headquarters Allied Powers Europe) – met regularly on the level of officers from the various European military intelligence services in order to discuss questions relating to stay-behind and secret warfare. Both ACC and CPC operated beyond democratic checks and balances, as national parliamentarians were, as a rule, completely unaware of their existence.

A SHAPE directive, unavailable to academics until now, regulated the details of the stay-behind armies, as Gladio commander Serravalle explained. This directive

> related to the training of Gladiators in Europe, how to activate them from the secret headquarters in case of complete occupation of the national territory and other technical questions as, to quote the most important one, the unification of the different communication systems between the stay-behind bases. The CPC was…a centre with primary mission to co-ordinate in time of war the national resistance units at a specific moment between the occupation and the counter-offensive.[55]

Both the CIA as well as US Special Forces took part in these meetings, according to Serravalle.

> At the stay-behind meetings representatives of the CIA were always present. They had no voting right and were from the CIA headquarters of the capital in which the meeting took place… Or members of the US Forces Europe Command were present, also without voting right.[56]

Thomas Polgar, who had retired in 1981 after a 30-year-long career in the CIA, explained with an implicit reference to CPC and ACC that the stay-behind programmes were coordinated by 'a sort of unconventional warfare planning group linked to NATO'. In these two clandestine planning groups, senior officers of the

CIA, MI6 and NATO regularly meet with senior officers of European intelligence services, at times represented by the director of the intelligence service, as 'each national service did it with varying degrees of intensity'. According to Polgar, the ACC and CPC representatives 'would meet every couple of months in different capitals', adding that 'in Italy in the 1970s some of the people went a little bit beyond the charter that NATO had put down'.[57]

When the stay-behind networks were discovered in 1990, the press observed that the 'story seems straight from the pages of a political thriller'[58] and argued that this large international covert action programme represented 'the best-kept, and most damaging, political-military secret since World War II'.[59] The European Parliament debated the legal, social and political implications of the discovery. In a special resolution passed on 22 November 1990 the Parliament made it clear that it condemned

> the clandestine creation of manipulative and operational networks and [called] for a full investigation into the nature, structure, aims and all other aspects of these clandestine organisations or any splinter groups, their use for illegal interference in the internal political affairs of the countries concerned, the problem of terrorism in Europe and the possible collusion of the secret services of Member States or third countries.[60]

During the debate in the Parliament, Italian parliamentarian Falqui had insisted that

> ...this Europe will have no future if it is not founded on truth, on the full transparency of its institutions in regard to the dark plots against democracy that have turned upside down the history, even in recent times, of many European states. There will be no future, ladies and gentlemen, if we do not remove the idea of having lived in a kind of double state – one open and democratic, the other clandestine and reactionary.

French parliamentarian Dury shared these concerns and added, 'What worried us in this Gladio affair was that these networks were able to exist out of sight and beyond control of the democratic political authorities. That, I think, is the fundamental issue which remains.' And Greek parliamentarian Ephremidis concluded,

> the democracy we are supposed to have been enjoying has been, and still is, nothing but a front... The fine details must be uncovered, and we ourselves must establish a special sub committee of inquiry to hold hearings and to blow the whole thing wide open so that all the necessary steps can be taken to rid our countries of such clandestine organisations.[61]

Due to the prominent role of both the Pentagon and NATO in the secret operation, the European Parliament in its resolution stressed that it '[p]rotests vigorously at the assumption by certain US military personnel at SHAPE and in NATO of the right to encourage the establishment in Europe of a clandestine intelligence and operation network'. As the Parliament itself had no authority to investigate security affairs which remained within the sovereign domain of each EU member state, it urged that further investigations into the affair should be carried out in all countries concerned. Therefore its resolution requested

...all the Member States to take the necessary measures, if necessary by establishing parliamentary committees of inquiry, to draw up a complete list of organisations active in this field, and at the same time to monitor their links with the respective state intelligence services and their links, if any, with terrorist action groups and/or other illegal practices.[62]

Yet today, the data on the stay-behind networks, and particularly their numerous alleged links to crime and terrorism, still remain fragmentary, as most states have refrained from investigating the stay-behind structures in detail, and have refused to present public reports.

CONCLUSION

Academics, one might as well admit, face great difficulties when it comes to the analysis and description of the secret side of international politics. Shadow governments, including those few like the P2 that are on the historical record, and their links to paramilitary secret armies like Gladio, are extremely difficult to pin down. Many questions remain, only fragments can be collected and ordered into a narrative of limited coherence, which can only offer glimpses into the abyss of deceit and manipulation. Noble as it might be, the aim to penetrate and illuminate the world of parallel structures and secret warfare still has a long way to go, as most universities do not even teach and research the secret side of international politics as a field of enquiry. Judged from that perspective, one of the most important factors with regard to future international conflicts might lie in the emergence of a global conviction that we must not only strive for honesty and truth, but above all try to solve conflicts through transparent and peaceful means. For, clearly, violent solutions stand a more than reasonable chance of being manipulated in one way or another by clandestine groups.

NOTES

1. See below, on the stay-behind army Gladio in Italy. For an international overview, compare Daniele Ganser, *NATO's Secret Armies: Operation Gladio and Terrorism in Western Europe* (London: Frank Cass, 2005). The book was translated into Italian and published by Fazi in Rome in August 2005 (*Gli eserciti segreti della Nato. Operazione Gladio e terrorismo in Europa occidentale*). Then in October 2005 the Turkish translation was published in Istanbul by Güncel Press (*NATO'nun gizli ordulari. Gladio Operasyonlari, Terörizm ve Avrupa Güvenlik Ilkeleri*). In July 2006 Ciceron translated and published the book in Slovenia (*Natova Skrivna Vojska. Operacija Gladio in terorizem v zahodni Evropi*). Greek and Estonian translations were published in 2007 by Antilogos Publishing and Tammerraamat, respectively.
2. Kathryn Olmsted, *Challenging the Secret Government: The Post-Watergate Investigations of the CIA and FBI* (Chapel Hill: University of North Carolina Press, 1996), p. 9.

3. Official CIA homepage, https://www.cia.gov/cia/public_affairs/faq.html#7 (accessed 1 January 2007).
4. Christopher Andrew, *For the President's Eyes Only: Secret Intelligence and the American Presidency from Washington to Bush* (New York: HarperCollins, 1995), p. 171.
5. Arthur Darling, *The Central Intelligence Agency: An Instrument of Government to 1950* (University Park: Pennsylvania State University Press, 1990), p. 245.
6. United States Senate, *Final Report of the Select Committee to Study Governmental Operations with Respect to Intelligence Activities*, Book IV, 'Supplementary Detailed Staff Reports on Foreign and Military Intelligence' (Washington, DC: US Government Printing Office, 1976), p. 36.
7. William Corson, *The Armies of Ignorance: The Rise of the American Intelligence Empire* (New York: Dial Press, 1977), p. 299. As the operation was secret the money was dirty and had to be laundered first. Corson explains that this was done by first withdrawing $10 million in cash from the Economic Stabilization Fund, laundering it through individual bank accounts and from there 'donating' it to a variety of CIA front organisations.
8. Corson, *The Armies of Ignorance*, p. 298.
9. Ibid., p. 298.
10. National Security Council Directive on Office of Special Projects, 18 June 1948 (NSC 10/2). Formerly Top Secret. Contained in full in Thomas Etzold and John Gaddis (eds), *Containment: Documents on American Policy and Strategy 1945–1950* (New York: Columbia University Press, 1978), p. 125.
11. Andrew, *For the President's Eyes Only*, p. 198.
12. Quoted in Andrew, *For the President's Eyes Only*, p. 171. Allen Dulles, Director of CIA from 1953 to 1961, privately reminded Truman that he had always authorised CIA covert action. To the CIA legal counsel, Dulles wrote on the subject that '[a]t no time did Mr. Truman express other than complete agreement with the viewpoint I expressed'. Ibid.
13. Andrew, *For the President's Eyes Only*, p. 198.
14. Quoted in Regine Igel, *Andreotti: Politik zwischen Geheimdienst und Mafia* (München: Herbig Verlag, 1997), p. 233.
15. Quoted in Igel, *Andreotti*, p. 233, and the Italian newspaper *Corriere della Sera*, 17 January 1994.
16. *Observer*, 21 February 1988.
17. No author specified, 'Aufatmen in Rom nach der Aufsürung Gellis. Ein Leben wie aus einer vergangenen Zeit', in the Swiss daily *Neue Zürcher Zeitung*, 12 September 1998.
18. Paul Ginsborg, *A History of Contemporary Italy: Society and Politics 1943–1988* (London: Penguin Books, 1990), p. 423.
19. Philip Willan, *Puppetmasters: The Political Use of Terrorism in Italy* (London: Constable, 1991), p. 60.
20. British daily television news programme *Newsnight* on BBC1 on 4 April 1991.
21. Percentage of the national vote of the Partito Comunista Italiano (PCI) during the second half of the Cold War: 1968: 26.9%; 1972: 27.1%; 1976: 34.4%; 1979: 30.4%; 1983: 29.9%; 1987: 26.6%. After the end of the Cold War, the PCI changed its name to Partito Democratico della Sinistra (PDS), which got 16.1% at the 1992 polls. Source: Ginsborg, *A History of Contemporary Italy*, p. 442.
22. Senato della Repubblica Italiana, *Relazione della Commissione Parlamentare d'Inchiesta Sulla Loggia P2*, Roma 1984.
23. Sergio Flamigni, *Trame Atlantiche: Storia della Loggia massonica segreta P2* (Milano: Kaos edizioni, 2005), p. 261.
24. Igel, *Andreotti*, p. 229.
25. In an interview with Willan. Quoted in Willan, *Puppetmasters*, p. 55.
26. Quoted in *New Statesman*, 21 September 1984.
27. Ibid.
28. *Le Monde Diplomatique*, December 1990; *Reuters*, 1 August 1990; *Der Standard*, 24 July 1990. RAI broadcasted four interviews with Dick Brennecke between 28 June and 2 July 1990.
29. *Reuters*, 1 August 1990.
30. *Reuters*, 2 August 1990.

31. A copy of Cossiga's letter to Andreotti was leaked to the press, as so often happens in Italy. The Italian political magazine *Panorama* published it and the Presidential Palace confirmed that it was genuine. Quoted in *The Times*, 24 July 1990.
32. Igel, *Andreotti*, p. 243.
33. Quoted in Igel, *Andreotti*, p. 231.
34. Quoted in Flamigni, *Trame Atlantiche*, p. 261.
35. Igel, *Andreotti*, p. 231.
36. Frank Gigliotti was powerful enough to advise President Harry Truman, allegedly a fellow Freemason, to fire CIA Director General Bedell Smith. In his letter to Truman, dated 30 September 1952, Gigliotti wrote: 'My dear President Truman' and then in a commanding tone noted:

    Some months ago while talking with Margaret Vaughn at their home I told her that I felt that General Bedell Smith would let you down the first opportunity that he had… I want you to know, my dear President, that we have loved you and respected you and defended your flank in season and out of season, through the churches, through political organisations, and before the general public… [but] The statement of General Bedell Smith last night that 'There is no security organisation in the government of the United States into which communists have not infiltrated themselves' is a shame upon him… What has he been doing all this time besides nursing his ulcers…? You will remember that a little over a year ago I made the statement that what we needed to head Central Intelligence was a man who gave ulcers to the enemy and not one who allowed the enemy to produce ulcers in his own system and in the thinking of the Nation. I feel that…now as Chief of CIA he [Smith] has been a perfect dud… I think, along with many others of your friends, that the Intelligence of the United States as centralised in Bedell Smith is at the lowest ebb it has ever been in the history of the United States… I am sending you this information as your friend, and I am asking these question not only as your friend, but as one who has consecrated and dedicated his life to helping make our beloved America a place where future generations will be proud of the fact that you were President of the United States… Mr. Smith should be brought to task… I feel that he has betrayed all of the confidence that you have placed in him. With regards and prayers, I remain Your friend Frank B. Gigliotti.

    (Document found by the author. Papers of Harry S. Truman, Harry S. Truman Library, White House Central Files, Confidential Files.) The letterhead gives Frank Gigliotti's address as: 3777 Gigliotti Drive, Lemon Grove, California.
    On 20 January 1953, Eisenhower as new President entered the White House and replaced Truman. On 9 February 1953, Bedell Smith was fired and Allen Dulles replaced him as Director of Central Intelligence.
37. Flamigni, *Trame Atlantiche*, p. 36.
38. Aldo Beolchini to *La Republicca* on 21 December. Also in Igel, *Andreotti*, p. 51.
39. *Relazione della Commissione parlamentare d'inchiesta sugli eventi del giugno-luglio 1964*, Roma 1971, p. 67. Quoted in Igel, *Andreotti*, p. 51.
40. *Commissione parlamentare d'inchiesta sugli eventi del giugno-luglio 1964, Relazione di minoranza*, Roma 1971, p. 307. Compare Igel, *Andreotti*, p. 53.
41. Quoted in Igel, *Andreotti*, p. 232; *Observer*, 18 November 1990; French weekly *Le Monde Diplomatique*, December 1990. Both Gelli and Haig were furious about this SISMI report and the promising career of Emilio Santillos, director of the SISMI anti-terror office, ended abruptly soon after the report of April 1983. Also the biographies of his fellow investigators took a tragic twist. SISMI Colonel Florio died in a mysterious car accident. SISMI Colonel Serrentiono left the service 'for reasons of ill health'. Major Rossi commited suicide. Major Antonio de Salvo surprisingly left the anti-terror office in good health and joined the Freemasons; Compare: Igel, *Andreotti*, p. 234.
42. Igel, *Andreotti*, p. 239.
43. Jean-Francois Brozzu-Gentile, *L'affaire Gladio* (Paris: Editions Albin Michel, 1994), p. 28.
44. 'They were the agents who were to "stay behind" if the Red Army overran Western Europe. But the network that was set up with the best intentions degenerated in some countries into a front

for terrorism and far-right political agitation.' Hugh O'Shaughnessy, 'Gladio: Europe's Best Kept Secret', *Observer*, 7 June 1992.

45. William Colby, *Honourable Men: My Life in the CIA* (New York: Simon and Schuster, 1978), p. 81.

46. International news service *Associated Press*, 14 November 1990.

47. Brozzu-Gentile, *L'affaire Gladio*, p. 28.

48. For an international overview, compare: Ganser, *NATO's Secret Armies*.

49. Colby, *Honorable Men*, pp. 81 and 82.

50. General Serravalle's testimony in front of documentary film-maker Allan Frankovich's camera. Serravalle speaks Italian; the English translation is by the film company (subtitles). See Allan Francovich, *Gladio: The Puppeteers*, second of three Francovich Gladio documentaries, broadcast on BBC2 on 17 June 1992.

51. Serravalle, in Francovich, *Gladio*.

52. Ibid.

53. *Independent*, 1 December 1990.

54. Philip Willan, 'Terrorists "Helped by CIA" to Stop Rise of Left in Italy', *Guardian*, 26 March 2001.

55. Gerardo Serravalle, *Gladio* (Roma: Edizioni Associate, 1991), p. 78.

56. Ibid., p. 79.

57. Jonathan Kwitny, 'The CIA's Secret Armies in Europe', *The Nation*, 6 April 1992, p. 445.

58. *The Times*, 19 November 1990.

59. *Observer*, 18 November 1990.

60. Resolution of the European Parliament on the Gladio Affair, 22 November 1990.

61. Debates of the European Parliament, 22 November 1990. Official transcripts.

62. Resolution of the European Parliament on the Gladio Affair, 22 November 1990.

Notes on Contributors

Robert Cribb is Convenor and Senior Fellow, Division Pacific and Asian History, Research School of Pacific and Asian Studies at the Australian National University. His research interests focus mainly on Indonesia, though he has some interest in other parts of Southeast Asia (especially Malaysia and Burma/Myanmar) and inner Asia. He has published widely and the themes of his research include mass violence and crime; national identity; environmental politics; and historical geography. He has held research positions at the Australian National University, the Netherlands Institute for Advanced Study and the Nordic Institute of Asian Studies, where he was also director for two years.

Howard Dick is a Professor in the Department of Management and Marketing at the University of Melbourne, and a co-director of the Australian Centre for International Business at the same University. His research interests include Asian business; corruption and governance; institutional development; global logistics; urbanisation in the Asia-pacific; and maritime history and policy. By background an economist, economic historian and economic geographer, Howard specialises in Indonesia, Southeast Asia and Japan with research interests in international business, logistics, urbanisation, development and governance. Recent publications include *Cities, Transport and Communications: The Integration of Southeast Asia since 1850* (with Peter Rimmer); *Surabaya, City of Work: A Socioeconomic History, 1900–2000*; *The Emergence of a National Economy: An Economic History of Indonesia* and *Corruption in Asia: Rethinking the Good Governance Paradigm* (with Tim Lindsey). In 2003, Howard was appointed Editor of the Asian Studies Association of Australia Southeast Asian Publications Series.

Guilhem Fabre is Professor of International Affairs at Le Havre University, France, and a member of Institut Universitaire de France. He is the author of *Criminal Prosperity: Drug Trafficking, Money Laundering and Financial Crisis after the Cold War* (RoutledgeCurzon, 2003). Professor Fabre is also Senior Research Associate at Ecole des Hautes Etudes en Sciences Sociales (EHESS) China Centre in Paris.

Mark Findlay is the Director of the Institute of Criminology at the University of Sydney. He is also a Research Professor at Nottingham Law School and a Senior Associate Research Fellow at the Institute of Advanced Legal Studies, University of London. An experienced socio-legal researcher, Mark has worked as a research consultant for international agencies, governments and private consortia in many jurisdictions. He is the author of *The Globalisation of Crime* (Cambridge, 1999) and his most recent book, co-authored with Ralph Henham, is *Transforming International Criminal Justice: Retributive and Restorative Justice in the Trial Process* (Willan Publishing, 2005).

Daniele Ganser is a Swiss historian who specialises in international relations and international history since 1945. His research interests are peace research, geostrategy, secret warfare, resource wars, globalisation and human rights. He teaches at Swiss universities, including the History Department of Basel University and he has been a Senior Researcher at the Centre for Security Studies at the Swiss Federal Institute of Technology (ETH) in Zurich. His current research focuses on the so-called 'war on terror' and peak oil (www.peakoil.ch). He has published books in several languages and is the author of *NATO's Secret Armies: Operation Gladio and Terrorism in Western Europe* (Frank Cass, 2005).

Henner Hess is Professor of Sociology at the University of Frankfurt. His publications include the influential monograph *Mafia and Mafiosi: Origin, Power and Myth* (Crawford House Publishing, 1998).

Rensselaer W. Lee III is a Senior Fellow at the Foreign Policy Research Institute in Philadelphia, and President of Global Advisory Services in Virginia. He is the author of *Smuggling Armageddon: The*

Nuclear Black Market in the Former Soviet Union and Europe (St Martins Press, 1999); *The White Labyrinth: Cocaine and Political Power* (1990); and, with Patrick L. Clawson, *The Andean Cocaine Industry* (1996).

Alfred W. McCoy is J.R.W. Smail Professor of History at the University of Wisconsin-Madison. Professor McCoy has spent the past thirty years writing about Southeast Asian history and politics. His publications about this region have focused on two topics – the political history of the modern Philippines and the politics of opium in the Golden Triangle. The first edition of his book, published in 1972 as *The Politics of Heroin in Southeast Asia*, sparked controversy, but is now regarded as the 'classic work' about Asian drug trafficking. Now in its third revised edition, this book has been translated into nine languages, including, most recently, Thai and German. Three of his books on Philippine history have won the Philippine National Book Award: *Philippine Cartoons* (1985), *Anarchy of Families* (1994), and *Lives at the Margin* (2001). In 2001, the Association for Asian Studies awarded him the Grant Goodman Prize for his career contributions to the historical study of the Philippines.

William Reno is an Associate Professor at Northwestern University, Illinois. He is a specialist in African politics and the politics of 'collapsing states'. He frequently travels to conduct his research to places including Somalia, Sierra Leone, Congo and Central Asia, where he talk to insurgents, government officials and foreigners involved in conflicts. His books include *Corruption and State Politics in Sierra Leone* (Cambridge, 1995) and *Warlord Politics and African States* (Lynne Rienner, 1998).

Vincenzo Ruggiero is Professor of Sociology at Middlesex University and Co-Director of the Crime and Conflict Research Centre at that University. His research interests include social movements and urban sociology; drugs and drug networks; prisons; comparative criminology; racial matters; organised crime; and political violence. He has published extensively in English and Italian. His latest book is *Understanding Political Violence* (Open University Press, 2006). He has been nominated as Distinguished International Academic by the American Society of Criminology.

Peter Dale Scott is an English Professor at the University of California, Berkeley, and a former Canadian diplomat. An anti-war speaker during the Vietnam and Gulf wars, he was a co-founder of the Peace and Conflict Studies Program at his university and of the Coalition on Political Assassinations. He is a poet as well as a prose writer, and has written several investigative books on 'deep politics', focusing on US covert operations, their impact on democracy and their relations with the JFK assassination and the global drug traffic. He is the author of *The War Conspiracy: The Secret Road to the Second Indochina War* (1972); with Jonathan Marshall, *Cocaine Politics: Drugs, Armies, and the CIA in Central America* (1991); *Deep Politics and the Death of JFK* (1993); *Coming to Jakarta* (1988); *Listening to the Candle* (1992); *Minding the Darkness* (2000); and *Drugs, Oil, and War* (2003). His latest book is entitled *The Road to 9/11: Wealth, Empire and the Future of America* (University of California Press, 2007).

Francisco E. Thoumi is an independent consultant and former Professor of Economics and the Director of the Research and Monitoring Centre on Drugs and Crime at the Universidad del Rosario, Bogotá. He is an expert, researcher and writer on drug policy issues. He has previously held high-profile academic positions at California State University and George Washington University, as well as important positions within the Inter-American Development Bank and the World Bank. Between 1999 and 2000, he was a research coordinator for the former United Nations Office on Drug Control and Crime Prevention under their Global Programme Against Money Laundering, and between 1993 and 1996 he was a regional coordinator under United Nations Drug Policy's UNDP Research Programme on the Economic Effects of the Illegal Drug Industry in Bolivia, Colombia and Peru. Dr Thoumi is also the author of *Illegal Drugs, Economy and Society in the Andes* (2003); *El Imperio de la Droga: Narcotráfico, Economía y Sociedad en los Andes* (2002); *Las Drogas: una Guerra Fallida. Visiones Críticas* (with A. Camacho and A. López, 1999); *Political Economy and Illegal Drugs in Colombia* (Lynne Rienner, 1995). He is the editor of *Drugs, Crime and Armed Conflict in Colombia, Journal of Drug Issues* (Winter 2005),

El Rompecabezas de las Drogas Ilegales en Estados Unidos: Una visión ecléctica (with A. Guáqueta, 1997); and *Drogas Ilícitas en Colombia: su Impacto Económico, Político y Social* (1997).

Ola Tunander is a Research Professor at the International Peace Research Institute, Oslo (PRIO). He has written, edited and co-edited several books on history, geopolitics, political philosophy and military strategy. He is the author of *The Secret War Against Sweden – US and British Submarine Deception in the 1980s* (Frank Cass, 2004). He has also given numerous lectures at universities, military staff schools and ministries.

Eric Wilson is a Senior Lecturer in International Public Law at the Faculty of Law, Monash University. He has a PhD in History from the University of Cambridge, an LLB from the University of British Columbia and an LLM from the University of Washington and in 2005 was awarded the SJD from the University of Melbourne. His current subject interests are in the history and philosophy of international law and critical jurisprudence. He is the author of *The Savage Republic: De Indis of Hugo Grotius, Republicanism, and Dutch Hegemony within the Early Modern World-System (ca. 1600–1610)* (Martinus Nijhoff/Brill, 2008).

Index

Compiled by Sue Carlton